HIMMLER
NEVER GAVE ME
CHOCOLATE

THE LAST DAYS OF THE THIRD REICH

HIMMLER NEVER GAVE ME CHOCOLATE

THE LAST DAYS OF THE THIRD REICH

Extraordinary stories by
NIGEL BANCE

With additional research by
DIANA PETERSEN-BÜCHSE

Print & Online Solutions

COVER PHOTOGRAPHS

Inside front cover – inside this shed, Hans Heinrich Otzen (inset), then a young boy, chatted away with Heinrich Himmler who sat in his car listening to news on the car radio. Hans Heinrich held an abiding memory of Himmler: he never gave him chocolate unlike his SS guards who were inside the family farmhouse forging new identity and travel documents necessary for their escape to the south.

Inside back cover – this former school in Hamburg had become a notorious SS killing centre in the final weeks of the war. In its basement and in the room with the half-open metal door (inset), 20 Jewish children, the youngest aged five, were hung over clothes hooks on the wall: one of the foulest wartime atrocities.

Back cover – More than 1,000 concentration camp prisoners were burnt to death in a barn in Gardelegen. The blame for this mass slaughter lay not only with the SS and Luftwaffe paratroopers. The Volkssturm, Germany's huge part-time army, young boys in the Hitler Youth and Gardelegen's firemen had a part in the massacre. 'The people of Germany' were responsible, wrote a US army doctor who attended the handful of survivors from the inferno.

THE STORIES

HIMMLER NEVER GAVE ME CHOCOLATE

First published in Great Britain in 2021 by
MWM PRINT
Unit 9 Orwell Court,
Hurricane Way,
Wickford SS11 8YJ

ISBN 978-1-5272-8695-5

Design, typresetting and production: Roger Kohn Designs, Sunningdale
Printed and bound in Great Britain by Clays Ltd, Elcograf S.p.A.
Maps drawn by Peregrine Bush

CONDITIONS OF SALE

FOREWORD

For millions, World War II never ended. Vivid memories remain of death, torture, humiliation, starvation and incarceration. For the survivors who worked in the Third Reich's slave labour camps, held in the concentration and death camps, and who endured the death marches, there has been no closure.

As a re-invigorated West Germany grew out of the post-war chaos, a compliant state legal system, stuffed with prosecutors, judges and lawyers, who once held high Nazi office or military rank, obfuscated attempts to prosecute those responsible and ensured that only a few ever faced justice.

To its collective shame, German industry that collectively employed millions as slave labour, hid behind this skewed legal system and only begrudgingly offered up a measure of financial rectitude, money that could never compensate for the brutality and hardship. Many of those companies, now major global corporations, never even offered an apology.

In the death-throes of the Third Reich, atrocities continued even though it was clear that Germany was finished. The SS was not solely responsible. The police, fire service, other essential services, and civilians waded into the bloodletting even though they knew they would be accountable. Several of our accounts are graphic in the telling, never shying away from the horrific nature of each of them.

The first story - *Himmler never gave me Chocolate* - isn't about an atrocity *per se* but it is about the man who directly or indirectly ordered them, and his final week of life hiding up in the hamlets that dot the German/Danish border in Schleswig-Holstein.

Much of what we uncovered in our six accounts has never before been published. We were shown family documents and photographs and our search of official government documents, some only recently made public, was thorough. Above all, so many people were prepared to share their recollections with us and to them we are very grateful.

Four other stories - *Twenty little Suitcases, Chasing down the Hares, The Charnel House,* and *The Camp the World Forgot* - share a common theme. Many of the architects in the terror were never brought to justice, free to live out the rest of their lives. The final account - *The Village that Keeps its Secrets* - follows on from *The Camp the World Forgot* and describes the efforts we made to discover the whereabouts of one SS camp guard who was forever remembered by the survivors she brutalised.

GLOSSARY

SS RANKS AND EQUIVALENTS

Reichsführer	Chief of the SS – Heinrich Himmler
Obergruppenführer	General
Obergruppenführer	Infantry General
Gruppenführer	Lt. General
Brigadeführer	Major-General
Standartenführer	Colonel
Obersturmbannführer	Lt. Colonel
Sturmbannführer	Major
Hauptsturmführer	Captain
Standortarzt	SS medical doctor, usually a Captain rank
Obersturmführer	Lieutenant
Untersturmführer	Second Lieutenant

OTHER RANKS

Sturmscharführer	Staff Sergeant-Major
Hauptscharführer	Senior Sergeant
Rapportführer	Usually Sergeant, head of discipline
Oberscharführer	Sergeant
Scharführer	Lance-Sergeant
Unterscharführer	Corporal
Rottenführer	Lance Corporal
Sturmann	Private 1st class
SS-Mann	Private

OTHER SS RANKS

Ortsgruppenleiter	Group leader in small townships
Schutzhaftlagerführer	Camp chief operating officer
Stützpunktleiter	Area commander for satellite camps
Blockleiter	Head of individual blocks in the camps
Aufseherin	Female SS concentration camp guard

OTHER TERMS

Begleitkommando	Personal bodyguard – all the top Nazis had one
Kreisleiter	City or town administrator during the Nazi era, usually SS
Kreisleitung	Administration building for staff
Bürgermeister	Mayor, some held SS rank
Ortsbauernführer	Village Nazi who upheld strict party discipline

FIRE SERVICE RANKS

Unterbrandmeister	Squad leader in the volunteer fire service

POLICE RANKS

Hauptwachmeister	Senior sergeant
Wachmeister	Sergeant
Oberwachmeister	Junior sergeant
Unterwachmeister	Constable

OTHER GERMAN TERMS USED IN THIS BOOK

Arbeitskommando	Work party or detail
Häftlinge[n]	Concentration camp prisoner[s]
Hof	Farmhouse
KZ	A term used for concentration camp
Muselmänner	Concentration camp inmates deemed unfit for work
Ostarbeiter	Slave labourer
Vertriebene	Displaced Persons (DPs)
Zoglinge	So called 'Pupils' in Uckermark Youth Camp
Zuchthaus	Prison

I

HIMMLER NEVER GAVE ME CHOCOLATE

STORYLINE

For too long, Heinrich Himmler's eight days in Flensburg during May 1945 have been shrouded in intrigue and mystery.

We reveal the extraordinary story of what happened here between May 2 and May 10, an account recanted through the lens of the people who lived in the hamlets that dot this ancient farming landscape. Their memories supplemented by never-before-seen photographs and documents provide the testimony to Himmler's last days before his flight south, to capture and suicide.

This story, the first of six that describe events that took place in the last days and weeks of the Third Reich, is framed against the background of the Dönitz administration in Flensburg, the city in Schleswig-Holstein that butts up to the Danish border. Without Allied recognition, this 21-day rump Nazi government had operated for two weeks after the official unconditional German surrender was signed on May 8 in the Rheims schoolhouse.

A file in the British archives on one of Himmler's top aides provided us with extraordinary detail as to the whereabouts of 'Himmler's treasure', a term used by British intelligence officers in their European-wide efforts to locate two large metal strongboxes that stored his valued private possessions. That file was only declassified upon the aide's death in 2007. We disclose where these strongboxes were stored, even their contents, and the names of the two SS officers who hid them in May 1945. One returned, 20 years later, and the heated exchange with the farmhouse owner was overheard.

We visited the private property in which Himmler stayed during those eight days in May and to view the strip of land where Himmler's briefcase was buried by one of his bodyguards. That leather briefcase had never left Himmler's side.

A villager, a young boy at the time, had never before told his story of talking to the former Reichsführer-SS in another commandeered farm. While Himmler's bodyguard were in the family home falsifying new identity papers to make good their escape, Himmler took the boy for a drive.

◀ Heinrich Himmler in SS uniform.

▲ The track to Hühölz with the Lorenzen Hof in the distance, home to former Reichsführer-SS Heinrich Himmler and some of his entourage for eight days in May 1945. *Source: Nigel Bance*

DOWN THIS TRACK, the British came. The house owner and his family had no warning of their coming.

Only on April 11, 1946 had Captain Owen, a British military intelligence officer, discovered the significance of the Lorenzen Hof in Hüholz. A former member of Heinrich Himmler's Begleitkommando, or bodyguard, had broken ranks with his detained colleagues and talked. On April 23, exactly 11 months on since the British army had forcibly terminated the last vestige of Nazi government in Flensburg, the two lorries rumbled down the track on a search mission.

Accompanying Owen were members of 318 FSS, the seasoned Field Security Section that two months earlier had captured Rudolf Hoess, the former commandant of Auschwitz, working him over before he confessed to his real identity. The present owner of the Gottrupel property, near Flensburg, where Hoess had been employed as a farm labourer, still recalls his wife's grandfather vividly describing the screaming emanating from the barn where Hoess had slept.[1]

According to the report sent to British Intelligence in Bad Oeynhausen, its headquarters in Germany, Nikolaus Lorenzen, the owner of the Hüholz farmhouse, and his 21-year-old daughter, Greta, were subjected to 'high-pressure' interrogations.[2] At first, Lorenzen denied he was aware of the identity of his houseguest but he broke under questioning admitting that Himmler had stayed in his home from May 2 until May 10, 1945. The 318 FSS turned over the house and lifted up the floorboards before the former Begleitkommando member took Captain Owen to the grassy area behind the barn. Long strips were sectioned off and the digging began. The FSS hadn't finished with Lorenzen. He spent the night in a cell in Flensburg's main police station undergoing a further grilling.[3]

Hüholz had marked the beginning of the end for Himmler.

---

[1] The barn was pulled down in 1960 and replaced. After his detained wife had given up the location of her wanted husband, the British had arrived at the property at 11pm, banged on the door, and went straight to the barn where Hoess was found in his pyjamas. Hoess was found with his leather jacket and this was later donated to a local museum.

[2] 'High-pressure' was the actual term used in the post-raid military intelligence report.

[3] For many years, it was agreed in the family that it would keep silent over Himmler's time in the house.

The eight days that Himmler, with his 14-strong Begleitkommando and his group of key aides, spent in the agricultural hamlets that adorn the south of Flensburg is still vividly recalled by some that were there. Then, they were young children but old age hadn't dulled their memories, Hans Heinrich Otzen being one, aged 10 at the time.[4]

Heinrich Himmler, wearing shabby civilian clothes, sat in the four-seater military Steyr in the shed in the courtyard of the Otzen Hof, a farmhouse in the hamlet of Mariengaard, listening to the car radio pumping out the usual propaganda on military successes on the Eastern Front against the Red Army. The former Reichsführer-SS knew otherwise, he had realised many months earlier that the course of the Third Reich had run. By his side in the Steyr was his leather briefcase. The door of the shed was firmly closed to keep out the inquisitive. Refugees had flooded into the area, breaking into outbuildings in a desperate search for food and a space to rest a tired body.

While Himmler listened to the radio, his men were inside the farmhouse checking up on progress on the top floor where the SS had established a workshop to replicate travel documents and identities to get through the British lines when the time came to escape. When the SS had first arrived to commandeer the house, Elizabeta, Hans Heinrich's mother, had been ordered to maintain a ready supply of hard-boiled eggs, their yolks vital in the inking process. Out in the courtyard, an SS guard kept watch over the Volkswagen Kübelwagens, the army utility vehicles that had become a regular feature in the hamlets. None of Himmler's group remained in the Otzen Hof overnight.

To the young and impressionable Hans Heinrich, the SS and its reputation had no significance but his mother did urge caution. At first she had been unaware to the identity of her regular visitor but soldiers from the Wache-Marine-Battalion, the navy military that had moved into the area to protect the fields and farms against food theft, had revealed his name. Hans Heinrich had continued to chatter away to Himmler in the shed but it was a one-way conversation. Himmler

---

[4] Sadly, Otzen died shortly after our interview.

found him a nuisance and on the rare occasions he did respond, he was gruff in tone.

Away in the Wehrmacht, Hans Heinrich's father, Peter, served as a truck driver in a regiment that had fought at Stalingrad but withdrawn before the ignominious surrender in February 1943. Later, held as a PoW, Otzen had managed to escape to the Polish coast and cross the Baltic to Flensburg, arriving home after Himmler had left. In his long absence, Elizabeta had managed the farm.

The top of the farmhouse was out of bounds to the curious Hans Heinrich but when he did venture upstairs he was taken aback by the sight of SS officers attempting to scrape away their blood type, tattooed on the inside of the left arm. When he wasn't checking up on the activities of the farm's visitors and cadging chocolate from Himmler's men, he queued at a local field kitchen serving goulash soup, taking his place with the military and other villagers. Hans Heinrich was forever hungry.

On one of the days that Himmler had parked up, Hans Heinrich had dared to climb into the Steyr but Himmler roughly shoved him out. The young boy was desperate for a ride and surprisingly Himmler relented. No longer did Hans Heinrich remember whether Himmler or one of his bodyguards drove but he never forgot the experience. They took the road behind the Otzen Hof and visited another commandeered farmhouse before returning to drop off the boy and pick up the milk, which his mother always left for Himmler to take back to his hideaway in Hüholz.

The Otzen Hof has barely changed externally since May 1945. There is a new owner, but Hans Heinrich was granted permission to show us the shed in the courtyard, which still stands. The weather was achingly bitter as Hans Heinrich, well into his eighties, took us through a door in the back portraying a boyish excitement to be sharing this untold extraordinary wartime experience. Where Himmler had sat in the Steyr, a modern tractor now stands on a concrete floor.

Hans Heinrich has two over-riding memories of his time with Heinrich Himmler.

'Himmler never gave me chocolate', he recollected and nor did Himmler ever lose sight of his leather briefcase.

◀ The central police station in Flensburg became the key centre for distributing new identities and Wehrmacht uniforms to SS, Gestapo and SiPo members.

▶ Despite being handed the portfolio of interior and security minister by Dönitz, Himmler felt he was far better qualified than anyone else to lead a post-Third Reich government. Himmler had chosen the conference room in Flensburg's central police station on May 5 to outline his political ambition. The next day Dönitz fired him.

▶ The Feuerwehrschule, fire-training centre, in the Flensburg suburbs was Himmler's SS headquarters. It was here where he addressed his loyal members of the Concentration Camp Inspectorate, including Rudolf Hoess, and other senior SS officers in the city, for the final time.

▲ The shed in which Hans Heinrich Otzen chattered to Himmler at the Otzen Hof in the hamlet of Mariengaard still stands. We visited on an achingly-cold day.

▶ Hans Heinrich stands in the exact location where Himmler's Steyr was parked up, now concreted over.

7

FLENSBURG OFFERED A SAFE HAVEN

The bumpy track down to Hüholz from the Winderatter Weg has been replaced and the three large chestnut trees that once adorned the front of the property have long gone. The Lorenzen Hof was a perfect place to hide up from preying eyes as the Steyr and four Kübalwagens drove slowly down it on May 2, 1945, three days after Hitler's death in his Berlin bunker.

Himmler with his Stab Heeresgruppe B and Begleitkommando – personal staff and bodyguard – had relocated several times around Germany with Himmler growing increasingly paranoid for his safety. Berlin was no longer safe and he visited only rarely as the vultures circled, with Reich ministers distancing themselves from the architect of widespread murder and destruction. With a military defeat imminent, Himmler faced the stark realisation that the Allies had ranked him top in the United Nations listing of most wanted Nazis that would face war crimes. More than ever, and especially after the BBC announced that he had put out strong feelers with the British and Americans for peace talks, Himmler needed the protective shroud of his loyal Begleitkommando.

An old friend, SS-Obergruppenführer (General) Curt von Gottberg, had identified Hüholz as a suitable Flensburg hideout for the former Reichsführer-SS, who had been promised a role in the administration led by Hitler's chosen successor, Grand Admiral Karl Dönitz. Gottberg, the orchestrator of the Jewish pogroms in occupied Belarus and the Baltics, was not only trusted, he was very familiar with the Flensburg area after farming land in the nearby hamlet of Grundhof. He also probably knew that Nikolaus Lorenzen could be relied upon to keep silent about his future guest.

In November 1944, the Himmler entourage had been in Aigen, a district of Salzburg, laying up in the Villa Trapp. A month later, it moved on to Triberg, in the Black Forest, and then for a short spell to a village in the Deutsche Krone, in Pomerania. Prenzlau was the next location followed by Wustrow, near Rostock, on Germany's north coast. Himmler's private and well-prepared train now secretly departed for Bavaria, the plan being that it would await him at a later date either at Berchtesgaden or Bayrischzell, near the Austrian border.

It reached neither location, being delayed at Pilsen due to intensive Allied bombing where it remained in a siding guarded by members of the Begleitkommando.

After Wustrow, the entourage had moved into the Hartzwalde estate outside Hohenlychen, 75 miles north of Berlin, a large property previously requisitioned by Himmler as a gift to his personal doctor, Felix Kersten. Himmler had added to his Stab, his personal staff: the much-decorated Sturmbannführer (Major) Heinrich Springer was transferred in as ordnance (weapons) officer from the Begleitkommando staff of Field Marshal Walter Model. Prior to that posting, Springer had served in Belgium in 12-SS Panzer Division, the Hitler Youth, as one of its Waffen-SS commanding officers. In his fighting war, Springer had been wounded six times.

With continuing worries over his safety, Himmler had further expanded his Begleitkommando to 24, which included Wilhelm Walter, a former Oberfunkmeister (Senior signals petty officer) in the U-Boats. The transfer, as Walter later related to a British interrogation officer, had come as a complete surprise. Both Springer and Walter will figure prominently in this account of Himmler's eight days in Flensburg.

While at Hohenlychen, Walter had participated in one of the most audacious SS missions of the war, Himmler tasking his Begleitkommando with breaking through to Hitler's bunker in Berlin and bringing out the Führer. Sturmbannführer (Major) Heinz Macher, the Begleitkommando chief, successfully led the armoured convoy into the besieged capital, but Hitler was resolute in remaining. Hitler had looked drawn and grey, Walter had recalled. The Begleitkommando returned to Hohenlychen but only after fighting a ferocious rear-guard action with Red Army units who had given chase.[5]

On April 28, the Himmler entourage moved into a villa in Krakow-am-see, in Mecklenburg, and two days later, it took over a house in Klutz, near Lübeck. This stay lasted barely hours before it drove in convoy the 30 miles north to Plön, where Dönitz had established his HQ.

---

[5] This operation to extract Hitler from Berlin was disclosed by Walter during his interrogations by the British.

Upon Hitler's death, Dönitz had relocated to Flensburg, to set up his new government in the naval complex in Murwick on the south of the Flensburg fjord. When Himmler and his staff arrived, he preferred for his base the seclusion of the Feuerwehrschule, the fire training school, in Harrislee, to the west of the city and just a short distance to the Danish border. The 24-strong Begleitkommando had been reduced to 14 at this point with several now stiffening the defence of the Kiel Canal. A team had also been ordered south, to Salzburg, to extract Himmler's crates hidden in the Aigen caves. One of Himmler's senior officers, Standartenführer (Colonel) Paul Baumert, was entrusted to safely escort Himmler's wife, Margarete, and eldest daughter, Gudrun, to Italy.

Springer had travelled ahead to Flensburg to prepare for Himmler's arrival. His wife, Ursula, and their three young children, Anke, Güda and the recently born Herwig, were already in the area after being bombed out of their Berlin apartment. Ursula had been employed as a domestic in the village of Grundhof and it is unclear whether that might have been in General Gottberg's home. Later, Ursula had rented the granny annex across the courtyard from the Festesen Hof in Mariengaard, not far from the Otzen Hof, and a short drive from Hüholz. Heinrich Festesen could be trusted just like Nikolaus Lorenzen. He was the deputy bürgermeister, mayor, of Lutzhöft and Mariengaard, and his orders carried weight in the villages. Few dared to cross him.

Himmler's key aide in the Stab was Standartenführer (Colonel) Rudolf Brandt, who after the war would be charged with war crimes. He had ordered the medical experiments in Dachau where prisoners were submitted to excruciatingly painful temperature experiments conducted by Dr Sigmund Rascher, a Luftwaffe doctor, to simulate the effect of flying at high altitude. Just days before the Himmler party arrived in Flensburg, Rascher had been arrested by the SS and executed at Buchenwald, probably ordered by Brandt to conceal his own culpability.

Always in attendance were the two Stab adjutants, Werner Grothmann and Herbert Dürring, both with the rank of Obersturmbannführer (Lt. Colonel). Grothmann had stepped into the role in August 1941 as Waffen-SS officer, Joachim Peiper, returned to fighting duties. Post-war, Peiper was accused of war crimes in Belgium and Italy. The 21-year-old Dürring had joined in July 1942 after a spell at the SS training school in Schleissheim. In June 1941, he had been wounded in the first weeks of the invasion of the Soviet Union.

Never wanting to be out of contact, Himmler had two communications experts in his entourage, Sturmbannführer (Major) Heinz Schmaloer and Brigadeführer (Major General) Wilhelm Keilhaus. Providing medical assistance was the 67-year-old Dr Max Müller. Himmler's secretariat numbered four. Heinz Schreiber, the confidential secretary, oversaw all private papers and documents received from Hitler's office and other ministries, and Fraulein Doris Mähner with her assistant, Fraulein Hintze, dealt with the correspondence. Another secretary, Fraulein Lorenz, who had worked for Himmler since 1938 and knew his every secret and foible, was not in the party at Flensburg. She had been in the group sent to Salzburg to hide Himmler's crates and other personal items. Rumours had long persisted that Himmler had affairs with his female secretarial staff, as his marriage to Margarete, a former head of a Berlin nursing home, grew distant after 1938.

The Begleitkommando kept a close guard on Himmler and his Stab but Sturmbannführer (Major) Josef (Sepp) Kiermeier, a policeman, stuck closer throughout the war. He had been regularly photographed with Himmler, including the trips to Auschwitz, Treblinka and Sobibor.

Flensburg had offered a safe haven for Himmler. The city and its hamlets in this part of the historic Angeln were loyally 'Brown'. Local bürgermeisters, councillors and other officials demonstrated sycophantic allegiance to National Socialism and Hitler. In the schools, the greeting of 'Heil Hitler' had replaced the informal 'Moin, Moin'. In the early Nazi years, young men proudly wore and paraded in the brown uniforms of the SA – the Sturmabteilung – the paramilitary arm of the NSDAP that with its bullyboy tactics had propelled Hitler into electoral power. Later, the uniforms were exchanged for the Hitler Youth. Young girls were swept up in the adulation. The Bund Deutscher Mädel, the League of German Girls, paraded in great numbers throughout Schleswig-Holstein.

BDM girls sewed for the cause in the Arbeitsraumen, the

workrooms, and they travelled around the country. A parade in the Lüstgarten in Berlin in 1933 attracted nearly 100,000 young girls. Midsummer was celebrated with BDM marches but more sinister were the regular guided tours of Dachau, the first concentration camp to be built in Germany. The importance of increasing the birthrate was celebrated with the award of an Ehrenkruz der Deutschen Mutter, a cross of honour for German mothers. It was presented in bronze for four children, in silver for six and in gold for eight.

In and around Flensburg, Nazi flags adorned homes and businesses on Hitler's birthday every April. Most homes had a Volksempfänger, an easily affordable radio promoted by Goebbels, the propaganda minister. Manufactured by Siemens and Telefunken, moulded on its front was the Reichsadler (the imperial eagle) and swastika. All other radios were banned and listening to the BBC from 1939 was an offence harshly dealt with.

In Lutzhöft, Georg Jacobsen, the newly appointed bürgermeister was behind the construction of the Hitler Platz, a celebration of Hitler's accession to power. It was constructed in 1934 on a grassed area in front of the Gastwirtschaft, the guesthouse. A stonewalled garden had been laid out with an upright stone in its centre with the year 1933, the Reichsadler, and the swastika chiselled into it. On the opening of the Hitler Platz, the villagers had turned out in force, the boys and young men in SA uniforms, including Georg Andresen, a Nazi mouthpiece who accepted payment for snooping on his neighbours. Andresen was one of the many in the village gathering who had proudly clicked his heels, stood to attention, and raised a straight arm in the Nazi salute. There were dissenters, amongst them Richard Kmostak. He had hurt his hand and out of the bandage he subtly extended a middle finger in contempt. A staunch communist, Kmostak had decorated his living room table with the Bolshevik flag. Another nonconformist was the more rational and respected Hans Diederichsen, an army veteran of WW1, whose family had never bought into Nazi ideology and what it stood for.

Diederichsen and his wife, Margaret, had several children and on one of our research trips to Lutzhöft, we met two: Marlene, aged 13 at the end of the war and Johannes, then aged 10. They showed us unique documents and photographs of the time. Another daughter,

Ingeborg, aged 12, had in an extraordinary observance recorded the hamlet's activities during these uncertain and anxious days. Sitting on a cushion in a large elm in the front garden of the Diederichsen Hof, she would many years later write a highly-illuminating account on what she and her family had witnessed, entitled *De Sack in de Boom* and translated as 'the Sack in the Tree'.

Unlike many Lutzhöft residents, Hans Diederichsen and Margaret demonstrated sympathy and humanity to those who required it. One who would be forever grateful for that support was Annie Lenker, a young woman who milked the cattle on the farm and had a room behind the farmhouse. Annie had risked public humiliation by having a relationship with Michel, a Serbian PoW, who worked on a farm owned by Hans' brother, Nicholas. She fell pregnant. The risk for Michel was almost certainly a lynching. A similar incident had occurred in another Flensburg village, and the PoW had been hung over a tree bough. The German girl had her hair hacked off before she was positioned in an open cart packed high with manure, and paraded around the village enduring the vitriol and spittle.

Fearful of a similar retribution towards Annie Lenker for her liaison with an Eastern European PoW, Diederichsen kept her working in a bid to conceal her growing condition. That couldn't last and someone in Lutzhöft gave her up but she steadfastly refused to disclose the name of the father. In the summer of 1944, Annie faced a tribunal in nearby Grundhof. Briefed by Diederichsen, Annie, who was well liked in the village, related to members a plausible story that one day she had helped a frightened German soldier who was off to war. In a show of pity she had agreed to sleep with him, but only once, and she never knew his name. That soldier was probably now dead on the Eastern Front, she pleaded. Through Diederichsen's help, that defence was sufficient to avoid the public dishonour in the manure and no one in authority ever discovered Michel's identity. Continuing to work on the farm, Annie gave birth to a son and she was able to show off the new-born to Michel through the wire fencing of his PoW camp.

We readily accepted the invitation to visit the latest Jacobsen generation in the Jacobsen Hof where we viewed material relating to Georg Jacobsen's war, much of it unseen by the gathered family.

Jacobsen, still in post as Lutzhöft bürgermeister throughout the war, had several absences with his deputy, Heinrich Festesen, filling the position. Post-war, Jacobsen when asked about his wartime experiences responded that he had merely promoted German agricultural methods in occupied Estonia and Denmark.

That was a fiction. The documents confirmed that Georg Jacobsen, the bürgermeister, had joined SS Division Totenkopf, the 'Death's Head'. Klara, his daughter, now well into old age, surprised the gathered family by sharing an untold story about her time in Talinn, the Estonian capital, accompanying her father and mother. She quietly reminisced that as a 15-year-old she had often played with the children of the SS and Gestapo chief, Hinrich Möller. Formerly the chief of police in Flensburg, who had personally taken part in Jewish manhunts during the 1938 pogroms in Schleswig-Holstein, Möller had chosen one of the grandest villas in Talinn as his living quarters and Klara described it as being heavily protected by Ukrainian SS and German SS troops. Under Möller's watch in Estonia, the nation's Jewry was systematically massacred. In a number of photographs, Jacobsen looked resplendent in SS uniform with his colleagues, their smiling faces demonstrating the utmost loyalty to their cause. In front of the group, weapons are carefully stacked. While in Estonia, Jacobsen was granted home leave on compassionate grounds when his wife was ill. A second posting took him to Copenhagen, Denmark, and by the end of the war, Jacobsen held the rank of Hauptsturmführer, or captain.

During the years of the Third Reich, Hans Diederichsen and Georg Jacobsen declined to socialise with each other, unusual for a hamlet the size of Lutzhöft. Even when Jacobsen's aggressive Alsatian attacked his dog, the incident was never mentioned between them. Diederichsen believed that Jacobsen protected him, tolerating his anti-Nazi tendencies, as he did with other villagers.

No Nazi flag flew outside the Diederichsen Hof, even on Hitler's birthday, a protest that really rankled with the village die-hards. Occasionally Diederichsen met a small group of like-minded in the hunting room of his house to secretly discuss the state of the war. Diederichsen's father, who lived in the granny annex and was a former Lutzhöft bürgermeister, risked daily listening to the BBC and the family was very familiar with the 'bongs' that always presaged the news. During one broadcast, there was a dangerous moment when the grandfather didn't hear his front door open as a villager named Nielsen, known as the 'biggest Nazi in the area', entered. At the last moment, the grandfather was able to close down the illicit radio and hide it. The grandfather kept on listening but he took greater caution.

THE SS HIDEAWAYS IN HÜHOLZ, LUTZHÖFT AND MARIENGAARD

The Feuerwehrschule, the fire training school in Harrislee, was Himmler's SS base in Flensburg but Himmler needed the isolation of the farming communities of Hüholz, Lutzhöft and Mariengaard to billet himself, his Stab and the Begleitkommando. In Hüholz, Himmler, Grothmann and Brandt had taken over the living room and two of the bedrooms in the Lorenzen Hof. Anne Marie, Lorenzen's wife, and Greta, his 21-year-old daughter, made do with the remaining rooms. Dürring, Schreiber, Kiermeier, Macher and some others bunkered down in the outbuildings including the barn. Behind the property, a track led to the Winderatter See and its boggy wood.

Himmler's weapons officer, Springer, was ensconced with his family in the granny annex of the Festesen Hof in Mariengaard and Georg Jacobsen was able to billet the remainder of the entourage across the two hamlets. His home in Lutzhöft, behind the village pond, became the central meeting point for the SS. Meals were taken here and escape plans discussed.

Doris Mähner and Fraulein Hintz, two of Himmler's secretaries, moved into the Festesen Hof and a day later, Dürring and Macher had moved over from Hüholz.[6] The Festesen family moved into the rear of the main house leaving most rooms to the growing SS presence. Müller, the SS doctor, Schmaloer and Keilhaus, the

---

[6] Heinrich Springer confirmed these movements and the billeting of Himmler's personnel in his January 1947 interrogation in Neuengamme, the former concentration camp near Hamburg. British Intelligence and the Central Intelligence Agency only declassified these interrogation files in 2007, upon Springer's death.

communications experts, were in Lutzhöft with others in the Begleitkommando and Stab.

The contingent swelled when the remnant of Hitler's Begleitkommando arrived after fighting their way out of Berlin, obeying the order to report to Himmler.[7] There is an account of SS in a black Mercedes arriving in Lutzhöft and asking directions for the Festesen property. They were probably billeted in the Wree Hof opposite the Diederichsen Hof. Jacobsen requested that Diederichsen accommodate three SS officers. At first, Diederichsen and Margaret were disinclined to do so but they felt it prudent to accede to the bürgermeister's wishes and the officers were provided with rooms overlooking the garden. During the day, the officers spent time in the Jacobsen property. Diederichsen left his 'guests' alone, never asking their business.

Diederichsen had other 'guests', which he put up in his barn. These were Wache-Marine-Battalion soldiers and they had to fend for themselves. On one occasion Margaret was asked to cook three hares they had caught which she did. Brazenly, the soldiers reduced the large beech in front of the house to a stump to use as firewood. The Diederichsen family employed a cook at the time and she took a shine to one of them. He remained in the village after the war as the relationship had developed.

Neither the SS nor the Wache-Marine-Battalion were aware that right under their noses Diederichsen was shielding a young naval defector, Johannes Hessler, who would have been shot if found. Hiding in the hayloft, with the soldiers below, he later used a window onto the roof to escape and in an extraordinary corollary to the story, he returned to the Diederichsen Hof a half century later. He had been in Flensburg and seen a car sticker advertising Lutzhöft. Hans Diederichsen was now dead but the family warmly received him. Not for the first time did the family hear an account of their parents bravery by standing up to the Nazis. Hessler, after his escape, had made his way to Plön in the south and later joined the British army as a

---

[7] Wilhelm Walter, a member of Himmler's Begleitkommando, in his later interrogation by the British, revealed that several had made it to Flensburg to join Himmler's group. Walter didn't disclose their names.

signalman. The family had been unaware of the deserter in the hayloft.

The 10-year-old Johannes Diederichsen and his friend Fritz, who lived in the village guesthouse, revelled in the excitement of the SS takeover of the village. Fritz had told him about an exciting discovery in the field behind the Jacobsen Hof. The field was dotted with deeply dug holes where chalk was traditionally extracted to use as fertiliser but in recent weeks these holes had a different use: stored inside were armouries of weapons. Tentatively, the boys approached one but a menacing shout from an SS soldier soon had them scurrying away.

Word had quickly leaked out that Himmler was in Hüholz and within 24 hours of his moving in, the windows of the Lorenzen Hof were smashed. Recollections of what happened on May 3 are now hazy but the perpetrator might have been a refugee holed up in the outbuildings. No one knew if the SS had found the culprit but it is safe to assume that if they did, the refugee would not have lived long.

EARLIER DAYS…
HIMMLER'S PEACE OVERTURES

Few in British Intelligence had doubted Himmler's assertion that he was the most resourceful and assertive of any in the Third Reich leadership. Through the SD, the counterintelligence arm of the SS, Himmler ran an organisation the equal of the Abwehr, the established state intelligence service, even if its methods were often brutal. Himmler had opened 'back channels' to the British and Americans offering military surrender of all German forces but with conditions. The first dialogue was in August 1943, brokered by Jacob Wallenberg, a senior member of the Swedish banking and industrial dynasty. The Wallenberg family, with its worldwide assets, was enjoying a profitable war, selling manufactured product and vital ores to both the Axis powers and the Allies. Supposedly neutral, Sweden never shied away from doing deals with Nazi Germany.

Felix Kersten, Himmler's personal doctor, and Brigadeführer (Major General) Walter Schellenberg, Berlin's SD chief, had travelled to Stockholm to meet an officer in the OSS, America's intelligence service. Schellenberg was onside with the growing military opinion

◀ The unveiling of the Hitler Platz in Lutzhöft, constructed in 1934 as a celebration of Hitler's accession to power and the beginning of the '1,000-year Reich'. Villagers had turned out in force, the boys and young men, on the right, in SA uniforms. The ceremony has yet to begin and the large carved stone in its centre remains covered with a Nazi flag. *Source: The Diederichsen family*

▲ The barn (left) of the Diederichsen Hof in Lutzhöft housed some of the Wache-Marine-Battalion soldiers, who had moved into the hamlets to guard the fields and safeguard the crops. Unknown to the soldiers, a deserter had hidden in the rafters and he eventually escaped over the roof, returning to the property several decades later. Georg Jacobsen, the bürgermeister, who had returned from his Waffen-SS duties in Copenhagen, had also ordered Hans Diederichsen to billet members of the SS in a rear building. These men, one of whom would later threaten Diederichsen with a bullet in the SS breakout, took their meals in the nearby Jacobsen Hof with their colleagues billeted in the hamlet. *Source: The Diederichsen family*

▲ The Jacobsen Hof beyond the pond in Lutzhöft was the daily meeting place for members of Himmler's Stab and Begleitkommando and behind it, hidden in the deep chalk pits, was an SS arms dump.

▲ According to his SS records, Georg Jacobsen was a volunteer in the Waffen-SS. He is among members of his unit in this photograph but it is unclear were it was taken. *Source: The Jacobsen family*

that Germany needed to extricate itself from war with the Western Allies as a matter of urgency and that Hitler must be deposed in whatever manner possible. Two of Hitler's closest ministers, Joachim von Ribbentrop, the foreign minister, and Martin Bormann, the Reichsleiter, despite the state of the war, still advocated an extension of hostilities with an invasion of Switzerland, enabling access for German forces into Italy and the Mediterranean.

When Herschel Johnson, the US ambassador to Sweden, heard about the discussion with Himmler's emissaries, he vociferously objected but was overruled by the OSS headquarters in London. Schellenberg had outlined the proposal to the OSS officer and it was predicated on a full military surrender to Britain and America. After surrender, said Schellenberg, the German military could combine with their forces to confront the Soviet Union. In this utopia, Himmler would become the new Reichsführer of Germany. The initiative was quickly dismissed in Washington and London, so not to offend Moscow.

As the war entered its final months, Himmler had orchestrated an attempt through the 'back channels' to deflect responsibility for the concentration camps in Germany and occupied Europe. The world had recoiled at the scenes in July 1944, as the Majdanek camp outside Lublin, Poland, was the first such extermination centre to be liberated. Auschwitz was liberated the following January. There had been an alternative to the camps, Himmler had claimed through the 'back channels'. Hitler should have adopted the scheme to deport Europe's Jewish communities to neutral countries outside Europe, mainly Madagascar. Himmler further accused Karl Kaltenbrunner, a bruiser of a Nazi, and director of the Reich Main Security Office, as the real supremo of the pogroms, the camps, and the atrocities that had become the hallmark of the regime.

Since February 1945, Himmler, although reluctant at first, had entered into talks with Count Folke Bernadotte, the deputy chairman of the Swedish Red Cross. With Sweden neutral, Bernadotte urgently wanted Himmler to allow the release of Norwegians and Danes from the camps and give them asylum in his country. There were also a number of Swedish women, married to German men who had died in the war, who wished to return home.

Bernadotte, in June 1945, chronicled in detail his meetings with the Reichsführer-SS that had been choreographed by Schellenberg.[8] Berlin was the venue for the first, in early February that year. For secrecy, it was not arranged formerly through the Swedish Legation and channelled through von Ribbentrop's office in the foreign ministry as protocol demanded. With Hitler against any contact with Sweden, as it trained Norwegian policemen to be part of the Norwegian Resistance, Schellenberg went through Wagner, von Ribbentrop's personal secretary, whom he knew well. Himmler had agreed to see Bernadotte but only on the condition that Kaltenbrunner and von Ribbentrop met him first.

Kaltenbrunner received Bernadotte in a grand house on the Wannsee, a smart Berlin suburb, putting the Swede at ease with a Chesterfield cigarette and a Dubonnet with Bernadotte musing that the bottle must have been looted from France. Not wanting to disclose his real intentions, Bernadotte merely alluded that he wanted Swedish Red Cross access to some of the camps. The meeting had gone better than expected with Kaltenbrunner recommending to Himmler that Bernadotte should be given a hearing. So far, so good, believed Bernadotte but he hit his first major snag. News of Bernadotte's real intentions to repatriate the Scandinavians had reached Bormann, who argued that the nation would be grossly offended by the sight of Swedish Red Cross vehicles criss-crossing Germany.

That was a setback as was Bernadotte's meeting with von Ribbentrop. Bernadotte found the Reich's senior diplomat arrogant, ridiculous and insufferable. He further had to endure a long lecture on why Germany must win the war if Bolshevism was to be liquidated. Von Ribbentrop forecast that if Germany lost, within six months Russian bombers would be blasting Stockholm.

Finally, on February 12, Schellenberg telephoned Bernadotte with more helpful news: Himmler had agreed to meet him and he would drive him to Hohenlychen, Himmler's latest base, the medical and research facility that had been one of seven in the T-4 euthanasia

---

[8] 'The Fall of the Curtain', Last Days of the Third Reich, Cassel and Co, London, June 1945, including 'Schellenberg's Story'. The notorious Stern Gang in Jerusalem murdered Bernadotte in September 1948.

programme that up to the programme's closure in 1941 had murdered tens of thousands of the mentally unwell and disabled. The facility then took on different purposes, one equally as murderous. SS officers recuperating from war wounds and Reich ministers needing a rest occupied the wards and private rooms but the laboratories were given over to experimentation on concentration camp inmates. SS-Brigadeführer Karl Gebhardt was its medical director and he administered his own programme in nearby Ravensbrück where women had their legs deliberately smashed with a hammer and infected to determine the spread of gangrene.

Gebhardt had greeted Schellenberg and Bernadotte on their arrival, looking thoroughly miserable and announcing he was suffering from pneumonia. He took them on a tour of the wards, explaining that every bed was now occupied with German refugees from the Eastern Front, mainly children, of which some 80 had needed amputations through frostbite and bullet wounds.

Himmler suddenly appeared and Gebhardt introduced him to Bernadotte, who was instantly taken aback.

'When I suddenly saw him in the green Waffen-SS uniform, without any decorations and wearing horn-rimmed spectacles, he looked a typical unimportant official, and one would certainly have passed him in the street without noticing him. He had small, well-shaped delicate hands, which were carefully manicured, although this was forbidden by the SS.'

Over the course of the next two and a half hours, Bernadotte amended that first impression. He found the SS chief 'humorous, vivacious, and amusing'. When the conversation turned awkward, Himmler cracked a joke. 'He spoke warmly of Hitler but his relationship with what he called the inner circle of the leadership had become a serious headache', recalled Bernadotte, who was encouraged to hear that Himmler had opposed an attack on Sweden despite von Ribbentrop being in favour. Himmler had described the military situation as very grave but his Waffen-SS was plugging the growing gaps in the defence of the Oder line against the Red Army.

Bernadotte broached the question over the Scandinavians in the camps and Himmler's tone turned sharp. '"If I were to agree with your proposal the Swedish papers would announce with big headlines that the war-criminal Himmler, in terror of punishment for his crimes, was trying to buy his freedom.'" If there was to be a release, stated Himmler, Sweden and the Allies must pay financial compensation and provide an assurance that Norway's Resistance would cease sabotaging installations and attacks on the German military. Any such deal, responded Bernadotte firmly, was out of the question. Himmler belied Bernadotte's claim that the number of Scandinavian prisoners held in Germany totalled 13,000, it was only a few hundred he countered. As to the matter of Swedish women who had lost their German husbands and wanted to return home, Bernadotte handed over their names. Schellenberg was detailed to look into it.

The meeting over, Himmler asked Schellenberg whether he had organised a competent chauffeur to take Bernadotte back to Berlin as the roads were strewn with tank traps and barricades. Himmler made another Swedish headline crack, more as a joke this time. '"He really didn't want to read that war-criminal Himmler murders Count Bernadotte.'"

Later, Schellenberg had some positive news for Bernadotte. Swedish-born women might receive exit visas and for the Danish and Norwegian prisoners held in the concentration camps there was a possibility of repatriation but there was a catch. The Scandinavians were to be held in Neuengamme concentration camp after first assembling in Friedrichsruh, in the grounds of the palatial manor owned by the Bismarck family, to the east of Hamburg. Bernadotte now had a glimmer of hope that Himmler might just deliver. Kaltenbrunner threatened to scupper the proposals so Bernadotte flew again to Berlin, on March 5, to discuss with Schellenberg how he could be circumvented. 'The gloves were off', recalled Bernadotte.

Construction began on the huts in Neuengamme to house the Scandinavians and the Swedish Red Cross planned to mobilise a convoy of 12 lorries and 12 coaches, attended by a fleet of ambulances and mobile field kitchens. Each vehicle was painted white and clearly marked Swedish Red Cross. The convoy left Malmö, in Sweden, on March 11, reaching Flensburg and then Friedrichsruh without incident. The Swedish military, which had exchanged their uniforms for Red Cross ones, provided the escort.

The expected interference by Kaltenbrunner hadn't materialised and by March 23, the vehicles had already collected 200 Danes and Norwegians from Sachsenhausen and 600 from Dachau. Rescuing 1,990 imprisoned Danish policemen needed a major logistical effort, and the convoy was expanded to 35 vehicles.

Obergruppenführer (General) Günther Pancke, the SS chief in Denmark, had rounded up these policemen with his henchman, Otto Bovensiepen, as retribution against the attacks by the Resistance and as a lesson to the Danish population. Bovensiepen had for months conducted his own brand of terror, employing 'clearing murder squads' around the country, leaving bodies in their wake. A sham air-raid warning at 11am on September 19, 1944 was the signal for 'Operation Möwë' as Gestapo, SS, Wehrmacht and German police moved against every police station in the country but thanks to an overnight tip off, large numbers had avoided the purge and gone into hiding. In Amalienborg and Odense the police resistance was bitter with many killed in the firefights. Those taken endured brutal interrogation in Copenhagen's main police station in Politigaden and at the Gestapo headquarters in the Shellhus, the commandeered Shell Oil building. Kaltenbrunner sent the detained policemen first to Buchenwald and then to camps around Dresden.

In their Nazi black uniforms, the notorious Hilfspolizei (Hipo) auxiliary police, a bunch of collaborators and released criminals, took over the Danish streets. Pancke's lesson to the people back-fired as the Resistance took out key Copenhagen landmarks including the Tuborg brewery. Bovensiepen carried on with his murder squads, one entering a hospital in Odense to shoot the doctors. The Danish nation would never forgive the Hipos and many fled to Flensburg in the final weeks.

With Friedrichsruh the assembly point for his Scandinavians, Bernadotte based himself at Schönhausen, north-west of Berlin, and commuted by car. During these trips he witnessed the death rattle of a country on the verge of defeat. Time came to visit Neuengamme to monitor progress in the hut construction and Bernadotte dreaded the meeting with Standartenführer (Colonel) Max Pauly, the commandant. Bernadotte pulled no punches in graphically describing this SS officer as 'one of the revolting creations of the Third Reich, very smart and efficient, but with the reputation of being one of the very worst'. Pauly, a commandant of Stutthof camp from September 1939 until August 1942 before his transfer to Neuengamme, had become the major supplier of slave labour for Hamburg's industry. Now, Neuengamme was in the process of being emptied on the orders of Himmler, the prisoners forced into the death marches.

Pauly was in no mood to accommodate the Swedish Red Cross request that every Scandinavian transferred from Friedrichsruh must be properly recorded and medically examined. As Bernadotte inspected the huts he warned Pauly that the stay in Neuengamme must be very temporary and evacuation to Flensburg and the Danish border was a priority.

Himmler looked nervy and grave when Bernadotte saw him again at the Hohenlychen hospital on April 2. The war situation had become critical, he told Bernadotte, with Schellenberg in attendance. Himmler wanted to discuss how to save the German nation but he broke off to answer the phone. In his absence, Schellenberg urged the Swede to immediately contact Eisenhower and arrange a ceasefire. The Western Allies wouldn't agree, they would demand a full surrender, remonstrated Bernadotte. Himmler returned from taking the call and his mood hadn't lightened but he did enquire on the progress in collecting the Scandinavians from around Germany. Bernadotte commented that the conditions were wretched at Neuengamme, insisting to Himmler that he must agree to an immediate evacuation. Hitler had refused and Kaltenbrunner remained a roadblock, responded Himmler, they must remain in Germany. Himmler did concede that if Bernadotte could promise that if the Scandinavians were interned in Sweden and not released, he might just swing it with Hitler.

'I AM DESCRIBED AS THE CRUELLEST AND MOST SADISTIC MAN ALIVE'

Before they parted, Himmler ruefully admitted that Germany had catastrophically underestimated Britain and its determination to fight on after early setbacks, further reflecting that the international criticism aimed directly at him was both prejudiced and mistaken. "'I am described as the cruellest and most sadistic man alive'", he said quietly to Bernadotte. In the drive back to Schönhausen, Schellenberg had warned the Swede to watch his back. Kaltenbrunner had tapped his phone and was dangerous.

A week later, Himmler had news that the exodus out of Berlin of Hitler's inner circle was underway with Schellenberg adding the detail that Hitler might be in the final stages of Parkinson's disease. Sensing an opportunity, Bernadotte pushed Himmler to agree to an evacuation from Neuengamme for his Scandinavians. Himmler was in partial agreement but stipulated that Denmark, not Sweden, must be the ultimate destination for them.

Bernadotte and Schellenberg drove out to see Himmler in Wustrow, near Rostock, on April 13, and the three strolled through the woods quietly discussing the state of the war. Himmler was again pensive. In the course of the following week, Schellenberg carefully sounded out several of Hitler's ministers on how to deal with the impending defeat, assiduously avoiding anyone close to Keitel and Jodl, the military chiefs, who adamantly insisted that the two large armies in Norway and Denmark, numbering more than 500,000 troops, must immediately return for the defence of the nation. Schellenberg took a chance with Count Luis von Krosigk, Hitler's finance minister, despite the bad blood that had long existed with Himmler. Surprisingly, Krosigk offered a reconciliation agreeing that Hitler should be immediately replaced, an opinion shared by Franz Seldte, the minister for labour. What Schellenberg didn't share with anyone was the idea for a full SS takeover of government, which he and Himmler had frequently discussed in private.

The distant thunder of Russian guns had grown louder as Bernadotte and Schellenberg arrived in Hohenlychen on April 20 for a meeting scheduled for 9pm. Gebhardt, its medical director, met them relaying the message that the Reichsführer-SS was away until 6am the following morning. When Himmler did pitch up with his Begleitkommando, he looked worn and tired, offering the excuse that he hadn't slept properly for days. Now, more than ever, said

Himmler, he feared for his safety.

Breakfast was a simple but excellent affair, recollected Bernadotte, with Himmler persistently tapping his front teeth with his fingernail, a sign, confided Schellenberg later that he was anxious. Bernadotte again sought permission for the Scandinavians to go to Sweden, but Himmler again refused, citing Hitler as the reason but if Denmark became a battleground with the British, that order could be rescinded. Bernadotte asked whether all French women prisoners interned at Ravensbrück might also be released to the care of the Swedes.

The next day, Bernadotte flew to Padborg, just over the border into Denmark, to inspect the receiving arrangements for the Scandinavians in the Froslev concentration camp.

Remaining in Denmark, Bernadotte had an interrupted sleep that night. At 3am the phone rang and he took the urgent call from Standartenführer (Colonel) Hans Hinsch, Flensburg's Gestapo chief: Schellenberg was in Flensburg and needed to see him. Bernadotte arrived in the afternoon. Hitler was finished, related an upbeat Schellenberg, he would be gone in a day or two. Himmler now wanted Bernadotte to urgently arrange a meeting with Eisenhower telling the US army supremo that he now had the authority to surrender all German forces, including those in Denmark and Norway, to Britain and America. Bernadotte promised to pass on the proposal but first he needed to sound out the Swedish Foreign Office.

Within hours, Bernadotte had travelled to Lübeck, to the south of Flensburg, and Himmler arrived at the Swedish legation about midnight, moments before the RAF hit the city. They hurried down into the basement where a small number of Swedes and Germans had gathered. "Himmler was not recognized," recalled an amazed Bernadotte.

The raid lasted an hour and returning upstairs the electricity was out so they sat in candlelight and talked. Himmler said that Hitler was probably dead and reaffirmed that he would never surrender German forces to the Soviet Union. Bernadotte asked him to at least confirm the capitulation proposal by letter to Gunter, the Swedish foreign minister.

In the early hours of April 24, they left the legation with Bernadotte accepting a lift to Lübeck's airfield. Himmler had insisted on driving but he quickly lost control of the car, much to the Swede's concern, and ran into the barbed wire surrounding the building.

Later, back in Flensburg, Bernadotte met up with Schellenberg before flying to the airfield at Kastrup, outside Copenhagen, in a plane laid on by the Swedes, where he saw Gunter and informed him of the meeting in Lübeck. The Swedes did send a message to Eisenhower about Himmler's proposal. Harry Truman, the new US President, in office since April 12 after the death of Roosevelt, refused to even consider it.

On April 27, Bernadotte flew to Odense, Denmark, to meet Schellenberg and pass on Truman's reaction. Schellenberg shared with Bernadotte the rumour from Berlin that Hitler had died that day by injection, but there was no confirmation. Hitler certainly wasn't dead and Bormann recorded in his diary that day that Himmler and Jodl had delayed the promise to send in an SS division to defend the centre of Berlin. 'They sacrifice their Fuhrer – Shit, what scum',[9] he had written.

The BBC, with its network of contacts, had latched onto the Himmler proposals and Churchill was pressured to respond. Churchill wasn't forthcoming apart from informing Parliament that any developments would be publicized and debated. In reality, London and Washington had already vetoed Himmler's proposal and had immediately informed Moscow to defray any charge of collusion with the Nazis. In further damage limitation the British Foreign Office released a press report reiterating that no unconditional surrender could be discussed without Russian cooperation. Bernadotte was angry at the news seepage to the BBC and so was Himmler who wrongly accused Schellenberg as the source. Bormann's diary recorded the fury in Hitler's bunker at Himmler's capitulation tender.

---

[9] The diary of Martin Bormann had been located in Hitler's bunker by the Red Army. It is never displayed in Moscow but I have a full copy of the document that relates to 1945 and ends May 1. It was published in Russian as Communism collapsed in a booklet with a very limited circulation.

Bremen was the location of what was to be the final meeting between Bernadotte, Himmler and Schellenberg: April 29 would also be a seminal date for the leaders of the local communities surrounding Bergen-Belsen and Buchenwald. Professing no knowledge of the hideous war crimes, they were forced to view the horrors in their own backyards, the souvenirs of human skin and half-burnt, part-cannibalised corpses. Hundreds were still dying from the effects of starvation and disease. At Buchenwald, 1,000 German women were forcibly marched into the camp and they sang loudly in protest. Prodded past piles of emaciated bodies that bravado evaporated into a whimper.

Himmler said he would immediately order the German army in Denmark to surrender to the British but Bernadotte was starting to doubt whether he carried the authority to do so. However, Bernadotte with Schellenberg flew that day to Copenhagen to seek the co-operation of Obergruppenführer (General) Werner Best, the Plenipotentiary (Nazi administrator) for Denmark. Best, a seasoned SS governor, had been in post since November 1942 and under his watch Froslev was built. Earlier in the war, he had served with Reinhard Heydrich in Poland before commanding an extermination unit. Loyal as ever to the Nazi cause, Best proved typically uncooperative.

After the disappointment of Copenhagen, Schellenberg immediately flew back to Germany to consider his next move with Himmler over the Scandinavian prisoner release. They had talked long into the evening. Himmler's mood was dark and it didn't improve the following day – April 30 – when the news came through that Hitler was dead in his Berlin bunker and Dönitz had been nominated to succeed him with von Krosigk replacing von Ribbentrop as foreign minister. Himmler called Dönitz at his base in Plön and considered whether he should resign as Reichsführer-SS. According to Bernadotte in his revealing memoir written just weeks after the war's closure, Himmler had steadfastly promoted capitulation but was there another motive? If successful, might orchestrating surrender to the Western Allies mitigate the inevitable charge of war crimes?

That day Himmler contemplated suicide.

BERLIN FALLS, AND THE EXODUS NORTH BEGINS

Germany was now entering its end game. American tanks rolled into Munich and the British army crossed the Elbe. In Berlin, the Red Army had clawed its way into Berlin's Tiergarten with the Reichstag in its sights.

Himmler and Schellenberg were in Plön on May 1 for a conference with Dönitz, enduring a treacherous journey through a battle zone, recalled Schellenberg. The news of Hitler's death was shared with the nation. The Stockholm correspondent of *The Times,* the Swedish capital monitored all news emanating out of Berlin, reported that the broadcast had all the tension of Götterdammerüng, the Richard Wagner opera, and was a Hitler favourite. The announcer declared that none but German gods and the German race could fight in so helpless a position "except, perhaps the British, who did not flinch in 1940 when they seemed inevitably lost". The defenders of Berlin had rallied around the Führer and sacrificed themselves for him, reported the announcer gravely.

Loud intermittent bangs interrupted the broadcast followed by silence. The announcer broke in to say an important statement would follow. For 30 minutes, Wagner then filled the airwaves before the announcer interrupted to report that Hitler had been killed, fighting in the defence of Berlin and that Dönitz had assumed authority as supreme commander of all German forces. He was ready to continue the fight. It ended with the slow movement of Bruckner's 7th symphony. London treated the claim that Hitler had died on April 30, leading the fight against the enemies of the Reich, as a joke as did Moscow who reacted that it was a fabrication allowing him time to escape the clutches of the Red Army and the NKVD.

The day before he died, Hitler had dictated his testament, denouncing Himmler as treacherous and stripping him of all rank and responsibility including the Volkssturm, the home army that had come under his remit. Karl Hanke, the 'Hangman of Breslau' became the new Reichsführer-SS. Göring had been dismissed from post several days earlier.

In Plön the atmosphere was tense. Von Krosigk agreed with Himmler to solicit immediate talks with the British and Americans.

Dönitz objected, supported by Keitel and Jodl, the army chiefs. There were arguments on whether the Wehrmacht in Norway, commanded by Colonel-General Franz Böhme, should give up without a fight. Dönitz finally caved in over Norway leaving it to Schellenberg to arrange a meeting with Böhme on the Sweden-Norway border in an aircraft supplied by the Swedish military. As in Copenhagen, the talks proved fruitless with Böhme refusing to consider any notion of surrender to the British.

Dönitz took to the air at 10.20pm, quelling all rumour of surrender in every theatre of war: 'He had to save the German people from Bolshevik destruction and as long as the British and Americans hamper us from reaching this end, we shall fight and defend ourselves against them as well.' There was no reference to Himmler or Göring. London now believed that Himmler had lost his power base.

For Count Bernadotte, his discussions with Himmler did have a positive outcome. The 'Swedish Camp' in Neuengamme had become an oasis of hope and under the care of the Swedish medical professor, Gerhard Rundberg, the inmates received decent medical care, food and clothing. Their treatment was comparatively humane unlike the barbaric conditions on the other side of the fence where SS thugs, commanded by Max Pauly, exercised absolute power over life and death.

In the days before Hitler's death, Himmler had given the green light to finally evacuate the Scandinavians north to Flensburg, then to Copenhagen and to final sanctuary in Sweden, via ship to Malmö. Bruno Kitt, the SS doctor in Neuengamme who previously had medical responsibility for the women's camp in Birkenau and had worked alongside Dr Josef Mengele, accompanied the convoy. As the 30-truck and bus convoy loaded up on April 20 with 4,000 prisoners, heavily armed RAF fighters swooped in over Neuengamme, waggling their wings as a gesture to the thousands of inmates who remained that liberation from Nazi tyranny was not far off. Churchill had provided an aerial escort.

The day after Dönitz had broadcast to the nation, Berlin fell but the ministries had already emptied. With the Luftwaffe airfields in Schleswig-Holstein still open and operational, the tide of the exodus to the north grew. Hamburg, Germany's second city, defended by the

Wehrmacht, paratroopers and Hitler Youth, was now under immediate threat from the British. With the British also close to Lübeck, Dönitz and his staff evacuated further north to Flensburg taking over the naval cadet sports school in Murwick where he established his new government with von Krosigk as leading and foreign minister. Von Krosigk, a former Rhodes scholar at Oxford, spoke excellent English, attributes that Dönitz believed might endear him to Field Marshal Montgomery and lead to more lenient surrender terms. Von Krosigk had other skills: his finance ministry in Berlin had quite literally funded the war. The Waffen-SS had been particularly grateful, von Krosigk exempting it from the chore of submitting regular expenditure allocations.

War can disguise many secrets and only later in the Ministries Trial in 1948, the 11th of the 12 Nuremberg trials, with 20 key figures in the dock, did the prosecution forensically unpick von Krosigk's financial wizardry. As 177 synagogues and 7,500 Jewish-owned stores had burned on November 10, 1938, von Krosigk ensured that all insurance payments would be diverted into the coffers of the SS-Main Economic Administration Office as a Jewish 'act of atonement'. His office had financed the building of the concentration and death camps including Auschwitz-2, the Birkenau site with its four crematoria, eight gas chambers and 46 ovens. With his usual thoroughness, after the July 1944 attempt on Hitler's life, with the conspirators either shot or hung on meat hooks in the execution chamber in Berlin's Plötzensee prison, von Krosigk assiduously confiscated their property and assets.

Laundering of the SS wealth through the Swiss banking system had been managed with the help of Wilhelm Stuckart, a key SS official in the ministry of the interior, who Dönitz would make a minister in his Flensburg administration. Together they orchestrated the 'War Booty Office' with proceeds directed into the "Max Heiliger" account at the Reichsbank. This was a conduit account handled exclusively by the secretive Maedel section within von Krosigk's finance ministry, concealing the beneficiaries, one of whom was Himmler. Von Krosigk and Stuckart probably also benefitted.

In the 1948 trial, one identified transaction, a consignment of dental gold extracted from cadavers in the death camps, did shed some light into the account's operation. This 1943 transaction was the 10th into the account and in charge of its conveyance to the Reichsbank was SS-Brigadeführer (Major General) Melmer. The court heard that von Krosigk's department couldn't decide on whether Melmer should be in civilian clothes or uniform. Von Krosigk would deny all knowledge of "Max Heiliger" and other evidence put to him by the Nuremberg prosecution.

Establishing contact with Montgomery had become a priority for Dönitz and on May 2, several high-ranking Wehrmacht officers sought permission to come though the British lines to Montgomery's headquarters on Lüneburg Heath. Allowed through, Captain Derek Knee, an intelligence officer and proficient German speaker, was hastily called in by Montgomery. Knee would recall post-war that Montgomery had ordered that the German officers should be made to wait under the symbolic headquarters' flagpole. When Montgomery did emerge from his caravan he addressed Knee sharply: "'What do these people want?'" The officers handed over a letter of introduction from Field Marshal Keitel and Knee instantly translated it. It contained nothing of substance, he told Montgomery who retorted that any surrender must be unconditional. Glowering at the German officers, Montgomery stated that if he didn't get it, "'he would be delighted to go on fighting'". With that, Montgomery turned on his heel and returned to the caravan. Knee entertained the German officers to a good lunch with wine and brandy before sending them back through the lines.

Hamburg fell to the British the next day, after two weeks of stiff resistance. Kiel and Flensburg were now targets and the impotent defiance of Dönitz was collapsing by the hour. Aerially, few bombs fell on Flensburg but one that did missed its target and took out a school with the tragic loss of 35 children. Out in the Baltic Sea an even more deadly attack was to unfold. Low-flying RAF Typhoons attacked three large passenger ships at anchor offshore Lübeck, believing they only contained escaping SS enroute to Flensburg. There were SS, but guards from Neuengamme with 9,000 prisoners. After the attack, German trawlers followed by British vessels rescued 350 from the *Cap Arcona*, which had keeled over, as well as 400 SS men and 20 SS women. Skeletons would be washed up for decades and the Ministry of Defence files in London on the sinking remain closed.[10] Out in the Flensburg fjord, a huge explosion rent the air. The German destroyer, Z 43, blew up after the crew had set charges. The ship quickly sank in waters 24 metres deep.

On May 4, the senior German officers again came though the lines to Lüneburg Heath and this time the war correspondents observed the confrontation. With Knee beside him, Montgomery sat at the head of the table, silently observing the faces of Admiral Hans-Georg von Friedeburg, General Eberhard Kinzel, Rear Admiral Gerhard Wagner and Lt-General Fritz Polack. Knee had helped Montgomery draft the surrender document of all German forces in northern Germany, which the German officers duly signed in turn.

Dönitz had entertained no thought of surrender to the Red Army in the east where the full reality of total war continued to rage. In Murwick, Dönitz now had his team of ministers in place and out of the 350 key staff, 230 were either SS or SD. Himmler, no longer in contact with Count Bernadotte, was handed the portfolio of the interior and security by von Krosigk, the senior minister. To head up industrial reconstruction, von Krosigk had relied on the experience of Albert Speer, Hitler's munitions minister. Himmler promoted the argument to Dönitz and other ministers that Prague in the east, still held by Army Group Centre with 900,000 men, was more appropriate than Flensburg as the new centre of command. Speer was sympathetic but Dönitz was unmoved.

Schellenberg met Dönitz, von Krosigk, Himmler, Keitel and Jodl in Murwick in what turned out to be a bad-tempered affair. Dönitz must immediately surrender all German forces still fighting or on a war footing in Holland, north-west Germany and Denmark was the advice of the SD chief. Better to surrender now, he argued, rather than be conclusively beaten. As usual, Keitel was against any capitulation.

Whether Dönitz gave the order on what would unfold in the fiord, offshore Nordgaardholz and close to the Flensburg Lightship, in the early hours of May 5, is unclear. The codename was 'Rainbow'.

---

[10] Recent research has revealed that these vessels never had enough fuel to sail far, a deliberate ploy by the SS. Essentially, they were death ships.

What remained of his deadly U-Boat fleet was to be scuppered. The first came to the surface at 4am with the crew lining up on deck to face the shoreline before scrambling into dinghies with whatever could be removed. Once ashore, the explosives detonated and with the flood valves opened, the U-Boat slowly slid into the depths. In total, 52 U-Boats were sunk. Standing off, the British navy witnessed the spectacle and sent boats to arrest the sailors. In the U-Boat pens and construction yard at Hamburg-Finkenwerder, 11 were deliberately scuttled and altogether, 225 U-Boats around Schleswig-Holstein and north Germany went to the bottom between May 1 and May 9. [11]

THE FLENSBURG RATLINE

The city had become the last haven for hardened and bitter Nazis – a ratline. The swagger was tempered with the inevitability of defeat as armed troops strutted around the winding streets, drinking in the bars and giving the Nazi salute. Any insults to the now-dead Hitler, even loose talk, could invariably result in summary execution. Standartenführer (Colonel) Hans Hinsch, the Gestapo chief since August 1942, still claimed authority but the sight of the reviled Gestapo uniforms grew scarcer.

Himmler and Heinrich (Gestapo) Müller had issued orders in mid-April to concentration camp commanders and Gestapo heads to evacuate and head for Schleswig-Holstein. Flensburg's central police station, under Gestapo and Sicherheitspolizei (SiPo) control, was issuing new IDs of dead soldiers with pay books and shabby Wehrmacht uniforms to those who needed to abscond into the melee of a defeated army.

The process of exchanging identities proved remarkably straightforward, as identified by a later interrogation of five members of the Volkssturm, the home army. A blank soldbüch, or pay-book, and civilian clothes had been handed to each of them in Flensburg's Kreisleitung, the administrative office for the NSDAP. Now formerly

---

[11] Some U-Boats were salvaged. Three U-Boats were located in 1985 under the Elbe U-Boat bunker in Hamburg.

discharged from the Volkssturm and with a new name in the soldbüch, each man applied to the bürgermeister for a Fluchtlingsausweise, or refugee certificate. On the strength of these certificates the group obtained travel documents to leave Flensburg.

Clearly, there can only be estimates of how many new IDs were dispensed from the central police station, the naval barracks in Murwick, Himmler's fire training school base in Harrislee, and the Kreisleitung. One estimate runs as high as 5,000. Among the war criminals in the city, several were notable names. Paul-Werner Hoppe, the commandant of the Stutthof and Wöbbelin camps, was just one of many who had collected his new identity at Flensburg's central police station. It isn't clear if Max Pauly, the Neuengamme commandant, was masquerading under a new identity when the British military police later picked him up in Flensburg.

Managing the ID exchange in the central police station was the SiPo chief, Hauptsturmführer (Captain) Hans Bothmann, who had previously commanded the Chelmno death camp in Poland and introduced the gassing vans, the predecessor of the gas chambers. Later, he had cleared the Lodz ghetto. Other SiPo officers desperate for a change of identity included Standartenführer (Colonel) Ludwig Oldach whose police responsibilities had encompassed the Ravensbrück concentration camp, 60 miles north of Berlin, and Uckermark, the nearby police camp for women deemed 'disruptive' or 'deviant'. The decision was made in January 1945 to liquidate Uckermark and crematorium construction workers moved onsite. The following month the ovens were operating at full capacity. Before Uckermark was liberated in April some 5,000 young women had been slaughtered in just three months – more than 400 a week. Oldach had fled with other Gestapo and SS north to the coast and caught a boat to Flensburg.

In the same murderous league was Sturmbannführer (Major) Kurt Stawitzki, whose SiPo career had extended back to the German invasion of the Soviet Union in June 1941. After Lemberg (L'vov) was taken, his men had ruthlessly cleared out the Jewish community to the Belzec death camp in Poland. In the final months of the war in the Flossenberg camp in Bavaria, Stawitzki murdered many German officers who Hitler and Himmler considered traitors, including Admiral Wilhelm Canaris, the Abwehr chief. Loyal to the bitter end, Stawitzki and his group had executed the remaining prisoners in Berlin's notorious Lehrter prison.

The largest SS group in the exodus to Flensburg was the staff of the Concentration Camp Inspectorate that had been based in the Sachsenhausen camp outside Berlin. Under the command of Gruppenführer (Lt. General) Richard Glücks, the Inspectorate reported into Obergruppenführer (General) Oswald Pohl in the SS-Main Economic and Administrative Office. The actual number in the convoy from Sachsenhausen has never been clarified but Obersturmbannführer (Lt. Colonel) Rudolf Hoess, who worked in the Inspectorate after relinquishing command of Auschwitz-1, helped in the travel logistics.

Hoess had been the longest serving commandant at Auschwitz, leaving before the main influx of 430,000 Hungarian Jews into Birkenau, known as Auschwitz-2. During his time he had helped establish Auschwitz-3, Monowitz, which used inmates for the German firms manufacturing nearby. Hoess was to boast at Nuremberg, as a witness against Kaltenbrunner, that his killing process at Auschwitz was way more productive than at Treblinka, the extermination centre that murdered 870,000 in its two camps. When asked in court how many had been liquidated in the Auschwitz complex of camps, Hoess estimated 2.5 million with another half a million dead through starvation or disease. Claimed Hoess, the Concentration Camp Inspectorate, based in Sachsenhausen, had managed 900 camps but the actual figure was nearer 15,000, according to Yad Vashem when all the satellites are included. Himmler had visited Auschwitz in 1942 and 'watched in detail one processing from beginning to end', Hoess described in his extraordinary handwritten memoir before his hanging by the Poles in the very camp that had earned him notoriety.[12]

In the Inspectorate convoy to Flensburg were two vehicles stuffed with boxes of documents and wireless equipment. Wives and children were on the trip but Hoess had chosen to leave his dependents

---

[12] Hoess was hung on April 16, 1947, his last hours spent in the 'Bunker', also known as the 'Death Block', in Auschwitz-1, a block very familiar to him.

behind in the family home outside Ravensbrück. The trip to Flensburg was tortuous, wrote Hoess, and the convoy was forced to split after incessant harrying by the RAF. Hoess took charge of one but he soon ran into trouble. Two lorries broke down in Rostock, including the one with the wireless equipment, and with no time to fix them with British troops in the area they were abandoned. 'For days on end we scurried from one clump of trees to the next, as low-flying planes continually machine-gunned this principal escape route', wrote Hoess. Glücks fell ill and became an additional worry. Driving through Wismar, the city on the Baltic, the convoy met Keitel's entourage, which was also heading for Flensburg. Army deserters had been apprehended on the streets and Keitel insisted on setting an example for others who were running away. All were summarily executed with Hoess observing the shooting. Keitel and Hoess moved on. Flensburg was still 225km distant and the British and Canadian armies were edging ever closer.

Sheltering in a farmhouse, somewhere enroute, Hoess had heard the devastating news that his beloved Führer was dead. Both Inspectorate convoys finally arrived in Flensburg and Himmler was delighted that it had arrived more or less intact. Hoess and Gerhard Maurer, the Inspectorate's deputy head, who had managed the department that deployed camp prisoners for Speer's factories, immediately took Glücks to the naval medical centre in Murwick, very close to the Dönitz headquarters.

Pohl, Glücks' boss, had been in the Inspectorate convoy as was Dr Karl Gebhardt, the Hohenlychen medical director, whose job was to manage the accompanying wives and children. Once in Flensburg, Gebhardt set about arranging false papers for the families to escape over the border into Denmark. Arthur Liebehenschel, who had taken over from Hoess at Auschwitz-1 before moving on to Majdanek, was another in the convoy. When the Red Army had liberated this extermination centre, Liebehenschel had long gone.

A large contingent of SS doctors had assembled in Flensburg. Werner Heyde, a former head of the of the T-4 organisation would be grateful for his new name and with the papers of a Fritz Sawade, he promptly disappeared into the city and there he would remain for the next 14 years, protected by friends in power who knew his real identity. Die Welt often used the term 'Flensburg Kamaraden' in describing the level of post-war protection seemingly offered by the state.

So certain was Heyde of maintaining his cover, he contributed medical opinions to the Schleswig-Holstein State Insurance Agency from his Flensburg home. He was a regular expert witness in court cases and practised as a psychiatrist.

Dönitz was personally responsible for Hitler's long-time personal physician, Karl Brandt, who had fallen out with his leader in April after trying to send his family through the lines to US forces. The Gestapo had arrested him and after sentencing by a military court he was sent to Kiel. Dönitz had him released on May 2 and Brandt had joined him in Flensburg. Leonardo Conti, Germany's senior health officer, had reported into Brandt, and his record marked him out as one of the worst of the SS doctors in T-4. Nanna, Conti's mother, had joined her son in Flensburg and her record as the head of the German midwifery association and of referring to T-4 the names of mentally ill and disabled children, further condemns Germany's medical profession.

Even by the horrific standards of some SS doctors hiding out in Flensburg, Enno Lolling, a senior physician in the Inspectorate who appointed doctors to the camps, justifiably stands out. Lolling initiated a programme to study skin infection after tattooing. Prisoners were then killed and the bodies skinned. In another programme, Lolling had asked camp doctors to decapitate prisoners and develop methods to shrink their heads. Lolling had been a member of the Inspectorate group that had visited Auschwitz in September 1944 at the inauguration of the SS hospital.

Siegfried Hanloser, the head of the Armed Forces Medical Services, would later be found by the British military police and he would join 22 other SS doctors in a special Nuremberg trial that assessed the profession's contribution to mass murder. Given Hanloser's extensive responsibilities, the US prosecution lawyer needed a 42-page closing briefing to summarise his role in the Concentration Camp Inspectorate. When graphic descriptions of typhus experiments in Buchenwald were described in court, Hanloser had argued that they were justified to prevent infection of

▶ The Christiansen Hof in Kollerup was commandeered by Field Marshall Ernst Busch, the Wehrmacht commander of all German forces in northern Germany. Himmler visited and demanded that Busch must provide Wehrmacht travel documentation. Busch had refused.

▲ Busch arriving at the Christiansen Hof.
Source: The Christiansen family

▶ Busch in the garden.
Source: The Christiansen family

▲ Only on April 11, 1946, 11 months after Himmler had left, had Captain Owen, a British military intelligence officer, discovered the significance of the Lorenzen Hof in Hüholz. A member of Himmler's Begleitkommando, Wilhelm Walter, had broken ranks with his detained colleagues and talked. The Lorenzen Hof was turned over by 318 FSS.

▲ At this site behind the barn, Himmler's briefcase had been buried, according to Walter; 318 FSS carefully dug this area in strips, now concreted over.

41

German troops on the Eastern Front. Desperate to avoid the death sentence, Hanloser had described himself as a reluctant medical doctor who found killing repulsive, but he was forced to admit that he hadn't made any attempt to stop the experiments.

Flensburg was not only filling up with SS, SS doctors, SiPo and Gestapo. German resident communities in Denmark were emptying and crossing the border. They knew that Denmark would exact retribution if anyone was found to have aided the Germany military or the collaborative Danish Hipo police. Adding to the influx were emaciated and desperately ill prisoners from Neuengamme, Stutthof and Sachsenhausen on death marches.

One group was from Sandbostel, a Neuengamme satellite, and it had begun on April 20. On reaching the Kiel Canal, the 1,000 prisoners were escorted aboard the steamer, *Olga Siemers*, and the conditions were rank. The steamer sailed into the Baltic Sea and berthed in Flensburg on April 30. Those still deemed capable were loaded onto a goods train for onward transit but with Allied aircraft straffing the trains and stations, it was forced to a halt at the railway station in Weiche, to the south of the city.

A second train joined the chaos and squalor in Weiche. On April 30, a death march of 600 inmates from Neuengamme had started out for Lübeck but with that route no longer secure, they boarded a train to Flensburg only to stop at Weiche. Some 1,600 prisoners were now holed up in the stationary trains where they would remain until May 4 until Flensburg's bürgermeister cleared out the station. The *Rheinfels*, a passenger steamer moored in Flensburg harbour, became the final destination but the conditions were as bad as the trains. Many of the SS guards deserted leaving the prisoners locked up and starving.

A similar predicament faced prisoners from the Stutthof concentration camp near the Polish city of Gdansk. They had been shipped to Flensburg on-board the barge *Ruth*. During the five-day Baltic crossing, 330 of the 960 had succumbed from dehydration or asphyxiation as the SS guards had battened down the deck hatches. The now-moored vessel in Flensburg quickly earned the reputation as the 'SS Death Ship'.

The outcome was immeasurably more positive for 200 German

Jews from the Riga ghetto in Latvia. Count Bernadotte had negotiated their safe transit through the Krusau border post 6km north of Flensburg into Denmark, with final sanctuary in Sweden.

THE WEHRMACHT TAKES OVER KOLLERUP

Kollerup in May 1945 was a farming community near Flensburg with 77 inhabitants, seven farms, a guesthouse, a blacksmith and a pub that doubled up as a meeting place. Already swamped by a tide of refugees vying for space in a barn or attic, similar to other hamlets, the sudden appearance of 350 Wehrmacht officers and soldiers, artillery and armoured vehicles alarmed both the residents and refugees who faced the stark realisation that the war was far from over.

A Wehrmacht billeting officer had arrived at the end of April to commandeer accommodation for Field Marshal Ernst Busch, a 60-year-old army careerist, who Dönitz would later promote to C-in-C of all forces in northern Germany, Denmark and Norway. Armed roadblocks were set up on the two roads into Kollerup, schoolchildren were barred from travelling to school in nearby Estrup and farmers on their tractors had to show IDs. Most residents were reticent in venturing outside their homes. Kollerup was sealed tight.

The Christiansen Hof, a farmhouse with a magnificent dining room and murals on its ceiling, became the telecommunications centre and chosen as Busch's personal quarters with an adjacent room as his bedroom. Busch was ill, his chronic heart condition worsening by the day, so he needed Dr Liebartz, his personal doctor, close. Liebartz had a room, as did Busch's adjutant and two orderlies. The Christiansen family and the nanny, Adel Braun, remained in the house. The nanny lived in a small space outside the dining room and she overheard many of Busch's conversations. After the war she married a Scotsman and now aged 100 she lives in Australia.

General Staff used the Jacobsen Hof as its headquarters, which also housed the typing pool and the cartographers who were busy drawing up maps. Troops dug a wide defensive trench around this Kollerup farmhouse against a British attack. Dönitz visited and on one occasion the young Helga Jacobsen observed him sitting on the entrance steps in his uniform, deep in thought. The shy Helga wanted to talk to him but she thought better of it. The Wild Badger pub opposite was utilised by the general staff.

A sole British jeep drove slowly through Kollerup on May 5 in a recce with a white flag on the windscreen. It didn't stop and nor did the wary Wehrmacht make any attempt to intervene.

That very day, Grand Admiral von Friedeburg, the navy chief in the Dönitz government, was in Lüneburg to accept Montgomery's terms for unconditional surrender in the Netherlands, Schleswig-Holstein, the Friesian and Heligoland islands, and Denmark. In the Christiansen Hof, the highly charged atmosphere heightened during the course of the day and late in the evening, three senior Wehrmacht officers arrived for an urgent meeting with Busch. The dining room door was quickly closed but Adel was listening. The telephone rang and voices rose sharply. She heard that at 8am the next day, all German troop movements were to cease. Excited, Adel rushed to see the family and gushed out the news.

For Dönitz and his ministers in Murwick, it was business as usual on the Eastern Front. After six years of a murderous and barbaric Reich occupation, the Prague Uprising had begun. The huge Red Army offensive on Dresden would quickly follow. Military discipline remained strict. Three sailors from the destroyer, *Paul Jacoby,* were taken ashore to face a firing squad in Flensburg. They were accused of sabotaging the ship's compass.

Kollerup would shortly witness another visitor, this time the victor. Alma Möllgaard-Langmaark, whose family owned the Langmaark Hof, saw a Jeep cruising slowly through the village. It was Montgomery. From their vantage points, the 350-strong Wehrmacht contingent watched. It had still to formerly stand down.

HIMMLER'S FINAL ADDRESS

Despite being handed the portfolio of interior and security minister by Dönitz, Himmler felt he was far better qualified than anyone else to lead a post-Third Reich government. Himmler had chosen the conference room in Flensburg's central police station on May 5 to outline his political ambition.

Who attended is unclear but one Himmler loyalist who did pitch up to listen and no doubt applaud was Alfred Wünnenberg, the 54-year-old former Waffen-SS commander turned head of the Ordnungs Polizei, Germany's uniformed police service. His reserve police battalions had eliminated entire Jewish communities in Poland and the Ukraine. Wünnenberg had blood on his hands. Reports of Himmler's incendiary declaration quickly reached Murwick. He had arrogantly proclaimed a new sovereign state from Flensburg to the River Eïder, stretching from the North Sea to the south of Kiel.

The sacking came as no surprise the following morning. Dönitz had found Himmler's very presence in Flensburg a hindrance and an embarrassment. In Himmler's hideaways in Hüholz, Mariengaard and Lutzhöft, the Stab and Begleitkommando stepped up plans for escape. Several times, Himmler, with Rudolf Brandt, his key aide, had visited Kollerup to discuss the war with senior Wehrmacht officers and in what would be the final confrontation with Busch, Himmler went alone to the Christiansen Hof to demand Wehrmacht travel documents for his people to get through British lines.

Adel Braun, the Christiansen family nanny, probably heard every word. Busch, never a Himmler supporter, refused any assistance and Himmler had stormed out. That might have been the day when the young Liesel Höck witnessed him outside the Höck Hof, her home adjacent to the Christiansen Hof, in earnest conversation with a number of German officers.

Germany's surrender was officially confirmed on May 8. Jodl and von Friedeburg had travelled to Rheims, northern France, to sign and in the evening, von Krosigk broadcast the terms from the Post Office communications room next to Flensburg's central police station.

With time now running out, Himmler summoned the Concentration Camp Inspectorate, camp commandants and other loyal SS to the fire training school in Harrislee for what was to be his final address. Himmler's mood was surprisingly upbeat, as witnessed by Rudolf Hoess. 'Himmler was beaming and in the best of spirits, yet the world had crumbled beneath our feet. He told us to hide in the Wehrmacht and disappear.'

Himmler then returned to Hüholz leaving his loyal cadre of mass murderers to make their own arrangements. Hoess didn't choose a Wehrmacht identity, opting instead for the naval ID of Franz Lang, a dead seaman. Within hours of saying his farewell to Himmler, he headed west to Sylt, an island in the Friesian archipelago.

On that day – May 8 – the Red Army took Dresden.

THE BRITISH ARRIVE AT THE 'ANT HEAP'

Victory in Europe (VE) Day – May 9 – was barely celebrated by the British 159th Brigade, commanded by Brigadier Jack Churcher, which was moving up from the Kiel Canal. The brigade was battle-weary, landing on Juno Beach in Normandy on D-Day plus 6 and participating in the bloody battle to take Caen. It moved into Belgium and was the first to enter Antwerp. The Rhine was crossed on March 28 and Osnabruck was taken. On April 12, the brigade had witnessed the piled corpses at Bergen-Belsen concentration camp.

Montgomery had given the order to move on Flensburg and by this time, Churcher's soldiers were inured to the sight of German atrocities. An advance party had tentatively ventured inside the city and reported back that no accommodation was available. No shots were exchanged. The entire brigade of 2,500 in strength set up camp four miles to the south. Churcher needed to confirm what the advance party had witnessed. 'The place was full to overflowing just like one would imagine an ant heap. Everywhere, men and women crawled all over the place, in uniform, not in uniform. It was a most fantastic sight', he wrote in his military papers.[13] The sight of large numbers of heavily armed German naval and military police and army buses lurching through the streets full of troops was disturbing. The Luftwaffe airfield remained operational.

Churcher entered the office of the Flensburg bürgermeister, Ernst Kracht, who stood proudly in his SS uniform: his desk adorned with a framed photograph of Hitler. Churcher ordered it be removed before his visit the next day. Asked for an estimate of the strength of the German military in and around the city, Kracht estimated 50,000. Churcher gave him the day to find accommodation for his brigade.

---

[13] Churcher's papers are held in the Liddell Hart military archives at King's College, University of London.

On that second visit – May 10 – the photograph had gone and surprisingly, Kracht had located some billets. To create an impression, Churcher now sent the brigade's band into the main square and the brigade was trucked through the city with armoured carriers, the soldiers alert. The roads were lined with the curious and the anxious. Roadblocks were set up and troops barred all crossings into Denmark. Out into the Flensburg fjord, no ship could escape as the British and Soviet navies put on an equal display of force.

In Flensburg's central police station there was a rush to vacate as word soon spread that Churcher was to commandeer the building as his headquarters. The assorted Police, SiPo, and SS had moved out but not before dumping documents in the courtyard in the rear for burning. Churcher and a detachment from the British navy, facing the challenge of dealing with over 2,000 vessels of all sizes in the harbour, moved in, wary of any nasty surprises deliberately left behind. A building nearby was requisitioned as the Officers Mess.

British troops quickly located the *Rheinfels* steamer and liberated the prisoners. What SS guards that had remained on-board were arrested. The *Ruth*, described as the 'SS Death Ship', was also located and in the months to come the British authorities were determined to bring the perpetrators of this war crime to book. In Berlin, General Ivan Serov, the head of the Russian NKVD in the city, was asked to extradite several guards who had fled to the comparative safety of the Soviet Occupation Zone. One was Kurt Wanserski who had escaped Flensburg for Hagen before joining his parents in Schwerin to live under the family name of Jantzen. In the trial that eventually took place in Flensburg, city lawyers defended the 13 SS guards, demanding acquittal for all. Almost all were, but two were executed.[14]

For Churcher on May 10, a trip to Murwick and the other military centres on the southern side of Flensburg's fjord was paramount. London needed briefing.

First on his list was the Naval Torpedo and Signal School. Moored

---

[14] Some of the bodies of those on the *Ruth* were later recovered by the British and buried on Friedenshügel, the Peace Hill, in Flensburg. The trial had taken place at the Saal des Deutschen Hauses.

alongside was the luxury liner, the *Patria*, where Dönitz and his ministers socialised. The Naval Cadet School was a short drive away. Its commanding officer had gladly given up the sports block to Dönitz to use as administration offices and it was heavily guarded by the Wache-Marine-Battalion, the navy military.

At first the guards barred his way but Churcher strode through the main gate, climbed the steps to the front door of the sports block and went inside. The sight of members of the British army brought stunned staff out of their offices into the corridor. Churcher was startled to see Himmler who was top priority to locate and arrest. Himmler hastily retreated. Churcher loudly called for Jodl and when the military chief did finally appear, he vehemently denied that the former Reichsführer-SS was in the building. Concerned about the large military presence, Churcher ordered Jodl to immediately reduce the naval troops in Murwick to no more than 300 and to prioritise the construction of detainment camps.

Next on Churcher's drive of discovery along the coastline was Glücksburg Castle, the grand residence of the Mecklenburg family, used as living quarters by several of Dönitz's ministers. Churcher chose not to enter the Marine-Kaserne complex hidden in the woods at Meierwik, where the SS were housed including the group from the Concentration Camp Inspectorate. He didn't want to instigate a confrontation.

Glücks, the SS head of the Concentration Camp Inspectorate, who Hoess had brought through the Allied lines, was the first to commit suicide and avoid capture. Later that day, he bit into his phial of cyanide poison. His immediate superior, Otto Pohl, one of the top officers in the SS hierarchy, also knew his days of freedom were numbered and he went on the run, hiding out in the Flensburg hamlets where in the weeks to come he would work as a farmhand.

"ARREST THE LOT AT ONCE AND LIQUIDATE IT AS SOON AS POSSIBLE"

Back at his headquarters at the central police station, Churcher called his divisional commander to report, no doubt mentioning the sighting of Himmler. Two hours later Montgomery called him and the British Field Marshal didn't mince his words. "'Arrest the lot at once and liquidate it as soon as possible'", ordered Montgomery, in a typically tetchy mood. Not possible, replied Churcher, he simply didn't have the military resources. "'Make a plan then, what help do you want?'" came the blunt response.

Churcher's unexpected appearance in Murwick was the signal for Himmler and his group to break. An SS ratline into Italy was already established with a compliant Vatican providing new identities and travel documents to Argentina, via the port of Genoa. But first, Himmler needed to relocate to Friedrichskoog at the mouth of the Elbe, on the south-west coastline of Schleswig-Holstein, a distance of 140km.

According to the later British interrogation report for Werner Grothmann, Himmler's primary adjutant, the reason why Himmler had been in Murwick on May 10, despite his sacking by Dönitz, was to hand Jodl a note to be immediately couriered to Montgomery. Its content acknowledged that Britain and the other Allies had beaten the Third Reich militarily but enormous effort was now needed to re-establish a stable Germany. He pledged to assist Montgomery, placing the Waffen-SS at the disposal of the British to fight the Soviet Union, and requested a private meeting. Himmler had asked Montgomery to courier his response to Friedrichskoog.

That note was not delivered to Montgomery. It never left Murwick. Jodl never had any intention in sending it.

In Murwick, even after the appearance of a senior British officer, it was business as usual for this rump government. Dönitz and his ministers remained committed to a fighting retreat from the Red Army.

On that day – May 10 – three sailors aboard the German vessel *Buea* faced a firing squad. Before the May 8 capitulation, they had deserted with a fourth colleague at Svendborg in Denmark but caught by the collaborative Danish Hipo police and handed over to the German authorities on Funen. In what was to be the very last court-martial in Nazi Germany, the ship's captain, Rudolf Petersen, ordered them shot. He had contemptuously brushed aside the plea from one of the accused, the 20-year-old Alfred Gail, that the war was over. His body was later washed ashore at Nordgaardholz in the

Flensburg fjord.[15] The fourth sailor was sentenced to imprisonment but it wouldn't be served.

THE RATS SCUTTLE AWAY

Himmler's people had for days planned the escape. One of the Kübelwagens had returned to Lutzhöft from Himmler's SS base in Harrislee with an assortment of uniforms for distribution in the general exodus.[16] Documents in the fire training school were destroyed. Activity accelerated in the Otzen Hof in Mariengaard, the impromptu SS workshop on the top floor that supplied forged travel documents.

In the Diederichsen home in Lutzhöft, the three SS officers billeted in the property were amongst the first to leave demanding a lift in Diederichsen's horse and cart to the railway station in nearby Husby. That short trip almost cost Diederichsen his life. As the horse and cart manoeuvred down the track, the senior SS officer began a bitter tirade towards him on why he wasn't on the Eastern Front fighting the Red Army. Diederichsen ignored him yet the officer wasn't done, boasting about his own actions in the 'Ausland' and why the killing of women and children in Poland had been perfectly acceptable. This time Diederichsen did take offence and only the quick interjection by the others averted a bullet in the nape of the neck. Diederichsen seized the moment, ordering them out and speeding home leaving the SS to walk. He'd been lucky.

Heinz Macher, the Begleitkommando chief, had assembled his men in Lutzhöft, probably at the Jacobsen Hof, to outline the escape plan. The party would split up and take several routes south to hold up in Bavaria. Grothmann and himself would take personal charge of the former Reichsführer-SS. Safely in Bavaria the Begleitkommando would regroup and go underground creating havoc among the occupying Allies especially the hated Red Army. Not discussed was whether Himmler had an ultimate escape destination.

---

[15] A memorial stone dedicated to Alfred Gail is on the fjord bank.
[16] This was confirmed during the interrogation of Walter, a member of Himmler's Begleitkommando, in April 1946.

'HIMMLER'S TREASURE'

Himmler had personal items he needed to conceal for retrieval at a later date when safe to do so. British Intelligence would term it 'Himmler's treasure' when it launched an intensive European-wide search to locate it.

Heinrich Springer, Himmler's ordnance officer, and Herbert Dürring, Himmler's deputy adjutant, had driven to the forest in Leck, 28km to the west of Flensburg, to meet up with Bartels, the forestry manager, who had been a frequent visitor to the Lorenzen Hof in Hüholz in recent days. Bartels advice had been sought in burying Himmler's weapon collection. Springer would list the items in his interrogation by the British in January 1947, an interrogation record that would remain secret until 2007, the year of his death in Schleswig-Holstein. Carefully wrapped up and buried in Leck were two prized shotguns, two light MGs, several revolvers, a dozen hand-grenades and a quantity of ammunition.

The destruction of Himmler's papers in Hüholz was the responsibility of Heinz Schreiber, his confidential secretary. He burnt them behind the barn at the Lorenzen Hof and he ordered Wilhelm Walter, a Begleitkommando member, to dispose of Himmler's briefcase, also behind the barn.[17] This was the briefcase observed by the young Hans Heinrich Otzen in Himmler's parked-up Steyr in the shed at the Otzen Hof in Mariengaard. Walter buried it deep and covered over the area so it would appear undisturbed.

In the hiding of the most priceless component of 'Himmler's treasure', Springer had chosen a temporary home in his granny annex in the Festesen Hof in Mariengaard. Springer and Dürring had driven the two metal strongboxes over from the Lorenzen Hof, containing gold, jewellery, including a priceless pearl necklace, a collection of diamond-faced watches and a large amount of money in convertible currencies.[18] Under the watchful gaze of Ursula, Springer's wife, the two Himmler aides pulled up the floorboards to expose the deep void below. They dug deep into the sandy soil.

---

[17] Walter's interrogation had confirmed the order from Schreiber.
[18] Confirmed by Springer.

▶ A *Sunday Graphic* photographer took this photograph of Werner Grothmann and Karl Heinz Macher in British custody, shortly after their arrest with Himmler.

THE THUGS are Himmler's bodyguards, captured with their chief. When a "Sunday Graphic" cameraman took this picture both men were believed to have poison phials in their mouths.

▲ Springer was a much-decorated Waffen-SS officer before joining Himmler's Stab. While in British custody, he was accused of committing war crimes in Belgium, torching homes and executing civilians. Springer was No.18 on the United Nations War Crimes List No.11. Springer with his wife Ursula. Escaping twice from the Neuengamme detention centre, shoot on sight when cornered was the Allied military instruction if Springer became a threat to life during his second escape.

▶ Herbert Dürring's post-war movements are unknown. The Bundesarchiv in Berlin provided his SS file and photographs. Upon Springer's arrest at the Festesen Hof, the second visit from the FSS, Dürring fled, later organising the retrieval of the strongboxes from the granny annex.

▲ The former Festesen Hof in Lützoft was commandeered by a number of Himmler's Stab and Begleitkommando, who occupied almost every room. Heinrich Festesen was the wartime deputy bürgermeister, or mayor.

▲ The granny annex sits at the entrance to the Festesen property where Himmler's weapons officer, Heinrich Springer, and Herbert Dürring, one of his two adjutants, buried Himmler's two metal strongboxes under the floorboards. Springer returned to the Festesen Hof in 1965, his unexpected meeting with Festesen both acrimonious and lengthy.

Springer had taken the decision to remain in Mariengaard with his family and take his chances but had told his wife that he would shoot himself if the Soviets moved into Schleswig-Holstein. Earlier, Springer had hidden his own weapons in a nearby copse: two 7.6mm pistols, one given to him by Ursula six months before.

Inside the Lorenzen Hof, no clues would remain of Himmler's time in the property. The outbuildings where some of the Begleitkommando had slept were systematically cleansed. A Kübelwagen not needed in the breakout was driven out to the Winderatter wood close to the Lorenzen Hof, an area studded with deep pools of water, and dumped, but its roof remained visible.[19] The Steyr command vehicle was left in the Otzen Hof in Mariengaard. It was later taken to a secluded farmhouse in the Weigab, a boggy area 7km away, where Himmler had visited, according to Otzen. The significance of this property during Himmler's time in the hamlets has never been explained. What eventually happened to the Steyr remains the subject of local speculation.

By early evening – May 10 – Himmler's party was almost ready. In the Lorenzen Hof, Himmler had shaved off his trademark moustache and replaced his glasses with an eye-patch. The SS uniform had for some days been exchanged for a civilian jacket, field grey trousers and boots. To anyone who would now ask his identity, Himmler was Heinrich Hitzinger, a sergeant in the Feldpolizei, the Wehrmacht's secret police that rooted out counter-espionage and sabotage, trying to make his way home.

Three Volkswagen Kübelwagens left the Lorenzen Hof at 10.30pm. The group had decided it was safer to travel at night. Aside from Himmler, his party included Rudolf Brandt, Werner Grothmann, Josef Kiermeier, his personal bodyguard, as well as Begleitkommando members, Heinz Macher, Dr Max Müller, Eduard Schmid, Rudolf Böttcher, Nicholas Lorenz and the SS Feldwebel, Lüngen. Dürring was to remain in the Festesen property in Mariengaard with Springer.

---

[19] We spoke to 84-year-old Anna Maria Lorenzen who confirmed that the vehicle had remained in the pool for a number of years but it was gradually stripped back by local children.

In the hamlets, the camaraderie extended towards Himmler and the SS was now tempered by expectation that the British were very close. Papers were destroyed in the Jacobsen Hof in Lutzhöft, and weapons disposed of. Not yet would Georg Jacobsen, the SS bürgermeister, have to defend his war record as a member of the SS Division 'Totenkopf' in Talinn and Copenhagen. Jacobsen continued with his mayoral duties. Andresen, the brown-shirted Nazi who had strutted around the village in his supposed importance and paid by the NSDAP to snoop on the residents, put away his uniform and buttoned his lip. Abandoned in the barns and farmhouses were SS uniforms, IDs, unused fuel drums, weapons and an assortment of personal items.

Lutzhöft's Hitlerplatz was now a shrine to a bust and broken Nazi ideology and Jacobsen, in a bid to cover up the 'Brown' support, wanted the centre-piece stone commemorating Hitler's ascension to power in 1933, dug out and buried. Jacobsen cynically ordered the village pacifists to do the digging but Hans Diederichsen objected, as did other sympathisers called up for the task. Diederichsen bluntly told Jacobsen that his Nazi cronies should do it instead, but they eventually gave in and dug to keep the peace.

Not all the SS had left the village and the sight of villagers tearing down the upright stone emblazoned with the Reichsadler and swastika enraged two officers who strode over from the Wree Hof, revolvers raised and shouting. The diggers were accused of treason and for the second time in a matter of days, Diederichsen dodged a bullet in brazenly facing off the SS, reasoning that the war was over. Willy, another digger, angrily retorted that as the order had come from the SS bürgermeister he should be the first to be shot. Cheekily, Diederichsen suggested that the young officers might lend a hand. They strutted away, fuming. Those men may have been the remnants of Hitler's Begleitkommando that had escaped Berlin to join Himmler in Lutzhöft.

Johannes Diederichsen, aged 10 at the time, recalled the day the British army arrived. With his good friend Fritz from the guesthouse, they heard the rumble getting closer and within moments an open jeep with armoured cars pulled up at the Hitler Platz. Both boys stood back, staring, as the soldiers climbed down and waved.

According to Johannes, the soldiers sat on the grass and prepared a breakfast of white bread sandwiches offering one to the boys. Johannes had never seen white bread before. A British officer walked over to the Diederichsen Hof and introduced himself to Hans Diederichsen and his wife, Margaret, who celebrated the occasion by serving up tea in the best silver to their visitor. All the local bürgermeisters and councillors would remain in post until checks were made into their past, said the British officer. Georg Jacobsen, for the moment, was safe.

The Diederichsen family made an intriguing discovery. In the shed behind the house, that the billeted SS had used, a walking stick was found with a 'W' whittled into it. Did that refer to the 'Werewolves', Hitler's group of fanatical Hitler Youth that was formed in 1944 to hide behind the Allied lines and create mayhem? British Field Security Sections were already scouring the Flensburg area looking for Nazis whose names were on the UN war criminal lists. Alfred Wunnenberg, the head of the Ordnungs Polizei, was in the bag on May 13.

A Belgian FSS, all fluent German speakers, had pitched up at Flensburg's central police station on May 11, briefed to help assess what was going on in Murwick. Montgomery had agreed that the 'liquidation' of the Dönitz administration would take place on May 23, allowing Churcher 12 days to plan. Annoyingly for Churcher, Montgomery had dispatched an Allied Control Mission from SHAEF[20] to advise on the roll-up. A further aggravation was Field Marshal Busch's national broadcast from Murwick, arrogantly announcing that as well as being in charge of the German army in Schleswig-Holstein he also had the remit to run the large area occupied by the British military. 'All German military and civilians are subordinated to me', Busch had declared. 'Utter fiction', Churcher later wrote in his war papers and he sent in army technicians, with guards, to dismantle the Murwick communications centre. Dönitz had been shut down, for good.

The Allied Control Mission duly arrived: an American general,

---

[20] Supreme Headquarters Allied Expeditionary Force.

Lowell Rook; three Russians – a general, an admiral, and a senior airforce officer; a British brigadier and a French colonel. Churcher was immediately wary of the Russians but the first concern was to find suitable quarters for the Mission and its staff. The British navy came to his rescue by bringing down the *Patria*, with its full crew, from its mooring in the Naval Torpedo and Signal School, and berthing at the quayside in the centre of the city. Churcher gave it only one gangplank so the Russian movements could be easily monitored. Trust quickly became an issue as the Russians pursued their own agenda and were deliberately obstructive.

On the Eastern Front, Prague, the last Nazi bastion, fell to the Red Army, nine days after the fall of Berlin and three days after the surrender at Rheims. The partisan uprising in Prague had been a success but everywhere in Central and Eastern Europe, the German tyranny was being replaced with another. The NKVD and Smersh were moving into buildings vacated by the Gestapo to enforce the Soviet brand of enforcement and government.

'THE ONLY SANE MAN IN A GERMANY THAT HAD GONE MAD'

After Himmler's party left the Flensburg hamlets on May 10, the group had split. Only Macher, Grothmann and Lüngen now accompanied Himmler. Macher drove and using the side roads they arrived in Friedrichskoog at the outflow of the Elbe at 6.30am the next day. Finding a secluded hut they rested up and ate their tinned provisions hoping that the courier from Montgomery agreeing to a meeting would pitch up. Montgomery, of course, never received Himmler's note in Murwick: Jodl had seen to that.

After two days and still no courier, and in a position surrounded by British troops, Himmler decided they should head further south, cross the Elbe, and head for the Harz Mountains. A local fisherman, Willy Plett, was paid 500 Reichsmarks to take them across the mouth of the Elbe to the village of Otterndorf on the night of May 16. From now on they were on foot. Himmler dismissed Lüngen.

Macher and Grothmann walked ahead while Himmler trudged behind, in character with the weariness of others filling the roads.

Their dress was typical: Grothmann and Macher wore Wehrmacht greatcoats and Himmler looked the part in his shabby Wehrmacht Feldpolizei top and civilian trousers. The outskirts of Bremervörde were reached on May 18. The others had also reached the town. Kiermeier, Müller, Schmid, Böttcher and Lorenz headed into Bremervörde on a scouting mission.

There are differing accounts as to the circumstances of Himmler's arrest, but I prefer the one, dated June 13, 1945, written down by a British interrogation officer after interviewing Grothmann at length.

> *The arrest occurred on May 21 near Meinstedt* (south of Bremervörde and south west of Hamburg), *by three Russian soldiers who were attached to a British security control. Himmler was wearing civilian clothing and had a black patch over an eye, while Grothmann and Macher were dressed partly in uniform, tunics and greatcoats, without badges of any kind.'*

The arrest was timed at 5pm. Continued the British officer:

> *'In view of this disguise, they were not recognised by the Russians, who handed them over to the occupants of a British army car. They were driven to a camp at Seelos-bei-Bremervörde and remained unrecognised. Grothmann said this was not surprising, since Heinrich Himmler in civilian clothing and without his glasses appeared as an ordinary type of middle-aged German and was definitely difficult to identify.*
>
> *'On the following day – May 22 – the three men were taken to another camp at Bremervörde where they were briefly interrogated. The British officers supposed them to be either German civilian refugees or Wehrmacht deserters. Himmler gave his name as Hitzinger, whilst Grothmann assumed the identity of his elder brother Eduard Grothmann. He had three brothers in the Wehrmacht, Eduard, Otto and Günther.*
>
> *'Himmler, Grothmann and Macher were subsequently transferred the next day to Westertimke camp, north-east of Bremen, in a group of 20 German civilians and military prisoners from a number of locations. While all were being searched, the camp commandant was told that one urgently needed to talk to him. It was Grothmann, still assuming the name of his brother.*

'Grothmann told Captain Smith, the chief interrogator, that he was SS and he with his two colleagues wanted to speak privately. Curious, Smith isolated the three from the others and the man calling himself Hitzinger introduced himself as Heinrich Himmler and admitted that Grothmann and Macher were aides. Himmler said he needed to speak to Field Marshal Montgomery.

'The commandant left them under an armed guard in a side room to make urgent telephone calls. Returning with two other British officers, the three were ordered to strip. Himmler removed his horn-rimmed glasses and eye patch. An examination of Himmler's rucksack revealed a change of underwear and a small glass phial with a colourless liquid that Himmler said was to treat his severe bouts of stomach cramps. The phial was taken away for examination. Himmler's examination ended at 18.40 hours on May 23'.

Himmler was hauled away to the prison in Bramstedt, south of Bremerhaven, where he remained for a very short time under close guard. Colonel Murphy, head of British Second Army Intelligence, collected him and in a three-car convoy they arrived at a semi-detached house in Uelzener Strasse, Amelinghausen, a requisitioned property to interrogate special prisoners. The stooped figure of Himmler emerged, swathed in a British army blanket and wearing army boots, accompanied by Colonel Murphy. Himmler had been offered a British battledress at Bramstedt but had refused it.

In the building, CSM Edwin Austin, a fluent German speaker, spoke firmly to Himmler and he was led into a room where Captain Wells, a British army doctor, awaited. Himmler was again stripped. When Wells began examining his mouth for a poison phial, Himmler objected but not before the doctor saw a blue object wedged between the lower teeth and gums. Yanking open Himmler's mouth, Wells attempted to prise out the phial but Himmler bit deep and painfully into the doctor's finger and crunched into the phial. As Himmler convulsed, his legs were grabbed and he was hung upside down with his mouth dunked in a bowl of water in a vain attempt to save him. According to the official report, Himmler died at 23:14 hours on May 23 within '25 minutes of taking poison'.

One of the British sergeants present exclaimed, 'the bastard's beaten

us'. The naked body lay under a blanket on the bare floorboards in the room overnight, fully visible to the inquisitive. He was photographed with his glasses for the records, the glasses soon disappearing as a war trophy, before being quickly replaced. At one stage, the blanket was pulled fully back to expose the SS chief, the man responsible for the deaths of millions. The next day the body was dumped unceremoniously in a leafy grave in a forest outside Amelinghausen by two British army sergeants who were sworn to secrecy on its location. [21]

In London, *The Times* ran an obituary on May 25, headlined 'Power through Terror'. Himmler had been clever it reported: even in the early days of the Third Reich he made no public speeches, wrote no books or articles, preferring to perpetuate the mystery and imagery of a secret state, run by him. The newspaper concluded that in one of his conversations with Count Bernadotte, 'Himmler is said to have described himself as the only sane man in a Germany that had gone mad'.

At least Himmler's suicide was witnessed. Only charred remains existed for Hitler outside the door of his Berlin bunker, and to this day there are doubts on authenticity. Bormann died in the Berlin ruins, his teeth identified by his dentist in 1972 after a body, seemingly his, was found buried in wasteland being excavated for an exhibition park near Lehrter railway station. Like Hitler, there are doubts. Heinrich Müller, the Gestapo chief, was never located and respected veteran KGB officers I knew for several years confirmed that he was secretly picked up by the Russians and run by the NKVD in Moscow, assisting in the interrogation of captured high-ranking German military.

Back at Westertimke, Grothmann and Macher now underwent intense questioning. Grothmann's interrogator handed him the photographs of the British army's liberation of Bergen-Belsen but Himmler's senior adjutant nonchalantly dismissed them as Allied

◀ Himmler's body, following his suicide

---

[21] Those two British sergeants, Ray Weston and Bill Ottery, returned to the building in 1977 and visited the woods where Himmler's body was buried. They were still under instruction never to reveal the exact site.

propaganda. When bluntly told that the photographs had been taken not by the army but by accredited photographers attached to the British units, Grothmann studied them more carefully and finally shook his head in disbelief. Himmler, too, stated Grothmann, had been in blissful ignorance of what had occurred in the concentration camps. The interrogator recorded the lies.

The interrogator also noted that Grothmann was a 'tough customer' in every sense with a demand that none of Himmler's Stab or Begleitkommando should be prosecuted for war crimes. All were entitled to the military privilege of rank as prisoners of war. Macher, the head of the Begleitkommando, in his interrogation, reiterated that in the last weeks of the war Himmler only wanted to assist the Allies and those efforts needed recognition. By chance, a British photographer was at Westertimke and he took a unique picture of Grothmann and Macher in their leather trench coats, talking together. [22]

The day *The Times* ran its Himmler obituary, General Karl Oberg, known as the 'Butcher of Paris' had been picked up hiding on a farm in Kitzbühel, near Innsbruck. Renowned for his barbarity, Oberg was a personal friend of Himmler and the Gestapo's most senior officer next to his chief. Oberg would twice be sentenced to hang but each time the death penalty was rescinded. Also that day, in London, the Polish authorities made a statement that it would be seeking the highest level of retribution for 15,000 war criminals.

Günther Pancke, the notorious and brutal Gestapo chief in Denmark and a long-standing friend of Himmler, had been taken. His wife, Adda, had rented a house in Barg, to the south-east of Flensburg and Pancke had regularly visited. Oddly, the British would embargo the news of his arrest until June 11.

On May 21, the British army torched almost every barrack in the Bergen-Belsen concentration camp, such drastic action necessary to control the typhus that remained rife amongst the inmates. Since this German atrocity had been liberated, the stinking and rotting bodies had been buried in large pits. Almost all the thousands of dead had no name.

---

[22] The photograph is in the Grothmann interrogation file and it was published in the *Sunday Graphic* under the heading of 'The Rogues Gallery'.

ROLLING UP THE LAST NAZI BOLT HOLE

In the spacious lounge bar of the *Patria*, the headquarters for the Allied Mission, Churcher laid out to its American, British, French and Russian members the details of *Operation Blackout*. It was the eve of what Montgomery had referred to as the 'liquidation'.

The American, Rook, true-to-form, had strapped a loaded and cocked revolver around his thigh, resembling a gunslinger. 'Rook gave me the creeps', recalled Churcher later in his military papers. Churcher had expected some dissention from the Russians, as did Rook, but its three representatives signed up to his plan for the following day – May 23. The only Russian stipulation was that the list of everyone arrested must be shared. Arresting Himmler was paramount. At this point, Allied intelligence was unaware that Himmler had fled the Flensburg area on May 10, the day that Churcher had seen him in Murwick. Intelligence reports also placed Heinrich Müller and Martin Bormann hiding out in the Flensburg area. Dönitz, Jodl, Keitel, von Ribbentrop, Alfred Rosenberg, the Nazi Party ideologist, and William Joyce, the American-born Irish broadcaster, who had pumped out anti-Allied propaganda from Berlin, Luxembourg and Hamburg, were also among Churcher's immediate targets.

News came in during the day that the German fleet had finally disarmed in Copenhagen's port: a prize of 135 warships including the *Prinz Eugen*, the 10,000-ton cruiser and the light cruiser, *Nürnberg*. An additional 600,000 tons of merchant shipping was delivered into the hands of the Allies. Every ship was to be made ready with skeleton crews to sail to ports in England. *The Prinz Eugen* was then to sail to Boston in the US, and was destined to end its days in the Pacific in early atomic bomb testing.

Maintaining secrecy of the intended roll-up of Murwick on May 23 was overriding but Churcher realised he could never keep the lid on for long. The press had sniffed a major breaking story and 50 war correspondents descended on Flensburg. Luckily one was Chester Willmott of the *Daily Telegraph* who Churcher trusted, so he took him aside in the hope that he might co-ordinate the others. In exchange, Churcher offered the full inside story to Willmott after the operation.

Flensburg was sealed, telecommunications blocked, the runways of the Luftwaffe airfield expertly disabled by a 50-man detachment of the RAF Regiment led by Squadron Leader Mark Hobden whose group with eight others had secured 16 airfields in Schleswig-Holstein in the past week. In the rush to Flensburg, Hobden's force had been held up on the bridge across the Kiel Canal at Rendsburg by an SS Panzer battalion with its tank commander steadfastly refusing to accept that for him and his men the war was over. Hobden wouldn't be deterred and only after what Hobden would recall many years later as 'an hour of forthright discussion', did the German colonel give way. The RAF Regiment was a tough bunch, a well-trained fighting unit with a reputation to match any other in the British military.

Before Churcher concluded his briefing in the *Patria* lounge, the annoying Rook piped up that he was pulling rank over the British brigadier, insisting that he would arrest Dönitz. Churcher was angry.

A message was sent to Murwick. Dönitz, Jodl and von Friedeburg must attend a meeting on the *Patria* the next day at 9.30am. Out in the Baltic, the British and Russian navies patrolled in line abreast blocking any breakout.

'THE LAST SIX MINUTES OF THE THIRD REICH'

Churcher described the arrests.

> 'Punctually at 9.30am, three grey limousines with Wehrmacht number plates emerged from the German headquarters and headed for the Patria. In the first car was Grand Admiral Dönitz, the second, Grand Admiral von Friedeburg, C-in-C of the German Navy, and in the third, General Jodl, C-in-C of the German Army. As they reached the quay, Dönitz's adjutant resplendent with gold tassels, got out of the first car and held the door open. Carrying a gold-tipped baton, Dönitz emerged, and the party went aboard and shown into the lounge bar.
>
> 'Before them was a long table, covered by a white tablecloth. Dönitz, Jodl and von Friedeburg sat down. Dönitz by now had smelt a rat. "It's easy to guess", he said, "why we've been asked here today". They

sat alone in silence for six minutes, while their adjutants paced the linoleum floor of the corridor outside.

'These were the last six minutes of the Third Reich', recalled Churcher.

'When the SHAEF members entered the lounge bar, Dönitz and his commanders rose to their feet. No one saluted from either side. As the arrest details were read out, Dönitz listened impassively, turkey-necked and tight-lipped as ever. Jodl, his face reddened and blotchy, let a sheaf of papers fall through trembling fingers to the floor. Von Friedeburg was on the verge of tears. Dönitz was asked if he had anyway to say. "'Any word from me", he replied, "would be superfluous"'.

The surrender concluded, the German party filed out and it walked resignedly down the gangplank where a posse of armed British officers and soldiers awaited them. Responsibility for Dönitz had been assigned to Captain Derek Knee, Montgomery's trusted German speaker who had helped the British commander draft the surrender document of all German forces in northern Germany on May 4 at Lüneburg Heath.

Churcher's orders were very clear. The British officers must stay close to their charges, watching every move. The Reichsführer's pennant that had previously adorned the bonnet of the Grand Admiral's car had now been removed. In convoy and accompanied by British jeeps, Dönitz, Jodl and von Friedeburg were driven back to their respective living quarters in Murwick to collect the minimum of luggage.

Dönitz took his time and when he reappeared from the commandant's villa, he resembled the 'Michelin Man', reminisced Knee. The wife of the former head of this last vestige of Nazi government had advised her husband to wear several layers of underclothes fearing he might be held in a PoW camp for some time. A batman struggled with the number of suitcases. 'You aren't going on holiday, you're going to prison and you have the choice of one suitcase', Knee had warned. Dönitz was visibly upset. He did choose one but he chose badly. When the suitcase was examined later it contained nothing but more underpants and vests.

This 'comic opera', the Dönitz administration so previously

described by Churcher, had run its course, lasting for 21 days. It had operated without Allied recognition for 15 days after the official unconditional German surrender was signed in the Rheims schoolhouse on May 8.

Operation Blackout was in progress, some 12 hours before Himmler had given himself up in the south. Churcher had taken no chances given the large number of Wache-Marine-Battalion soldiers he had seen on his earlier visit. The King's Shropshire Light Infantry, the Hereford Light Infantry, Hobden's RAF Regiment and a British Field Security Section were fully prepared to respond if attacked.

'My tanks and armoured vehicles had rolled forward in force, my troops advanced with fixed bayonets, and the enclave had surrendered without firing a single shot', wrote Churcher in his papers. The sports complex that housed ministers and staff was locked down, soldiers blocking any exit apart from the front door. As each office and corridor was secured, the FSS scoured each face. Everyone, including the female secretaries, was ordered to face the wall, hands in air, before filing outside to be searched for cyanide or potassium capsules. The search was on to locate the prime targets: Himmler, Heinrich Müller and Martin Bormann. The substantial Murwick grounds were thoroughly searched for runaways. British Pathé recorded the scene for the newsreels back home providing the visual record that the Third Reich was finally dead.

Wilhelm Stuckart, who had taken over Himmler's position as interior and security minister, was amongst those in the bag. A lawyer who had co-authored the Nuremberg Laws, anti-Semitic legislation designed to keep the nation pure, Stuckart had been in agreement at the Wannsee conference in Berlin in January 1942 to exterminate European Jewry. Otto Georg Thierack, the minister of justice, who had gained notoriety for ordering the installation of eight meat hooks in the execution shed in Berlin's Plötzensee jail, was also accounted for. Julius Dorpmüller, the minister of postal affairs and Herbert Backe, minister for food, were in custody but Franz Seldte, the minister of labour, a position he also held under Hitler, had fled. Rosenberg had been located in the Murwick naval hospital ward suffering with a sprained ankle. There was a report that he was drunk. Neither von Ribbentrop nor Joyce, high on the wanted list, was found.

At Glücksburg Castle, a rabbit warren of hiding places, the Belgian FSS had gone in with British infantry. Speer was located. An uncorroborated report said he had been found luxuriating in the bath. The Duke of Mecklenburg was located in this grand castle on the fjord with 40 other members of the German aristocracy who had taken refuge.

By midday in Murwick, 6,000 were held in the grounds and waiting to be trucked away to temporary PoW camps, built by the German military. Among the senior Nazis arrested all but Dönitz had concealed a poison phial. The only casualty had been von Friedeburg. His quarters were at the Marine-Kaserne in Meierwik, but after the arrests on the *Patria*, von Friedeburg had asked his escorting officer, Captain Davies, if he could first go to Murwick to pick up some items from his office. As the jeep came to a halt, von Friedeburg requested to use the toilets and in a locked cubicle, the 50-year-old bit down on his cyanide phial and choked, dying within seconds.

Job well done, and with only one death, that of von Friedeburg, later in the day Churcher ordered in the 15/19th Hussars to parade its armoured vehicles through Flensburg. 'This created a most impressive spectacle and the whole atmosphere changed', he said. 'It was rather like a beehive with the lid lifted off'.

Dönitz, Speer and Jodl had another date with British Pathé, this time joined by the world's press. The three were escorted up the steps of the central police station in the city and made to wait in a cell before being led out to the courtyard in the rear where the camera bulbs flashed. They stood awkwardly and silent, Knee remaining close to Dönitz. On the courtyard walls, troops had mounted machine guards. After the photo-call, they were then led back inside and Dönitz and some ministers were taken away for a flight from the Luftwaffe airfield to the Palace Hotel at Mondorf-les-Bains, Luxembourg, now transformed into a high security area manned by the US military, and nicknamed the 'Ashcan'. The British had other plans for Speer, he would be taken to the British PoW camp named 'Dustbin' in Castle Kransberg in the Taunus Mountains that had previously served as one of Hitler's intelligence centres.

In London, *The Times* wrote: 'Dönitz was not the type of man to be trusted to lead Germany'. Its report on the roll-up read like an end of regime obituary. Curiously, Montgomery wasn't at his Lüneburg headquarters when Churcher's soldiers went in. He had returned to London for a few days and in the evening of May 24, he was at the theatre. The audience, on seeing Montgomery take his seat, stood as one and gave the field marshal a rapturous ovation.

Back in Flensburg, Otto Ohlendorf, head of a key department in Himmler's Reich Main Security Office and the domestic head of the Sicherheitsdienst or SD, had undergone interrogation. His part in the massacres in the Southern Ukraine, Crimea and the Caucasus, commanding Einsatzgruppe D, had already been well recorded. Enno Lolling, the odious SS doctor with a penchant in the camps for skinning prisoners after tattooing, and for shrinking heads, had also been located, his life terminating on May 27 through taking poison. The British had picked up Curt von Gottberg, friend of Himmler and mass murderer, in the hamlet of Hattlundmoor, close to Flensburg. Von Gottberg, who had arranged the Lorenzen Hof in Hüholz for Himmler, chewed into his capsule and avoided the inevitability of a later date with the hangman. Joyce was eventually picked up but completely by chance. A British unit combing the woods near the Danish border, accompanied by a war correspondent, came across him and his wife living rough. The correspondent immediately recognised Joyce's severe facial scar. The whereabouts of von Ribbentrop remained unknown. He had fled south to Hamburg to live rough in the city ruins.

Kollerup was closed down. Busch, the Wehrmacht commander, had already left for Montgomery's headquarters before the Murwick roll-up, vacating the Christiansen Hof to the newly-arrived General Georg von Lindemann, the head of all German forces in Denmark. Curiously, Busch's adjutant had returned to the property requesting food provisions for his now departed chief. A nervous Johannes Christiansen, the head of the family, had tackled Busch when he left on the possible outcome for the villagers when the Wehrmacht left. 'From my experience the British troops will flatten the village', came the blunt response. It wasn't, of course, but the village was far from returning to normality given the volume of displaced persons. We were cordially invited into the Christiansen Hof by the present family and their local friends, and shown original photographs of

Busch's time in this grand farmhouse that became his operations centre. The dining room, with its wonderful ceiling mural, remains almost exactly as it was in May 1945. The door into the adjacent room, which Busch used as a bedroom, is blocked with a painting resting on an easel.

Three days after the roll-up, Churcher was informed that a battalion of up to 1,000 armed Hitler Youth, ready to attack the British when the signal was given, had concealed themselves, two to three at a time, on numerous yachts in the harbour and vessels further down the fjord. Every boat now needed careful searching and the boy soldiers were escorted down the line to PoW camps.

The unexpected death in custody of the Duke of Mecklenberg, a cousin of King George VI, was an embarrassment. The Duchess insisted on a full-scale national funeral in Flensburg but Churcher refused. Instead, the family had to settle for a small private affair much to her anger and she stormed into Churcher's headquarters. She contemptuously slung her husband's British GCVO insignia (the Grand Cross of the Royal Victorian Order) across Churcher's desk, demanding its return to George VI. Churcher courteously walked her off the premises. The GCVO was sent down the line to the general staff and the driver who took it had to get a signed receipt.

Dealing with the huge number of displaced persons in Flensburg and the hamlets proved a mounting difficulty. Russia was given the responsibility for expatriating those whose countries were now under Soviet occupation, a situation that Churcher felt uneasy with. At the Soviet marshalling points for pick-ups he placed British officers to ensure no coercion and he was right to do so. In one location, a Red Army officer shot dead a Pole who jumped off a lorry. Immediately disarmed and charged with murder, the officer was handed over to the Soviet military.

Another ugly incident involved Captain Lutz, a much-decorated former U-boat commander used by Churcher to log vessels in the fjord. 'I thoroughly disliked him and my men never trusted him', recalled Churcher. Billeted in the city, Lutz was found murdered one night and who killed him was never discovered but Churcher denied any British involvement.

Disarming the 250,000-strong German army in Denmark and

bringing it down to Flensburg needed careful planning. Busch, in a last order from Kollerup, had instructed no surrender to the British and even ordered it to immediately dispatch troops to the Eastern Front, an order quickly countermanded. Churcher handed the logistics for the disarmament to a German general and a small Wehrmacht staff working out of his central police station headquarters. Within days, the entire occupation army in Denmark walked in long convoys on one allotted road down to the German border. At the rear of each convoy, an open horse-drawn wagon held provisions.

Handling the weapons required very careful thought. All vehicles and heavy artillery had to be abandoned in Denmark but Churcher agreed that the army should keep their guns in the convoys but on reaching the checkpoint they would be confiscated, with the rifles stripped of firing bolts. It was soon clear to the British that the Wehrmacht in Denmark had been poorly equipped. Most rifles were ancient Austrian Steyrs, a model first manufactured in 1894, and Churcher intended to dump them into the Flensburg fjord. In a surprise move, the British general staff in Lüneburg overruled him as the Chinese army had agreed to buy the entire consignment. The walking convoys continued south to PoW cages near Plön. The entire operation took several days.

Assisting the Danes became a priority. The Danish government wanted to rebuild its army so Churcher allocated British NCOs to instruct, which went well until the question of rations was raised. With food supplies in Denmark scarce, the NCOs had to contend with the minimal rations as per the Danish soldiers and Churcher objected, causing a diplomatic rumpus. The NCOs remained until Churcher's brigade was ordered south to Krefeld in December 1945.

There were concentration camps in and around the Flensburg area. Froslev, just over the Danish border in Padborg, was taken over by the British as a holding centre for many of those arrested at Murwick. Ladelund, a Neuengamme satellite north-west of Flensburg, was already empty. It had operated for just three weeks until December 16, 1944 when the SS returned the rump of the 2,000 prisoners back to Neuengamme. The regime under SS-Untersturmführer (Second Lieutenant) Hans Griems had been brutal and at least 300 died in the camp's short existence, the majority of them Dutch.

Bistoft, close to Kollerup, was the least known local camp. Based in the village bahnhof and served by a single track from Flensburg, from 1942 it housed Soviet and Ukrainian PoWs, including women.[23] The station's booking hall and waiting area served as sleeping quarters and the inmates worked on the local farms to replace the labourers who were now in the military. The men returned every night but the women were allowed to sleep out on the farms. A young Ukrainian woman worked in the Jacobsen Hof in Kollerup and slept in the barn. Suddenly taken gravely ill, the Jacobsen son put her on a sledge and pulled it to the nearest doctor but it was too late. She is commemorated with a gravestone in the cemetery of Bistoft church. On the day of the burial all Bistoft's prisoners were given the day off to attend her funeral. Today, local villagers tenderly care the gravestone.

RAIDING LUTZHÖFT AND MARIENGAARD

After the interrogation of Grothmann and Macher in Westertimke, the British were now piecing together Himmler's last days. Both aides had given up the locations of the Flensburg hamlets where the Himmler entourage had stayed, bar one. The Lorenzen Hof in Hüholz would remain a secret and neither had disclosed the names of their colleagues.

Within hours, a British Field Security Section moved into the hamlets searching for SS. Jacobsen, the Lutzhöft bürgermeister, was arrested on May 24, and interned for interrogation at the Neumünster detainment camp for SS and Gestapo in the south of Schleswig-Holstein. The Jacobsen Hof was searched for documents and weapons, and Hans Diederichsen was immediately asked by the British to take over as bürgermeister with a portfolio that included neighbouring Grundhof. Jacobsen was later transferred to Eselheide, another detainment centre. After nearly two years of internment, he agreed to pay a fine for membership of the SS and participate in a De-Nazification programme.

On May 26, another FSS unit raided the Festesen Hof in

---

[23] It is no longer a station. The single track was pulled up years ago. All that now identifies the building is a frieze of a train on the front.

Mariengaard with the knowledge that it had billeted a large number of Himmler's entourage. Springer, Himmler's weapons officer, was the target, his identity now known in the community. As the FSS had pulled up their trucks and jeeps in the courtyard, Springer had bolted out of the rear of the granny annex, where he lived with his wife and young children, and hid up behind a hedge. Facing a wary large dog in the courtyard, a British soldier shot it dead. In the main house, Dürring, Himmler's deputy adjutant, who had also remained at the Festesen Hof after Himmler's break to the south, carefully stood away. Curiously he was never asked to identify himself and was never questioned.

With Springer missing, the FSS left and Springer later crept back into the granny annex. He had only deferred his arrest. The FSS did get its man, returning the next day. Again, Dürring wasn't quizzed, implying that the British were unaware of his connection with Himmler. Once the FSS had left, Dürring packed a bag. Next time, the FSS might return for him.

Diederichsen's first priority as bürgermeister was to collect up the weapons and setting an example, he gave up the family collection of rifles and pistols dating back to the Franco-Prussian war in 1870. He demolished what remained of the Hitler Platz, distributed dumped fuel left in the barns by the SS and the Wache-Marine-Battalion, and reopened the schools. Accommodating the refugees that continued to flood into the area was an on-going problem and his decision to house 17 in the now empty front rooms of the Festesen Hof angered the Festesen family. After sufficient time had elapsed, Diederichsen established an evening school in Grundhof to explain what had been behind Nazi ideology. In an area so 'Brown', it wasn't surprising those seminars were poorly attended.

Aboard the *Patria* moored in Flensburg's harbour, the Allied Control Mission's staff sifted through the mountain of captured documents. The files of the Ober-Kommando Wehrmacht (OKW) found in Murwick were particularly extensive. Located in Dönitz's own files was the signed order from Hitler for the June 1941 offensive on the Soviet Union. Included in that document was Hitler's declaration that once Russia was defeated, Germany would again turn its attention to invading Britain. To determine the culpability of those who had committed local war crimes, the mission had agreed that an Atrocity Investigation Unit should be established in the city.

On May 29 – six days after the Flensburg roll-up – the mission had concluded and the celebration aboard the *Patria* was lavish with General Trusov, the senior Russian delegate, its host. The correspondent of *The Times* described the party as 'vigorous', as the vodka and caviar flowed. Trusov loudly led the toasts to the Allied cooperation, in particular the success of the respective air forces that had brought the Third Reich to its knees.

The following day, the *Patria* was emptied as the mission delegates left Flensburg leaving behind a small staff to move into the *Calabria*, a smaller passenger liner moored alongside. The search for Nazi documents would continue. At 16,000 tons, the *Patria*, once the pride in the Hamburg-Amerika line on the South America route, and later camouflaged as a submarine depot ship, was earmarked as an Allied troopship.

As the summer of 1945 came to its end, the British authorities brought all the newly appointed bürgermeisters and local councillors together, ironically in the Feuerwehrschule, the fire training school in Harrislee, once Himmler's SS headquarters in Flensburg. With basics scarce, the guests were asked to bring milk and cake: the British contributed the coffee. Hans Diederichsen recorded in his diary that the event proved quite a social occasion.

Personal sorrow was never far from the Flensburg story. Many of its young men who fought for the Reich never returned and for Ursula Pülschen, then a 16-year-old schoolgirl who lived in Estrup, the final days and weeks of the war remain raw. Ursula's brother, Ludwig Möller-Unruh, aged 15, had been taken out of a Flensburg grammar school in March and with other boys forcibly enrolled in the Grenadier-Ersatz- und Ausbildungs-Battalion No 65, based in Delmenhorst near Bremen. The training was short before they were pitched into battle. One of the Flensburg boys was wounded and Ludwig was allowed to visit him in hospital. Both boys had contemplated desertion.

Ludwig had sent only one letter home but as the war ended there was only silence on his whereabouts. For many years, the Möller-Unruh family contacted the German military authorities but with no luck. Eventually, in the Möller-Unruh graveyard in the nearby Grossolt church, a plague was placed for Ludwig in his memory. Wehrmacht records report that the March 1945 intake into the battalion had reinforced other infantry in desperate rear-guard actions against the Red Army in the Halle an der Saale area. If he had earlier died in fighting the British around Hamburg, there would be a record. Given his death was never recorded by the German authorities, Ludwig might have ended his days in a Gulag work camp with names replaced by prisoner numbers. The outcome for several of the 100 similar-aged boys who received basic army training in the playground of Estrup junior school, close to Kollerup, in late April 1945, was no better. They, too, had been forcibly marched off to war.

WHAT HAD DÖNITZ ACHIEVED?

Captain Knee had escorted Dönitz to Luxemburg, and on the flight Dönitz told him that his wife had put some sausage in his briefcase but he had nothing to cut it. Knee loaned him his penknife.[24] As the Nuremberg trial of Nazi leaders began in November 1945, the afternoon of the eighth day was intentionally graphic. The defendants, many wearing sunglasses to mask their eyes from the full glare of the world's press and the intensive lighting, were ordered to face the large screen to watch newsreels. An American psychologist in court detailed their reactions on the Allied liberation of Bergen-Belsen and Buchenwald.

Hess, Hitler's deputy before he fled to Britain, had glared at the screen 'looking like a ghoul with sunken eyes'. Keitel had 'wiped his brow, taking off his headphones' and von Ribbentrop 'closed his eyes, and looked away' only returning to the screen 'as a British army officer related that he had already buried 17,000 corpses' in the horror that was Bergen-Belsen. Göring 'didn't watch most of the time', preferring to lean on the balustrade in front of him. Frank, the head of the barbaric General Government in occupied Poland, and one of the worst mass killers in the SS, had 'swallowed hard' before cynically crying uncontrollably at the sight of the naked corpses of dead women

---

[24] An account told by Knee in his post-war reminiscences.

tumbling into the mass burial pits. During the trial, Frank underwent a conversion to Catholicism. Some thought it was a fruitless attempt to save his life. Speer 'looked very sad, and swallowed hard', already resigned to the death penalty reported one observer. He would be spared that capital punishment despite in later life admitting he had first-hand knowledge of the death camps.

Dönitz had sat impassively with his head bowed, not caring to watch the relentless images of emaciated bodies but like Speer, he wouldn't have a date with the hangman. Dönitz could not refute the charge that on taking command he had ordered the army to fight on, especially against the Red Army. His argument in doing so was to allow more German military and civilians to escape to the comparative safety of the British and American lines, the point he had first made on May 2 to Montgomery. 'I had to buy time', he pleaded at Nuremberg.

Why had the British waited 15 days after the general capitulation to terminate his Flensburg regime? Churcher in his papers was clear that he wanted no violence, no shooting and no deaths in his roll-up. He had needed to plan and factored into his decision was how Dönitz might deploy the 250,000-strong occupation army in Denmark, which could have overwhelmed Churcher's brigade.

Montgomery had demanded an immediate 'liquidation' but he had accepted Churcher's argument that planning was vital. There was an obvious downside in the delay. The timing allowed several thousand of the guilty to flee through the Flensburg ratlines courtesy of new IDs.

HUNTING 'HIMMLER'S TREASURE'

The first to confirm that Himmler had left behind valuable items in Hüholz, Lutzhöft and Mariengaard was Begleitkommando member, Wilhelm Walter, the former U-Boat Oberfunkmeister unexpectedly drafted into the bodyguard in the final months. Walter wasn't in the Himmler breakout. He with other Begleitkommando had left the area independently. Walter had taken a vehicle getting as far as Lüneburg until running out of petrol.

For the rest of the journey to Magdeburg to join his wife he walked or thumbed lifts. Using a false identity, Walter landed a job as a policeman that lasted until December 1945. Leaving his wife behind, he moved to Hannover and it was here where he met Heilmann, another Begleitkommando member, who hadn't been in Flensburg. Through Heilmann, Walter met up with others in an arch under Hannover's railway station, which they nicknamed 'the bunker'. Beerfelden, near Heidelberg, was Walter's next location and it was here where the British tracked him down as part of *Operation Globetrotter*, the operation to locate all members of Himmler's Begleitkommando and Stab. In an interrogation on April 11, 1946, he opened up to Captain Owen, a British Intelligence officer, disclosing names of Begleitkommando hiding out in Hannover, Brunswick and Göttingen.

If that wasn't sufficient a prize, what Walter additionally yielded up to the British about Himmler's last days in Hüholz and the burying of Himmler's briefcase on the orders of Heinz Schreiber, Himmler's confidential secretary, was definitely worth pursuing. The British, despite their numerous searches of properties in the Flensburg hamlets, had never discovered Himmler's Hüholz hideaway.

Himmler had first driven down the track to the Lorenzen Hof on May 2, 1945. Now, almost one year later, on April 23, British army vehicles trundled down the same track for the first time. Owen had brought Walter up from Beerfelden and in a carefully planned operation with 318 FSS, commanded by Captain Hallfurt, they drove to Hüholz. Nikolaus Lorenzen had no warning of their coming. This same unit in March had grabbed Hoess, the commandant of Auschwitz, from a barn in Gottrupel to the west of Flensburg and worked him over.

According to the report sent to British Intelligence in Bad Oeynhausen, its headquarters, Lorenzen and his 20-year-old daughter, Greta, were subjected to 'high-pressure' interrogations. Only then did Lorenzen 'reluctantly' admit that Himmler had stayed in his home. The 318 FSS turned over the house, including pulling up floorboards, and outbuildings before Walter led them to the grassy area behind the barn. Long strips were sectioned off and the digging began.[25] Without corroborating evidence from Schreiber, who the

---

[25] The area excavated by 318 FSS remains but much of it is now concreted over.

British hadn't located, the dig ended. The FSS hadn't finished with Lorenzen. He spent the night in a cell in Flensburg's police station and his watch was confiscated. News of Lorenzen's arrest spread quickly and a villager from Estrup came forward to plead his innocence. Allowed to leave, Lorenzen refused to do so unless his watch was returned and had to point it out in a drawer full of watches.

Walter had a further use. Using his contacts, 318 FSS needed him to unearth names and locations for members of Himmler's entourage that might still be in the area. This part of the operation was certainly productive. The British arrested one Begleitkommando member who had inveigled himself into a job in the Oberlandesgericht (court) in Flensburg. Heinz Henning was another picked up. He had set a false trail as to his whereabouts by writing home that he was living in Helmstedt in the south. Fritz Schuman had done likewise, corresponding with a girlfriend that he was living safely in Salzburg. He, too, was picked up by the FSS. Walter had located the address for Kleinert, now living in Adolf Hitler Koog, a new village constructed near Husum in 1937 to honour Hitler. An SS gauleiter who operated in Reichsgau Sudetenland, the Nazi name for annexed Czechoslovakia, was also in the net after a Walter lead. He was found working as a farm labourer outside Flensburg, just like Hoess.

If Walter's interrogation had facilitated unknown personal detail of Himmler's eight days in Flensburg, Heinrich Springer's interrogation in January 1947 while being held with other SS accused of war crimes in Neuengamme, the former concentration camp now used by the British[26], proved a revelation.

After Springer was captured in the granny annex of the Festesen Hof on May 27, 1945, he was first taken to the Barkelsby internment camp and then to Neuengamme. In an audacious escape using a rubbish lorry, Springer with 12 other SS broke out on February 18, 1946, and he paired-up with Arwed Flegel, who had passed his time in the camp as its masseur. They hid up in a 'safe house' in Hamburg before moving on. Both men were eventually re-captured on July

---

[26] Known as No. 6 Civil Internment Camp.

29, and returned to Neuengamme.

As to why, six months later, Springer divulged to the British military authorities the secret operational details of the Nazi ratlines that operated out of Flensburg, Heide and Hamburg with links to other German cities, we can only speculate. During his time at liberty, Springer had used three aliases – Ludwig Müller, Ludwig Richter and Otto Grigo – and Arno Scheller, the black-marketeer and criminal who was the mastermind behind De Chelard, the ratline with the most extensive network, shielded him. Springer had blown the names: Scheller was arrested and jailed, as were the heads of the Axmann and Leute des Meghin ratline groups. If known, Springer would have been at risk for the rest of his life, which might have been the main factor why the British authorities classified his interrogation file for 60 years until his death in Oelixdorf in Schleswig-Holstein.

Exposing the ratlines was most certainly a coup but Springer's admission of a Himmler cache instigated an immediate Europe-wide investigation to uncover more on his two metal strongboxes once stored in the granny annex of the Festesen Hof in Mariengaard. Strangely, Springer had also implicated Ursula, his wife.

After Springer's strongbox disclosure, a British Field Security Section returned to the Festesen Hof where 21 months earlier they had picked him up, to conduct a vigorous search of every building on the property but the chances of finding them was slim. Was Heinrich Festesen, the wartime deputy bürgermeister, aware of the strongboxes buried under the floorboards in his granny annex by Springer and Dürring? On our visit to the Festesen Hof, we had asked one family member with a memory of the war that very question. We didn't get an answer, but what had transpired in 1965 suggested he did.

British Intelligence now scoured the internment camps across the occupation zones to interrogate all Begleitkommando and Stab members in custody. Heinz Schmaloer and Wilhelm Keilhaus, Himmler's two communications experts named by Springer as being billeted in Lutzhöft were grilled at length in their internment camps. Schmaloer had been on the run until his capture in March 1947 and given his wartime record, he was one of the last high-profile prisoners transported to the 'London Cage' in Kensington.[27] He denied any knowledge of 'Himmler's treasure'. Keilhaus went through the same process at the Recklinghausen holding camp.[28] Dr Max Müller, then aged 70, was also in Recklinghausen. Billeted either in the Festesen Hof or in Lutzhöft, he had nothing to say on the strongboxes. Another Himmler aide in Flensburg, Adolf Gutgesell, was interrogated in March 1948 in Fallingbostel[29] and the response was similar.

Werner Grothmann, Himmler's chief adjutant, held in the 'Bunker' section in Dachau as a witness in the impending Dachau trial of guards, brushed aside any notion of a cache but he did reveal the existence of one strongbox that Himmler had built into his personal train to use as a safe. Right up to his death in 2002, Grothmann spurned all interviews about his role under Himmler. Heinz Macher, the Begleitkommando chief, also in custody, had feigned surprise that Himmler had anything of value in Flensburg.

Doris Mähner and Fraulein Hintze, the two Himmler secretaries billeted in the main house in the Festesen property were also questioned in depth. The former, who had escaped Mariengaard with the ID of a Wehrmachthelferin – army communications – had been tracked down to Eberhausen in Munich and interrogated in 1948. Again, the response was negative. Neither had she seen any of Himmler's valuables in his house in Gmund on the Tegernee.

The interrogation of Fraulein Lorenz, the closest secretary to Himmler, revealed an illuminating perspective on Himmler's stash of crates in the Hallein cave in Aigen, Salzburg. Himmler had tasked Lorenz with six members of his Begleitkommando in mid-April to extract certain items and hide them elsewhere. The group made it through to Salzburg and removed three crates marked 'Himmler' holding rare china and books, and other items, much of it looted from occupied countries and dispossessed German Jews. Stored crates

---

[27] London Cage was run by MI19, a section of the War Office responsible for gleaning information and confessions from PoWs. In total, 3,573 men, all SS and Gestapo, passed through the Cage, of which more than 1,000 admitted to war crimes.
[28] No. 4 Civil Internment Camp.
[29] No. 3 Civil Internment Camp.

General Churcher (left) with Colonel Corbett in Flensburg on the day of the capture.

◀ Brigadier Bryan Churcher's brigade entered Flensburg on May 9, 1945. 'The place was full to overflowing just like one would imagine an ant heap' he wrote in his memoir. *Source: Churcher's papers, Liddell Hart military archives, King's College, University of London*

▲ British troops entered Murwick's naval sports complex on May 23, brushing past the Wache-Marine-Battalion guards on the door. *Source: Imperial War Museum*

▲ Outside, everyone was searched for cyanide or potassium capsules. By midday in Murwick, 6,000 were held in the grounds and waiting to be trucked away to temporary PoW camps. Among the senior Nazis arrested all bar Dönitz had concealed a poison phial.
Source: Imperial War Museum

▶ As each office and corridor was secured, the Field Security Section scoured each face. The search was on to locate the prime targets: Himmler, Heinrich Müller and Martin Bormann. Everyone, including the female secretaries, was ordered to face the wall, hands in air. Notice the framed Dönitz photograph on the wall.
Source: Imperial War Museum

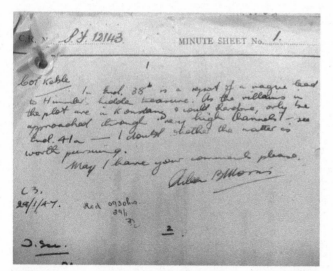

◀ This handwritten document from a file in the British Archives refers to a 'vague lead to Himmler's hidden treasure' and that it should be investigated through 'very high channels'.

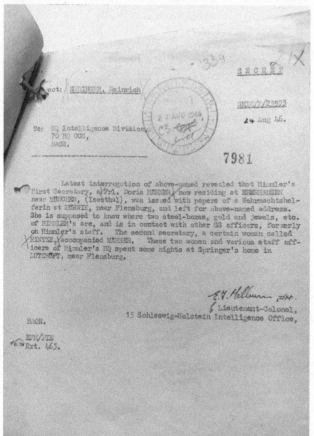

◀ In the extraordinary and revealing Heinrich Springer file, only released by the British after his death in 2007, Doris Mähner, one of Himmler's closest secretaries billeted in the Festesen Hof in Lutzhöft, is identified as a key source in the British hunt for the two strongboxes hidden under the floorboards in the granny annex occupied by Springer and his family.

that belonged to Stab members were also loaded onto the lorry.

Concealing this large number of bulky crates locally proved a problem so Lorenz decided it should be taken to Neukirchen where she lived. Once there, she had related to her British interrogator, the Begleitkommando stored the crates 'in a wooden shack', but where it was she refused to elaborate. Once the task was accomplished, the SS party had spilt up and had gone to ground. Lorenz then returned to her home, named 'Steger', and it was here where the British had picked her up in 1948, her neighbours none the wiser of her past. Lorenz claimed that the shack had been broken into sometime in June 1945 with nothing recovered. Of the two metal strongboxes that had accompanied Himmler to Hüholz, she offered the standard denial apart from alluding that as her colleague, Mähner, had been with Himmler in the final weeks of the war, she would be better positioned to know whether these strongboxes actually existed. Himmler's wife, Margaret, and Gudrun, the eldest daughter, were brought back from Italy under guard and taken to Nuremberg for questioning.

Ursula had visited Springer several times in Barkelsby and Neuengamme, he had told his interrogator in 1947. Once, she had cycled to Barkelsby to tell him that Dürring had immediately fled the Festesen Hof after his arrest on May 27, 1945, and gone into hiding. A few days later, in the middle of the night a man had knocked on the door of the granny annex. Declining to reveal his name he brought greetings from Dürring and said he had been ordered to collect the two strongboxes. The man then left.

Springer had told Ursula to locate his two pistols hidden not far from the granny annex and dump them into the nearest river. He suggested that a friend, Siegfried Saul, might help, and as to who he was and his involvement with Springer we have been unable to clarify. Springer later smuggled out of Barkelsby a sketch map for Ursula on where to locate them.

Soon after that Barkelsby visit, Springer had been transferred to Neuengamme and for a time was unwell which required a hospital stay in Bergedorf, near Hamburg. Ursula had seen him on the ward in October 1945 and in hushed tones, she admitted that the sketch map hadn't helped. She and Saul had been unable to find the pistols.

Springer then concluded that Dürring must have taken them. In December, Springer had another visitor in Neuengamme, Bartels, the Leck forestry manager who had identified the hiding place for Himmler's private weapons. Bartels related that the arms dump had remained untouched.

Whilst on the run from Neuengamme between February to July 1946, using one of his aliases, Springer took a chance and caught a bus from Hamburg then to Flensburg. He stayed in Hohenaften at the home of his cousin Vellguth, who was eager to provide any assistance to his relative. The following day, Vellguth cycled to Mariengaard to see Ursula and to give her a list of items her husband required. Later, Ursula cycled to Hohenaften to find her husband in quite a state. Constantly looking over his shoulder, moving regularly around 'safe houses' and avoiding arrest, had taken its toll. He might cross the border into Denmark and disappear, he told her, using contacts with the pro-German Danish community in Flensburg.

Just weeks after Springer's extraordinary admissions in Neuengamme, he was on the run for the second time in a bid to avoid the charges of war crimes laid against him by the Belgian War Crimes Group. Belgium had demanded his extradition to stand trial on charges of 'rape, looting and murder' of civilians in Annevoie, Yvoir, Godinne, Hun and Dinant. As a senior officer in the 12th SS Panzer Division, essentially Hitler Youth with Waffen-SS officers, the fighting in the Ardennes Offensive was fierce and Belgian civilians felt the brunt. In several locations where Springer had fought, homes were torched and residents lined up and shot. In Annevoie, alone, the SS destroyed 58 homes. Springer was No.18 on the United Nations War Crimes List No.11. His commanding officer, Kurt Meyer, already had form in executions. The day after the D-Day landings, his men had summarily shot 18 Canadian soldiers in the grounds of the Ardenne Abbey.

Shoot on sight when cornered was the Allied military instruction if Springer became a threat to life during his second escape from Neuengamme. He was eventually picked up in Tübingen in the French Occupation Zone in December 1947. Under an armed guard, he was escorted to Recklinghausen for interrogation, then to

Fischbeck and finally to a cell in Hamburg's Altona jail. When Springer's solicitor received a letter stating that the Belgians had seemingly rescinded the charges, he immediately petitioned the British authorities for the immediate release of his client. It was granted.

Tracing 'Himmler's treasure' turned cold through lack of solid leads. Had Springer traded the whereabouts of Himmler's cache, the ratlines, and other Himmler secrets, maybe even whether Hitler or a 'double' had died in Berlin, against the dropping of the Belgian war crimes charges?

The one person who definitely did know the whereabouts of the strongboxes, Herbert Dürring, had gone to ground. He may have been one of the many thousands of SS who had fled to a safe haven outside Europe, maybe even with their contents that would have ensured a wealthy post-war life style. The Bundesarchiv in Berlin provided me with details of his wartime career. Born in December 1923, he joined the Hitler Youth at the age of 10 before signing up for the Waffen-SS in April 1941. Posted to SS Division Germania, he trained in Hamburg before moving to SS Der Fuhrer, a unit in the thick of it in the invasion of the Soviet Union. By September 1941, Der Fuhrer had been decimated and Dürring was wounded. Recovered, Dürring took a course in the Waffen-SS officer training school in the baroque palace of Schleissheim from March 16 to July 17, 1942 and at the young age of 19, Himmler had seen his potential and appointed him as his second adjutant. At the time he was single and in a handwritten application to the SS Race and Settlement Main Office the following year, seeking permission to marry,[30] Herbert Wilhelm Walter Dürring wrote up his life story. In joining Himmler's Stab, he had sworn absolute loyalty to the Reichsführer-SS.

The Dürring family home was in Hannover, an apartment in the large Dingelstedtstrasse block, where his parents, Paul and Hermione, lived. Had Dürring fled Mariengaard to Hannover before escaping elsewhere with a new identity? Given his boyish looks and slender

---

[30] Standard SS requirement.

frame, characteristics observed in the photographs in his SS file, he could easily have passed himself off as a member of the Hitler Youth – an organization he knew well.

With more than seven decades now past, we shall probably never know why Dürring had remained with Springer in the Festesen Hof in Mariengaard as the Himmler group fled. Springer had family ties but Dürring had no need to stay and risk capture. Had Himmler trusted his loyal young adjutant to retrieve the treasure, later, and reunite it with him somewhere in Bavaria, or indeed, elsewhere? Himmler never made it out of northern Germany so what did happen to the two strongboxes, which British Military Intelligence had referred to as 'Himmler's treasure'?

In an intriguing postscript, Heinrich Springer pitched up unannounced in Mariengaard in 1965 and his visit to the Festesen Hof was both acrimonious and lengthy. We spoke to the person who overheard that heated conversation and there is more to reveal on what had transpired between the wartime deputy bürgermeister and one of Himmler's key aides.

More recently, a local carpenter extensively renovated Himmler's hideaway in Hüholz. No item relating to Himmler's eight-day stay in the Lorenzen Hof was discovered and nor would there be. British military intelligence, led by Captain Owen, with two lorry-loads of 318 FSS, had torn the house apart during the fruitless search on April 23, 1946, just days after Walter had broken ranks with other detained bodyguard colleagues and revealed the property's significance. The grilling of Nikolaus Lorenzen, the owner, and Greta, his 21-year-old daughter, was intense before Owen obtained the admission that Himmler and some of his entourage had moved into the house and outbuildings.

The carpenter did make a discovery under the attic floorboards in another property, finding a battered suitcase stuffed with Reichsmarks. As to determining the location in the nearby Winderatter wood where one of Himmler's bodyguards had dumped a vehicle before the escape to the south, thanks to local knowledge we were able to locate the once waterlogged bog. The area still remains only accessible by foot through a field behind the Lorenzen Hof, which is why the bodyguard had needed to find an access track between the trees off the Winderatter Weg. The attempt to sink it completely had failed and over the years much of the vehicle had remained visible for the local children to clamber over. A farmer ripped out engine parts for his tractor, openly boasting that the steering wheel belonged to a vehicle once driven by Himmler.

What of Himmler's briefcase buried behind the barn of the Lorenzen Hof?

The 318 FSS had left empty-handed after it ransacked the house and dug the area where Walter had said he had concealed it. With no corroboration from the still-missing Heinz Schreiber, Himmler's confidential secretary, the British had only Walter's word as to location but had he lied?

Nikolaus Lorenzen's son, Heinrich, a 17-year-old in the army, after the British released him from a PoW camp on the Rhine, was later to recall that three local lads had discovered it but as to where he didn't elaborate. An anxious father of one of the boys, worried about the repercussions, reportedly destroyed the briefcase.

There is another, more plausible, explanation that Captain Owen and the 318 FSS would have considered. If Walter had told the truth, and his revelations to Owen did yield positive leads as to the whereabouts of several SS hiding out in the Flensburg area and the identities and locations of other Begleitkommando, might Nikolaus Lorenzen have recovered it? Very likely, Lorenzen witnessed the flurry of activity on the day of Himmler's departure, May 10. SS uniforms and IDs were discarded and burnt, weapons and vehicles surplus to requirement were dumped, Schreiber destroyed documents and Walter had buried the briefcase.

Lorenzen might have passed it on as a prized and unique wartime possession. Intriguingly, even now, the briefcase that Himmler never let out of his sight, maybe even with his most private papers, might be hidden away in a dusty recess of an attic in a local hof.

Clearly, the Flensburg hamlets of Hüholz, Lutzhöft and Mariengaard have yet to fully surrender their wartime secrets.

H HIMMLER'S FINAL MOVEMENTS

Southern Germany late 1944

Northern Germany late 1944 - 1945

Flensburg and its hamlets May 2-10, 1945

STORY CHARACTERS: POST-WAR

DÖNITZ AND HIS FLENSBURG MINISTERS

★ Dönitz, Grand Admiral Karl: Convicted for war crimes at Nuremberg, Dönitz served his full 10-year sentence and after release in 1956 he lived near Hamburg where he died in December 1980 at the age of 91. Thousands attended the funeral, mainly WW2 naval veterans. Dönitz had always denied any involvement in war crimes, even denying knowledge of them.

★ Jodl, Generaloberst Alfred: Sentenced at Nuremberg he was hung in October 1946, his body taken to Munich for cremation. He was 56. Posthumously, a West German De-Nazification Court cleared Jodl in February 1953. Under US pressure, that decision was revoked.

★ Krosigk, Count Luis von: He was amongst those tried in the Ministries Trial that lasted the best part of 1948 and was sentenced to 10 years. After release, he enjoyed a long retirement, writing his memoirs and contributing to German debate on economic policy, dying in Essen in March 1977, aged 90.

★ Speer, Albert: Released from Spandau in October 1966, after serving his 20 years, he remained in denial of being party to any war crimes. A letter, however, surfacing in Britain in 2007, finally nailed the so-called 'good Nazi', the post-war nickname for him. Speer had written this letter to Hélène Jeanty, the widow of a Belgian resistance leader, dated December 23, 1971, and confessed that he had been at a conference with Himmler revealing plans to exterminate all Europe's Jews. "There is no doubt" he said in the letter, "that I was present as Himmler announced on October 6, 1943 that all Jews would be killed. Who would believe me that I suppressed this?" If Speer's guilt had been known at Nuremberg, he, too, might have had a date with the hangman. After Spandau, he made a career in writing his three memoirs that sold millions of copies, turning him into a very wealthy author. Speer died on a trip to London in September 1981, at St Mary's Hospital, Paddington, aged 76.

★ Stuckart, Wilhelm: Tried in the Ministries Trial, he later went

through De-Nazification in 1951 and died in a car crash in
Hannover in November 1953, aged 51. There was the suspicion
that the crash was staged.

★ Thierack, Otto Georg: Arrested but committed suicide by
poisoning at Sennelager, Paderborn, age 57.

★ Seldte, Franz: He died in a US military hospital in 1947 before
formal charges at Nuremberg were laid against him. He was 64.

★ Dorpmüller, Julius: Captured by the British several days before
the May 23 roundup, he was tasked by the British in running the
German railway system. In post for only two months before
succumbing to cancer in July 1945, age 75.

★ Backe, Herbert: He hung himself in his Nuremberg prison cell
in April 1947, aged 64.

SS, GESTAPO, SIPO AND OTHER NAZIS

★ Best, SS-Obergruppenführer Werner: Testifying at Nuremberg,
he was later extradited to Denmark and in 1949 he was sentenced
to death. Commuted to five years, of which four had already been
served, there was outrage so he was re-sentenced to 12 years but
released in 1951 after serving only two. Returning to Germany he
was fined DM70,000 by the De-Nazification court in 1958. The
Danish courts weren't done with him and he was charged in
March 1969 with committing mass murder with a trial set for
1972. Claiming ill health, he was released, dying in Mulheim in
June 1989, aged 85.

★ Bothmann, SS-Hauptsturmführer Hans: Captured by the British,
he committed suicide in April 1946 while being held in Heide,
Schleswig-Holstein, aged 34.

★ Brandt, SS-Standartenführer Rudolf: Himmler's aide was
prosecuted at Nuremberg but denied knowledge of medical
experiments in Auschwitz, Dachau, Buchenwald, Ravensbrück,
Sachsenhausen, Natzweiler, Bergen-Belsen, Treblinka and others.
His standard defence was 'I cannot remember'. Sentenced to death,
he lodged an appeal but he was eventually executed at Landsberg
prison on June 2, 1948, with his body buried at the Spottinger
prison cemetery. He was 49.

★ Dürring, SS-Obersturmbannführer Herbert: The post-war movements of Himmler's second adjutant are unknown.

★ Gottberg, SS-Obergruppenführer Curt von: While in custody he committed suicide on May 31, 1945, aged 49, and was initially buried in the church cemetery in Grundhof. Some years later his remains were reinterred in Hamburg.

★ Griems, SS-Untersturmführer Hans: The Ladelund concentration camp commandant escaped British custody in 1945. The Flensburg prosecutor finally decided to investigate him for war crimes in 1963 and located him in Hamburg-Bergedorf, in 1965, living under his real name. The Hamburg authorities took over the case but only in 1971 was he charged. He died before the trial started, aged 69.

★ Grothmann, SS-Obersturmbannführer Werner: Himmler's primary adjutant denied any involvement in the building of the Reinhard death camps in Poland and entered the De-Nazification Programme in March 1949. Post-war, he enjoyed a long business career and declined all interviews, dying in February 2002, aged 86.

★ Gutgesell, SS-Obersturmbannführer Adolf Himar: Arrested in Flensburg, this Himmler aide was interrogated on March 11, 1948 at Fallingbostel internment camp about 'Himmler's treasure'.

★ Hoess, SS-Obersturmbannführer Rudolf: Fleeing from Flensburg to Sylt, he later returned and found work as a labourer at the Hansen Hof in the village of Gottrupel, west of the city. With the help of his brother-in-law he kept in touch with his wife but he was aware that the British maintained a close watch on her in the Ravensbrück home. Hoess was arrested in Gottrupel on March 11, 1946, his location given up by his wife fearing that if she didn't, she and her son would be handed over to the Soviets and sent to a prison camp. He kept a phial of poison on him but it broke two days before his arrest. Hoess underwent two days of intense British interrogation before being handed to the Americans and taken to Nuremberg as a witness in several trials including those of Ernst Kaltenbrunner and the IG Farben pharmaceutical company. Handed over to the Poles in May 1946, Hoess was first taken to Cracow and then to Warsaw. Allowed paper and a pencil, he penned an extraordinary account of his wartime activities. *The Commandant of Auschwitz* was first published in Polish in 1951, the publisher ensuring that all royalties went to an Auschwitz survivor charity. Hoess was hung in April 1947 on the gallows in Auschwitz-1, next to the gas chamber and ovens, aged 46.

★ Hoppe, SS-Obersturmbannführer Paul-Werner: This commandant of Stutthof escaped Flensburg with a new ID but was later captured by the Americans and taken to Camp 165 in Caithness, Scotland. He escaped, making his way to Switzerland and worked as a landscape gardener. Returning to West Germany in 1952 in the belief that he wouldn't be recognised, he reverted to his original name but was arrested a year later and jailed for five years, later increased to nine. He served just over seven and on release he found a job in the insurance industry, dying in Bochum in July 1974, aged 64.

★ Hintze, Fraulein: The British located Himmler's second secretary in 1948 and interrogated about 'Himmler's treasure'.

★ Jacobsen, SS-Hauptsturmführer Georg: Lutzhöft's bürgermeister was arrested on May 25, 1945 and sent to the SS internment camp in Neumünster and then Eselheide. Released on September 12, 1947, he entered the De-Nazification Programme in Schleswig-Holstein.

★ Joyce, William: Charged for treason, he was hung in Wandsworth jail, London, on January 3, 1946. He was 39.

★ Jüttner, SS-Obergruppenführer Hans: This Begleitkommando member was captured by the British on May 15, 1945. He died in Bad Tölz, Bavaria, in May 1965, aged 71.

★ Kiermaier, SS-Sturmbannführer Josef (Sepp): Himmler's personal bodyguard post-war wrote a book entitled *'Himmler'*. He died in 1991, aged 87.

★ Kracht, Ernst: Flensburg's SS bürgermeister, and die-hard Nazi, enjoyed a long life post-war, dying in the city on February 1983, aged 92.

★ Liebehenschel, SS-Obersturmbannführer Arthur: This commandant of Auschwitz and Majdanek was tried and later executed in Krakow in January 1948. He was 47.

★ Macher, SS-Sturmbannführer Karl Heinz: The chief of

Himmler's Begleitkommando died in Schenefeld, Schleswig-Holstein, December 2001, aged 81.

★ Mähner, Fraulein Doris: Himmler's first secretary had fled Flensburg with the new ID of a Wehrmachthelferin (communications). Found in Eberhausen, Munich, in 1948, she was interrogated over 'Himmler's treasure'.

★ Maurer, SS-Standartenführer Gerhard: The deputy head of the Concentration Camp Inspectorate avoided capture in Flensburg but was eventually found in March 1947 and was a witness in several war crime trials before extradition to Krakow and execution in April 1953, aged 46.

★ Müller, SS-Obersturmbannführer Max: Another member of Himmler's Begleitkommando later interrogated over 'Himmler 'treasure'. His later movements are unknown.

★ Ohlendorf, SS-Gruppenführer Otto: Condemned to death at the Einsatzgruppen Trial at Nuremberg – he ran Einsatzgruppen D – and sentenced to death in June 1951. He was hanged in Landsberg jail. Aged 44.

★ Oldach, SS-Standartenführer Ludwig: The British arrested this Gestapo chief whose patch included Ravensbrück and the Uckermark camp for 'deviant' women. He provided a useful account of the functional structure of the Gestapo and SS organisations. At his trial in 1948, Oldach was sentenced to a lowly three years, considered served by the time already in detention. Amnestied in 1954, he lived in Flensburg until his death in January 1987. He was 99.

★ Pancke, SS-Obergruppenführer Günther: Arrested in Flensburg on May 21, he was later deported for trial in Copenhagen and sentenced to 20 years in September 1948. He had been a frequent visitor in the last days of the war to the Flensburg hamlet of Barg to visit his wife. Pardoned and released in 1953, Pancke died in Hamburg in August 1973, aged 74.

★ Pauly, SS-Standartenführer Max: Arrested in Flensburg and sentenced to die with 11 others in the Neuengamme trial at Hamburg's Curio Haus in May 1946. Hung in Hamelin jail in October 1946 by Albert Pierrepoint, the prodigious British hangman. Pauly was 39. Pauly was described by Bernadotte as 'one of the revolting creatures of the Third Reich'.

★ Pohl, SS-Obergruppenführer Oswald: The head of the SS-Main Economic and Administration Office disappeared in Flensburg and worked as a farmhand. He was arrested by the British in May 1946 in Bremen, sentenced at Nuremberg, and hung at Landsberg Prison in June 1951, aged 58.

★ Ribbentrop, Joachim von: With a new ID, Hitler's foreign minister escaped Flensburg but was eventually captured on June 16, 1945 in a Hamburg boarding house, found asleep with a metal canister of poison strapped to his thigh. In his possession were three letters, addressed to Churchill, Anthony Eden, the British foreign secretary, and Montgomery, which was a rant on British foreign policy. Tried at Nuremberg he was hung on October 16, 1946. He was 53.

★ Schellenberg, SS-Brigadeführer Walter: This SD chief and Himmler confidant was arrested by the British, tried at Nuremberg and sentenced in November 1949 to six years jail. Released two years early due to illness, he died in Turin, Italy, in March 1952, aged 42.

★ Schmaloer, SS-Sturmbannführer Heinz: Arrested by the British on March 3, 1948 for war crimes, he was taken to the infamous London Cage for interrogation. He was closely questioned over 'Himmler's treasure'.

★ Springer, SS-Sturmbannführer Heinrich, Adolf: He died in Oelixdorf, Schleswig-Holstein, in October 2007, aged 92. That same year, his full file held in the National Archives, Kew, London, was declassified as were papers held by the Central Intelligence Agency in Washington.

★ Stawitzki, SS-Sturmbannführer Kurt: Using the identity of 'Kurt Stein' he fled Flensburg and later arrived in Bad Godesberg. The West German authorities only discovered Stein's real identity in 1970, but it was too late to bring him to trial for war crimes, he had died in the city in September 1959, aged 58.

★ Tiefenbacher, SS-Standartenführer: Part of the final Himmler group in Flensburg. Went missing after the Flensburg round up.

★ Walter, Oberfunkmeister Wilhelm: After the British took him back to the Lorenzen Hof in 1946 to search for Himmler's

▲ Heinrich Springer – the Himmler aide responsible for hiding 'Himmler's Treasure'. His interrogation files were only released in 2007, the year of his death.

briefcase, the later movements of this Begleitkommando member are unknown.

★ Wegener, Gauleiter Paul: This former SS gauleiter of Bremen, Norway and Weser-Ems was arrested in Flensburg. He died in 1989, aged 74.

★ Wunnenberg, SS–Obergruppenführer Alfred: Held in Froslev, he was interrogated over war crimes. He died in Krefeld in December 1963, aged 72.

SS DOCTORS

★ Brandt, Karl: Not to be confused with Rudolf Brandt, Himmler's aide, he was arrested in the May 23 roll-up in Flensburg. At the 'Doctors' Trial' in Nuremberg, titled the *'United States of America v. Karl Brandt et al'*, he was sentenced to death and executed at Landsberg jail in June 1948, aged 44.

★ Conti, SS–Obergruppenführer Leonardo: After capture in Flensburg, he was imprisoned in Froslev. Taken to Nuremberg to await trial he hung himself in his cell in October 1945. He was 45.

★ Gebhardt, SS–Brigadeführer Karl: Also sentenced to death at the 'Doctors Trial' and hung at Landsberg, aged 50.

★ Hanloser, Professor Dr. Siegfried: In the Doctors' Trial at Nuremberg, he avoided the hangman but received a life sentence – later commuted to 20 years. Suffering from terminal cancer, he was released in July 1954 and died the following month in Munich, aged 59.

★ Heyde, Werner: The 'euthanasia professor' as he was known before his trial, hung himself in Butzbach jail on February 13, 1964. He was 61.

★ Kitt, SS–Hauptsturmführer Bruno: He was arrested by the British and charged with 46 other SS members in the Neuengamme trial in Hamburg that began on March 18, 1946 and ended on May 13. With 11 others sentenced to death, Kitt was hanged in October 1946. He was aged 40.

★ Lolling, SS–Standartenführer Enno: He committed suicide at an army hospital in Flensburg on May 27, 1945. He was 56. Lolling was named many times in the Ravensbrück trials.

WEHRMACHT AND KRIEGSMARINE

★ Böhme, Generaloberst Franz: Commander of the army in
Norway, he was taken to Nuremberg for trial but after Yugoslavia
demanded extradition for his prior massacres and reprisals in
Serbia, he jumped to his death in prison in May 1947. He was 62.
★ Busch, Field Marshal Ernst: After vacating Kollerup, the British
transferred him to Aldershot in England for interrogation with
several of his staff officers. Busch died on June 17, 1945 at
Aldershot just weeks after his arrival and is buried at the Cannock
Chase German Military Cemetery, near Wolverhampton.
★ Keitel, Field Marshal Wilhelm: Sentenced at Nuremberg and
executed in October 1946, aged 64.
★ Lindemann, Generaloberst Georg von: Wehrmacht general in
charge of all German forces in Denmark. After vacating Kollerup,
he was arrested. The Danes were allowed to interrogate him in
August 1946 while being held in Nuremberg prison. Released in
1948, he died in West Germany in September 1963, aged 79.
★ Petersen, Captain Rudolf: This Kriegsmarine officer who had
performed the very last court-martial in Nazi Germany was tried
with four other naval officers in Frankfurt in August 1949 on a
charge against humanity. He was sentenced to two years jail less
time served in custody. Two others received 18 months and two
were acquitted. Petersen died in Flensburg in January 1983, aged 77.

BRITISH AND US MILITARY

★ Churcher, Brigadier John Bryan: After the war he served in
Palestine, Germany, and was the commanding officer of British
forces in Egypt at the time of the British and French takeover of
the Suez Canal. Later roles included adjutant to King George V1
and Queen Elizabeth. Retiring with the rank of Major General, he
died in 1997 at the age of 92.
★ Hobden, Squadron Ldr. Mark: This RAF Regiment officer, 20
years later, was again on the front line this time in Cyprus as
violence erupted between Greek and Turkish communities.
Hobden drew the line on a map denoting factional division. That

'Green Line' was to become infamous, dividing not only Nicosia but also the rest of the island and still exists. He retired from the RAF, as Group Captain, in 1972, and died May 13, 2013, aged 91.

★ Knee, Captain Derek: Montgomery's valued translator and Dönitz's escort later viewed Himmler's body. He returned to Cambridge University at war's end to complete his interrupted degree. He died in March 2014, aged 91.

★ Rook, General Lowell: This US mission member in Flensburg, who Churcher described as a 'gunslinger' with a strapped-on revolver, served in the UN National Relief and Rehabilitation Administration post-war and on retirement he befittingly became a cattle rancher. He died in January 1973, aged 79.

SOURCES FOR THIS STORY

Local sources, especially the reminiscences of people who lived through the last days of the Third Reich in Flensburg, have been paramount in the writing of this story.

MARIENGAARD:

Hans Heinrich Otzen, who had permission from the now owners of the Otzen Hof, took us inside the shed where he observed Himmler sitting in his military vehicle. The day we visited the weather was appalling and biting cold but he was still prepared to relate his unique story for the first time.

The Schmidt-Hollander family kindly received us in the former Festesen Hof to share their knowledge of the days when Himmler's entourage was billeted in the farmhouse.

LUTZHÖFT:

The Jacobsen and Diederichsen families provided a unique insight into the hamlet during the years of the Third Reich, allowing us to peruse family documents and photographs.

KOLLERUP:

The Christiansen family spent several hours with us, providing first-hand knowledge of the time when the house was requisitioned by

Field Marshal Busch, the Wehrmacht commander, who used the dining room as his command centre.

Ursula Pülschen, who as a schoolgirl in Bistoft, had witnessed the events of Kollerup and other hamlets in the area. Ursula's long-time friend, Lieselotte Thomsen, who lived in the Hock Hof in Kollerup during the war, also provided a valuable insight. Ursula later wrote a well-researched chronicle of the area.

HÜHOLZ:
The current owner of the Lorenzen Hof in Hüholz kindly allowed us access to the exterior of his property that had served as Himmler's accommodation during eight days in May 1945. The inside has been extensively remodelled.

FLENSBURG:
Ulf Bartelsen, a knowledgeable and serving policeman in Flensburg, gave us a guided tour inside the central police station during operational hours.

AMONG THE PRIMARY SOURCES

★ Brigadier Churcher's papers held in the Liddell Hart military archives in Kings College, University of London

★ Count Bernadotte account of his meetings with Himmler. *'The Fall of the Curtain'*, was published in June 1945. SS-Brigadeführer Walter Schellenberg, the SD chief, had contributed a chapter

★ British military files on Heinrich Springer [only declassified in 2007), Stab, including military correspondence, charges of war crimes in Belgium, full details of his time in internment and jail, and his extraordinary statement in January 1947, recorded by a military interrogator in Neuengamme

★ Military correspondence and interrogation records for: Werner Grothmann, Stab, Heinz Macher, Begleitkommando, Wilhelm Walter, Begleitkommando, Adolf Gutgesell, Stab, Doris Mähner, Frauleins Hintze and Lorenz, all secretaries in the Stab – and other members of Himmler's Stab and Begleitkommando

★ Extensive British military records and correspondence for Heinrich Himmler held in the National Archives

★ War Crimes Bulletins issued regularly by the British and American military in Germany, 1945–1946

★ Bundesarchiv, Berlin, for SS records

★ US Holocaust Memorial Museum, Washington DC

★ US National Archives and Records Administration, Maryland, US

★ *The Times* archive

★ *Flensburg Nachrichten*

★ *'De Sack in de Boom'*, written by Ingeborg Jacobs, a member of the Diederichsen family, who as a young girl sat on a cushion (that looked like a sack) high up in the elm tree in the front garden, observing

II

TWENTY LITTLE SUITCASES

STORYLINE

Drugged with morphine, the 20 Jewish children, ranging from five to 12 years in age, were led or carried one-by-one into the gloom of the largest room in the basement. The first to be strung up over a clothes-hook on the wall, at around midnight on April 20, 1945, was the eldest, a Slovakian boy. As one SS guard pulled the noose around his neck, another held onto the trunk and legs. The body was dumped behind a partition, out of sight of the next victim. According to one of the SS killers, not one child cried. The children's four camp carers had earlier been hung over water pipes from the ceiling in the nearby boiler room. Soviet PoWs were also brought to the building that night and when the killing was done, 47 bodies lay stacked in piles in the basement of this empty former school in Bullenhuser Damm, an industrial area in Hamburg.

The hangings rank among the foulest atrocities committed by the SS in the final days and weeks of the war. The notorious Dr Josef Mengele had personally selected 20 children in Auschwitz-Birkenau for transfer to the Neuengamme concentration camp, outside Hamburg. Here, another SS doctor had subjected the children to horrific medical experimentation. In a hurry to cover up his war crimes before the British army arrived at Neuengamme's gates, Pauly, the commandant, was tying up loose ends. The children had to die.

Neuengamme's doctor was tried for his crimes but the SS-Obersturmführer in charge of the hangings was never brought to justice as sclerotic West German bureaucracy stymied every attempt to do so. The relatives of the child victims, many of whom were survivors of the death camps, would never have their day in court to confront him.

The twenty little suitcases arranged in an oval in the basement of the Bullenhuser Damm building are not only poignant named memorials to the children who were slaughtered here, they are epitaphs to the depravity, brutality and blood-lust that was the Third Reich.

Two suitcases are devoid of any detail.

◀ Little has changed in this basement room in which the 20 Jewish children were individually hung. *Source: Nigel Bance*

'THE CHILDREN had to undress in a room in the basement, and then they were led into another room where Dr Trzebinski gave them an injection, so they fell asleep. Those who were still showing signs of life after the injection were carried to another room. There, a rope was placed around their necks and, like pictures, they were hanged on hooks on the wall. This was done by Jauch, Trzebinski, Dreimann, Strippel, and myself.

'At midnight another transport arrived from Neuengamme, this time with 20 adult Russians. They were led into a room in the basement and we hanged them. A rope was slung around a pipe, which ran beneath the building. The noose was placed around the neck and they were pulled up. Their bodies remained in the room. At 6am all the Russians were dead and I went to bed'.

This grotesque admission was part of the deposition made by SS-Rottenführer Johann Frahm, an SS corporal, during his interrogation by a British war crimes investigator on May 2, 1946. Frahm had placed the rope around the necks of 20 terrified children, who had already endured gross and painful medical experimentation in Neuengamme concentration camp.

The building still remains in Bullenhuser Damm in Hamburg, in the final year of the war converted to a satellite camp of Neuengamme. Previously, it had been a school. The 20 children, the youngest aged five, the eldest 12, were hung close to midnight on April 20, 1945. Identities and backgrounds were painstakedly uncovered after the war, thanks mainly to the efforts of a German investigative journalist and his wife, a lawyer. The nationalities of the children were 14 Polish, two French, two Dutch, one Italian and one Slovakian. Two French doctors and two Dutch orderlies, who had looked after the children in Neuengamme and accompanied them to Bullenhuser Damm, were hung not long before the children. As to the identities of the Russian PoWs nothing is known, like so many murdered by the Germans across the USSR and Europe. The bodies of the children were returned to Neuengamme on April 21 – the day of Hitler's 56th birthday – for immediate cremation.

With the British just hours away from taking the city, SS-Obersturmführer Arnold Georg Strippel, the Stützpunktleiter, or area commander for the 14 Neuengamme satellite camps in Hamburg, ditched his SS uniform in the realisation that he would be a marked man. Torture and serial killing had come naturally to this concentration camp careerist, beginning in 1934, a year after Hitler gained power. Prior to his final posting to the Spaldingstrasse satellite of Neuengamme, he had been a guard or held a senior position in Sachsenhausen, Buchenwald, Peenemünde-Karlshagen, Ravensbrück and Salzgitter-Drütte in Germany, Natzweiler-Struthof in France, Majdanek in Poland and Vught in Holland.

A Strippel favourite in the camps was to rope the arms of an inmate behind the back and attach the rope over the bough of a tree. The victim was left to hang in excruciating pain with the arms slowly detaching from their sockets. If the inmate didn't succumb, the injuries were appalling. Strippel thrived on spectacle. Another specialism was strapping an inmate over a saw bench and thrashing the back with a thick leather whip.

Just as guilty for the Bullenhuser Damm murders, even if he wasn't one of the five hangmen, was an ambitious 39-year-old SS doctor who had embarked on a scientific study in an effort to impress his medical peers. Based in the Hohenlychen medical facility, 75km north of Berlin, Dr Kurt Heissmeyer, like the majority of the 250 doctors attached to the Concentration Camp Inspectorate, had eschewed all normal medical vows to help and heal the sick. For the concentration camp inmates he experimented upon, Heissmeyer was a harbinger of excruciating pain and suffering. With a ready and compliant human resource, Heissmeyer could advance his work unhindered by traditional medical safeguards and ethics.

With the Red Army closing in on Hohenlychen, the majority of the medical staff made plans to escape. Medical records concerning concentration camp experiments conducted by its doctors were destroyed. Karl Gebhardt, its director, had joined in the Concentration Camp Inspectorate exodus to Flensburg but Heissmeyer, his deputy, had contrary plans. Proud of his TB experiments in Neuengamme and vainly hoping to attain international recognition for his work, he had no intention of burning his records, including photographs of victims undergoing treatment. Unseen, Heissmeyer buried a large zinc-lined box in the facility's garden to be retrieved at a later date. In civilian clothes, he now headed south to Sangerhausen, Thuringia, and into the protection of his family to join his father's medical practice. Living in plain sight, the patients were none the wiser as to his wartime back-story or his forthright racial opinions. In a post-war East Germany, free of scrutiny, Heissmeyer's practice flourished.

Nazi loyalties had come easy to the Heissmeyer family. An uncle was SS-Obergruppenführer (Infantry General) August Heissmeyer, no stranger to persecution of racial minorities in Germany and in the occupied East. His wife, Gertrud Scholtz-Klink, headed the National Socialist Women's League: both had fled as Germany collapsed and remained at large until 1948. After a short imprisonment, August Heissmeyer would aspire to become one of Coca Cola's top executives in West Germany.

To tell the story of what happened in the basement of the former Hamburg school we need to roll back into early 1944, to Blocks 4 and 4A in the main Neuengamme camp.

'HEISSMEYER'S BLOCK'

The experiments taking place in Block 4A, next to the sickbay, Block 4, could never be kept secret in a concentration camp the size of Neuengamme. Strictly off limits to the curious, camp inmates referred to it as 'Heissmeyer's block'.

Heissmeyer had needed approval for his tuberculosis trial from Gebhardt and Dr Leonardo Conti, the Reich's senior medical official, before the proposal could be submitted to Himmler who had to endorse all medical experimentation conducted by SS doctors. The Hohenlychen doctor had internally circulated several papers, drawing heavily on the pre-war theories of two Austrian researchers, Kutschera and Aichbergen, that live and virulent tuberculars implanted into human nodes might enhance immunity and even aid recovery for existing TB sufferers.

Approval was given to run a trial on humans to run parallel with a comparative study on guinea pigs. Jews and captured East Europeans and Russians were perfect specimens, Heissmeyer had argued, being racially inferior and more susceptible to TB than Aryan Germans. Heissmeyer was advised by Conti and Gebhardt to use male prisoners in Ravensbrück, a camp not far from Hohenlychen, and it is unclear why that inmate source was changed to Neuengamme. In Dr Alfred Trzebinski, Neuengamme's senior doctor with the SS medical rank of Standortarzt, Heissmeyer found a willing and experienced supervisor. Trzebinski had previously worked in Auschwitz and Majdanek.

Two French PoWs in Neuengamme were ordered into the trial as medical assistants, Professors Gabriel Florence, a 58-year-old eminent biochemist, and Rene Quenouille, a 60-year-old radiologist. Both men had distinguished medical backgrounds. Pre-war, Florence had been nominated for a Nobel Prize.

Arrested by the Gestapo as an active member of the Comité Medical de la Resistance, a group of doctors involved in the French Underground, Florence had been imprisoned in Montluc, the Gestapo torture jail near Lyon. The Gestapo transferred him to Neuengamme and he was put to work in the sickbay. As a fluent German speaker, the SS utilised him as a camp translator. Quenouille had also taken risks with France now occupied, being party to helping British agents evade capture. The Gestapo eventually uncovered Quenouille's covert activities and he was sentenced to death at the Fresnes jail near Paris but his execution wasn't carried out. In October 1943, he was moved to Mauthausen as a camp doctor. Mauthausen had just completed an infirmary, set up just outside the main camp, given the spread of epidemics that were ravaging the starving prisoners. That infirmary, however, became an execution selection centre with SS officers moving along the bunks looking for 'malingerers'. Quenouille was transferred to Neuengamme where his skills as a radiologist marked him out as a valuable PoW asset for Trzebinski.

Orderlies for the TB trial were also required and among those used by Trzebinski were two Dutchmen. Dirk Deutekom and Anton Hölzel had both been picked up by the Gestapo and sent to Buchenwald, arriving in Neuengamme in June 1944, the month that Heissmeyer began his experiments.

For his first trial, Heissmeyer selected 100 Russian PoWs.

Heissmeyer visited weekly from Hohenlychen to conduct the implanting and injection of the infectious tubercle bacilli. Safety precautions for the orderlies were neglected as the live bacilli culture, obtained from a Berlin laboratory, was mixed in a saline solution in porcelain mortars. The prisoners were forcibly restrained as Heissmeyer thrust a rubber tube down the throat and into the lungs to implant the tubercle suspensions, checking his positioning on the X-ray screen. Sometimes, Heissmeyer injected straight under the skin or rubbed into scratches. Post-war, Heissmeyer would argue that his procedures were ethically sound.

Tubercular nodes in the lungs spread quickly and when Heissmeyer needed to harvest the organs for autopsy, the victims were hung in batches in what other Neuengamme inmates referred to as 'Heissmeyer days'. The bodies were dumped in the morgue to await autopsy with organ parts sent to Heissmeyer's colleague in Hohenlychen, the pathologist, Dr Hans Klein. This particular pathologist had been a key participant in the earlier euthanasia programme that culled 30,000 of Germany's mentally ill and disabled. Klein was transferred to Hohenlychen in 1944 from Berlin's Rudolf Virchow clinic to work with Heissmeyer. Copious notes and photographs of the TB trials were maintained in Hohenlychen.

It soon became clear to Heissmeyer that his experiments on those with existing TB had only worsened their condition. Heissmeyer needed a fresh and quite different replacement stock and there was no one better placed to offer advice than Josef Mengele.

JOSEF MENGELE HELPS OUT

For his second trial Heissmeyer required children.

Birkenau was winding down with the Red Army close. Large numbers of inmates had been transported or death marched to Bergen-Belsen and the demolition of the gas chambers and crematoria, ordered by Himmler, was almost complete.

A request to Mengele was submitted by Heissmeyer on November 28 and he was specific in his choice: a mix of boys and girls, some related and in a spread of ages. Mengele, no stranger to selection, chose

10 boys and 10 girls, among them the two Hornemann brothers from Eindhoven in Holland and Roman and Eleonora Witonski, a brother and sister from Radom, Poland. Eleonora, aged five, was the youngest of the 20 chosen. In the Radom ghetto, she and Roman had witnessed the massacre of all its men by the SS on March 21, 1943.

Transport of the chosen to Neuengamme was arranged. A separate railcar was attached to a regular train to Hamburg. Accompanying the children was an SS guard with a Belgian PoW doctor in Birkenau, Paulina Trocki, and three PoW nurses. Block 4A in Neuengamme had been made ready to receive the children with its living conditions way better than in other Neuengamme huts. It had been a two-day train-ride to Neuengamme and on its arrival the three nurses were immediately strung up on the Neuengamme gallows on the orders of SS-Standartenführer (Colonel) Max Pauly, the camp commandant. Trocki was sent to another camp.[1]

Within a week, the children had settled into their individual bunks, a luxury compared to Birkenau where inmates had to scramble and fight for sleeping space. Trzebinski had allotted each child a trial number applying the same number to a guinea pig in a comparative study group. Heissmeyer regularly visited and conducted the injections of live bacilli with dosage differing by child and age. Florence, in a desperate attempt to save the children, often sabotaged the bacilli suspensions by boiling them before injection despite the risk to his own life if caught.

As this new trial progressed, the condition of the children deteriorated and extra food to increase resistance levels failed to reverse the decline but despite the setback, Heissmeyer and Trzebinski sustained the programme of injections. The children by now were dulled into full acceptance of their treatment, and the pain.

THE BULLENHUSER DAMM SATELLITE

There were 14 camp satellites of Neuengamme in the centre and suburbs of Hamburg, the largest being Spaldingstrasse holding 1,800 mainly Jewish prisoners at its peak. Once a grand building, the inmates

---

[1] Trocki survived the war.

◀ The rear of the former Bullenhuser Damm school in Rothenburgsort. To the left, two of the basement windows are visible with bars still on the windows. The SS guards from Neuengamme probably escorted the children, their carers and the Russian PoWs through these rear doors.

▶ Wartime photographs of the school are rare but this one in 1943 shows the extensive roof damage after an RAF raid on Hamburg.

◀ A side view of the damage.

▲ The basement.

▼ A drawing of the school transferred into a satellite of Neuengamme drawn by a former inmate. The 'skolan' is the school block.

▲ The steel door of the boiler room where the carers and PoWs were hung from the overhead ceiling pipes remains firmly closed to the curious. Entrance is allowed to the room on the right where the children were strung up over the clothes hooks.

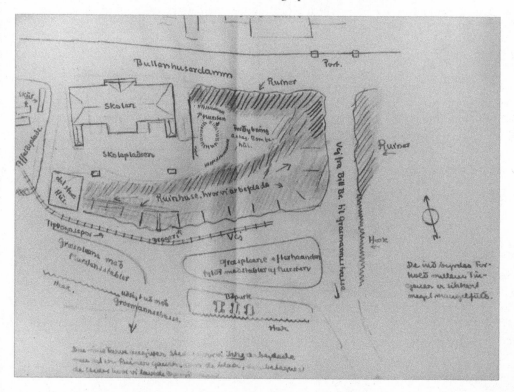

were housed in six blocks in the rear. In the middle of the complex was an uncovered corridor and in the front were rooms for the SS guards. Strippel, the Stützpunktleiter, or area command leader, had his office here.[2] The rooms were large and the prisoners only returned to them at night to eat and sleep. During the day, they were engaged in rubble clearance on the Hamburg streets. Paul Loéhac, a French doctor imprisoned in Neuengamme for being a member of the French Resistance, had been transferred to Spaldingstrasse and his medical workload was tough. Strippel had imposed a brutal regime and an estimated 800 died either in the camp or in the rubble clearing with the persistent danger of collapsing buildings.

Amongst these satellites were six women-only camps with Veddel, the first established in mid-July 1944. Its 1,500 women, mainly Hungarian and Czech prisoners from Birkenau, cleared bomb rubble at the commandeered Ebano-Oehler and Rhenania Ossag petroleum refineries, owned pre-war by Esso and Shell respectively: highly dangerous work that carried an ever present risk of sparking an explosion. At Steinwerder, 600 Veddel prisoners were used as slave labour in the Blohm + Voss shipyard, the company that had built over 200 U-boats from 1939 until March 31, 1945 when the last was commissioned into service.

Flogging was the order of the day at the women's camp in Sasel. Ida Römer, the superintendent who ran the camp after a five-day SS training course in Neuengamme, relished in the whippings she handed out, often on a whim. Around 500 Jewish women were transported in from Birkenau in September 1944 and used as forced labour for Möller, the construction company. When they weren't on the production lines, they cleared rubble in the St. Pauli and Altona districts, and in the S-Bahn stations. The women constructed a prefabricated housing settlement in the Poppenbüttel suburb of Hamburg for the homeless.[3] Many would later perish in Bergen-Belsen.

---

[2] Spaldingstrasse No.160 is now a hostel and has two panels in the foyers dedicated to its Nazi past. An Allied bomb devastated the front of the building in April 1945.
[3] An original prefabricated building built by the women prisoners still stands and is now a museum.

In the Tiefstack camp, 500 women manufactured concrete slabs in the local cement factory for makeshift housing at the Diago plant. Additionally they dug anti-tank ditches around Hamburg with the British army close. Allied bombing destroyed Tiefstack in early April 1945 and the subsequent death toll is unknown. As in several other satellites, the final destination for inmates was Bergen-Belsen. Unexploded bomb clearance led to a high mortality rate for the women in the Hammerbrook camp.

Work conditions in all the 14 satellites run by Georg Strippel, the Stützpunktleiter, from his office in Spaldingstrasse, were brutal and there is no real estimate on the death toll exacted on the male and female prisoners who lost their lives in the fruitless attempts to maintain Germany's industry and infrastructure.

Bullenhuser Damm in Rothenburgsort, an industrial centre, 3km away from Spaldingstrasse, still remains largely unknown amongst the post-war generations. The school was built in 1910 and during the years of the Third Reich, the children who filled the 30 classes stood enthusiastically to greet their teachers with the Nazi salute. Genetic theories and Nazi racial ideology figured prominently on the curriculum. In the playground, the boys and girls were kept apart by a wall down the centre. With the onset of war, part of the basement was renovated into an air raid shelter with airtight heavy metal doors installed.[4] The janitor was Wilhelm Wede, who had moved into basement rooms with his family in 1935. Wede had previously been in the police service for 12 years. After the building work his family was given better living quarters on the ground floor and the space vacated was used as the girls changing room for its gymnasium. In the evenings, Wede worked in the canteen at the local DAF community centre.

After the school was evacuated, DAF, the German Labour Front organisation, requisitioned the gymnasium in the spring of 1941 to house Italian labourers and later, living space was also allocated for workers from the Bill Brewery, opposite the school, and workers employed in the local Still forklift company. During the five-day RAF

---

[4] These doors remain.

bombing campaign on Hamburg in July 1943 – 'Operation Gomorrah' – Rothenburgsort was one of several industrial areas targeted and Bullenhuser Damm sustained bomb damage. Hamburg's first firestorm caused by incendiaries took place during the night of July 27 with 780 bombers overhead. Two days later, 770 bombers created another. Throughout the city 30,000 died and much of Hamburg was evacuated, including the Bullenhuser Damm school.

Despite its condition, Neuengamme took over the building in November 1944, turning it into the Bullenhuser Damm satellite. A workforce of 50 prisoners was brought in to fit bars to the windows, fortify the ground floor and construct the electrified fence. That labour force was doubled within days given the scale of the conversion. The former school had become a camp fortress and the SS filled its floors with Polish, Soviet and Danish prisoners, all engaged in body recovery from the surrounding area or hacking out stone for Deutsche Erd- und Steinwerke, the construction company. Medical responsibility for the Bullenhuser Damm satellite came under the remit of Dr Trzebinski, the chief doctor in Neuengamme, and in one of his reports he stated that the inmate complement on March 29, 1945, was 592 men of which 200 were Danes.

What was left of German industry was being systematically blown apart by March 1945. Hamburg, Bremen and Wilhelmshaven were hit with a massive raid that month as 1,400 US Flying Fortresses with an escort of 900 fighters took out U-boat yards and other targets around the ports. An RAF spokesman in London announced that strategic tonnage dropped over Germany during the month had broken all monthly records. RAF Bomber Command had dropped 67,500 tons with the Americans not far behind with 65,625. Hamburg and Berlin had borne much of the brunt.

That aerial bombardment didn't let up. On April 3, a force of 750 Flying Fortresses and 650 Mustangs bombed industrial centres in Hamburg and Kiel. Rothenburgsort by now was reduced to rubble. Two buildings on the school grounds that housed prisoners, the school itself, and the Bill Brewery were badly hit. Evacuation of Bullenhuser Damm inmates began on April 9 with the prisoners marched to the Sandbostel satellite and within three days, the camp was empty. The Danes had been evacuated as part of Count Bernadotte's deal with

Himmler to transport all Scandinavian prisoners to Sweden.

In charge of Bullenhuser Damm had been SS-Oberscharführer (Sergeant) Ewald Jauch who reported into Strippel in Spaldingstrasse. Jauch was a camp guard for the duration of the war, beginning with Sachsenhausen. In 1944, he was a roll-call leader in Neuengamme's typing pool hut before Pauly, the commandant, sent him to Bullenhuser Damm to manage the satellite.

With the prisoners gone and the school almost reduced to a shell with its roof partially destroyed and the windows blown out, only Jauch and Johann Frahm, an SS corporal, remained as did the janitor, Wilhelm Wede. Pauly earmarked the building to tie up loose ends in Neuengamme before he joined the SS exodus of camp commandants to Flensburg. One was the elimination of witnesses and study victims in Heissmeyer's TB experiments. Pauly wanted the 20 Jewish children killed, but away from the preying eyes of Neuengamme inmates.

There is no written testimony that the former Bullenhuser Damm school was already a killing ground but given it had been a concentration camp, prisoners must have been tortured or hung in the basement. Jauch and Frahm were probably accomplished Nazi hangmen.

'I'LL TAKE HIM TO BED NOW'

Trzebinski was ordered on April 20 to prepare the Heissmeyer children for travel and in the late evening the truck was loaded up. The two French doctors and the two Dutch medical orderlies accompanied them, as did Trzebinski who had a large supply of morphine. It isn't clear whether the inclusion of six Soviet PoWs in the party was a last-minute decision.

The SS escort had been deliberately chosen, all enjoying their status in exacting terror and willful murder of the helpless and vulnerable. Willi Dreimann, a Rapportführer, or camp sergeant, with responsibility to dispense discipline, revelled in his reputation as 'Executioner'. Formerly Dreimann had been a Hamburg policeman. Rottenführer (Lance Corporal) Adolf Speck, known for extreme violence against camp inmates, had run the Neuengamme brickworks since mid 1944 and under his watch the death rate in its labour force had soared. Little is known about Unterscharführer

▶ The old Bill Brewery opposite the school in Bullenhuser Damm was another Neuengamme killing ground during April 1945. Just days after the school hangings, 60 Russian PoWs were brought here and hung over the water pipes in the basement by Strippel and five Spaldingstrasse guards.

▶ Inmates from all the Neuengamme satellites in the city were used to clear bomb damage. This photograph is of Hammerbrook inmates.

◀ The entrance to what was the former Spaldingstrasse satellite of Neuengamme. Strippel maintained an office in the building. The children were first brought here where Strippel awaited them.

▶ The rear of the building has undergone renovation. The section to the left was badly bomb damaged in April. The building on the right, which housed the inmates, is now a hostel and two plaques in its foyer illustrate some of its notorious wartime history.

▼ Pauly's previous camp command was the notorious Stutthof. The photograph shows him greeting Himmler on a visit. Note the 'SS - 1' number plate on Himmler' vehicle.

▲ Tying up loose ends at Neuengamme before fleeing to join other camp commandants in Flensburg, Max Pauly ordered many killings including the elimination of the 20 children in Blocks 4 and 4a. Here, he is seen with his wife outside the commandant's block.

▲ A veritable rogues gallery of SS mass murderers. Auschwitz inmates had constructed a 'guesthouse' for SS officers at Solahuette, 29km from the main camp. Anton Thumann, second in from left, had a brutal reputation in Gross-Rosen and Majdanek, and after a short spell at Birkenau when this photograph was taken, he was transferred to Neuengamme where as Schutzhaftlagerführer, or camp chief operating officer, he relished his reputation as the 'Sadist of Neuengamme'.

Thumann had instructed Petersen, the SS driver who took the children from Neuengamme to Bullenhuser Damm, to bring back the bodies for cremation in the Neuengamme crematorium.

For interest, on the left, is Josef Kramer, the commandant of Auschwitz-2, Birkenau, who would later be transferred to Bergen-Belsen to run Camp 1 and on Thumann's right is Karl-Friedrich Höcker, the commandant of Auschwitz-1. Far right is Franz Hössler, the Schutzhaftlagerführer of Birkenau, who after Auschwitz became the commandant of Camp 2 at Bergen-Belsen.

Thumann, Kramer and Hössler would hang but Höcker would live long, dying in 2000, aged 88, and right up to the end he denied any involvement in mass murder. Photographs of Solahuette gatherings only came to light in 2007 after Höcker's photo album of his time at Auschwitz was presented to the US Holocaust Memorial Museum.

(Corporal) Heinrich Wiehagen who joined the killing squad but his later actions aboard a ship attacked by Allied fighters, when he shot Neuengamme prisoners jumping into the sea to save themselves, mark him out as an SS guard devoid of decency and humanity. Chosen as driver was Corporal Hans Petersen, the regular driver for Neuengamme's post office.

Florence, anticipating what was in store, shook the hands of the remaining prisoner orderlies who worked in Blocks 4 and 4A. One, Paul Weismann, remembered Florence's whispered final words. 'I don't believe we'll see each other again. Au revoir.'[5]

First stop was Spaldingstrasse where Strippel awaited them. Pauly had tasked him to oversee the killing. Under later interrogation by the British, Trzebinski claimed that he made it clear to the Stützpunktleiter that he wanted no part in what was to happen but Strippel had angrily retorted that he was a coward. Trzebinski, supposedly, was in two minds but he remained with the children. The truck continued to Bullenhuser Damm, through a city under total blackout. Strippel went ahead by car.

It was 10pm when the truck arrived. Jauch had already alerted Frahm to what was expected of them. Frahm was in his office when Jauch entered and said, 'they have arrived'.

The first to be hung were Florence, Quenouille, the two orderlies, Deutekom and Hölzel, and the six Soviet PoWs. Using the rear door of the former school they were taken into the basement and through to the boiler room. That room still exists but the metal door is kept firmly locked to keep out the curious, visitors like myself. Frahm admitted to British interrogators that Dreimann, Wiehagen, and himself were the hangmen. A rope was thrown over the overhead water pipes, the bodies dumped in another room.

Now it was the turn of the children.

They had been assembled in what used to be the girls changing room in the basement and the children were visibly upset by the dark and threatening surroundings. Trzebinski took each child aside to inject them with a strong dose of morphine to calm them down.

---

[5] Professor Gabriel Florence was posthumously awarded the prestigious Prix Henri Labbé award for biochemistry from the French Academy of Sciences in 1953.

Some immediately fell asleep or became drowsy but others remained alert. Frahm had come from the boiler room and told the children to undress. It was close to midnight.

Trzebinski's interrogation testimony described how the children had met their end. The first to die was the eldest, Walter Jungleib, a 12-year-old Slovakian boy.

'Frahm lifted the boy up in his arms, saying to the others "'I'll take him to bed now'"'. Trzebinski accompanied Frahm and the boy down the steps into the basement proper, past the boiler room and into the largest room. Waiting were Jauch and Dreimann, with Wiehagen by the door. Strippel joined them.

'This room was six to eight metres from the common room', said the doctor.[6] 'I saw a noose on a hook. Frahm put the sleeping boy's neck into the noose and then clung to the boy's body, bringing his full weight to bear on the noose'.

If Trzebinski still had qualms about murdering children, Frahm fully implicated him. With the rope wrapped around the neck of each child and positioned on the wall hook, one held onto the victim pulling it down, another pulled from the other side. Dreimann was involved in the first two deaths, according to Frahm. After each hanging, the body was unceremoniously dumped behind a partition with Walter Jungleib at the bottom of the pile. When done, there were 30 bodies in the two killing rooms. There were to be more before Strippel and his fellow SS killers were done.

Wede, the janitor, who post-war lamely claimed he had remained in his office on the ground floor, was seemingly oblivious to what was taking place in the basement.

Another truck had arrived from Spaldingstrasse, a group of 20 Russian PoWs, which Pauly wanted to be disposed of. Jumping down from the truck, three ran for their lives and Wiehagen and Speck gave chase. They were quickly rounded up and shot.[7] The rest

---

[6] This is a reference to the former school changing room.
[7] Speck would say during interrogation that one of the prisoners had thrown salt into his eyes in the bid to escape. With Wiehagen, he had chased down the escapees, which took several hours. Using that defence, Speck argued that given the timing he couldn't have participated in the hangings.

were taken into the basement and one-by-one they were strung up over the water pipes in the boiler room. There is no record of their names, as there isn't for the six hung earlier.

In the early hours of April 21, there were 47 bodies in the basement and the three upstairs. One of the hangmen, in his testimony, admitted that he and his colleagues were exhausted by their efforts. Strippel was the first to leave, returning to Spaldingstrasse. At 7am, Trzebinski returned to Neuengamme on his own to report to Pauly.

Shifting all the bodies out of the basement to the truck was strenuous. Petersen, the Neuengamme driver, must have helped as would Wede, even though there is no record of them doing so. As the bodies had been stripped, Wede probably burnt the clothing in the building's boiler.

Petersen had been instructed to deliver all the bodies to the Neuengamme crematorium on the orders of Schutzhaftlagerführer Anton Thumann[8], justifiably referred to as the 'Sadist of Neuengamme' by inmates. This camp chief operating officer had previously worked in Majdanek and Birkenau. In charge of the Neuengamme crematorium, the morgue and the registry was Unterscharführer Wilhelm Bracke, a corporal who thrashed inmates with the thick end of his bullwhip. Albin Luedke, an SS colleague, described Bracke's role to his interrogator on February 27, 1946. Bracke had had his own unit of prisoner Kapos: a work party of 25 Dutchmen, Russian and French prisoners, who with horses and carts daily collected the camp dead. In the Neuengamme mud, the carts frequently were bogged down but Bracke simply whipped the men to pull harder.

Pauly hadn't finished tidying up his loose ends. Between April 21 and 23, a transport of 58 men and 13 women transferred in from Fuhlsbüttel prison were immediately hung on Neuengamme's gallows. A week later, there were further killings in Bullenhuser Damm, this time in the abandoned Bill Brewery opposite the former

---

[8] Effectively, the camp's chief operating officer responsible for all the prisoners and their 'well-being'. The Schutzhaftlagerführer was in day-to-day control.

school. Trucks carrying 60 inmates from Neuengamme arrived in the Spaldingstrasse camp at 2.30am. They were mainly Polish PoWs classified as 'political prisoners', denoted by three red triangles sewn into their clothing. Eduard Bonitz, a 55-year-old Spaldingstrasse guard, a tobacconist before the war, described the sequence of events.

Arriving separately by car, an unnamed SS officer from Neuengamme brushed past the SS guards on the Spaldingstrasse gates and headed directly for Strippel's office with Pauly's order that the group be liquidated immediately because 'these prisoners were dangerous'. Within 10 minutes, the 60 were made ready for immediate dispatch to the Bill Brewery. A Spaldingstrasse inmate whispered to one of them that Bullenhuser Damm signalled death.

Strippel and five Spaldingstrasse guards, two known to Bonitz as Unterscharführer Lorentzen and Rottenführer Zimmermann, had taken the prisoners to the brewery. The trucks had arrived at 3am and the hapless 60 were taken down into the spacious basement and hung over the water pipes from the ceiling. Their names are unknown. Later that day, Strippel had sent over 30 prisoners from Spaldingstrasse to clean up the mess. The bodies were taken to Neuengamme where Bracke and his Kapos disposed of them in his ovens.

HUNTING DOWN THE KILLERS

The British army was closing in on Hamburg. To the west, the British 11 Armoured Division had crossed the uncompleted autobahn linking Hamburg to Berlin, reaching the village of Mühlenrade on May 1. The Scots Guards entered the town of Stade in the east to find the bürgermeister waving the flag of surrender. Unexpectedly, amongst the prisoners taken in Stade was Lt. General von Wulhhich, on the staff of General Friedrich Christiansen, the commander-in-chief in the Netherlands. Wulhhich had ditched his uniform in an attempt to evade capture. Christiansen would later face war crimes for his torching of Putten, a Dutch village, in October 1944, in retaliation for the killing of a Wehrmacht officer by the Dutch Resistance. The Wehrmacht and SS destroyed more than 100 houses and deported 661 men mainly to Neuengamme, with only 48 surviving the war. They spoke of beatings and incarceration in tiny metal punishment cages: such was the brutality of Neuengamme under the command of Pauly.

On May 2, Neuengamme was empty, the sickbay cleared with those too ill to travel summarily dealt with. The SS and the remaining prisoners had gone. A British reconnaissance unit arrived at the gate that day and reported back that the barracks were empty apart from stragglers. Count Bernadotte's Scandinavian prisoners had left in April with 4,000 onboard the legendary white buses that had picked up from Flossenburg, Theresienstadt, Bergen-Belsen, Ravensbrück, Dachau and Sachsenhausen and several of the satellite camps. Two final death marches had left Neuengamme for Flensburg: 400 on April 24 and 350 on April 30. The biggest exodus of prisoners was the rail transport of 9,000 prisoners on April 26 to Lübeck to board the *Arcona, Thielback* and *Deutschland* ships. Some prisoners had been left behind with a skeleton SS guard to clear up and eradicate evidence of mass murder in the camp. The barrack blocks had been scrubbed, the straw that served as mattresses burnt and the flogging trestle and gallows dismantled. Pauly had driven to Flensburg in his DKW staff car.

As for the three ships at anchor in Lübeck Bay, the RAF had targeted them on May 3 after faulty intelligence reported that the ships were stuffed with escaping SS, desperate to flee to the protection of the Dönitz government. Some 6,600 prisoners died in the air raid.

The remaining German forces in Hamburg surrendered without a fight on May 3 and British armour parked up in strength in front of the Rathaus. Within the day, Karl Kauffmann, Hamburg's notorious SS Gauleiter since 1933, was arrested. Under his watch, Hamburg's Jews had been transported to Poland [9] and Neuengamme had grown to become one of Germany's largest concentration camps. Kauffmann, a friend of Hitler, would never lose his admiration for fascism. [10]

Hamburg's 'Reichssender', the public radio broadcaster that had transmitted propaganda for the duration of the war, was taken over.

---

[9] During the war, 18 trains had departed from Hamburg with 6,150 Jews. As the war ended only 645 remained in the city.

[10] Post-war, Kauffmann linked up with Dr Werner Naumann, the former state secretary in the Reich's propaganda minister under Goebbels, and was later charged with political conspiracy to return West Germany to Nazism.

The announcer, in post for two years, broadcast that all public traffic and vehicles on the streets were barred at 12 noon the following day with only workers in the public utilities able to break the curfew. On a sombre note, he stated: 'It is improbable that I will be allowed to continue in this role and I wish all Hamburgers the best that one can wish for in the present situation. Long live Hamburg and long live Germany'. An Allied-controlled newspaper, the *Hamburger Nachrichten Blatt*, was quickly in print its headline proclaiming 'The War is Finished'. This first edition notified the Hamburg public of Britain's aim to establish a military government in the short-term.

Pauly and other known Neuengamme officers were already on wanted lists and by the end of May, the enormity of the slaughter in Bullenhuser Damn was apparent to the Judge Advocate General's office in the headquarters of the British Army of the Rhine (BAOR). It had to be prosecuted as a war crime, like no other, believed Major Anton Freud of the No.2 British War Crimes Unit based in Minden. 'This murder is outstanding for its utter ruthlessness and for the cold bloodiness of the accused', he wrote in a report.

On false papers, Trzebinski, Heissmeyer's supervisor, had disappeared into North Friesia on the Danish border, a region that had long been supportive to the party. He had scraped away his blood group tattooed under an arm, denoting SS membership. To anyone that asked, he had been a doctor in the Wehrmacht. Later caught up in a British military trawl, Trzebinski was detained at the Hesedorf camp near Bremervörde, and allowed to treat other inmates. Trzebinski felt secure enough to pose for photographs with his wife and young daughter in November after they visited him in Hesedorf.

The past did catch up with this SS doctor who prior to Neuengamme had earlier worked in Auschwitz and Majdanek. Held in Fuhlsbüttel jail in Hamburg, Trzebinski was interrogated by the British in February 1946 and admitted he had been a participant in the Neuengamme killing machine. As to the hanging of the 20 children, the fault wasn't his, he claimed. Heissmeyer had ordered the hangings to cover up his TB experiments.

Pauly was also locked away in Fuhlsbüttel, this pre-war shopkeeper in a village not far from Hamburg had hidden up in Sankt-Jürgen-Platz, an area in Flensburg's city centre, in a flat owned

◀ Kurt Heissmeyer had established a private tuberculosis clinic in Magdeburg, East Germany, post-war, living in plain sight but his patients were none the wiser to his murderous past. *Stern* blew apart that cloak of secrecy in 1959, running an investigative article revealing that West German schoolchildren were oblivious to the war crimes committed by SS doctors during the war. Cited was the tuberculosis trial on children in Neuengamme.

◀ What finally condemned Heissmeyer was his extraordinary admission that before he fled Hohenlychen he had buried a large zinc-lined box, containing not only personal items but also documents and photographs, including a ring binder, relating to his experiments on the Neuengamme children. Heissmeyer never had returned to Hohenlychen to collect the cache and it had remained *in situ* in the garden of this SS medical facility. It was one of the most comprehensive hoards of SS medical experiments discovered by the German authorities, East or West.

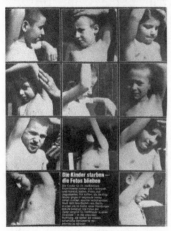

▲ Some of Heissmeyer's photographs of the children recovered from the box. Each of his child victims was photographed with the arm lifted so the post-operative scar of the operation to remove the lymph nodes was visible. The children each had around their necks the Neuengamme prisoner number and an experiment number. For his records that he had kept in his buried box, Heissmeyer always used the experiment number rather than a child's name.

▲ Those same photographs adorned the front cover, alongside Strippel's photograph, of an anti-fascist magazine in May 1986.

▲ Strippel and his wife.

▲ The decision to release Strippel from jail in April 1969 while serving his Buchenwald sentence was an earlier landmark in the leniency expended towards him by the West German legal system. Strippel's lawyer had been able to strike out the testimonies of several witnesses. Only the charge against the Buchenwald commandant, then dead, on the shootings of the 21 inmates, was allowed to stand. Strippel was freed and incredibly this SS killer pocketed DM121,500 (US$ 12,680 at the-then currency exchange) compensation for his time spent in jail. There was public outrage but Strippel didn't care, he had been cleared of a war crime and thanks to the state he was now moderately wealthy. SS-Obersturmführer Arnold Strippel died on May 1, 1994 in Frankfurt am Main, aged 84. He would be long remembered as a serial mass murderer in every concentration camp he had served in. We didn't find any newspaper record of his death.

◀ Alfred Trzebinski, Neuengamme's SS doctor, who managed the TB experiments for Heissmeyer, first administered the large doses of morphine to the children before participating in the hangings. He had fled north into North Friesia on the Danish border and scraped away his blood group tattooed under an arm, denoting SS membership. To anyone that asked, he had been a doctor in the Wehrmacht. Later caught up in a British military trawl, Trzebinski was detained at the Hesedorf camp near Bremervörde, and allowed to treat other inmates. Trzebinski felt secure enough to pose for photographs with his wife and young daughter in November 1945 after they visited him in Hesedorf.

123

by his brother-in-law. The location was compromised and two armed plain-clothed British military police pitched up on May 23. Pauly had answered the door. He was initially detained in the Neumünster internment camp that had rapidly filled up with SS and Gestapo.

Major Freud interrogated Pauly on January 9, 1946 and what Pauly signed in his testimony was short and dismissive. 'Experiments on 12 children were performed by Professor Heissmeyer but I didn't know that such experiments had been carried out on humans. The children were sent to Bullenhuser Damm when the camp was being evacuated. There, Dr Trzebinski killed them by means of injection'. It was 20 children, not 12, and cause of death was hanging, as Pauly knew full well. To him, Trzebinski was the culprit.

Frahm, the Bullenhuser Damm blockleiter who had placed the rope around each child's neck, had fled Hamburg seeking refuge with his family in Kleve, a town very close to the Dutch border. The British found him and he was taken to Neumünster. Describing his pre-war occupation simply as a 'worker', his deposition to British interrogators was damning, implicating his co-participants in the hangings.

Jauch, the Rapportführer in command of the Bullenhuser Damm satellite, had remained in Hamburg to take his chances but had been quickly rounded up. With so many SS and Gestapo in the city, the British had commandeered Neuengamme and it became No.6 Civil Internment Camp. On interrogation, Jauch denied any involvement in the child slayings arguing in his defence that he had poor mobility at the time, suffering with a bad foot condition. With Frahm's full admission, however, Jauch's culpability was clear. Also denying any responsibility was Petersen, claiming he was merely the Neuengamme driver who took the children to Bullenhuser Damm and returned the bodies to the Neuengamme morgue.

Speck and Dreimann had been ordered to accompany the final death march of prisoners from Neuengamme to Flensburg. Once in the city, Speck was one of many who exchanged his SS uniform in the central police station for a new identity. He now wore the uniform of a Hamburg policeman, maybe the same uniform he had used before he became an SS guard in Neuengamme guard in 1940. The British picked both up.

Wiehagen would never face justice, meeting a violent end

onboard one of the three prison ships at anchor in Lübeck bay. This former Duisburg schoolteacher was one of several SS bludgeoned to death as they shot prisoners jumping into the sea during the attack.

A living witness to Heissmeyer's experiments in Neuengamme had been located. Tadeuss Kowalski, a Polish PoW and a doctor, had been on Trzebinski's staff. After liberation, he worked in the Polish hospital in Haffkrug, the small coastal town north of Lübeck. A survivor of Auschwitz before his transfer to Neuengamme in April 1943, he was interviewed by a British interrogator in December 1945.

Kowalski had observed the children in the X-ray room under the supervision of Florence and Quenouille, with bacilli incisions either on the left or right breast or on the arm, which looked painful and swollen. He confirmed in his testimony that Heissmeyer had tasked Dr Doslie Bogumil, an inmate from Prague, to extract the glands under a local anesthetic and place them in sterilized test tubes for later examination in Hohenlychen by Dr Hans Klein.[11] Kowalski chillingly concluded '… all the children were taken away, along with the doctors …'

Why the children were not liquidated in Neuengamme is unclear but the empty satellite camp in Bullenhuser Damm offered a more secure and unobserved killing ground. The only witnesses, wrote the British War Crimes Investigation Unit, were seasoned killers who had no qualms in committing murder, even on a child as young as five.

The absence of Strippel, however, created a major legal hurdle for JAG. There were doubts that a case could stand up if the officer in charge wasn't in custody. Strippel had been shielded by the SS kamaraden, living on a farm and working as a farmhand. When he considered it safe to travel, Strippel travelled south to Frankfurt am Main, moving into Wielandstrasse No.37 on December 4, 1946.[12] This city like many others lay in ruins and a thriving black-market quickly developed alongside the US army occupation. In the chaos Strippel freely moved around, in plain sight.

---

[11] Klein never faced war crimes, enjoying an unhindered university career in Heidelberg.
[12] This address would later be confirmed by the city's Polizeipräsident in an Einlieferungs-Anzeige, a 'Wanted Notice'.

BRINGING STRIPPEL TO JUSTICE

What did proceed was the Neuengamme trial and 14 officers and guards stood accused in Hamburg's Curio-Haus when it opened on March 18, 1946. Appropriately, Pauly had No.1 around his neck for identification purposes. Amongst the 14 were Trzebinski, the doctor, with Frahm, Jauch, Dreimann and Speck; the SS guards directly implicated in the Bullenhuser Damm hangings. Thumann, involved in the cremation of the bodies, was also in the dock. All 14 in the Neuengamme trial were found guilty with death sentences imposed on 11.

In the course of the next four years, the Curio-Haus would host 188 military trials with 504 defendants, 59 of whom were women. Most cases involved the concentration camps and massacres in northern Germany but several concerned murdered RAF flying crew who were lynched by revengeful SS and Wehrmacht.

Albert Pierrepoint, the British hangman, had been brought over to carry out the hangings from the start and the army gave him the honorary title of Lt. Colonel. The military gave him an assistant, Sergeant Major Richard O'Neil. Gallows were erected in the West Wing of the jail in Hameln, to the south of Hamburg, of 'Pied Piper' fame, modelled on the apparatus in Pentonville jail in London with a trapdoor wide enough for a double hanging.

First to test those gallows on December 13, 1945 had been 11 former SS guards at Bergen-Belsen. On Tuesday, October 8, 1946, 14 were hung including 12 from Neuengamme. Among them were Pauly, Thumann, Dreimann, Trzebinski and Speck. The following Friday, Jauch and Frahm had a date with Pierrepoint. [13]

The hunt was still on for Strippel and Heissmeyer. The British had put out a high-priority countrywide alert on the former in May 1946, which did yield one lead. A Wilhelm Strippel was in No.7 Civil Internment Camp, in Eselheide, and in late June, a JAG officer visited to check his identity, but the birthdate of this Sicherheitsdienst agent,

---

[13] Up to the last hanging on December 6, 1949, Pierrepoint and O'Neill had hung 191 men and 10 women, the women executed singularly unlike the men. In 1950, Hameln was handed back to the German authorities and the West Wing with its condemned cells was demolished in 1986. The remainder of the prison would later become a hotel.

Arnold Strippel in Düsseldorf: Im Majdanek-Prozeß ist er angeklagt, an der Erschießung von 84 sowjetischen Kriegsgefangenen beteiligt gewesen zu sein. Der SS-Mann Strippel war von 1934 bis 1945 in vielen KZs tätig

Der SS-Arzt und die Kinder (6. Teil)

Arnold Strippel – eine KZ-Karriere

Ein Bericht von Günther Schwarberg
Dokumentation Daniel Haller

In derselben März-Woche 1979, in der die Abgeordneten des Deutschen Bundestages vor dem Hintergrund des Völkermordes an den Juden über die Nicht-Verjährung von Mord diskutierten, fällten zwei Frankfurter Gerichte Entscheidungen, die mit den NS-Verbrechen im Zusammenhang stehen. Ein Schöffengericht sprach den rechtsradikalen Vorsitzenden des „Kampfbundes deutscher Soldaten", Erwin Schönborn, frei. Er hatte das Tagebuch der Anne Frank als eine „Fälschung" bezeichnet und als das „Produkt einer jüdischen antideutschen Greuelpropaganda, um die Lüge von den sechs Millionen vergaster Juden zu stützen". Solche Äußerungen seien in der Bundesrepublik durch das Recht auf freie Meinungsäußerung gedeckt, sagte das Frankfurter Gericht.

Die 3. Zivilkammer des Frankfurter Landgerichts verurteilte den STERN zu 100 000 Mark Geldstrafe, weil er den Namen des SS-Obersturmführers Arnold Strippel im Zusammenhang mit der Ermordung von 20 jüdischen Kindern genannt hatte. Strippel gab eine eidesstattliche Erklärung ab, in der er jede Kenntnis und Beteiligung am Kindermord vom Bullenhuser Damm von sich weist und auch bestreitet, für das Hamburger Außenkommando Bullenhuser Damm des KZ Neuengamme überhaupt zuständig gewesen zu sein.

Nach allen bisherigen Feststellungen der Hamburger Staatsanwaltschaft hatte Strippel aber doch die Aufsicht über das Lager Bullenhuser Damm.

Die Frankfurter Richter Jürgen Schwichtenberg, 41 Jahre

▲ Strippel was a concentration camp careerist, said this newspaper.
Source: Barbara Hüsing

the SD counterintelligence arm of the SS, differed from Arnold Strippel, the fugitive. The real Strippel remained at large. Wrote the commanding officer of No. 2 British War Crimes Investigation Unit, 'very little is known about him.'

Strippel, believing he was safe, now attempted to expunge his wartime record by handing himself in to the Americans at the Darmstadt detention centre near Frankfurt to gain official release papers. Throughout the country many were doing the same. Strippel's lies were convincing and release papers were stamped but he remained vulnerable and instantly recognizable to the survivors of the nine concentration camps he had served in. A sighting was inevitable and on a Frankfurt street on December 13, 1948, a former Buchenwald prisoner, who had undergone a Strippel torture, spotted him and informed the police. Strippel was arrested.

Frankfurt's city's prosecutor was compelled to try a case against him over his participation in the murder of 21 Jewish prisoners at Buchenwald. That trial began on May 31, 1949 with the charge that SS guards in the camp, led by Strippel, had commemorated the failed assassination attempt on Hitler in November 1939 in the Munich beer hall with the execution of inmates. Strippel, reportedly drunk, had selected the names of the victims. The 21 were lined up and shot in the back of their heads. Strippel vehemently denied the charge and during the trial the prosecutor further questioned Strippel over Bullenhuser Damm, given he had been named by other participants in the child hangings in their respective interrogations. In a show of defiance, Strippel claimed no knowledge of any such episode even though it had been reported in the Hamburg press not long after the war had ended. With Buchenwald survivors giving stirring testimony, the judge handed down to Strippel a life sentence, to serve at least 21 years plus an additional 10. Strippel was sent to Butzbach prison to serve his time.

HEISSMEYER IS FOUND

Heissmeyer had established a private tuberculosis clinic in Magdeburg, East Germany, but *Stern* blew apart that cloak of secrecy in 1959, running an investigative article revealing that West German schoolchildren were oblivious to the war crimes committed by SS doctors during the war. Cited was the tuberculosis trial on children in Neuengamme. That article sparked nationwide interest and prompted East Germany's general prosecutor's office to arrest Heissmeyer on December 13, 1963. From his East Berlin prison cell this former SS doctor refuted all charges of murder.

What finally condemned Heissmeyer was his extraordinary admission in March the following year that before he fled Hohenlychen he had buried a large zinc-lined box, containing not only personal items but also documents and photographs, including a ring binder, relating to his experiments on the Neuengamme children. Heissmeyer never had returned to Hohenlychen to collect the cache and it had remained *in situ* in the garden of this SS medical facility. It was one of the most comprehensive hoards of SS medical experiments discovered by the German authorities, East or West.

Heissmeyer's court trial had begun on June 21, 1966 and nine days later he was sentenced to life imprisonment. He was jailed in Bautzen, a maximum security facility under the control of the Ministry of the Interior and the Stasi for high-profile criminals and spies. At the trial, Heissmeyer expressed neither remorse nor sense of moral culpability. 'For me there was no basic difference between Jews and guinea pigs and I did not think that inmates of a camp had full value as human beings,' he arrogantly argued, further emphasizing that if his experiments on the Neuengamme children had saved the lives of a similar number of Germans, the experiments would have been worthwhile. Heissmeyer's time in prison was short-lived, succumbing to a heart attack in August 1967. He was 62.

HAMBURG'S PROSECUTOR

Three months before Heissmeyer's death, Hamburg's prosecutor, Dr Helmut Münzberg, had reluctantly begun a preliminary hearing against Strippel over the child slayings and he interviewed Strippel in Butzbach. Yet again, this former Stützpunktleiter denied any knowledge of the Bullenhuser Damm hangings even suggesting that on the day, he had remained in his Spaldingstrasse office. Strippel would later amend his statement, claiming that he had only heard of the hangings after the war.

Some of Münzberg's conclusions on why he didn't instruct for a full trial were baffling and illustrated how West German authorities were often perceived as obfuscators, choosing not to bring Nazi killers to book. Münzberg chose to ignore the original British investigations and the testimonies of guilt from other participants in the hangings who had named Strippel as being in charge, countering that they had only minimized their own involvement. Equally crucial was the absence of living witnesses, argued Münzberg, yet he had declined to interview Wede, the janitor, who was in the empty former school at the time and probably helped in shifting the bodies out of the basement.[14]

One statement baffled all legal opinion and would blight the rest of Münzberg's legal career:

'No extraordinary pain or torture was inflicted on the children given they were unconscious after the morphine injection, and so, beyond the destruction of their lives, no further harm was done to them. In particular, they did not have to suffer especially long, either in body or soul'.[15]

When deputy attorney general of Schwerin in 1992, Münzberg claimed compensation of DM10,000 arguing that his legal career path had suffered by what he called grossly inaccurate interpretations of what he had said in 1967.

The decision to release Strippel from jail in April 1969 while serving his Buchenwald sentence was to be another landmark in the leniency expended towards him by the West German legal system. Strippel's lawyer had been able to strike out the testimonies of several witnesses. Only the charge against the Buchenwald commandant, then dead, on the shootings of the 21 inmates, was allowed to stand.

---

[14] Post-war, the former school was refurbished and used by Hamburg's meteorological service. It later reverted to its original purpose as a school. Wede was again the janitor, a position he held until 1956. A daughter, in a letter addressed to the Bullenhuser Damm memorial, dated October 19, 2011, recalled that her father maintained a fear of the basement and often broke down in tears. A former headmaster, Jonni Vogt, reminisced in 1979 that he had known nothing about the child murders until Wede told him. There is a personnel file for Wede in Hamburg's Staatsarchive. Wede died in 1967, aged 64.

[15] 'The Murders at Bullenhuser Damm', Schwarberg G., Indiana University Press, 1980, p132.

Strippel was freed and incredibly this SS killer pocketed DM121,500 (US$ 12,680 at the-then currency exchange) compensation for his time spent in jail. There was public outrage but Strippel didn't care, he had been cleared of a war crime and thanks to the state he was now moderately wealthy. He continued living in an apartment in Staufenstrassse No.4, Frankfurt, before moving to Kronthalerstrasse No.14 in 1979 and then moving again to Talstrasse No.10.

Stern, the magazine that had first brought the Bullenhuser Damm child slayings to the public's attention, wasn't done and in an article published in March 1979, headlined 'Der SS-Arzt und die Kinder' – 'The SS doctor and the children' – Strippel was named. Its author, Günther Schwarberg, a Hamburg-based investigative journalist, had extensively researched the case. Strippel's lawyer sought an injunction to prevent any further articles and in a civil case that was heard in Frankfurt on April 13, 1979, *Stern* was warned it would be fined DM100,000 each time any further article appeared. That injunction was ignored and Schwarberg wrote a further five, each time *Stern* refusing to pay. Underground Nazi publications added their support to Strippel.

The publicity generated a demand by several relatives of the dead children to attempt another application for a trial. Schwarberg's wife, Barbara Hüsing, a Hamburg lawyer in a small practice, relished the chance to help and agreed to work for the relatives purely on a *pro bono* basis.[16] A new witness to Strippel's camp methods came forward: Mei Versteegen, a Dutch prisoner in the Vught concentration camp, one of three in occupied Holland.

The Vught camp in much of its three-year existence had been a transit for deportation to the Sobibor and Birkenau death camps and was also a ready pool of labour for the giant Dutch manufacturing company, Philips, now under German control. Some Dutch prisoners had taken retribution in January 1944 against a German prisoner unmasked as a stooge and Adam Grünwald, the commandant, took revenge.

Strippel, then a guard in the camp, took charge in cramming 74 women into one of Vught's notorious 'Bunker' cells, squashed

---

[16] *Pro bono*: a lawyer would volunteer time and without charging a fee.

upright. Strippel himself pushed in the last before slamming the door, shamelessly oblivious to the terrifying screams of asphyxiation.

When that cell door was opened 13 hours later, women literally fell out leaving a pile of bodies of those who had fought, and lost, the fight for air from a small boarded window that had been clawed open. Surprisingly only 10 had died but that figure would rise. The survivors were barely able to walk. Later in the year Strippel was transferred to Neuengamme where its commandant, Max Pauly, was grateful for his talents.

Post-war, Grünwald was jailed and curiously when the Dutch authorities sought the extradition of Strippel, the American military in Frankfurt refused the request. Another Vught commandant was tried in West Germany in 1967 and the Dutch authorities sent a 6,000-page archive to Ludwigsburg relating to the SS atrocities committed in the camp. The boxes, however, merely attracted dust and ended up in Frankenthal. Hüsing got wind of its existence, realizing its value.

As to why in 11 years the German authorities had never consulted this cache, they simply claimed that the documents were in Dutch and no resources had been made available for a translation. Hüsing pleaded for a translation to be done given its importance to a potential case against Strippel yet the Vught material remained in their boxes. That was a setback and another would follow. The Frankfurt prosecutor debated whether the Bullenhuser Damm hangings should be considered as manslaughter not murder. If the former, the crime was out of time given the 10-year limitation period from it being committed.

Hopes were raised in 1976 with the onset of the Majdanek trial. Strippel, the concentration camp careerist, was one of the nine SS defendants in the dock.

MAJDANEK HORRORS

Düsseldorf had hosted the Majdanek trial and on the morning of July 1, 1981, the final day, the sentences were due.

Outside the court, the demonstration was noisy: the waving banners picked up by the raft of television cameras and press photographers. Yet for five years and seven months, almost as long as the entire war, the West German public had grown indifferent to its outcome, despite the trial being described from the outset that it would probably be the last of the major war crimes trials. To mitigate a public outcry of inaction, the authorities had issued a statement that investigations into 87,305 individuals were in progress and 6,449 had been sentenced since the end of the war. As the Majdanek trial had laboured on, the defence lawyers dragged their heels in the hope it just might be abandoned.

A group of 150 young people had turned up on that final day demanding maximum sentences for the nine accused: seven men and two women.[17] Strippel had been posted from Natzweiler to Majdanek in October 1941 as the Schutzhaftlagerführer – the camp chief operating officer – and promoted to Untersturmführer. Günther Schwarberg and some relatives of the Bullenhuser Damm children sat in the court with the expectation that Strippel might at least spend the rest of his life behind bars, albeit not for the slaying of the children.

In excess of 12,000 guards had been employed at Majdanek in the three years of its existence. Some 300 witnesses were called during the trial including 200 camp survivors and their testimony was grim. The trial was not only the most protracted in West Germany's history, it had been the costliest. Inside the court, the accused covered their faces as they were brought up into the dock for sentencing. The outcome was far from certain. Dr Günter Gogen, presiding over the five-judge panel, had suffered several collapses during the trial and according to *The Times* correspondent he had noticeably aged.

Strippel had been accused of personally murdering a group of 42 Soviet PoWs and on the days he was required to attend court he travelled by train from his home in Frankfurt. The court had provided a taxi for him at Düsseldorf station. During questioning, there were

---

[17] There were 16 guards originally charged in 1975. One died, another ruled unfit to stand trial, another was tried separately and four were acquitted in 1979 through lack of evidence.

▲ Roman Zeller and H. Wassermann have never been formerly identified and given no relatives have ever come forward, sadly who they were will probably never be known.

► Walter Jungleib was the eldest child and the first to be hung. He was the last child to be identified post-war.

▲ The suitcase memorials to Dr Rene Quenouille and Professor Gabriel Florence. Both men were French PoWs in Neuengamme, ordered into the TB programme as medical assistants. Quenouille, a 60-year-old radiologist, and Professor Gabriel Florence, a 58-year-old eminent biochemist, had distinguished medical backgrounds before their arrest by the Gestapo. Pre-war, Florence had been nominated for a Nobel Prize.

◀ In a bid to persuade the legal authorities that Strippel had to face war crime charges over the child hangings, Barbara Hüsing, a Hamburg lawyer, convened an independent tribunal to hear and assess all the evidence as to his guilt. The tribunal was filmed and ran for two days in April 1986. Hüsing had appealed the decision not to prosecute Strippel on medical grounds to Hamburg's Oberlandesgericht, the highest of all the city's courts, but it was rejected in January 1987. Again, Strippel was free to walk the Frankfurt streets and astonishingly the court even awarded him financial compensation for the 'stress' he had incurred. *Photograph by kind permission of Barbara Hüsing*

▶ Günther Schwarberg, married to Barbara Hüsing, was also indefatigable in trying to bring Strippel to court and in determining identification of some of the children. Schwarberg, seen here, wrote the seminal work on the child murders: *The Murders at Bullenhuser Damm*.

135

gasps from the public gallery, as Strippel expressed no knowledge of any killings or massacres in Majdanek. As to the use of the gas chambers he merely dismissed them as disinfectant rooms for inmates. The public gallery erupted and Gogen ordered the court be cleared. Strippel's defence lawyer had consistently demanded an acquittal on the grounds that his client had only carried out orders, the standard defence in war crime trials.

The atmosphere was palpable as Gogen began to read out the sentences, his firm voice failing to disguise his nervousness as his hands twitched violently. Loud cries of incredulity instantly sucked out any expectation that justice – 36 years after the end of war – would finally prevail. Only Hermine Braunsteiner Ryan, the daughter of a Vienna butcher, who had been extradited from the US, was given life.[18] Nicknamed 'The Stomping Mare' by Majdanek inmates given her penchant for trampling old women to a bloody pulp with her steel-studded boots, her actions epitomised the brutality of many SS women in the concentration camp system. Ryan took great pleasure in seizing young children by their hair and slinging them onto trucks for gassing.

The court had been appalled to what had occurred in Majdanek on November 3, 1943, named 'Operation Harvest Festival', as SS and the German Order Police shot down 17,000 inmates in open graves, accompanied to blaring music played through loudspeakers to drown out the noise. What happened in Majdanek was the largest single-day, single-location massacre during the Holocaust.

Aside from Ryan, sentences of between three and 12 years were handed down. One defendant was acquitted. The 12-year sentence was given to Hildegard Lächert, nicknamed 'Bloody Brigitta' by the prisoners she terrorised with her German shepherd dog and whip with a bullet she had woven into its tip. Gogan gave Strippel a mere three and half years and to compound the general disbelief in the court, he considered Strippel, aged 70, as unfit to serve the time imposing the

---

[18] Her first job was in a brewery before she worked for the giant Heinkel aircraft plant in Berlin, moving on to the Ravensbrück women's concentration camp in 1939, as the pay was better. *The New York Times* had revealed her past after discovering her whereabouts in Queens, in New York.

sole and derisible punishment of barring any travel outside the country. Yet again, the West German authorities had indulged this SS killer. Even worse, the opinion that he was too unfit would set a precedent and jeopardise any further trial on other charges.

Despite the ramifications, Schwarberg and Hüsing petitioned the Hamburg prosecutor claiming that the admissions gathered by the British interrogators in 1945 and 1946 were sufficient to prosecute a case on Bullenhuser Damm. Hüsing pushed the prosecutor's office into contacting the relevant agencies in Poland and Russia to search for camp prisoners who had witnessed or endured Strippel's methods in any of the nine camps in which he had served.

Trying to overturn the 'too unfit' precedent, Hüsing demanded that Strippel be subjected to medical examination. The prosecutor agreed and Strippel attended Frankfurt's University Clinic in 1985 to be assessed by three specialists including a neurologist. Strippel and his lawyer must have been encouraged when the doctors concluded that the former SS officer had hypertension and a trial would be a significant mental burden with a real danger that apoplexy might bring on a stroke.

The only option left to Hüsing was to appeal directly to Hamburg's Oberlandesgericht, the highest of all the city's courts, and to add weight to the appeal she convened an independent tribunal to review all the evidence against Strippel, including the medical opinion. Dr Klaus von Dohnányi, the-then mayor of Hamburg and politician, hosted the event and among the other participants was Martin Hirsch, a legal heavyweight and a former judge in the Federal Constitutional Court. The filmed tribunal ran for two days in April 1986. The relatives of the dead children also weighed in with their opinions by condemning the German legal system for its consistent inaction to bring Strippel to book.

The findings were put to the Oberlandesgericht but in January 1987, the court still threw out the appeal. The medical opinion of the three Frankfurt doctors hadn't helped. Again, Strippel was free to walk the Frankfurt streets and astonishingly the court even awarded him financial compensation for the 'stress' he had incurred. Hamburg's Bürgerschaft, the city's parliament, took an alternative view and handed Hüsing some compensation for her unpaid and painstaking efforts on behalf of the relatives. The Oberlandesgericht's decision had marked the end and no more appeals would follow. Hüsing had tried her best but each time she was thwarted by a legal system more interested in protecting Strippel than seeking justice. She continues to keep in touch with the relatives and attends the annual memorial to the children.

After the Oberlandesgericht ruling, Strippel for the last seven years of his life remained in Frankfurt, unpunished and protected by the state. He died on May 1, 1994, aged 83, with no national newspaper or journal reporting his death.

Schwarberg died in 2008. His book *'The Murders at Bullenhuser Damm – the SS Doctor and the Children'*, published in 1980, has become the seminal account of the dreadful events in this former school during the night and early morning of April 20-21, 1945. He is accredited with matching up the names of five of the children with their surviving relatives, a number of whom had endured their own harrowing years in the camps. The mother of Roman and Eleonora Witonski, a survivor of the Polish camps, had been laboriously searching for her children. The two were only identified as Bullenhuser Damm victims in 1982 after Schwarberg and Hüsing met the mother and showed her photographs of the victims that had been located in Heissmeyer's archive in Hohenlychen. In 2015, only the backgrounds of three children remained unknown but there was a breakthrough that year on one, Walter Jungleib, the first to be hung. An ageing sister came forward to furnish family details.

Only two identities of the slain remain unknown. A girl, probably Polish, is known as 'HW' and is likely to be H. Wassermann. She was aged eight when handed over by Mengele to Heissmeyer and put on the train to Neuengamme and Block 4A. The other is 'RZ', probably Roman Zeller, aged 12, and also Polish. All attempts to find their respective families have been in vain. In all probability they had lost their lives in Birkenau, Treblinka or Sobibor.

In the weeks after the British army occupied Hamburg, the Bullenhuser Damm school was requisitioned as a transit camp despite its condition. That use ended in 1947 and the building, now refurbished, was utilized by a meteorological service. Over the next decade, there were calls to erect a monument in the grounds and place a commemorative plaque on the front entrance but the Hamburg authorities opposed all plans, preferring to downplay the building's murderous significance during the last days of the war.

A plaque was finally allowed in 1963 but controversy ensued over the wording. What wasn't permitted was that the children were Jewish and nor did the plaque mention the death of the Soviet PoWs. Only in 1980 – 35 years after the event – did the authorities officially relent to allowing memorial status to the building and a rose garden was established in the rear five years later. Plans to sell the building to the private sector caused an outrage and given the protest they were abandoned.

In a private visit, with a guide from the city's Museumdienst, I was given access. I drew on the extensive knowledge provided to me by Dr Iris Groschek, who has written on the Bullenhuser Damm murders. The boiler room where the carers and the Soviet PoWs were hung from the overhead water pipes is off-limits but all other doors are open, their metal thickness impressive and built to withstand the Allied bombing. In the large room where the children were grotesquely hung on hooks there are quotations on the wall.

Where the 20 children were ordered to undress, this room has been transformed into an oval shrine of small and brightly coloured suitcases, their lids open. Inside are their names and known family details, some have photographs of earlier and happier times before they became the experimental playthings of Mengele and Heissmeyer. Appropriately, there are four other open suitcases with biographical detail for the two French PoW doctors and the two Dutch orderlies who were murdered in the boiler room.

This suitcase memorial angered some who believed the suitcases symbolize going on holiday or going away but it is far from that. It is poignant reminder that these children, like so many others, were far from their homeland. Sadly, the Wassermann and Zeller open suitcases are blank, apart from recording their probable names. For the 26 Soviet PoWs hung in the basement no names are known.

▼ OVERLEAF: The Twenty little Suitcases. *Source: Nigel Bance*

POSTSCRIPT: UNFIT TO STAND TRIAL, OTHER CASES

The question of unfitness to stand trial was tested in 2011 in the case of John Demjanjuk, the Ukrainian-born former car worker from Ohio, who post-war had built up a new life in the United States. Demjanjuk had been a member of the notorious Trawniki unit used as guards in the Polish death camps. His background came to light in 1981 and Demjanjuk was stripped of his US citizenship. Demjanjuk's lawyers argued for some years that he was not the brutal 'Ivan the Terrible' in Treblinka. Eventually deported to Israel to stand trial, Demjanjuk was deemed guilty to being party to extermination of Jews in the camp and sentenced to hang.

Israel's Supreme Court quashed the conviction in 1993 on the grounds that evidence against him was unsound, including a possible mistaken identity. He was returned to the US. Munich's public prosecutor moved against Demjanjuk in November 2008, stating it had enough evidence to prove his involvement in 27,000 deaths as a Trawniki guard in Sobibor and he was deported to Germany in May 2009. In the subsequent trial in 2011, Demjanjuk turned up in court in a wheelchair or carried in lying motionless on a stretcher. The Munich court was shown secretly recorded evidence that he could walk unaided and ruled against Demjanjuk being too unfit. The court found him guilty and Demjanjuk was sentenced to five years, the conviction later annulled because he died before an appeal could be heard.

More recently, the trial of the Rumanian Johann Rehbogen, a former SS guard in Stutthof, began in Münster in November 2018. Rehbogen was born in 1923 and joined the SS aged 18. After the war, he completed a PhD in business management and taught landscape gardening. Seventeen relatives of those who died in Stutthof had joined the prosecution as 'joint plaintiffs'. Several survivors had given statements. Aged 95, Rehbogen's lawyers argued that he was unfit to stand trial but the plea was overruled. The court sat for no more than two hours at a time for two days a week.

STORY CHARACTERS: AFTERMATH

★ Bracke, SS-Unterscharführer Wilhelm: Although he was not directly involved in the hangings, the British charged him as an accessory given he was responsible for the cremation of the bodies in Neuengamme.

★ Frahm, SS-Rottenführer Johann: In May, he had fled to Kleve, near the Dutch border, to join his family where he remained until the British picked him up in October 1945. Tried in the Curio-Haus and executed, aged 35.

★ Heissmeyer, Dr Kurt: His time in prison was short-lived, succumbing to a heart attack in August 1967. He was 62.

★ Jauch, SS-Rapportführer Ewald: Hung on October 11, 1946 in Hameln, aged 44.

★ Klein, Dr Hans: Never prosecuted for his part in the Heissmeyer TB experiments. In 1965 he was department head in the Heidelberg Institute of Forensic Medicine, dying in November 1984, aged 72.

★ Pauly, SS-Standartenführer Max: This pre-war shopkeeper from Dithmarschen in Schleswig-Holstein had been an SS careerist, joining the NSDAP shortly after Hitler came to power. Neuengamme commandant since August 1942, he claimed to his British war crimes interrogator that the decision to kill the children had come from Berlin and he merely passed on the order to Alfred Trzebinski. Sentenced to death on May 3, 1946, he was subsequently hung on October 8 in Hameln jail, aged 39.

★ Petersen, SS-Unterscharführer Hans: Not tried in the Curio-Haus trial and not used as a witness. He died in Sonderburg, Denmark, aged 70.

★ Römer, SS-Superintendent Ida: This brutal head guardian at the Sasel women's satellite camp was sentenced in 1946 to three years jail as part of the Curio-Haus trials.

★ Ryan, Hermine Braunsteiner: Ryan was arrested in Austria in 1946 and in 1949 tried for crimes in Ravensbrück. She was sentenced to three years but released early in 1950 with the Austrian government granting her amnesty against any further war crimes charges. In April 1959, she emigrated to the US and was granted citizenship in January 1963. Ryan settled in Queens, New York. Her past was finally revealed and the US authorities deported her to stand trial over her role in Majdanek. Reported *The New York Times*, neighbours knew this wife of an electrical construction worker from Maspeth as scrupulously house-proud and very friendly. As she fought deportation in 1972, the neighbours didn't believe she had had such a gruesome past. In jail after the Majdanek trial, Ryan refused to talk to other inmates, whiling away her time sewing dolls and soft toys. Ryan died in a Bochum nursing home, Germany, in April 1999, aged 79.

★ Speck, SS-Oberscharführer and Kommandoführer (work detail leader) Adolf: Hung on October 8, 1946 in Hameln, aged 35.

★ Strippel, SS-Obersturmführer and Stützpunktleiter (area base commander) Arnold: Died on May 1, 1994 in Frankfurt am Main, aged 84.

★ Thumann, SS-Obersturmführer and Schutzhaftlagerführer (the camp chief operating officer) Anton: This Neuengamme sadist was hung on October 8, 1946 in Hameln, aged 33.

★ Trzebinski, SS-Hauptsturmführer Alfred: Hung in October 8, 1946 in Hameln, aged 44.

★ Wede, Wilhelm: This school janitor, who was in the building during the hangings, was never interviewed. He died in Schleswig-Holstein in 1967, aged 64.

★ Wiehagen, SS-Unterscharführer Heinrich: Died in May 1945, beaten to death by prisoners on one of the ships at anchor off Lübeck. Aged 34.

★ Zimmermann, SS-Rottenführer: One of the Bill Brewery murderers. He was picked up by the British and held in Neumünster internment camp.

PRINCIPAL SOURCES:

★ Files and testimonies held at the National Archives, Kew, London, on Neuengamme and Bullenhuser Damm, including Curio-Haus trial records
★ Barbara Hüsing interview
★ Archives: *The Times, The Washington Post, The New York Times, Die Zeit*
★ US Holocaust Memorial Museum and Collections
★ KZ-Gedenkstätte Neuengamme, Hamburg, and its archive
★ Various archives in Israel
★ Günter Schwarberg, 'The Murders of Bullenhuser Damm', 1980
★ The Children of Bullenhuser Damm Association

NEUENGAMME'S SATELLITE CAMPS IN HAMBURG

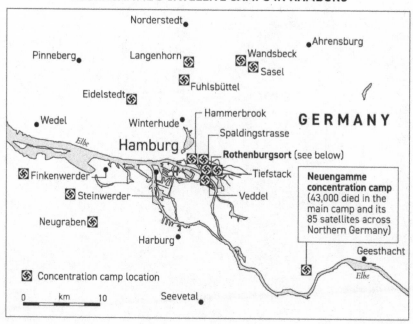

Rothenburgsort - Bullenhuser Damm, Hamburg

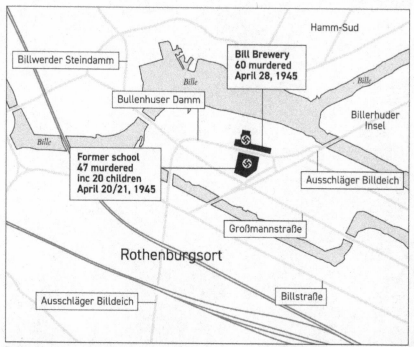

III

CHASING DOWN THE HARES

STORYLINE

What occurred in Celle in the dying days of the Third Reich is a dark and sickening reminder of the persuasive pull of Nazism and everything it stood for. National Socialism had pervaded into every level of Germany's social fabric and the systematic slaughter of concentration camp prisoners continues to cast a stain over this medieval town to the south of Lüneburg Heath.

For the witnesses prepared to attest that their neighbours and local police had aided and abetted the SS and Wehrmacht in committing murder, the lives of some would never be the same again.

When we approached the family of one witness, a 14-year-old at the time, we were informed that he had emigrated to the United States, still refusing to talk about his harrowing experience. Witnesses had been abused and threatened as the case eventually went to court with three of the accused sentenced to death.

The full account of what happened over two days in April 1945 can be told through the statements and testimonies given to Royal Air Force War Crimes investigators by both the witnesses and the accused. Emaciated concentration camp prisoners, many injured and sick, had just survived an Allied bombing raid on their stationary train in the Celle marshalling yards. Climbing out of their blazing open-top goods wagons, they had fled into the town and into the woods, to be clinically hunted down.

When caught, they were summarily shot in the back of the head or in the neck. The few survivors were taken to Bergen-Belsen.

Using primary sources that were kept secret for decades we can now reveal how the Celle massacre unfolded.

★ *A listing of characters is at the back of this story for reference.*

◀ Now a play area, over two days in April 1945 it rang with the incessant gun rattle of summary execution. Bodies still remain in these woods. Locals call this area the Mulde. *Source: Nigel Bance*

'*THIS CASE is a particularly strong example of the spontaneous and voluntary participation of German civilians in a revolting series of murders and it is most desirable that the perpetrators are brought to trial. Unfortunately, there is no satisfactory evidence as to the nationality of the victims, many of whom, in a futile appeal for mercy, protested that they were Germans.*'

This condemnation is in the report of the senior officer in charge of the War Crimes Group of the Royal Air Force.

The massacre over two days in April 1945 is recalled locally as 'The Celle Hasenjagd', or the 'Hare Chase of Celle'.

CELLE ZUCHTHAUS: DECEMBER 1, 1947

Celle jail, the Zuchthaus, retains its reputation as one of the toughest in northern Germany. This imposing structure, which faces the green in the old part of Celle, has a history steeped in violence with its cells full of hardened criminals serving long sentences. In the immediate days and weeks after the British liberated the Belsen concentration camp on April 15, 1945, the jail was crammed with SS and Hungarian army guards accused of committing war crimes. Even after the verdicts were handed down in mid-November 1945 as the Belsen trial ended, the jail remained full.

On December 1, 1947, the atmosphere in the jail was edgy as 13 detainees nervously awaited the summons to the interview rooms. Hauptwachmeister Heinrich Stahl, a staff sergeant in the Celle police force, arrived, as did Sergeant Ernest Able and Corporal William Amos of the Special Investigations Branch attached to No 84 Royal Air Force, War Crimes Group. Peter Compass, a translator in the RAF team, joined them. That day marked the culmination of a painstaking investigative process by the team involving over 300 interrogations and interviews, since the tip off by the wartime Anti-Nazi-Group in the first days of occupation that a major massacre had occurred in the town.

Stahl took charge of the line up as sheepish witnesses, one-by-one, were brought in and instructed to point out anyone they had seen kill between Sunday, April 8, and Monday, April 9, 1945. Able, Amos and Compass observed.

History didn't record Stahl's reaction as he placed six fellow Celle policemen in the line up. They had been brought in from Allied civil internment camps and during their time in Celle jail, any past camaraderie had dissolved into recrimination while professing their own innocence in mass murder. Amongst the others in the line up was a Celle fireman, an electrician, who had worked at the Luftwaffe airfield, and a celebrated local boxer with 150 fights to his name. Also brought up from the cells to stand in the line was a former senior prison warden who had already served a seven-month sentence for beating up prisoners on his watch.

There should have been more in the line up, in particular a Hauptsturmführer, an SS captain, who had orchestrated much of the killing, and the leader of the local Hitler Youth who had openly bragged of shooting 28 häftlingen, the German description of concentration camp prisoners. Both remained missing. One policeman had committed suicide while in custody.

The German Criminal Police in Lüneburg had instigated its own investigation two months earlier on whether Celle's police had colluded with the SS and other military during the events that followed a Royal Air Force bombing raid on stationary trains in the marshalling yards on April 8. Unknown to the RAF, one of the trains had held 3,000 male and 400 female concentration camp prisoners, enroute to Belsen, and it was caught in the inferno. The prisoners had been guarded on the train by 200 male and 43 female SS. Survivors of the bombing had fled into what they believed to be the comparative safety of Celle's streets and Neustädter Holz, the local woods. The Lüneburg investigation bore every hallmark of collusion and the British authorities had deemed it a whitewash.

To accurately tell the story of what happened in Celle on two fateful days in April 1945, we need to roll back to late 1944. With British and American aircraft squeezing German supply lines in the industrial Ruhr, the push was on for a major uplift in the manufacture of munitions. Germany's requirement for slave labour had become insatiable.

UNQUESTIONABLE SUPPORT TO HITLER

Celle's inhabitants in this medieval town that sits on the southern fringes of Lüneburg Heath, with its enchanting old quarter and its moated castle, could never argue they were oblivious to the Nazi forced labour and concentration camp system. There were 30 labour camps in the town and 150 in the close vicinity, employing in excess of 26,000 slave labourers. Lower Saxony was littered with camps.[1] Belsen, the worst of them all, lay astride the perimeter fence of the large Wehrmacht Bergen-Hohne barracks. The 3,000-strong SS and Hungarian army that served as camp guards would have enjoyed breaks in Celle's bars and taverns.

In the final months of Belsen's operation, Celle had become a food source as regular stores from Hannover dried up. Defined as a Krankenlager by the SS authorities, a camp for the sick and the dying, and ordered to accommodate inmates from camps throughout northern and north-western Germany, Belsen was overflowing. Unterscharführer Müller, the NCO in charge of Belsen's food supplies, made several trips to Celle in February but what its bakeries could spare barely dented the quantities that Müller required. With Belsen taking in 30,000 more prisoners in April, further trips to Celle proved futile.

With several death marches to Belsen passing through or around Celle, the sight of these long columns could not have gone unnoticed. Two Belsen survivors would later give evidence to British interrogators on one of the most notorious.[2] Some 610 prisoners of mixed nationality from Klein Bodungen, a Dora Mittelbau satellite, had set out on April 5, 1945. Imperiously riding up and down the column on his motorcycle was SS-Hauptscharführer (Senior Sergeant) Stärfl, the camp commandant. His deputy was the murderous SS-Oberscharführer (Sergeant) Wilhelm Dörr. The SS

---

[1] *'German Concentration Camps, prepared by Counter Intelligence Sub-Division (G-2), Supreme Headquarters Allied Expeditionary Force'*, London. This report was prepared within months of the war ending with detail of camps in Germany and the Nazi-occupied zones.

[2] Bogumil Gruhmann, Czech, aged 40, and Ernst Poppner, a German prisoner, aged 31.

guard contingent totalled 40, which included three of Dörr's prisoner-henchmen, who had no compunction in killing if it meant saving their own skins. With no food or water on the march naturally there were stragglers and if there was no room on the accompanying handcart, Dörr or his henchmen dispatched them. Dörr's own speciality was to make his victims kneel down before him before putting two bullets into the backs of their heads. Prisoners were then ordered to dig shallow graves before the column commenced.

Winding its way through Herzberg, Brunswick, and Peine, the body count grew. On April 8, the day that the Allied aircraft bombed Celle, the column reached the town's outskirts. The halt was only temporary before Stärfl pushed on. It wound its way through Celle's medieval streets and headed north to the bridge over the Aller River. Taking the road to Bergen, the column trudged though the village of Gross Hehlen, where several executions took place. By the time the column staggered into Belsen on April 9, Dörr's personal tally had soared to almost 50, his two sidekicks accounting for a further 30 at least. [3]

Factories in Celle needed slave labour, including the ITAG plant [4] located in the rail marshalling yards, the Güterbahnhof. Founded in 1912 by the Rautenkranz family, the company manufactured specialised piping and valves and its products aided German petroleum exploration across Europe and in Mesopotamia. [5] In its Celle plant, ITAG put French, Belgian and Polish slave labourers to work, housing them in cramped barracks in the hamlet of Papenhorst, south of the town.

Celle was 'Brown', a euphemism for loyal Nazi support. It was further distinguished as one of the very few towns in Lower Saxony whose political and civic apparatus was not purged when Hitler's National Socialists gained power in 1933. Gauleiter Otto Telschow, the Reichstag member for the Eastern Hanover district, and a former Hamburg policeman, was propped up by successive Celle Kreisleiters – SS administrators – including its last, Willy Milewski, and Ernst

---

[3] Dorr and Stärfl would be accused in the Belsen trial and hung.
[4] The ITAG factory remains in Celle.
[5] Mesopotamia is now Iraq. The German oil concessions were around Mosul.

▲ Wehrmacht officer Paul Tzschökell who ordered the Celle manhunt.

Meyer, one of several regional Oberbürgermeisters, or mayors. Loyal industrialists like Rautenkranz lent support, viewing the German ambition for European conquest a profitable driver in expanding the balance sheet. Adding to the 'Brown' mix was the Nazi-diehard, Major General Paul Tzschökell, whose Wehrmacht garrison was based in the imposing five-story Heide Kaserne barracks, not far from the castle. The Adolf Hitler Platz at the top of Hannoverschestrasse dominated Celle's centre, a place where residents gathered to celebrate the Führer's birthday.

Local newspapers and publications were on-message including the *'Celler Kriegs- briefe'*, a monthly circulation military newsletter. In the December 1941 edition, the town's SS administrators and Tzschökell expressed Christmas greetings to every soldier fighting on the respective war fronts, ending with a stirring message: 'We have faithful trust in our Führer and in victory. May everyone feel that the Homeland is with him!'

The formation of the town's Volkssturm was celebrated in the November 1944 edition, the part-time army's inspiration, according to the publication, being the success of *Operation Stormwind* in Poland with the scorched-earth eradication of all opposition in the rural communities.[6] Tzschökell's wife, Erika, in an earlier edition, had put a positive spin on the latest failed attempt on Hitler's life. 'At the end of July, all of Celle expressed an overwhelming loyalty to the Führer with my husband's garrison marching down the Stechbahn, united in protest against the flagrantly cowardly crime of July 20', she had affirmed proudly. Yet even Erika Tzschökell would have found it difficult to spin what has happening in Belsen with trainloads of KZ häftlingen daily passing through Celle enroute to the camp.

The persecution of Jews and transportation was never far from Celle's support of the Third Reich and the town's Gestapo office had authority throughout the region. Bergstrasse, in the old town, has changed little. During the war, No 46 was the police station with No 45 the section house that provided living quarters. This

---

[6] Strebel, Bernard: This publication was used as a source by Strebel in his 2010 paper on Celle, published in Hannover. Much of his paper analyzed the Nazi backgrounds of Celle's dignitaries in the naming of many streets in the town: a contentious issue.

Bergstrasse police station will figure prominently in this story of massacre.[7] Embedded into the pavement adjacent and facing the front door of No 10, are five 'Stolpersteine'. These are pavement brass memorials, easy to miss, dedicated to Jews transported to the German death camps in Poland. On March 7, 1942, Rosa Cahn, aged 80, was dragged out of No 10, transported to the Lodz ghetto and later gassed in Chelmno. Elsa Kohls, aged 47, was arrested on April 24, 1942, and also taken to Lodz. Three other members of the Kohls family, Adolf, Edith, and Lieselotte, aged 46, 22 and 20 respectively, were picked up six days later from No 10 and boarded a goods train to Auschwitz.

BELSEN AND SALZGITTER

Concentration camps were classified into five designations; extermination, labour, sick, experimental and training. The position of Belsen at its inception was unorthodox, not falling into any. Initially, the prisoners were 'exchange Jews', that is those the SS had decided to repatriate or to leave Germany, usually after substantial payments had been paid into SS coffers. By the end of 1944, that distinction radically altered. Belsen was now designated as 'Sick' and as the numbers swelled with inflows from other camps so the conditions further deteriorated. Josef Kramer was its commandant from December 1944, after his previous command of Birkenau. As the Red Army had approached Auschwitz-Birkenau, Kramer and many of his key SS staff had evacuated to Belsen. There had also been a steady influx of häftlingen into Belsen from Birkenau arriving either by train or by death march.

There were two camps: Camp 1 and Camp 2, the short-lived latter established only in early April 1945 in the nearby Bergen-Hohne Wehrmacht barracks to accommodate the inflow from the Dora-Mittelbau camps. Franz Hoessler, who had often been in charge of the new arrivals selection process on the Birkenau ramp, became Camp 2 commandant.

Dr Schnabel, Belsen's sole SS doctor in Camp 1, had informed

---

[7] Bergstrasse police station was closed in 1960 and is now a Karstadt department store.

his successor, Dr Fritz Klein, who had arrived with Kramer, that the medical services 'were in a proper working order and the Red Cross orderlies were working well': a delusional assessment. There were barracks in the five compounds that were 'hospitals' but they lacked even the very basic medical facilities. Only the 80–100 prisoner-doctors[8] administered treatment when they could but with diseases running rampart, they were powerless. Within days of his new appointment, Klein had left for Neuengamme, returning in mid March just in time for the visit from three senior members of the Concentration Camp Inspectorate, Oswald Pohl, Rudolf Hoess and Dr Enno Lölling, the head of all medical services in the concentration camp system.

Klein showed them around. 'I didn't need to point out very much because they could see with their eyes how bad the situation had become', he would later say contritely at the Belsen trial. In the first week of April, Belsen held 60,000 inmates and thousands of dead littered the site. Those who could walk were skeletal, and what there was of the Red Cross supplies for the inmates was grabbed by the SS and Hungarian army guards or left undistributed.

Kramer had no intention of improving the living conditions in Camp 1, now bereft of running water, food, blankets, paliases or cooking utensils. Conditions were marginally better in Camp 2 but the Wehrmacht commander made no attempt to alleviate the worsening situation on the other side of the perimeter fence.

One Sunday afternoon, Kramer had escorted Rosina, his wife, to a demonstration of weaving skills in the women's camp. As Rosina had congratulated the weavers on their efforts, the camp orchestra entertained the couple with their makeshift instruments. Both had enthusiastically applauded. 'My husband had told me with great pride about the beautiful orchestra and how it played', testified Rosina in court as she gave evidence that her husband had expended an extraordinary level of humanity towards the camp's prisoners. Kramer had promised proper instruments from Auschwitz.

As the Allied front line moved closer, Kramer had phoned

---

[8] This number was provided by Klein in the Belsen trial that ran from September 17 to November 17, 1945 and held in Lindenstrasse 30, Lüneburg.

Richard Glücks, the head of the Inspectorate, for evacuation orders but Glücks would have none of it, insisting that Himmler had given orders for a further 30,000 häftlingen to be shifted into Belsen from other camps. Glücks did agree to assist on the overcrowding, leading to the establishment of Camp 2 and he told Kramer that a satellite camp might be established in some former barracks in Münster, a distance away. In a further instruction, Pohl instructed Kramer to destroy all documents in the camp Registry. [9]

To the south of Celle was the Salzgitter complex with its 67 camps of various sizes feeding labour into the huge Braunschweig (Brunswick) steel works, built in 1940 by its state parent, the Reichswerke Herman Göring (Hermann Goering Steelworks), and the large number of munitions companies. Watenstedt had been chosen as the site for the steel plant and an 18km branch canal was constructed to join the vital Mittelland Canal. Salzgitter now amalgamated with 27 adjoining villages into what became the city of Watenstedt-Salzgitter, almost fully reliant on its imported slave labour.

Situated close to the steelworks were the Watenstedt/Leinde concentration camps, like all the camps in the Salzgitter complex under the auspices of Neuengamme in Hamburg. The camp, set up in May 1944, held 3,500 prisoners of which 1,500 were women transferred in from Ravensbrück to work on artillery shell manufacture. In February 1945, 800 Hungarian women, temporarily housed in the stables of the empty SS Riding School, further swelled the labour force in this dangerous and gruelling work. They had already endured Birkenau and Belsen. Another influx, this time 500 Polish men, arrived from the Braunschweig Schillstrasse camp via Birkenau. In Salzgitter, they were put to work in the Büssing NAG plant, the bus and truck manufacturer given over completely to war work.

In the Salzgitter-Bad camp on the edge of the old centre of Salzgitter, some 470 women were on the ammunition production

---

[9] The document destruction was total and nothing survived. Only survivor testimonies later provided some element of record.

lines of AG für Bergbau- und Huttendarf. They had been picked up in the Warsaw Uprising and when they arrived in Salzgitter, via Ravensbrück and Belsen, the SS paraded them in the 3km march to their four huts.

Drütte, the camp that had expanded from an initial 250 men occupying the empty storage units underneath an elevated road running into the artillery plant, would hold 3,150 by early 1945. Amongst the Salzgitter complex of camps, Drütte was one of the worst. There were countless executions in what the SS guards would record simply as 'escape attempts'.

SALZGITTER EVACUATES

Across Germany, radio stations had become prime targets for the Allied armies, including the large transmitter in Luxembourg. The BBC could now broadcast unhindered across the German nation with a daily stream of news and programmes debunking the Third Reich myths of military invincibility and racial purity. Some Celle residents would have had illicit radios and tuned into the BBC which reported the British move into the Ruhr and the advance towards Hamburg, Germany's second largest city. The Gordon Highlanders regiment of the 15th Scottish Division was moving closer to Celle. In the final days of March, the division was outside Uelzen to the north.

The order finally came through to evacuate the Salzgitter camps.

Watenstedt/Leinde was emptied with inmates crammed into three goods trains, their wagons uncovered, for an unspecified destination in north-east Germany. In a hazardous journey lasting a week, with lifeless bodies tossed over the side to free up space, the trains arrived at Ravensbrück. Their stay was temporary, with Ravensbrück also evacuating, and within days they joined in the camp's death march walking west. Those that finally arrived at the hastily prepared Wöbbelin concentration camp near Ludwigslust, in Mecklenburg, a so-called 'reception centre' for death marches, were close to exhaustion or near death.

Belsen was the chosen destination for the Salzgitter-Bad and Drütte inmates with 3,000 male and 400 female prisoners herded onto a train, guarded by 234 SS, of which 34 were women.[10] Engine problems soon developed and the train limped into Celle and held in the Güterbahnhof, the marshalling yards south of Celle station. Deutsche Reichsbahn needed to keep the main line clear. The plan was to load more coal, fix the problem, and carry on to Bergen in the evening. [11]

THE RAF ATTACK

There is confusion over which Allied airforce was behind the bombing of Celle on Sunday April 8, 1945. An account of the raid, locally published in 1989, states that the US Ninth Army Air Force carried out the mission,[12] yet that account runs contrary to documents held in the British archives.

In a summary written by the RAF officer in charge of the War Crimes Group in the preparation of documents for the impending war crimes trial on the Celle massacre, he wrote that RAF aircraft had attacked the town at 18.00 hours beginning with a warning run to alert the townsfolk that a raid was imminent. The marshalling yards had been the target but the RAF had had no prior intelligence that the stationary Belsen-bound train was also in the sidings. The prisoner train had taken a direct hit from a large RAF bomb, admitted the RAF officer. Had this raid on Celle been a joint mission with the Americans? If it was, the British files don't say so.

Whoever was responsible, the attack on the Güterbahnhof and the stationary trains, one of which held munitions, was devastating. Many Celle residents were killed and the town's dead are buried in the Waldfriedhof cemetery. Homes in streets close to the railway line had suffered hits as had several factories including the ITAG plant in the rail freight depot, and vital infrastructure such as the gasworks

---

[10] These specific numbers were supplied by the RAF War Crimes Group.

[11] All the trains to Belsen ended at the ramp outside Bergen, where prisoners were either transported to the camp in lorries or they were marched. The ramp area remains visible. A commemoration of what happened here took place in April 2019, and a Dutch survivor was present.

[12] Bertram, Mijndert: 'April 1945, Der Luftangriff auf Celle und das Schicksal KZ-Häftlinge aus Drütte', Celle, 1989.

and the Neustädt Bridge.

With the raid still in progress, survivors of the burning Belsen-bound train somehow clamboured over the sides of the open wagons onto the track to face the SS guards, their weapons drawn. As another wave of aircraft approached, the SS took cover in the ditches yelling at the prisoners, many terribly injured, to run for the woods to rendezvous later. In the panic, many stood where they were but others scattered and fled for their lives. From the ditches, the SS mowed them down, having no intention of keeping their word. Many did escape into the Waldweg, the forest track on either side of the Güterbahnhof.

Running alongside the railway is a road aptly named 'der Hasen', or 'Hare' track.

THE MIDNIGHT CONFERENCE

In the ARP command post in Celle's castle, Lieutenant Albert Sievert had observed the Allied raid. Sievert, aged 43, was a member of the air-raid defence force, combining that part-time duty with his role as one of Celle's senior policemen. His home in Nordmeyerstrasse was very close to the railway sidings. From the castle command post, Sievert saw the billowing smoke from the direction of the Zuchthaus, the town's jail, and the station beyond.

Hauptwachmeister Jacob Decker, a 50-year-old staff sergeant, had been on night duty in the police station on Bergstrasse, very close to where he lived in Nordwall. As the bombs rained down, Decker had called the police commander, Major Hermann Oetzmann, who was at home, resting. Oetzmann had been on patrol earlier in the day, including driving around the Güterbahnhof, but had felt unwell and gone home to sleep.

Oetzmann ordered Decker to take a police car into the town in damage assessment, and to take Ernst Kramer, another sergeant, with him. With the roads crated and with buildings on fire, they cautiously attempted to reach the most devastated areas. They hadn't gone far when another wave of aircraft came in and they ran for cover, 'to save themselves', Decker would later recall. Splitting up, Kramer aimed for Kronestrasse, not knowing that in the pattern of the

▼ There is mention to Somerhough of a 'Monsieur Le Dereuillenac' as the first to report events in Celle. This is Harold Le Druillenec, the only British survivor in Belsen, who had been arrested with his family by the Gestapo in June 1944, the day before D-Day, in St. Helier, Jersey, the largest of the Channel Islands. A schoolteacher, Le Druillenec had harboured a Russian PoW for 18 months and tuned into an illegal radio. Various trains took Le Druillenec to the notorious Alter Banter Weg concentration camp in Wilhelmshaven, a Neuengamme satellite, where he was put to work as a welder in the shipyards. With the British army close, all 1,129 inmates were being evacuated, many to Flensburg.

Le Druillenec was among a contingent of 400 of the sickest inmates being transported by train but at Lüneburg, it was bombed in an Allied air attack on the town. Some 250 died and survivors, including Le Druillenec, were death-marched to Belsen where they arrived on April 5, 1945. The SS guards led by the odious Dane, Gustav Jepsen, executed those left behind in what was termed the 'Lüneburg Massacre'.

Not only did Le Druillenec articulate to the British the atrocities he witnessed in Belsen during 10 days before liberation, he shared with his questioners the reminiscences that he had heard from other inmates including the Celle manhunt and massacre. This invaluable information became the key driver in initiating a war crime investigation.

Le Druillenec with 4,000 other British survivors that had been held in German concentration camps, filed a compensation claim in 1964 against the West German government. After prevarication, it paid out a miserly £1 million to settle all claims. Le Druillenec died in Jersey in 1985, aged 73.

Le Druillenec was the first survivor to give evidence in the Belsen trial.

► Several sensitive files in the National Archives relating to the hunting down and massacre of concentration camp prisoners who ran from the bombed train have only been released in recent years. This introduction to a document addressed to Group Captain Somerhough, head of the RAF's War Crimes Group, specifically states that bombs from RAF aircraft had bombed the marshalling yards. This contradicts the local belief that the bombs were dropped by US aircraft. Note the reference to who was to blame for the massacre in the 'systematic manhunt' that followed: SS guards, the Celle policemen and civilian volunteers.

C-59502 A.C

▲ Somewhere in this devastation was the stationary train that held the inmates from the Salzgitter complex of concentration camps enroute to Bergen-Belsen. Note the turntable on the left.

BAOR/15228/2/C.940/JAG.

for the attention of Group Captain SOMERHOUGH.

                    This case which arises out of information supplied
to the British authorities at the time of the BELSEN trial by
Monsieur Le DEREUILLENAC.   It appears that on the 8th April 1945
a transport train containing KZ prisoners of all nationalities was on
its way through CELLE probably to BELSEN.   The transport on the train
consisted of 3,000 men and 500 women guarded by approximately 200
men and 34 women. / Owing to the railway difficulties the train was
placed in a goods siding by CELLE station, and at about 1800 hours on
the 8th April 1945 after one warning run the RAF delivered an accurate
bomb attack on some ammunition trains in the siding.   As a result many
prisoners and guards were killed and the rest were ordered to take
shelter by the guards in the nearby houses and woods, and later ordered
to rendezvous in a place in the woods.   Before the prisoners had the
opportunity to get to the point in the wood a systematic manhunt began
organised by the SS guards, the German police officers in CELLE with
numerous civilian volunteers.   A merciless and brutal shooting and
killing of the KZ prisoners then took place in and around CELLE.
Many wounded were made to lie down and received the next shot.   Some
prisoners tried to escape, but in their weak condition were soon caught
and in spite of requests for mercy were shot by SS, ordinary police
and civilians.   This persecution went on most of the night of the
8th April and did not finish until Monday the 9th of April. Civilians,
mainly women, who endeavoured to give first aid to wounded prisoners
were abused and threatened.   A party of 40 prisoners was taken into
a small dell in the woods, and made to lie down in two rows and were
all shot in the neck, or while running away. /

bombing, it, too, had taken some hits, and Decker sought safety in the basement of a friend's house in nearby Fuhesstrasse.

Decker later returned to the police station to find the duty room buzzing with adrenalin, tempered with anticipation on what the night would bring. The initial rumour that plundering Zuchthaus prisoners were on the loose had quickly evaporated as numerous reports came in that häftlingen had escaped from a train in the Güterbahnhof. The duty room was full with several policemen in casual dress given the haste to report in and all wore their sidearm. Decker set off again, this time with Lieutenant Otto Schwandt, a 50-year-old veteran of World War I, and an experienced policeman of 25-years standing. Schwandt, who had only been in Celle since February, lived in the section house next to the Bergstrasse police station.

On the Hindenburgstrasse, a Wehrmacht staff car pulled up alongside the two policemen. Major General Tzschökell sat in the back and he called over to Schwandt to ask if he had seen any häftlingen. Schwandt reported they hadn't and Tzschökell drove away. Schwandt returned to Bergstrasse. For the next hour, Decker with another colleague stood at the Adolf Hitler Platz directing the traffic away from the bombed area.

Schwandt, Sievert and Decker would be key participants in the Celle slaughter as would another policeman, Helmut Ahlborn, aged 31, who lived in Rolandstrasse, to the north of the town centre.

Allocated watch patrol on April 8, high up in the tower of the Town Church, in Celle market, Ahlborn was just moments away from the Bergstrasse police station. Keeping him company in the vigil were two young civilian messengers, runners to convey urgent reports to Oetzmann and his two second-in-commands, Senior Lieutenants Meyers and Koch. From his high vantage point, Ahlborn heard the engines of the aircraft and saw the first bombs drop. As the attack continued, Ahlborn himself attempted a run to Bergstrasse but halfway down the tower he turned back as bombs fell close, ripping his overcoat as he did so.

When the raid was finally over, Ahlborn did return to the station and immediately tucked into a prepared meal in the duty room only to be interrupted by Oetzmann calling an emergency meeting. A reluctant Ahlborn put away his half-eaten supper in his locker and climbed the stairs to Room 4, Oetzmann's office. On the orders of the Kreisleitung, Meyers had put together a squad, its specific mission to round up the escaped häftlingen. Lieutenants Schwandt and Sievert were in charge but at this time it wasn't fully clear who would give the orders.

Decker and Sievert would later provide the names of the squad members to RAF interrogators. Apart from the lieutenants there was a mixture of sergeants and constables, among them Ahlborn, Gustav Behrens, Edward Meyer, Ernst Kramer, Gottwald, Detzloff, Weu, Peters, and Meinken. The squad drew rifles from the armoury and filed out with Ahlborn hanging back to try and finish his supper. Oetzmann chased him out to the waiting crew car, which was driven by constable Ahrens.

Some of the squad Ahlborn didn't recognise given the transient movement of policemen in recent weeks. Many new faces had been seen in Bergstrasse including a group of six policemen transiting back to Hamburg. In the crew car, Ahlborn began a conversation with a squad member who was unfamiliar, intrigued by the tattoo on his lower arm, an emblazoned 'Adolf Hitler'. Ahlborn closed his eyes and dozed, assuming that Lt. Schwandt would make the decisions that night.

Ahrens parked up outside Trift No 20, a large building that housed the Kreisleitung, the SS administrative hub in the town, presided over by Willy Milewski, the Kreisleiter. Schwandt and Sievert went inside leaving the rest to form up on the pavement and stand guard. Some SS appeared out of the dark, said nothing, pushed by and went inside. Oetzmann was a late arrival. The meeting was held in the conference room on the first floor that faced the green. As to who was in the Kreisleitung that night, Sievert would report that apart from himself, Schwandt and Oetzmann, there were eight to 10 Wehrmacht, including Tzschökell, a group of SS guards from the häftlinge train, and three men in civilian clothes. One of those was Milewski; another was probably Ernst Meyer, the Oberbürgermeister. As the police waited outside, a colleague, constable Overbeck, arrived to give them an update on the damage in the town. A clothing store had been hit as well as the rations-card office. The police joked that it would have been useful if the

Celle authorities had installed a better air-raid alarm.

Tzschökell sat silently in the conference room as his adjutant, a First Lieutenant, described the situation, as he understood it. An SS Hauptsturmführer added further detail on the KZ häftlingen. In the next 24 hours, this unnamed SS captain would show no mercy when prisoners pleaded for their lives. There were häftlinge sightings in the Waldweg, the forest track that marked the southern perimeter of the town before turning into Neustädter Holz, the large wood, and in homes left empty as residents sheltered in their cellars or in the civic bunkers. Schwandt would later describe the häftlingen as 'habitual and big criminals, putting all the inhabitants in great danger'.

As the SS train guards were unfamiliar with Celle, Tzschökell ordered them to work closely with the police in the häftlingen clearance. It would start on the east side of the railway line, in the Waldweg, and together they would move towards the Güterbahnhof. Crossing the railway line, they would split, the SS moving north and then west into Lauensteinstrasse, the police clearing the fields either side of Forststrasse before meeting up with the SS at the Rotthagen Sports Ground. In a pincer movement, both squads were then to move on Neustädter Holz in the final clearance. The Wehrmacht would provide troops, especially around its shooting range in Neustädter Holz with tanks adding support to the SS and police. The Volkssturm, the Hitler Youth and personnel from the local Luftwaffe airfield would add to the Celle hare chase.

Orders given, the Kreisleitung meeting broke up. Recalled Schwandt later, Tzschökell had insisted that the KZ häftlingen were to be cleared from the town by whatever means, and '"shot if found looting or resisting arrest"'. Even for a policeman, assessed Schwandt, insubordination and disobedience to the Wehrmacht commander's order would incur a court martial and the firing squad.

Tzschökell had unleashed the hunt for häftlingen despite the British front line drawing closer and without thought for the consequences that would duly ensue. There was support from local newspapers. The *Lüneburger Landeszeitung*, in its April 9 edition, appealed to the civilian population of Celle to assist the military and police claiming that the häftlingen endangered local lives through their pillaging and threatening behaviour.

THE MASSACRE BEGINS

Celle's fire service hadn't been represented at the Kreisleitung but a fireman claimed an early kill. Alwin Schuchardt, a 45-year-old fireman from the suburb of Altencelle, had raced to his fire station at the Luftwaffe airfield in Wietzenbruch believing the airfield to be under attack. It had taken hits but the damage was insufficient to put it out of operation. Unterbrandmeister Heinz Hoffmann, the fire commander, and Schuchardt, had heard the earlier reports of Zuchthaus inmates breaking out and grabbing weapons from the prison guards. The firemen now knew that to be false and those on the run were häftlingen from a train in the Güterbahnhof. In case of encounter, Hoffmann told his men to carry weapons. Schuchardt and Hoffmann set off in the support vehicle, the fire tender behind, in the direction of Neustädt Bridge in the town centre. As Schuchardt drove his vehicle out into Fliegerhorststrasse he saw the billowing smoke against the darkening sky.

Running parallel with Fliegerhorststrasse was a railway track that ran daily supplies into the airfield and as it crossed into Fuhrbergerstrasse, a level crossing with signals ensured the safety of pedestrians and road traffic. What happened on that level crossing in the early evening of April 8 would lead to Schuchardt being charged with committing a war crime. Schuchardt had pulled up his vehicle as a woman desperately flagged him down, at the same time propping up an overcome and bloodied figure.

There were a number of civilian witnesses to what would unfold. Gertrud Reinecke, who lived in Hasenwinkel No 9, was one. She had already seen Louise Basse, the local air-raid warden, struggling on the crossing with the injured man. 'He was tall, slender, looked exhausted, and had a towel wrapped around his head to stem the flowing wound on his chin', was how she described him.

Hoffmann had wound down the window to question Basse and what he said to her made her run away in panic, her arms flailing over her head. According to Schuchardt's later account, from within the car, his fire commander pulled out his pistol and aimed at the man but the weapon misfired. In moments, both Hoffmann and Schuchardt jumped out onto the crossing. Schuchardt claimed that

Hoffman had yelled at him to shoot the häftlinge. In the fire tender behind, its driver, Heinrich Wegmeyer, had stared transfixed and his subsequent evidence would add further condemnation of his colleague. At point-blank range, Schuchardt shot the häftlinge through the right temple with Hoffmann firing a second shot into the already lifeless body from his now unjammed weapon. Dragging the body to the side of the road, the vehicles sped off in the direction of the Neustädt Bridge.

Apart from Reinecke and Wegmeyer, two others had observed this cold-bloodied murder. Erdmann Dzierzawa, a resident, had heard the prisoner shout out, "do not shoot, Kommissar!" in a desperate plea for mercy. Hermann Müller, another resident, had seen both firemen fire into the helpless man.

Approaching the bridge it was clear the area was badly cratered so Schuchardt parked up in nearby Bredenstrasse to fight house fires. With so many casualties and the hospital already full, Schuchardt loaded up his vehicle with wounded and drove them back to the airfield for treatment. Pulling up outside the duty room, he saw a large number of häftlingen under Luftwaffe guard. Unloading his charges, Schuchardt returned to the town centre and helped fight the fire at the LUKAS factory. The fate of the prisoners at the airfield is unknown.

In the early hours of Monday, April 9, Schuchardt was helping out with fires burning uncontrollably around the town before he was instructed to transport several female Wehrmacht personnel, caught up in the raid, to Gifhorn, a town 40km to the south-east of Celle. He returned home to his flat in Altencelle to await further instructions, assuring himself that he had done his duty in the past hours.

CLEARING THE WALDWEG

The police crew car, driven by Ahrens, had left the Kreisleitung after the midnight conference for the Adolf Hitler Platz before turning south into Hannoverschestrasse towards the Waldweg. Ahrens had to carefully dodge a large column of well-armed SS going in the same direction. Another group of SS had marched to the Rotthagen sports ground on the other side of the railway to establish a base to bring in häftlingen from the surrounding streets.

On reaching the Waldweg, Ahrens parked up. The area was badly cratered. The SS and police waited for Tzschökell's promised tanks and when they did trundle up, the häftlingen clearance began. In several lines abreast, the drive down the Waldweg towards the Güterbahnhof and the railway line resembled a front-line battlefield with tanks spearheading the advance through the fields. Fanning out 25 metres apart and proceeding with caution, Schwandt led the police advance into the darkness. In the distance, the Güterbahnhof still burned.

The time was 01.00 hours on Sunday morning, April 9.

With Sievert on his left and Behrens on his right, Decker soon found discarded clothing, mainly underwear. The three policemen warily approached a shed, their rifles raised. Kicking in the door, they found 12 cowering häftlingen. Only four were uninjured, the others badly burnt and bleeding. To the surprise of the policemen, several were German Jews from Hamburg. 'We then left them', said Decker, 'telling them I would inform the German Red Cross (GRC), and return later'. Decker claimed to his RAF interrogator that he did tell Haarstrich, the GRC leader, but he didn't return. Nothing is known about the fate of these 12. Decker and Sievert heard shots in the darkness, only admitting that the SS were firing. None of the policemen would later confess to any participation in the killings in Waldweg. This first stage in the häftlingen clearance had taken five hours.

At 06.00 hours, according to Sievert, the police squad had crossed the railway line. Very quickly, 30 häftlingen were discovered, standing or sitting in a huddle. Ahlborn later described the scene. All were searched and anyone found wearing civilian clothes or soled shoes was deemed a pillager. In the executions that followed, yet again, the police had denied any culpability.

Ahlborn was now allowed to split from the police squad, venturing up Denickestrasse to No 89, to see how his uncle and grandmother had fared in the airstrike. Almost every house in this street that ran parallel to the railway line was damaged. His relatives were missing so Ahlborn assumed they were in a bunker or nearby cellar. Lying in the cratered garden were two shattered pigs belonging to his uncle. Still separated from the rest of the police squad, Ahlborn

FROM:- 	Sgt. Able E., R.A.F.Police War Crimes Section
TO:- 	D.P.M. 84 Group R.A.F.Police Unit
SUBJECT:-

Investigations in the mass-killing of concentration
camp prisoners which took place in Celle on
April 8th and 9th 1945.

SIR,

I have to submit for your information the following
report:-

At Celle on January 18th 1946 acting on information
received investigations were instituted by this section
into the alleged mass-killing of concentration camp
prisoners which took place in Celle following an Allied
airraid directed against the railway-station and marshalling
yards.

Investigations were mainly carried out by Cpl.Amos W.,
R.A.F.Police and myself with Peter Coumpas as interpreter.

First information was received from members of an
Anti-Nazi-Group in Celle, who although they were not eye-
witnesses themselves, gave a description of the incident
and also the names of witnesses living in Celle.

Interviews of witnesses were commenced and during the
course of these investigations over 300 persons were
questioned, including one ex-concentration camp prisoner
a Polish Subject named Jacob Rosmarin who is a survivor
of this transport. His statement describing the journey
to Celle and the following action which took place is
attached. (Entered as general information.)

A description of the actual action taken against the
concentration camp prisoners is as follows:-

On Sunday 8.4.45 at approx. 18.00 hrs a transport train
of concentration camp prisoners consisting of 3000 men and
500 women of all Nationalities with a guard of 200 men and
34 women was standing in the marshalling yard of the Celle
railway-station, when the station was attacked by Allied
planes. One British soldier is known to have been one of
the prisoners. This transport was damaged by the bombs and
a number of prisoners and guards were killed. The remaining
prisoners were ordered by the guards to take shelter in
the nearby houses and woods, and later to gather together
at a point in the woods. After the raid was over and before
the prisoners could proceed to this gathering point a number
of SS, soldiers, and assisted by civilians commenced a
round up of the helpless prisoners. An unknown number of
prisoners were caught and shot. Others were beaten to death
while others who had gathered in groups were fired on at
random. The wounded were killed by a shot in the back of the
neck. Many prisoners tried to escape but were too weak to do
so, and were eventually caught and shot without mercy. Shooting
went on through most of the night, and continued until midday
Monday 9th of April 1945 no quarter being given to the
prisoners who were being hunted like animals. Many prisoners
were begging for mercy and pleaded to be allowed to live but
were laughed at by those taking part in this persecution, and
who shot the prisoners dead on the spot leaving the bodies

/laying...

▲ The RAF investigation into the Celle manhunt and massacre, headed by
Sergeant Able, begun in earnest on January 18, 1946, aided by information
provided by an Anti-Nazi Group in the town. When Able had concluded, with
over 300 people questioned, his introduction to his report clearly states that
prisoners had been 'hunted like animals' and 'laughed at' as they begged for mercy.

◀ The Kreisleitung, the town's administrative hub, at Trift 20 was the venue for the midnight conference. Celle's policemen had stood guard at its entrance.

▶ Bergstrasse 45-47 housed the Celle police station and police accommodation. The site is now occupied by a Karstadt store.

◀ The large public green opposite the Trift now includes a memorial to the train prisoners murdered in the manhunt. The large white building with its tower on the Trift is the Zuchthaus, or jail. During the raid, the false rumour started that its inmates had broken out.

met up instead with the SS guards, who were clearing Carstenstrasse, Hattendorfstrasse and Lauensteinstrasse.

With Ahlborn gone, Schwandt's squad had headed up Forststrasse and towards Rotthagen. The squad heard repetitive shooting in the area of Carstenstrasse and Lauensteinstrasse. 'Damned pig-affair!' retorted Sievert to Decker. The SS were leaving bodies in their wake: Hattendorfstrasse was littered.

Only Ahlborn later illuminated the horror that was the Rotthagen sports ground.[13] Bodies of häftlingen wearing typical camp striped clothing lay face down on the grass, shot through the head or neck. The SS guards moved amongst them finishing them off. A Wehrmacht tank stood guard at the sports ground entrance. Ahlborn had added to the total, bringing in a häftlinge he had apprehended nearby, wearing civilian clothes and gesticulating unconvincingly that he was a local resident. An SS officer, probably the Hauptsturmführer from the Kreisleitung meeting, came over to Ahlborn to greet him. Ahlborn handed over his captive, informing the captain that Lt. Schwandt and the rest of the police squad would shortly be arriving. Hearing the shots, curious but cautious local residents had ventured over, including another of Ahlborn's uncles, Paul Kommel, who lived in Rotthagen, to chat about the bomb damage in Denicketrasse. Even as they spoke, more häftlingen were being brought in from the surrounding streets to lay on their fronts.

Shortly after the police squad had arrived, the pincer move on Neustädter Holz began. The SS left the sports ground into Rotthagen that led into the top of Fuhrbergerstrasse, the police took another direction, moving into Amelungstrasse where there were shootings but the police, typically, repudiated the charge that this street had added to the Celle killing grounds.

THE CIVILIANS JOIN IN

Within hours of the Sunday raid, Celle's civilians had taken their own measures to deal with the fleeing häftlingen.

---

[13] The sports ground is now built over with several rows of post-war properties. The name of Rotthagen has gone.

Friedrich Lautenbach, a Hattendorfstrasse resident, had heard loud female screams for help as he was repairing the broken glass in his damaged front door. KZ häftlingen were molesting German women, he would recall to his RAF interrogator. Heinrich Luhmann, a Luftwaffe employee at the airfield, had also heard the screams. Lautenbach's later account to investigators of his role in the hare chase bordered on the farcical. Luhmann, in uniform, had supposedly raced to his home demanding his rifle but he had prevaricated. Under protest, Luhmann had grabbed it and set off in the direction of the screams, only returning the rifle the next day. Four bullets were missing from the ammunition clip and Lautenbach queried the loss. Luhmann later returned with four unspent bullets. Luhmann never needed Lautenbach's rifle, he had his own.

Deemed more credible by the British was the evidence of Ernst Bohlau, a Celle policeman, who lived nearby. He had seen Lautenbach and another of Lautenbach's neighbours, Karl Schmidt, 'shooting wildly at prisoners'. Several fell dead. When Bohlau had gone to their aid, both Lautenbach and Schmidt threatened him with their weapons. Lautenbach had finished off the wounded. Georg Gründer, a farmer, saw Luhmann and Schmidt chasing three häftlingen, their corpses adding to the growing tally in Hattendorferstrasse. Luhmann later boasted, 'that is the second man I've killed', but his personal count was already higher. Another resident, Wilhelmine Schmitz, witnessed Lautenbach, Luhmann and Schmidt shoot at least eight häftlingen.

Schmidt had threatened any resident who questioned his actions. He had aggressively approached Augusta Prater, who lived in Carstenstrasse No 85, to enquire whether any häftlingen were in her house or garden. There weren't, but Schmidt did see häftlingen running in the field opposite and gave chase. Augusta didn't dare look but before she retreated to the safety of her cellar she heard multiple shots. When she did warily emerge, eight bodies lay in the field with Schmidt standing over them. Looking up, Schmidt saw the shocked Augusta and he ran towards her, menacingly pointing his pistol.

Another who was openly hostile to concerned neighbours was Luhmann. Sitting in the porch with one, Dr Götee, Luhmann had bragged that his killing tally had reached seven. When Götee remonstrated, a snarling Luhmann turned on him thrusting his gun against his face. He further rounded on the wife of another neighbour, threatening to hand her over to the military and have her shot. When a prisoner was seen hiding in the hallway of a house, Luhmann summarily dealt with him, as he described later to his interrogator: 'the prisoner was very calm. I walked behind him, aimed and shot him between the shoulder blades. He fell on his face.' Wilhelmine Schmitz overheard a Luhmann exhortation to anyone in earshot: "'the häftlingen are criminals and we need to kill them all. Everybody, men and women, must help!'"

At some stage, Luhmann had operated with Oskar Carlowitz, a 55-year-old electrical officer working in the armoury section at the airfield. From his first floor flat in Fuhrbergerstrasse No 77, Carlowitz had seen the raid and the smoke from the inferno that was the Güterbahnhof. Not long afterwards, 15 häftlingen stood outside his block and he rushed downstairs to confront them. Another No 77 resident, Heinrich Giesemann, joined him, as did neighbours, Ortsgruppenleiter Mengershausen, a senior Party officer and staunch Nazi, and Friedrich Neuer. Giesemann had spent his war in the notorious Todt Organisation, the entity that quite literally had worked slave labourers to death building military infrastructure and concentration camps. With Todt now dissolved, Giesemann had joined Celle's Volkssturm, the civil defence force, and was regularly seen around Celle wearing jackboots, his long Todt overcoat and always with a holster strapped around his waist.

Carlowitz, Giesemann, and Mengershausen were to add to the growing body count. Carlowitz would later claim that he had shot no one and he had simply handed over häftlingen to the SS to deal with, but a witness who had observed him shooting heard him shout out, "'today, we will have a bloodbath!'"

Frenzy had taken over when a prisoner appeared from Birkenstrasse, a flailing overcoat revealing the striped clothing underneath. A gang of residents gave chase after one yelled that he had murdered a local child in the search for food. Hell-bent on retribution, Mengershausen brought the prisoner down and kicked him almost senseless. The killing of a child had been a fabrication but to Mengershausen that didn't matter. Luhmann, who was never far from any shooting, had quickly appeared on the scene and dragged the terrified häftlinge into the woods, and put a bullet in his head.

The next day – Monday – April 9, Carlowitz had awoken early and rode his bicycle to the airfield, arriving at 07.30 hours. The airfield had remained at action stations with the expectation of further raids in the softening up of the town before the British attack. Carlowitz didn't stay long and in his uniform and steel helmet, with a machine pistol over his shoulder, he and Giesemann joined the Volkssturm in Neustädter Holz, under the command of deputy company commander, Kuckuk. During the day, the Kuckuk group had rounded up 180 häftlingen but as night fell Kuckuk needed to temporarily house them. At first light, his plan was to hand the häftlingen over to the police or so Carlowitz said in his statement to the British.

Not far from the turn to the Luftwaffe airfield on Fuhrbergerstrasse is a coffee house. Now the Allertal-Café, in April 1945 it was the Kreikenbaum, a much frequented bar and restaurant. Behind it was a derelict building formerly utilised by the Luftwaffe. Kuckuk and Carlowitz told the bar owner that his barn was being temporarily requisitioned but he would have none of it. Carlowitz pushed him aside and the häftlingen were bundled into the building and the door locked. Many were horribly injured from the burning train but even with wounds they had been determined to run for freedom. All were desperate for food and water. Carlowitz would later insist to the British that he sourced bread and water but his interrogator dismissed the claim. As to the fate of the 180, they were later marched into Neustädter Holz and dealt with by the SS, admitted Giesemann, but he and Carlowitz would probably have assisted in the killings.

The following day – Tuesday – April 10, Carlowitz had been observed again cycling to the airfield, his machine pistol over his shoulder. He had passed several bodies still lying in Fuhrbergerstrasse. Once he arrived at the Luftwaffe armoury, he claimed that he begged Major Helms, his boss, to intervene with the military and police to end the bloodshed. Helms had refused saying that the police was now in control of the situation.

In the subsequent war crimes trial, Carlowitz wouldn't help his defence by declaring 'should my account be untrue, I am prepared to take any punishment'. His defence played on a sorry litany of illnesses, including heart disease, rheumatism and diabetes to obviate away from his actions.

Giesemann was to join Carlowitz in the dock, refuting the accusation that at one stage in the häftlingen clearance he had boasted that his personal tally of killings was substantial. A neighbour, Lieschen Müller, had bravely confronted him when she saw him about to kill another. 'Are you crazy?' she had protested, 'hasn't enough blood been shed?' Giesemann had stormed off and the prisoner fled. Within days, Giesemann and Mengershausen had quit the town, only returning several weeks later hoping that the British were too preoccupied with Belsen than to investigate the war crime in Celle.

Three witnesses, all women, had observed one killing that became one of the most controversial in apportioning blame. It was to fully test legal argument and interpretation in the later summary hearing, trial and subsequent mitigation plea.

Renate von der Marell lived with her mother, Berta Kniep, in Fuhrbergerstrasse No 79, a large apartment block on the corner of Birkenstrasse, and in the hours after the raid she had seen many prisoners running up Fuhrbergerstrasse and looking for a way into Neustädter Holz. At around midday on Monday, Renate saw an unidentifiable man, in uniform, pull up on his bicycle outside the house opposite. Within moments he and another man, again someone Renate didn't recognise, pull out a prisoner from within the house and onto the street.

Not giving up, the häftlinge somehow pulled away but he was quickly overpowered. With Renate watching from her window, the uniformed man on the bike pointed his pistol at the häftlinge's head but the gun jammed. Misfiring weapons were to become a typical defence employed by defence counsels.

Yet another uniformed man had now appeared on the scene, this one a motorcyclist, and seeing what had happened asked for the pistol, unjamming the firing mechanism and testing it by firing into the air. He then handed it back and sped away. The häftlinge was now shot in the head. Renate saw the man collapse yet he somehow summoned the strength to pull himself up before falling back and lie still. Everyone left. Blood ran in the street gutter.

The concentration camp inmate was not dead, but he was certainly dying. From her window, Renate saw his chest heaving. Fearing to venture out to help, she remained in her apartment and two hours had elapsed before another man arrived outside, and this one she did recognise. It was Fritz Joost, the slater from Birkenstrasse No 46, with a rifle. Joost would later claim that others were with him, one an unknown SS officer barking orders, but Renate's account doesn't mention any others. Joost later told his RAF interrogator that this officer had ordered him to fire into the häftlinge's chest at point-blank range. Renate had watched, horrified, as the now lifeless body was dumped in the ditch alongside the road.

Renate wasn't the only witness. Marta Homann, in Birkenstrasse No 22A, had also seen the prisoner still moving after the earlier shot to the head. Like Renate, she was too scared to help. 'He was bleeding and moved several times', Marta later testified. Then Joost had appeared. 'I first saw him when he crossed the road to where the prisoner was lying. He used an army rifle', confirmed Marta.

THE PRISON WARDER KILLER

Ernst Fischer was a 49-year-old master sergeant in the Zuchthaus, the tough jail in Celle that held hardened criminals. Married with three children, the family lived in a flat in Fuhrbergerstrasse No 50. On the day of the raid, Sunday, Fischer was off-duty and digging his garden. Hearing the aircraft above, the family ran to the nearby civic bomb shelter, which residents referred to as the bunker, to join the huddle of 60 neighbours. A stray bomb exploded close, amongst the trees, and its impact, even for this prison officer used to extreme violence, was 'frightening'.

The later appearance of a crowd at the bunker's entrance, in striped clothing, came as a shock. Sadly, Fischer didn't impart to his interrogator what subsequently happened, apart from confirming there had been a confrontation. What Fischer did recall was that he ran home, concerned it might have been bombed. It wasn't but the front door was wide open with the kitchen a mess, gone were the family food ration coupons and the store of sausage. Fischer was incensed.

Cautiously, Fischer walked into the main bedroom where he found a häftlinge going through his wardrobe eyeing up the suits and in the häftlinge's hand was his pocket-watch. Fischer tackled him and pulled him by his collar into the garden, the häftlinge lashing out with his fists. Around his waist, and attached by string, was a battered aluminium plate, a much-prized food utensil in the camps. In the ensuing scuffle, Fischer pulled the plate away smashing it repeatedly over the häftlinge's head, the commotion alerting members of the SS and the Volkssturm. One ran over.

Fischer denied any killings but as a prison officer he kept his pistol at home and whether he used it on this particular häftlinge, the RAF couldn't determine. A neighbour, Frau Hilbig, had witnessed the altercation and heard Fischer say to the soldier that the häftlinge must be shot as a looter. Albert Dümeland, another neighbour, saw Fischer marching the häftlinge into the heathland and a volunteer fireman, Ernst Just, observed him shooting the prisoner in the head.

CLINICAL SLAUGHTER IN NEUSTÄDTER HOLZ

At around 08.00 hours on – Monday – April 9, some 12 hours since the airstrike, the SS and police had left the Rotthagen sports ground. The SS had moved up Rotthagen, now renamed Welfenallee, to the top of Fuhrbergerstrasse, into the Lönsweg and Unter den Eichen. Some SS moved into a nearby road with the name of Texas and occupied its sports ground. Like the Rotthagen sports ground, this one became another killing ground. As planned, the police entered the Fuhrbergerstrasse from the direction of Amelungstrasse and Birkenstrasse to trap the häftlingen in a pincer movement.

Sievert had found a bag of laundry, full of baby clothes, lying in front of one house in Fuhrbergerstrasse, obviously dumped in the rush for shelter when the raid began. The police lieutenant knocked on the door and handed it back. The entire squad then entered No 40, the home of the cobbler, Lambrecht, his family, and the lodger, Frau Wolter. Within moments the squad was in the back garden and over the Gartenrand – the long garden fence behind the Fuhrbergerstrasse back gardens – into the heathland and the Neustädter Holz beyond. Already the gunshots were frequent in the 'Mulde' where the SS was lining up captured häftlingen before ordering them to lie on their fronts, the trademark SS style of execution. This part of the 'Mulde' killing ground is now the mini golf course.

The police squad had now entered the Lönsweg and it began rounding up häftlingen, assembling them at the private shooting club. Decker described them as sitting or standing in huddles with many wearing stolen overcoats or civilian clothes.

Many Fuhrbergerstrasse witnesses had seen prisoners being led through the Gartenrand. The hare chase of Celle had now entered its end game and the body count would significantly rack up. In the later testimonies to the RAF investigators, Ahlborn, Decker, Sievert and Schwandt provided detail of the appalling events that were to unfold in these woods but their statements never concurred in a bid to conceal their own culpability. Ahlborn did provide his investigator with a series of sketch maps, drawing in the positions of the police and SS, with crosses symbolising death.[14]

During the bombing raid on the Güterbahnhof, the SS guards had ordered the häftlingen to run for the woods to rendezvous later. For the hundreds that did reach the Neustädter Holz, that promise of a rendezvous had turned out to be a premeditated massacre. The killing grounds under the trees were numerous, even the pits in the heathland were full of bodies. Unter den Eichen, the 'Mulde', the Wehrmacht shooting ground, and the clearings around it, are synonymous with death. One of the accused, the former boxer, Otto Amelung, had also referred to 'the little firs' during his RAF interrogation and prisoners were also shot around the Alten Canal.

The shooting club in Unter den Eichen, or 'Under the Oaks', has been in existence since 1625 and is one of five in Celle. Its members participate in an annual championship with the winner receiving the

---

[14] The author obtained those maps and walked the routes to the Neustädter Holz killing grounds.

◀ Ahlborn, one of the three sentenced to hang in the war crimes trial, lived in Rolandstrasse, in north Celle. The day after he had played a significant role in the manhunt, he complained of being sick while on duty in the town. A colleague escorted him back to his flat where a neighbour cooked him a meal. Ahlborn informed neighbours that he had been sick during the day of the airstrike and barely capable of working. The RAF investigators had marked out Ahlborn as the worst of the police killers. At one stage in the manhunt Ahlborn was heard to boast: "'you shoot these prisoners, I have already shot 26!'"

▼ Amelung, the former boxer, was another sentenced to hang. He lived in this imposing property in Fuhrbergerstrasse. A witness had described Amelung as 'acting like a madman, with his mouth foaming and his eyes bulging'. Technically a civilian, he wore his Wehrmacht sergeant's tunic during the manhunt.

▲ Joost, a slater, the third member of the accused given the death sentence, lived in a flat in Birkenstrasse. The case against him proved to be legally controversial.

▲ Carlowitz lived in a flat in Fuhrbergerstrasse 77. Corporal Amos, one of the two RAF interrogators, would long remember his encounter in Celle jail with this 55-year-old electrical officer working in the armoury section at the Luftwaffe airfield. Entering the interview room, Carlowitz had stood proudly to attention, clicking his heels and arrogantly extending his arm upwards in the typical Nazi salute. Amos ignored the gesture, firmly believing that Carlowitz was one of the ringleaders in the massacre. A witness who had observed him shooting had heard him shout out "'today, we will have a bloodbath.'"

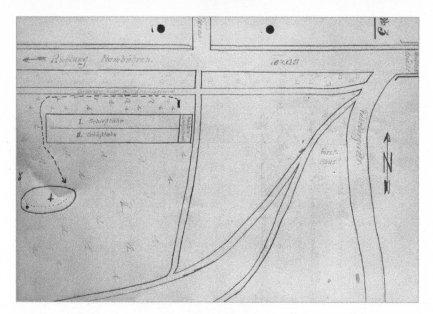

▲ Ahlborn drew several sketches for the RAF investigators on the route taken by the Celle police squad to the police killing ground in Neustädter Holz. On his third map, he has drawn in the clearing, denoted by the upturned cross. The stick figure refers to the stranger he encounters.
Source: National Archives Kew

▲ Moving down the track past the shooting range, a short walk took us to the clearing, identifiable by a fork in the track. Here Lt. Schwandt, the killing squad leader, ordered the victims to line down in two rows face down. Some ran for their lives, only to be gunned down by Ahlborn and others. The mass killing began, the police shooting the victims through the head and neck.

honour of planting an oak tree within the club's grounds. Where acorns have fallen outside the perimeter fence, oaks now mingle with the birch and pines. Inside the club premises, there is a bar, which leads into the four firing positions and the rifle rests are the 1925 originals. Before any shooting is permitted, club officials must check the perimeter wire fence for gaps as a safety feature. None of the members we spoke to were prepared to answer any questions on what had happened in the club's grounds in April 1945 and by the expressions on their faces our presence was very unwelcome.

Little has changed within the club's range which is flat and the sides banked. This wide hollow in the trees extends outside the shooting club and is known locally as the 'Mulde'. Running parallel is the Lönsweg, a favourite track for dog walkers. Occupying much of the 'Mulde' is the long-established Klause Lönsweg, a traditional restaurant, which now has a mini-golf course, and facing the building is the Wittesstrasse, mostly a track than runs up from Fuhrbergerstrasse.

The decision by the police to take the häftlingen they were holding outside the shooting club elsewhere in Neustädter Holz was never clarified to the RAF but Schwandt, as squad leader, and with general knowledge of the area, very likely made it. What was happening in the 'Mulde' had attracted attention from a number of Fuhrbergerstrasse residents, some of whom were children. They were witnesses to a mass slaughter. For Schwandt, he preferred a quieter area in the woods, away from prying eyes.

Ahlborn later drew a sketch map for his British interrogator on the route taken by the police with their captured prisoners from the Unter den Eichen to a clearing in the woods: a quiet place, away from prying eyes.[15] This route took them into Texas past its sports ground, before turning left into Sandweg, a sandy track running parallel with the Wehrmacht shooting range.[16] Ahlborn had marked

---

[15] Obtaining a copy of that map from Ahlborn's interrogation file, we walked that route and located the clearing, close to the modern-day Celle ring road that now cuts a wide swathe through Neustädter Holz.

[16] The Wehrmacht shooting range is now given over to fields and a storage area for the local authorities. Some wartime relics still remain, including the concrete structures at the end of the ranges that housed the targets.

a caravan in Sandweg 'with men inside' who might have been häftlingen but he doesn't say so. The area was swarming with SS and Volkssturm. Turning south off the Sandweg down another track, the group hit a fork, and just off was the clearing. The shooting elsewhere in the woods and the 'Mulde' was loud and incessant.

Decker, walking close to Sievert, later repeated an anxious conversation that had taken place enroute to the clearing. Sievert had told him '"Jakob, they have to be shot"'. Decker had snapped back, 'Albert, I won't do it!' He claimed that he then left his colleagues at the clearing and carried on down the path with the intention of returning to Fuhrbergerstrasse. When a volley of shots rang out, Decker turned around to see Schwandt, pistol in hand, shooting at escaping häftlingen. Decker saw two Volkssturm soldiers as he walked back alone through the trees, claiming to them that he had nothing to do with what was about to unfold in the clearing. The RAF investigators didn't believe his story.

Ahlborn's account of the shootings in the clearing was more descriptive. Sievert had ordered the häftlingen to form two rows and to lie down on their fronts, the feet of the first row pointing towards the feet of the other. About 15 ran off, screaming 'do not shoot, do not shoot!' chased by Schwandt who shot them down. That version differed completely from Sievert's account. He had accused Ahlborn, Decker, Meinken and Peters of chasing down and killing the runners, not Schwandt.

Once the runners had been dealt with, the bloodfest began.

'IT WAS ALL MADNESS'

Several policemen later accused Schwandt of giving the order, but the lieutenant denied he had. Ahlborn gave a personal perspective. 'My head was spinning and nerves ran away from me in this madness'. There was a collective hesitation amongst the squad and in the indecision more prisoners attempted escape and this time Ahlborn, alone, gave chase, finishing each one off with a bullet through the temple. That now signalled the shooting of the two rows of prisoners. Ahlborn claimed no part but Sievert in his testimony accused him of being a willing participant along with Peters,

Behrens, Weu and Detzloff.

As the guns fell quiet, the 60 or so häftlingen lay dead. Sievert would testify that he now left, passing SS and Volkssturm as he did so. Ahlborn headed south to the 'Mulde', with Peters not far behind. Decker, too, had left alone, or so he said, and headed for the Lönsweg. Approaching the Gartenrand, he was accosted by a frightened Fuhrbergerstrasse resident exclaiming that a häftlinge was holed up in her shed, refusing to move. Decker grabbed the man and took him back to the 'Mulde', before returning and encountering Otto Amelung, Celle's 32-year-old sporting celebrity.

Amelung had joined the Wehrmacht in 1937 after a boxing career with 150 fights under his belt, including one in London in 1935. In his interrogation statement, Amelung fondly recalled his eight days in the capital, making friends in the boxing world and embracing the British culture. As a soldier, he had fought the British in Norway and from 1943 was on the Eastern Front, and wounded three times. In April 1945, those Wehrmacht days behind him, he had settled down with his wife and seven-year-old son. The family lived in Fuhrbergerstrasse No 82 and during the bombing raid they had taken shelter in the bunker. Worried for his parents, the fit Amelung ran to their house just in time to see one of his father's chickens being pulled through a hole in the garden fence, decapitating it in the process. A policeman would later state that the sight of the chicken losing his head only heightened Amelung's lust to kill.

Wolfgang Helms, a young 14-year-old who lived in Fuhrbergerstrasse No 52, was naturally excitable, as any young boy would be with the sight of men with guns. He had already heard shooting and when he did venture out he had seen men in striped clothing running for the cover of Neustädter Holz. He had no idea who the runners were but Wolfgang recognised a chaser as Amelung. One of Wolfgang's friends, Helmut Born, joined him and together they gawped as several runners fell and stumbled in the hail of bullets. Four runners were seized by Amelung, Decker and Ahlborn and were dragged by their collars into Wolfgang's back garden. A policeman handed over his pistol to Amelung. 'I saw the prisoners getting down on their stomachs and Otto Amelung bent over them and shot them through the back of the neck', Wolfgang had recalled to his RAF interrogator. Those bodies would remain in the garden until April 11 – Wednesday – until family members buried them. A soldier later bragged to Wolfgang that he had broken a rifle over an häftlinge's head. Nearby lay the body, his head beaten to a bloody pulp. Wolfgang would observe further police, SS and Wehrmacht shootings.

In Amelung's own later statement, he reflected that what had occurred in Celle had born no similarity to his experience on the battlefield. 'I never saw anything like it, people should never have been killed in such a manner', he told his interrogator but Amelung eventually admitted that he had personally gathered up 10-12 häftlingen from the back gardens in the Fuhrbergerstrasse and escorted them into the woods. Countering the accusation that he had killed them, he attested that these prisoners had run away on hearing the shots in Unter den Eichen.

At one stage, Amelung had been in the clearing close to the Wehrmacht shooting ground with the policemen. He admitted his presence but denied any participation, despite being named by several policemen. In his first interrogation, Amelung had denied killing anyone but given there were witnesses he did admit to the four deaths observed by Wolfgang Helms. In his defence he blamed Decker and Ahlborn for goading him on. "Don't be a coward, you are an old soldier, go on, shoot them!" Ahlborn had chided.

'I HAVE ALREADY SHOT 26!'

Ahlborn had been marked out as arguably the worst of the police killers, even ingratiating himself with the Hauptsturmführer, the SS captain, who had been tasked by Tzschökell with the co-ordination of the häftlingen clearance. Amelung would recant the Ahlborn boast: "you shoot these prisoners, I have already shot 26!"

The role of Ludwig Einfeldt, a forester, as an accomplice in several of Ahlborn's killings has never been properly determined. In one episode, together they grabbed a cart in the garden of one of Einfeldt's neighbours and dumped a body in a heathland pit. Witnesses had also observed Peters and Ahlborn cornering a lone häftlinge cowering in the shop door of the baker, Wosianko. Ahlborn claimed that Peters had shot him where he stood, but both men were culpable.

At 10.00 hours on April 9, Schwandt had stood the police squad down and they returned to the crew car waiting outside the entrance of the Wehrmacht shooting range. In the drive back to Bergstrasse, no one dared speak but Sievert broke the silence by asking each policeman for his personal tally of shootings. All ramped up their number, fearful of a reprimand or ridicule if they went low. Ahlborn went high, as did Decker.

THE POLICE COVER UP

When Ahrens parked up, Major Oetzmann was waiting. Very tense was how one policeman later described the mood as Oetzmann called Schwandt and Sievert into his office. Ahlborn had returned to the half-eaten meal he'd left in his locker the previous evening. To his surprise Oetzmann called him in, Decker, too. If there was any sense of introspection, Oetzmann had little time for it, losing his temper when Ahlborn jokingly chipped in to say that he had encountered several members of his family during the clearance.

Oetzmann wanted a cover up, and fast. He insisted that all bodies must be collected. Every squad member had to be briefed and a collective defence constructed in an effort to suppress the truth. Not even colleagues who had been on duty elsewhere in the town could know. When asked, blame was to be placed squarely with the SS, especially the omnipresent Hauptsturmführer, who by now was taking survivors by truck to Bergen-Belsen. Even Oetzmann never knew his name.

The meeting broke up and Schwandt immediately left for Fuhrbergerstrasse, in charge of body collection. Ahlborn was detailed to follow later and deal with any eventualities.

When Ahlborn did arrive in Unter den Eichen, outside the entrance to the shooting club the collection was underway with bodies heaped high on the trucks. In the 'Mulde', the bodies still lay in this SS killing ground, their brains and blood soaking into the leafy ground. Bodies were slumped against the Gartenrand and in the back gardens of the Fuhrbergerstrasse homes. The heathland pits outside the Gartenrand overflowed.

Ahlborn was in the Lönsweg when he saw the vehicle speeding towards him, its driver gesticulating wildly and shouting, 'all of them are not dead!' A civilian, the driver blurted out, had found them in a clearing just north of the 'Mulde' and behind the Wehrmacht shooting range. Ahlborn ordered the driver not to return until he gave the order. The policeman knew exactly where to go, of course. As he crossed the 'Mulde', pistol in hand, he was curious about this civilian.

When Ahlborn saw him, the man was standing just outside the clearing, a cap partly shielding his eyes. A rifle was slung over his shoulder. Despite being Celle born and bred, and widely known around the town, Ahlborn failed to recognise him, standing as if maintaining a silent vigil. The policeman found his presence unnerving. They didn't converse. Ahlborn would later mark the stranger's position on one of his sketch maps he drew for his British interrogators.

Under the silent gaze of this stranger, Ahlborn scanned the clearing only now comprehending the enormity of the massacre that he had been a party to just hours earlier. The numbers of the dead in the clearing would vary in the later admissions of the police squad members. Ahlborn believed close to 40, the RAF War Crimes team estimated at least 60, but it fully realised that the real number was way higher. Ahlborn saw the bodies that still lay strewn in the bushes, cut down as they had attempted escape, some by him.

Ahlborn didn't say in his admission whether the stranger had pointed out those still alive but he knew what he had to do. No one could be left alive to later testify. Under the pretext of writing a report for his superior, Ahlborn informed the stranger that he needed to search each body for identification and valuables. Moving from body to body, he found little but one did have the ID of a Polish labourer in Celle's gas works, just one of many local slave labourers caught up in the häftlingen flight for freedom.

Four were still alive.

The face of one was cloaked in a handkerchief in an attempt to feign death. Ahlborn pulled it away and the häftlinge's eyes darted from side to side in panic. With the stranger looking on, Ahlborn told the häftlinge to run and clear off. The wounded man staggered away into the woods. For the three others, Ahlborn didn't later record whether the stranger had moved away before he pumped three bullets into each of their temples – the 'Gnadenschuss', or finishing shot. Job done, Ahlborn reported back to Schwandt, who said that he was off to the police house for something to eat.

Ahlborn remained until the air-raid siren wailed, and fearing another attack he also returned to Bergstrasse leaving the body collection detail to continue its work. The following day – Tuesday – April 10, he was back on the Celle streets in his usual duties. His colleague was Gustav Behrens, another member of the Schwandt squad. The two men shared little of the events over the past two days and Ahlborn had later complained of feeling very sick. Behrens escorted him back to his flat in Rolandstrasse No 17. As Ahlborn's wife wasn't home, Frau Foste, a neighbour, took him in and cooked the policeman a meal, which for someone supposedly very sick, he kept down. Ahlborn didn't share with Frau Foste the events of April 8 and 9 but he did allay to other neighbours that he had been sick during the day of the airstrike and barely capable of working.

Not sick, but certainly depressed, was Sievert. A colleague, Johann Schuldkamp, who had not been in the squad, had tackled him on the Neustädter Holz killings. The Bergstrasse police station had been awash with speculation, said Schuldkamp. 'Albert, were you in on it, too?' Schuldkamp had enquired. 'Yes', came the sombre response.

For those prisoners who had somehow survived the Güterbahnhof bombing and the hare chase – an estimated 500 – the SS train guards trucked them off to Bergen-Belsen where their number would be substantially reduced further in the camp's final week of horror. Celle's police soon solved the problem of where to bury the dead that littered the Güterbahnhof. As this area was so badly pitted the bodies were tipped into the craters and back-filled with rubble. Some of the dead in the hare chase around the town and in Neustädter Holz might also have been brought here on Oetzmann's instruction.

The Wehrmacht came up with the solution for the Güterbahnhof injured, and there were many with appalling blast and burns injuries. At the rear of the Wehrmacht's Heide Kaserne headquarters are two red-stone buildings, one with bars on its windows. The other had provided stabling for the Wehrmacht but in the last weeks of the war it was empty. Oetzmann brought the Güterbahnhof injured here on April 9, and he had no intention of providing any medical assistance, food or water. The police locked them in and stood guard. Oetzmann had left the häftlingen to die from their wounds. Only the following day did Oetzmann relent, allowing in a small supply of water and what passed as soup. The two Heide Kaserne buildings had become another Celle killing ground.

Oetzmann hadn't participated in the killings but in his actions afterwards, and in the cover up, he was as culpable as his men. In a clumsy attempt to further defray police responsibility, he ensured that the Bergstrasse station daybook omitted all details on the events of April 8-9. The Allied airstrike had no mention. The only incidents noted for April 8 in Oetzmann's daybook was a small fire and the death of two horses.

THE BRITISH ARRIVE

Unlike the occupation of Hannover and Bremen where the Wehrmacht, the SS and the Hitler Youth put up a frantic and stoic defence, the losses in Celle were light, with the town surrendering to the Gordon Highlanders on April 12. Amongst the deaths were three Celle policemen. In Bremen, the SS bürgermeister had had no intention of raising the white flag. The Scottish troops of the 52nd Lowland Division and battalions of the Manchester Regiment 'had to burn their way through the enemy before the city fell' reported a British war correspondent. In Celle, a post-war myth gained traction that Milewski, the Kreisleiter, and Tzschökell, the Wehrmacht commander, had personally saved Celle from total destruction in offering a minimal military response. That view is now fully discredited.

The prime target for the Gordon Highlanders was to secure the Heide Kaserne and the Wehrmacht surrendered without a major firefight. Learning of the horror in its stables, the doors were quickly opened. Those still alive were immediately transferred to a local hospital. Oetzmann was accused for the deaths and arrested. When he was interviewed several months later, the interrogator reported that he was uncooperative and deliberately vague in detail. On whom he had placed in charge of the police squad in the hare chase, Schwandt or Sievert, he claimed he had forgotten. Incredibly, Major Oetzmann was never indicted for war crimes.

Upon occupation, the Royal Military Police commandeered the building next to the stables in the rear of the Heide Kaserne and it would be used for such purposes until Britain scaled back military deployment in Germany from 2010. The RMP maintained its own newsletter and reports abounded over many years of strange sightings, noises and smells in the building, especially at night. To keep out the curious, the RMP had bricked up the basement as within this dark sanctum the SS had tortured many of the train survivors. Jewish symbols had been carved into the red brickwork, a lasting and stark reminder of Nazi brutality.

As the British army moved into Celle's castle and the Heide Kaserne barracks, the RMP scoured government buildings to locate SS administrators. The ones who were found experienced either the pleasure of a cell in the jail or a detainment camp, including Telschow, the odious regional SS gauleiter, but he would avoid an investigation into his backstory by slashing his wrists and bleeding to death. Milewski, the Kreisleiter, had done a runner and was last seen in the Lüneburg Heath area. No records are available as to his later whereabouts. Rautenkranz, the prominent industrialist and the owner of the ITAG factory, was arrested and would remain in custody for 13 months. Family assets and wealth were confiscated and in the coming months, Rautenkranz's company links with companies such as IG Farben, the manufacturer of the gas that had murdered millions in the camps, were investigated.

The day the British took Celle, some SS guards in Belsen deserted taking with them 150 prisoners of German origin, and as to what happened to them is unknown. Kramer, the commandant, with key staff, including the Aufseherinnen, the female guards, had remained. Inmates had formed themselves into militias, along ethnic lines, and armed with whatever they could find they inflicted revenge especially on the Kapos, the inmate prisoners who had accepted SS privileges in return for running the blocks. In one day, seven Kapos were beaten to death. The Ukrainians, in particular, were brutal, rampaging through the compounds in search of any remaining German prisoners. The SS and the 1,500-strong contingent of Hungarian army guards had lost control.

That SS defection in Belsen coincided with the arrival of two senior Wehrmacht officers through the British lines. Based in the Bergen-Hohne tank training school, part of which had become Camp 2, they brought an offer. Blindfolded they were taken to the British headquarters.

The Wehrmacht, numbering 800, would ensure Belsen was 'open' so both camps would not be defended when the British arrived. Belsen had become a human disaster, stressed the two officers, sabotage had cut off all power supplies from Celle, and typhus, typhoid, tuberculosis and gastroenteritis were endemic. Medical attention and supplies were vital. On its part, the Wehrmacht, using force if necessary, would ensure that the SS and Hungarian guards remained in their watchtowers and barracks as the British approached. Guards in the two entrances would wear white armbands and stand down. In the interim, warning signs of disease were to be placed on roads around Bergen.

There were conditions to this Wehrmacht offer. Its troops in the Bergen-Hohne barracks had to be released six days after British occupation with their weapons and vehicles returned. Upon the handover, the troops were to have unhindered access back to German lines.

The Wehrmacht officers returned to Bergen and three days later – on April 15 – an SAS squad in specially modified jeeps with mounted Browning machine guns, drove warily towards the town of Bergen to reconnoitre the strength of the military presence in and around the camp. At its head was a hardened 25-year-old veteran of many covert operations, Captain John Tonkin. With first-hand experience of dealing with the SS, he was taking no chances. In France, the SS had murdered 31 unarmed SAS colleagues who had surrendered. Maintaining a safe distance behind Tonkin's jeeps was an anti-tank regiment and a medical convoy. They were to proceed to the camp only on Tonkin's signal to do so.

In a revealing tape recording he made for the BBC radio archives,

40 years later, Tonkin spoke publically for the first time about entering Belsen. As the SAS had approached Bergen, said Tonkin, they caught the smell. Taking the road to Belsen from the centre of Bergen, that odour became overpowering.

Past the Wehrmacht barracks was the main entrance to the camp and unchallenged by the guards, the jeeps, their Brownings primed, carried on. 'The SS were either unconcerned or were simply unaware of us', he recalled. 'There were thousands of walking skeletons and pile after pile of dead', was Tonkin's initial reaction after quickly scanning the sight before him.

Equally disturbing for Tonkin was the sight of SS camp guards casually taking pot shots at prisoners, 'just for fun'. Tonkin reminisced, 'I have never been so angry in my life'. The SAS rounded up Kramer and others, placed them in a hut and Tonkin gave them an ultimatum. He didn't mince his words. 'Unless this shooting stops immediately, you will all die… rather horribly', and he meant every word. Sensing this SAS officer had every intention of carrying out his threat, the SS officers filed out into the camp. The shooting ceased.

Outside Kramer's office in Camp 1, German-speaking Lieutenant Sington had parked up his jeep, alongside a loudspeaker van. The broadcast of liberation in both English and German reverberated around the huts, a poignant message that would be long remembered by Belsen survivors, who now knew that for them the murderous German tyranny had ended. The British had arrived.

Lt. Colonel Taylor with his 63rd Anti-Tank Regiment surrounded the SS quarters and the watchtowers, aiming its guns, with an order to fire if fired upon. The sentries in the watchtowers meekly climbed down and surrendered their weapons. With Belsen now secure, the army medical convoy arrived, headed by Dr Glyn Hughes, whose staff over the coming months would be credited with saving thousands of lives.

It is worth recording Sington's first sighting of Camp 2, the Wehrmacht barracks, before he went to Camp 1. It was read out to the court in the subsequent Belsen trial that began five months later.

'When you first arrive you see magnificent barrack blocks, a beautiful theatre and hospital and beautiful military messes, but you soon find out that it was a Panzer Grenadier training centre. About a mile down a track there is Belsen Concentration Camp. It is roughly a kilometre and a half long, 300–350 metres wide and surrounded by wire. There were five prisoner compounds, three for the men and two for the women.'

Sington continued. 'The first approximation was that 12,000 men and 28,000 women were housed in 60 wooden huts. In all, there were five cookhouses, and three concrete ponds that held the water supply. Of the living conditions, I know of no words to truly paint a picture. The camp held a dense mass of emaciated scarecrows, living skeletons, lying, sitting and shuffling about the place. These living skeletons in rags did not properly understand what was happening. With no working latrines, excreta lay everywhere. Attempts had been made by the prisoners to bury the dead in large pits but 13,000 corpses lay around. In the weeks before liberation, many prisoners had resorted to cannibalism, stripping thigh muscle off corpses.'

Four days after its liberation, the German military reneged on its truce. Earlier in the day, the 800 Wehrmacht troops were released and escorted through the British lines but later, 10 Focke-Wulf 190 fighters flew in low to strafe the ambulances and other targets. The soldiers and the former prisoners ran for cover, many hiding under the field hospital vehicles. There were casualties and several ambulances were destroyed. Fire was returned.[17]

Before work begun on clearing the bodies scattered around the camp, many clumsily hidden in the last hours before occupation, Bergen's civilians were compulsorily brought in to view the thousands of cadavers piled on the ground and in open-sided lorries. There were to be 11 large burial pits. British-Pathé recorded the townspeople's reaction for a worldwide and shocked audience. Given the huge number of sick with disease, the British army converted a wing in the nearby Wehrmacht barracks into a hospital

---

[17] The adjutant of the 113th Light-Aircraft Regiment, Royal Artillery, Captain Pares, wrote an excellent report on the liberation of Belsen. His regiment had relieved the 63rd Anti-Tank Regiment on April 19, the day before the Luftwaffe raid. Given the concern that the surrounding area was still a fluid war zone, Pares' outfit had travelled 238 miles in 22 hours to get to the camp.

with many hundred more taken to Celle's general hospital. On April 23, six detachments of British Red Cross Society staff arrived and on the 30th, 100 volunteer medical students arrived from Britain to help out. In an attempt to bring typhus under control, the British had set fire to many of the huts in Camp 1 and on May 21, the troops ceremoniously torched No 41, as a final symbolic act.[18]

In the coming six weeks, despite the intensive British medical attention, a further 13,000 would die of typhus and dysentery.

In leg chains, Kramer had stumbled out of Camp 1 on April 21, accompanied by a British military policeman with his pistol drawn and a soldier walking attentively behind with his rifle pointed at the commandant's back. He was taken to Celle prison, continuing to protest that his arrest was against the conditions of the 'open' truce. Others would join Kramer in the cells that day, including Hoessler, the commandant of Camp 2. All the jailers were German. One of the accused remonstrated with the German sergeant major in charge of the jail that he was a German prisoner and had been falsely arrested. Kramer was later sent to a transit camp and to a secure detainment centre in Belgium where he was manacled day and night, still complaining that he must be treated more leniently as a prisoner of war. Kramer would become caricatured in the world's press as the 'Beast of Belsen', in the shape of a shambling gorilla – a sadistic beast in human form thirsty for the blood of his tortured victims.

As Belsen became the focus of a major war crime investigation, it was soon clear that it would also cover Auschwitz-Birkenau, given that its senior staff and some guards had transferred in from Poland in December 1944 when the Auschwitz complex of camps had been evacuated in the Red Army advance. The trial, the first to try Nazi war crimes, began in Lüneburg on Monday, September 17, 1945 and the court in a surprising finding believed that even though Kramer had little time for Nazi doctrines, he was personally unmoved by the dreadful fate of his victims and their suffering. That final court observation wasn't sufficient to save him from the gallows.

---

[18] Some huts did remain in Camp 1 and they were dismantled in the mid 1950s.

THE CELLE INVESTIGATION

In the first days of occupation, an uneasy peace descended on Celle. British army vehicles cautiously patrolled the empty streets, most residents preferring to remain in their homes. No one could possibly have forecast that Celle was to be a key British army garrison town in Germany for the next 55 years.

The survivors of Oetzmann's hellhole of the Heide Kaserne stables were beginning to share their harrowing experiences and what gave these statements further traction were the accounts from members of the Anti-Nazi-Group that had covertly operated in Celle during the war. Scores now needed settling. The British legal authorities, based in Herford, west of Salzgitter, were left in no doubt that a serious war crime had been committed.

At 8.15pm on May 28, a Royal Military Police jeep pulled up outside Birkenstrasse No 17, a street not far from Fuhrbergerstrasse, and popularized by apartment blocks. Corporals Hope and Vissers, with their interpreter, known as J.J., rang the doorbell for Hanni Dünsing. What Hanni related to the RMPs in the next 45 minutes was sufficient for them to knock on the door of fellow resident in the block, Friedrich Loth, Celle's stationmaster and rail traffic superintendent.

As the Allied bombing raid had grown in intensity, Hanni and others had decided to make a break for the bunker in the heathland and outside in Birkenstrasse they witnessed Loth, revolver in hand, shooting at runners. Hanni had yelled at Loth to stop, but he ignored her and the prisoners kept falling. She didn't know if they were alive or dead.

Loth immediately denied any killing, telling Hope "'I only fired two shots in the air'". He was hauled off to Celle's jail. Loth would later tell his RAF interrogator that he couldn't have shot any prisoners because he might have endangered the lives of the women and children who had gathered in the street.

Despite being weighed down by assembling evidence for the impending Belsen trial, Herford finally determined in July that events in Celle must be fully investigated mandating the experienced Special Investigations Branch of the RAF War Crimes Group. The

RAF had successfully run down SS that had murdered Allied aircrews.

The German Criminal Police, in Lüneburg, independently conducted its own assessment on whether Celle's police had been complicit with the SS and other military in committing mass murder. A Major Klein had pitched up in Bergstrasse to conduct interviews but with the statements so similar in detail, suggesting collusion, the RAF deemed it worthless apart from the evidence of one policeman, Ernst Bohlau, who had been prepared to record that he had personally observed shootings committed by Lautenbach, Schmidt and Amelung.

In the Bergstrasse police station, quiet conversations were left to more private quarters. Decker would recall one such moment in October. He was in his garden in Nordwall, tending to his rabbits, when a subdued Schwandt appeared with news that the questioning of the police was imminent. 'Now the matter of what happened in Neustädter Holz will begin', he told the master sergeant. 'But I never did any shooting, you know that?' responded Decker quickly. Schwandt made no comment. Before he left Decker to his rabbits, the police lieutenant had stressed that every police statement given to the British had to be consistent, no names could be mentioned, and no one must admit to even being in Neustädter Holz.

Amelung, too, was apprehensive. Technically a civilian, despite wearing his Wehrmacht sergeant's jacket during the häftlingen clearance, he had willingly co-operated with Decker and Ahlborn in several killings. He met up with the two policemen to agree a collective stance.

The three agreed that if questioned all blame had to be heaped on Schwandt as the squad leader and the SS Hauptsturmführer, who had threatened to report any insubordination to Major General Tzschökell. In another private moment but this time between only Amelung and Decker, Ahlborn was considered the weak link as he was widely known in the town and had been seen in the vicinity of Neustädter Holz several times during the killings. Solidarity amongst the police was now at breaking point, Behrens was one of several who claimed to colleagues that he couldn't possibly have killed any häftlingen as his pistol had been misfiring. Few listened.

Amelung was the first to be arrested by the Royal Military Police, on February 5, 1946 and from his jail cell, he loudly denounced every charge. Fischer, the senior prison warden, was charged the following day but he was already in a cell over allegations of brutality against prison inmates. The first policeman to be arrested was on February 7 – Ahlborn. It is worth recalling that he had boasted of killing 26 häftlingen at one stage in the hare chase. The former Todt and Volkssturm officer, Giesemann, was arrested at his home on February 11. By the end of the month, Luhmann, Carlowitz, Joost and Lautenbach had joined them in the Celle cells.

Schwandt was picked up on March 8 and 15 days later, Sievert was pulled in vigorously denying the Schwandt claim that he had been in charge of the police squad, given his familiarity with Celle's streets. Schuchardt, the fireman, who had callously murdered an already seriously wounded prisoner on a level crossing, in front of a raft of witnesses, was arrested on March 28.

Corporal Amos, one of the two RAF interrogators, would long remember his encounter in Celle jail with Carlowitz, the Luftwaffe's armoury electrical officer. Entering the interview room, Carlowitz had stood proudly to attention, clicking his heels and arrogantly extending his arm upwards in the typical Nazi salute. Amos ignored the gesture, firmly believing that Carlowitz was one of the ringleaders in the massacre.

Initially, no one confessed to any killing, the exception being Ernst Kramer, a policeman, who admitted from the outset shooting at least two prisoners. To his RAF interrogator, he came over as rather simple and didn't realise the seriousness of the charge against him. Others were also in the cells including Mengershausen, the party blockleiter. Throughout he was stubborn, expressing no remorse. Heuer, another civilian, divulged nothing. As the interrogations continued, the façade of complete innocence had peeled away. Some altered their stories, admitting partial blame, but the policemen never veered from the collective consensus that they had merely carried out orders.

Relationships worsened in the cells. Amelung claimed Ahlborn had 'acted like a madman' with Ahlborn counterclaiming that

Amelung had been 'at boiling point over the stealing of his father's chicken.' From his cell, Decker continued to peddle the myth that he hadn't killed. Heuer and Giesemann shared a cell and when Giesemann returned after his interrogation, a message had been scrawled in pencil on the cell: 'In this cell, even one's best friend becomes a traitor'. Heuer was released the following day. Kramer, aged 62, would commit suicide on April 20 while in custody.

On June 15, 1946, the 18 in the cells were transported to Fischbeck detention centre, one of several in northern Germany that held prisoners charged with war crimes. That number would be whittled down to 13 as charges were dropped against Behrens, Schmidt, Loth, Mengershausen and Hoffmann, the fire chief.

The Hitler Youth Leader, Karl Genthe, another to boast multiple killings – at one stage 28 – remained missing despite extensive searches of the detainment camps. Missing also was Edward Meyer, a policeman, who had gone into hiding somewhere in the Burgdorf area. The RAF team had to admit that it wasn't possible to trace any members of the SS, the Wehrmacht and the Luftwaffe, given the transient movements at this stage of the war. Curiously, none of the policemen named the ever-present SS Hauptsturmführer. Were they fearful of the reach of the SS even though the war was over?

The RAF interrogators switched their focus to finding witnesses and advertisements were placed in local and Hannover newspapers. Many witnesses had already come forward on their own volition. Each one needed interviewing, with statements taken. Nailing down every specific episode was impossible so the investigators concentrated on the killings with multiple witnesses. Once these interviews had concluded, the senior officer in the RAF's War Crimes Group had no doubt there was a case to answer.

Given the probability that the accused would be acquitted in a Military Court as the nationality of the victims in each proven incident of shooting couldn't be determined, the RAF sent the case to the Atrocities and War Crimes Section of the Control Commission, requesting that it be included 'among the 10 or so exemplary cases to be tried under Law No.10'. Very clearly, the RAF officer spelt out why. 'This case must not go untried, as it is a particularly strong example of the spontaneous and voluntary participation by German civilians in a peculiarly revolting and inhuman series of murders.'

Celle was now to rank as one of the very worst Nazi atrocities.

THE TRIALS

The RAF investigators had tried hard to locate any Belsen survivors who had been on the Celle train and one was found, still undergoing recuperation and awaiting repatriation. Jacob Rosmarin, however, was vague in his detail and the RAF gauged that his testimony wouldn't stand the scrutiny of a trial. Rosmarin did set off a peripheral line of enquiry. On the train, Rosmarin had struck up a conversation with a British serviceman, a Scotsman, but Rosmarin didn't know what had happened to him. With most of the Belsen documents destroyed by Kramer and his officers, the search proved next to impossible. Local hospitals that still nursed Belsen inmates were scoured but the Scotsman was never found.

To test the mendacity of the evidence from 39 witnesses, a military Summary Court was convened which started in Brunswick on December 2, 1947. At this time, all the accused had been returned to Celle jail from their respective detention centres. The day before the Summary Court opened, the RAF had held its identification parade of the accused in the jail.

Frieda Wolter, who lived in Fuhrbergerstrasse No 40, was a witness in the Summary Court and her testimony was powerful, highly graphic and compelling. On April 8, 1945, she said, at first she hadn't recognized the striped clothing worn by the half-starved and bare-footed men that had appeared outside her home, many with wounds. Guarding them had been an SS soldier who told her disdainfully they were "'criminals'" being taken into Neustädter Holz to be dealt with. Even as he spoke, other prisoners were running in the heathland behind her garden, some injured and supporting each other. One carried a child. Another had his head stoved in by a uniformed man with his rifle butt after being pinned to the ground.

Sickened by events, Frieda had taken to the safety of the cellar that functioned as a washhouse and shelter, to sit with her landlady.

WAR CRIMES TRIAL. HANOVER.

ACCUSED
&
Defence Counsel.

6th April, 1948.

1. Heinrich LUHMANN   -   Dr. GUTER and Dr. BALL
2. Friedrich LAUTENBACH   -   Dr. NEBELSIECK
3. Oskar GANLOWITZ   -   Dr. HOLDE
4. Karl SCHMIDT   -   Dr. JEROXL
5. Heinrich GIESEMANN   -   Herr ROMBERG
6. Ernst FISCHER   -   Dr. HOLSTE
7. Alwin SCHUCHARDT   -   Dr. WILLHAUSEN
8. Otto SCHWANDT   -   R/anwalt HOFFMANN
9. Albert SIEVERT   -   }
                                   } Herr ROMBERG
10. Helmut AHLBORN   -   }
11. Otto AMELUNG   -   Dr. HOLSTE
12. Jakob DECKER   -   Dr. NEBELSIECK
13. Fritz JOOST   -   Dr. ADRIAN.

3 German interpreters sworn.

Dr. Holste.   I ask that each accused be tried separately.

Dr. Nebelsieck is ill. I produce medical certificate.

Court.   Application that each accused be tried separately, refused
         as there is no reason to hold that any of the accused is
         prejudiced by being tried with the others.

Bard P. P. for D. of P.

         I will begin with witnesses who do not affect accused 2 or
         12, Dr. N's clients.

Pleas.   Court 1.

         All accused.   N.G.

                          Court 2.

         All accused.   N.G.

Bard P. P. opens.

         Train containing Concentration Camp prisoners in Celle Station.

         Bombing: Prisoners allowed to disperse.

◀ The accused in the war crimes trial included several policemen. The German Criminal Police, in Lüneburg, had conducted its own assessment on whether Celle's police had participated with the SS. A Major Klein had pitched up in Bergstrasse to conduct interviews but with the statements so similar in detail, suggesting collusion, the RAF deemed it worthless.
Sources: National Archives, Kew

▲ Renate von der Marell observed from Fuhrbergerstrasse 79, an apartment block on the corner of Birkenstrasse, Joost's killing of the prisoner in the road.

▲ The body of the prisoner was left on the side of the road opposite her flat. Blood flowed in the gutter. In Joost's plea against the death sentence, his lawyer persisted with the defence that Joost had fired into an already lifeless body.

▲ When British armour warily entered Celle on April 12, 1945, the Gordon Highlanders experienced little opposition but several Celle policemen were killed.

▲ On April 15, 1945, an SAS squad in their well-armed jeeps had driven warily towards the town of Bergen to reconnoitre the strength of the military presence in and around the camp. At its head was a hardened 25-year-old veteran, Captain John Tonkin. In a revealing tape recording he made for the BBC radio archives, 40 years later, Tonkin spoke publically for the first time about entering Belsen. As the SAS had approached Bergen, said Tonkin, they caught the smell. Taking the road to Belsen from the centre of Bergen, that odour became overpowering.

What really disturbed Tonkin was the sight of SS and Hungarian army camp guards casually taking pot shots at prisoners. The SAS had rounded up Kramer and others, placed them in a hut and Tonkin gave them an ultimatum, not mincing his words. 'Unless this shooting stops immediately, you will all die… rather horribly'. The shooting ceased.

Outside Kramer's office in Camp 1, German-speaking Lieutenant Sington had parked up his jeep, alongside a loudspeaker van. The broadcast of liberation in both English and German reverberated around the huts, a poignant message that would be long remembered by Belsen survivors, who now knew that for them the murderous German tyranny had ended. The British had arrived.

In this SAS photograph, Tonkin is third on the left.

▶ The army took no chances when Kramer, Belsen's Camp 1 commandant, was taken away in leg irons to a prison cell in Celle. *Source: Imperial War Museum, London*

Suddenly they heard movement in the room above and Frieda crept upstairs to be confronted by another group in striped clothing, gesticulating and crying out 'many bombs, many bombs!' Keeping her calm, Frieda told them it wasn't safe in the house. 'They left the house peacefully and went into the forest', she informed the court.

Further fugitives had appeared outside No 40, these ones guarded by a wounded SS soldier. The prisoners begged for water. 'We had taken a bath before the raid and there was only a small amount left in the boiler and the water supply was cut off', Frieda explained, but that didn't deter her from grabbing a bucket and extracting the last drops in the pipes even though it was still warm. Taking it outside, the SS guard roughly prevented her from dispensing it. '"These swine don't drink"', he had yelled at her. 'In that case you don't drink, either, you swine', she responded, passing around the bucket to the grateful prisoners.

As the night wore on, neighbours came in to share the cellar. At one stage, an injured prisoner stumbled into the house only to collapse in the cellar passage. The SS took him away the following morning. In another episode, a prisoner was dragged out of No 40 and stabbed to death with a fixed bayonet. 'I couldn't bear to watch', recalled Frieda. In the darkness, prisoners were still fleeing for their lives on either side of the house. One was shot behind the garden shed. Frieda heard in the darkness, '"what shall we do with him?"' Back came, '"give him a burst!"' A shallow pit just beyond the garden fence of No 40 had filled up with bodies.

Freda was bandaging the wounds of one prisoner when a policeman turned on her, pointing his pistol, ordering her to stop. That policeman returned several times as No 40 continued to attract fleeing prisoners. '"Are these swines still alive?"' retorted the policeman to Frieda. '"I will do the necessary"'.

Such was the number that Frieda had summoned the courage to stand amongst them in her back garden, hoping that her presence would deter further shooting. Sadly, such fortitude didn't stop an SS soldier pushing her aside and marching them out of the garden and into the wood. When asked in the Summary Court if she could identify the policeman who had threatened her with his pistol, Frieda had no hesitation. She pointed at prisoner No 8: Lt. Otto Schwandt.

Another who pointed accusingly at prisoner No 8 was Sergeant Ernest Able, one of the two Special Investigations Branch interrogators for the RAF who had conducted much of the questioning in Celle's jail. Able had been called back from Berlin where he now worked in the Criminal Investigation Department of the British Civil Police. The Summary Court had required him to elaborate on several aspects as to his interrogation of Schwandt in March 1946.

Clarification was necessary to determine whether Schwandt had been the police squad leader as he had continued to insist that Sievert had been in charge, on the basis that he had only arrived in Celle in February 1945 and Sievert had a better knowledge of the town. From his interrogations of other policemen, confirmed Able, there could be no doubt that Schwandt had given the orders. "'If my colleagues shift the blame from their own shoulders to mine, this is only to defend their own involvement'" had been the plank of Schwandt's defence, Able told the court, reading from his notes.

That led onto the court inquiring how Schwandt had interpreted Tzschökell's order in the Kreisleitung conference. During his interrogations of Schwandt, explained Able, the accused never had any doubt. Celle had to be cleared of the KZ prisoners by whatever means and the police had to follow military orders and take the lead from the SS. Schwandt had done so, fearing the dire consequences if they hadn't.

Further elucidating on Schwandt's attitude during interrogation, Able described him as combative, arrogant, aggressive and bitterly resentful to arrest. "'By no means did I think I would have to give account to a foreign power. My comrades and I are regarded as war criminals and we feel terribly hurt about that charge considering we never committed offences during our service. Perhaps our actions would not be viewed as a war crime if only Germans had been the victims. I therefore ask you not to compare us with real war criminals. Set us free to continue our good work.'"

The police lieutenant never accepted any liability, Able recalled, denying police involvement in the Waldweg, the roads enroute to the Neustädter Holz and the clearing near the Wehrmacht shooting ground. The SS, not the police, had conducted the shootings in the clearing, Schwandt had argued. Incredulously, Schwandt had claimed that none of the squad fired their weapons during the operation to recapture the camp prisoners.

Able was also required to elaborate on Ahlborn's first interrogation and his denial of culpability. Prisoner No 10 was identified by Able. Ahlborn had told him that he had arrived in the clearing after his police colleagues, a contrary account to his colleagues, to find Schwandt standing amongst the prisoners who were lying down on their fronts. "' Come on Ahlborn, we must shoot them!'" Schwandt had ordered. Ahlborn had denied any involvement in what ensued. The killers in the clearing on April 9 were Schwandt, Sievert, Decker, Peters and others, not him, insisted Ahlborn. He did later admit to shooting some prisoners who had run away.

There had been no shortage of witnesses to Ahlborn's actions on April 9. Wilhelm Fromme, a Volkssturm soldier, who lived in Wietzenbruch, gave testimony that provided further descriptive detail on the brutality that was the Celle hare chase. On duty during the raid, Fromme had deserted his post to take care of his family. The following day, he had testified, he deserted again after spending hours scouring the canal area for häftlingen in Neustädter Holz and around the Fuhrbergerstrasse back gardens. Fromme had discovered four wounded prisoners hiding in a pit behind one garden, one of whom threw up his hands for mercy and begged for a job as a farm labourer. Ahlborn had appeared out of Neustädter Holz, drew his pistol and proficiently shot all four through the temple. Fromme, supposedly, was shocked.

Despite lamely denying he had fired any shots during the two days, Decker was another Celle policeman who didn't escape the finger pointing in the Summary Court. Two women, Elfriede Klingemann and Louise Koninczeny, had been in no doubt on who they had seen kill on April 9, pointing out No 12.

The Summary Court wound up on December 12, deigning the evidence convincing enough to proceed to a full war crimes trial. Otto Amelung, Helmut Ahlborn, Oskar Carlowitz, Jakob Decker, Heinrich Giesemann, Ernst Fischer, Friedrich Lautenbach, Heinrich Luhmann, Otto Schwandt, Karl Schmidt, Alwin Schuchardt and

Albert Sievert now faced the real possibility of a death sentence by hanging. Missing from this group was Fritz Joost, the local slater, who had cold-bloodedly shot an already seriously injured prisoner, in front of Renate von Marell's Fuhrbergerstrasse apartment. He faced his own hearing on December 30.

Hannover was the High Court venue as that war crimes trial began on April 8, 1948, exactly three years to the day since the Allied airstrike on the Güterbahnhof. From the outset rancour ensued as defence lawyers petitioned that all charges be struck out as their clients were not being tried separately. The judge waved the petitions aside, pronouncing that being tried collectively was not prejudicial to any outcome. As the trial concluded on May 14, Ahlborn, Amelung and Joost were sentenced to death. In the case against Ahlborn, the prosecution had focused on just two of his killings. Amelung had been found guilty of killing four and there had been no doubt as to Joost's guilt. Schwandt was fortunate in receiving just 10 years given the prosecution couldn't nail down his actual involvement in Neustädter Holz. Decker received seven years, Schuchardt 10 and Sievert four. Carlowitz, Fischer, Giesemann, Lautenbach and Luhmann were acquitted, despite their participation in the häftlingen clearance.

Lawyers were quick to appeal the death sentences, submitting petitions for clemency to Dr Ohlhoff, the governor of Celle's jail. They wanted the governor to forward the petitions to the British Military Government Authority.

Amelung's lawyer claimed that Celle had been in a state of emergency and confusion after the bomb raid, with the KZ prisoners pillaging homes in the search for food and weapons. His client had blamed Ahlborn, who had "'acted like a madman, with his mouth foaming and his eyes bulging'" for chiding him on. Ahlborn had further goaded by exhorting "'don't be a coward, you are an old soldier, go on, shoot!'" The actual meaning of murder was another tack taken by Amelung's counsel stating that there was now a growing body of opinion in Germany that death sentences, even for war crimes, were no longer appropriate.

Schwandt had got off too lightly, was a key point raised by Ahlborn's lawyer: the lieutenant had been the one in charge and had given the orders to shoot. The lawyer further excoriated the evidence of two witnesses, Ludwig Einfeldt, the forester, and the 14-year-old Theo Lambrecht. Einfeldt's testimony against his client, argued the lawyer, was deeply flawed and suspect. As an example, he claimed, Einfeldt had failed to pick out Ahlborn in the identity parade in Celle jail the day before the Summary Court had convened: in fact, he said, the parade was a stitch up. Amelung had already influenced Sergeant Heinrich Stahl, the Celle policeman in charge, by telling him that Ahlborn had been one of the principals in the shootings. Einfeldt had also written to Ahlborn's wife confiding that he had seen an SS man carry out at least one of the shootings that her husband had been charged with.

Einfeldt should have been in the dock, not his client, insisted the lawyer, and two new witnesses had come forward who both lived in Fuhrbergerstrasse, Ruth Jürgen and Frau Sommel. Both women had seen Einfeldt kill on at least one occasion. Einfeldt's evidence needed to be set aside, it had no validity, and as to the evidence given by Theo Lambrecht, the lawyer described him as too young, impressionable and a Communist.

His client 'was not a Nazi fanatic as portrayed' and what he had done must be viewed in a different light as wartime rules prevailed at the time. In his opinion, the lawyer argued, there remained sufficient doubt as to the nationality of the victims who were killed. The prosecution in the trial never conclusively proved that the KZ prisoners Ahlborn had shot were not German nationals.

This issue had been a serious point of contention for the defence counsels in the trial, their argument being that seemingly Ahlborn and others wouldn't be facing a death sentence if only German nationals had been killed.

Highlighting Ahlborn's personal credentials in his submission, his client had excellent testimonials, had a friendly disposition, and was a twice-wounded war hero invalided out of the Wehrmacht in 1942. He had joined the police, a force 'he had served loyally' in the full knowledge that 'any act of disobedience would involve the gravest consequences for him'.

Members of Ahlborn's family had rallied around and added their weight to the plea. His mother in an emotional letter to the prison governor included a photograph of a very young and blond Helmut sitting on her knee. Helmut was the sole survivor of four boys: the others were killed in the war. Ahlborn's mother-in-law stated that Helmut, amongst all the policemen, had protested the loudest when Schwandt had given the order to shoot in the clearing. 'It had been madness', she wrote, 'yet it was the law of the front line with the British approaching'.

Joost's lawyer in his client's plea forensically eviscerated each witness statement in the Hannover trial that had led to a death sentence. In that trial he persisted with the defence that Joost had very probably fired into an already lifeless body that lay in Fuhrbergerstrasse. For the plea he continued with the same argument. 'The eyes were staring and lifeless', Joost had said, and before he shot into the body, he had lifted an arm, which dropped back immediately. Joost shouted at the prisoner but that, too, incurred no reaction. 'At the very moment when Joost fired at him, the prisoner was no longer capable of living', contended the lawyer, and from the distance they were, the witnesses could not have seen the bullet from Joost's rifle enter the body. Might his client have deliberately shot into the ground, further asked the lawyer?

Under 'In Dubio pro Reo', legal speak for the unreliability and contradictory nature of the evidence, the lawyer concluded, witness statements had to be disregarded in their entirety given the uncertainty on whether the KZ prisoner was alive at the time. Playing on a personal side, Joost was described as 'an orphan, a comparatively young man, who has his life still before him'.

Those clemency pleas for Amelung, Ahlborn and Joost were submitted to the Court of Appeal, in the Office of the Supreme Court, in Herford's Rathaus, and obviously swayed its members. Joost's plea had led to a full acquittal, Ahlborn's death sentence was commuted to 15 years, later reduced to 10, and Amelung would serve 20 years. Some of the other original sentences handed out were reduced. Schuchardt, the fireman, who had cold-bloodedly gunned down an already injured concentration camp prisoner on a level crossing, had his sentence reduced from 10 years to eight. Schwandt, the squad leader, also saw a reduced sentence.

WHERE ARE THE BODIES?

The British undertook a disinterment operation in August 1946, some 14 months after the shooting and several months after the interrogations, but from the outset it was poorly resourced. Under the auspices of the overworked British Tracing Office an order was given to select 12 former hardened Nazis, hand them each a spade and some rope and dig.[19] To ensure medical procedures were followed, two Celle doctors, Dr Gleser and Dr Histermann, were detailed to the squad. A local coffin manufacturer had been contracted and two lorries were put at the squad's disposal. Full support was demanded from the German authorities, including the disgraced Celle police force.

With its limited manpower, the squad could never undertake a full excavation of the Güterbahnhof bomb craters and Neustädter Holz. When a body was located, determining a name or nationality proved next to impossible. Few of the camp prisoners had any form of identity. The squad also disinterred bodies from the roads that led to Belsen, one being from the Klein Bodungen death march that had come through Celle on April 8.

Any bodies that were found were taken to Celle's Waldfriedhof cemetery in Wietzenbruch, their grave mounds discernible in a site bordered by small square stones with the simple message 'Unbekannt April 1945', or unknown: the wooden crosses placed on each grave have long rotted away. There are also graves for the Belsen victims who were later taken to Celle's general hospital.

In all, at Waldfriedhof there are around 300 graves. Very few are named.

Documents in the trial files held in the British archives confirm that 3,000 male and 400 female KZ prisoners had been on the train sitting idle in the Güterbahnhof and the RAF war crimes team had

◀ Celle's Waldfriedhof cemetery holds only a small number of the Hare Chase dead. *Source: Nigel Bance*

---

[19] "Betreuung von KZ-Häftlingen", Stadta CE, SP 11, Best 05 0 Nr. 01234, Celle archive.

estimated that up to 1,000 had died as a result of the Allied attack. No one knew how many had been dumped by the Celle police and Wehrmacht into the bomb craters that covered a wide area in and around the Güterbahnhof.

Standing on the bridge over the railway looking towards the Güterbahnhof, the modern ITAG factory, partially destroyed during the April raid, is dominant. Post-war the area has been developed into businesses, shops and homes but many bodies must lie under their foundations.

To compound the mystery of the bodies, there is no record on how many bodies were retrieved by Major Oetzmann's collection detail and nor is there information on where they were taken.

The disinterment squad hadn't properly searched the killing grounds in Neustädter Holz, given the large area. Metal detectorists have searched in vain, especially around the Wehrmacht shooting ground, partly now a civic spoil dump, but the majority of the escapees had nothing metallic on them to emit a signal.

Oetzmann, Schwandt, and other policemen, knew where the bodies were buried but they admitted nothing in their testimonies to the RAF's investigators. To do so would have been an admission of guilt in the massacre.

WHAT WAS THE DEATH TOLL?

Determining how many Celle survivors had been marched to Belsen by the SS is a key variant in the calculation. Given the camp's registry had been destroyed, no document is available for corroboration from that source. Post-war, an estimate of 500 has been generally accepted with recent research suggesting that the number that had to endure Belsen may have been up to three times higher. [20]

Sergeant Ernest Able, the RAF Special Investigations Branch investigator, who with his colleague, Corporal William Amos, had conducted more than 300 interrogations and interviews, was arguably the best qualified to define the overall Celle death toll. In his 12-

---

[20] 'Celle April 1945 revisited', Dr Bernhard Strebel, Bielefeld 2008.

page summary of events to the head of the RAF's War Crimes Group, dated April 16, 1946, he concluded that of the 3,400 concentration camp prisoners on the train, some 1,500 had survived, implying that 1,900 had died. It is unclear, however, whether that estimate includes the number that were marched to Belsen.

Of the number shot in the Celle hare chase, Able estimated 800.

Celle's killing grounds had been numerous. In the Güterbahnhof, the SS had cynically cut down many train survivors even though instructions were yelled to run for the woods for a later rendezvous. The Rotthagen and Texas sports grounds were killing grounds, as were the Waldweg, Hattendorfstrasse, Lauensteinstrasse, Amelungstrasse, Birkenstrasse, Carstenstrasse, Wittesstrasse and Fuhrbergerstrasse, with its back gardens and pits behind the fence, or Gartenrand as it was locally referred to.

Neustädter Holz, the Celle woods to the west of the town, saw some of the worst massacres, conducted by the SS, the Celle police, Volkssturm, Hitler Youth, Luftwaffe, Wehrmacht and civilians. The 'Mulde' was an SS site that claimed multiple lives. Shootings spilled over to Unter den Eichen, and in the clearing close to the perimeter of the Wehrmacht shooting range, the Celle police murdered an untold number, with Ahlborn cynically finishing off survivors hours later. Sporadic killings occurred around the Alten Canal in the woods.

Many had perished in the dying chamber that was the Wehrmacht's Heide Kaserne stables behind the garrison's headquarters in the town, its doors locked and guarded by Oetzmann's policemen.

The fate of the 12 prisoners discovered by Jakob Decker and Albert Sievert, cowering in a shed in the Waldweg, is unknown. The same applies to the 30 the police had encountered crossing the railway line from the Waldweg, as described by Helmut Ahlborn. As to the 180 prisoners held in the derelict building behind the-then Kreikenbaum restaurant, highlighted by Oscar Carlowitz and Heinrich Giesemann, almost certainly they were murdered in Neustädter Holz. The large number seen captive at the Luftwaffe airfield witnessed by Alwin Schuchardt, the fireman, may have shared the same fate.

Tzschökell's instruction to clear the häftlingen from the town by whatever means had developed into a mass slaughter. Clearly Celle has yet to fully yield up its secrets.

On a happier note, there is a report that some train escapees did outrun the hare chase in Neustädter Holz, helped by sympathetic families and farmers. A group of 30, despite their injuries, had reached the British lines.

MASSACRE ECHOES

Several survivors came forward in later years to describe their experiences. Joanna Kiaca-Fryczkowska, from Poland, related in 1994 that many had run from the burning train, escaping into gardens and the cellars of the private gardens. 'All we wanted was some bread and something drinkable', she recalled but no one came to their aid: 'German civilians betrayed us to the SS'. [21]

Otto Künder, a German survivor, had recalled in 1965 that 'as the bombs struck the train, the women screamed but as the planes turned away, more returned'. On jumping from his wagon, Otto had escaped the gunfire from the SS guards in the Güterbahnhof and ran for the forest where he met five women survivors, Poles and Russians. It was soon dark and all they could hear through the trees was gunfire. Cautiously walking down a footpath, they were later discovered by Wehrmacht soldiers. 'I told them that I was a German', said Otto 'and would rather die than return to a concentration camp'.[22] Otto being German probably saved all their lives.

Nadezhda Prokopenko's recall in 1998 vividly described when the bombs struck. The wagon she was in jumped up on the tracks and everyone ran shocked to the locked doors but the female SS guard yelled at them to stay back. Not easily swayed, the prisoners overwhelmed her and reluctantly the guard unlocked the doors. The prisoners jumped down onto the track and for a while, reminisced Nadezhda, prisoners and guards were temporarily united in the

---

[21] Account held in the Neuengamme Gedenkstätte.
[22] Ibid.

aftermath of surviving the horror of the bombing. The guards slaked their thirst with lemonade, even sharing some with the prisoners. Hanna was amongst the group later marched to Belsen.

Few can doubt the courage of those Celle witnesses who came forward to give evidence in the Summary Court and the war crimes trial, pitting neighbour against neighbour: with a number abused for doing so. Theo Lambrecht, one of the youngest witnesses, who lived in Fuhrbergerstrasse, emigrated to the United States and even now, well into his eighties, he refuses to discuss those trauma-filled days in April 1945. Many Celle residents were horrified and nauseated at the war crimes committed in the town's name.

Post-war, not everyone, including local politicians and councillors, had bought into redemption, seemingly indifferent to the worst excesses of the Third Reich. One newspaper had referred to Celle as a town of 'Ewiggestrige', or reluctant Nazi diehards. Streets still commemorate SS officials, such as the cul-de-sac named after Kurt Blanke, the notorious SS official, who became expert in confiscating assets of Jews in France, before their transportation to the death camps. Blanke, who lived long, dying in 1995, was never tried for war crimes and served as Celle's mayor from 1964 until 1973. The wartime SS mayor, Ernst Meyer, who might have been one of the attendees in that momentous midnight conference in the Kreisleitung, is commemorated through the Ernst-Meyer-Allee. There are other naming examples.

Echoes of the hare chase surfaced in the late 1980s as 11 residents vividly relived their experience in print, with the assistance of Celle's Bomann Museum and the Stadtarchive, the town's archive. None of these 11 had been witnesses in the Summary Court or trial but their interviews provided further powerful testimony. [23]

Elizabeth Henschel had sheltered in a bunker during the airstrike and when she emerged she was horrified at the devastation, the windows and doors blown out in every house in Sophie-Dorothea-Strasse. Entering her shattered home with her son, both were

---

[23] Bertram, Mijndert: 'April 1945, Der Luftangriff auf Celle und das Schicksal KZ-Häftlinge aus Drütte', Celle, 1989.

confronted by a small man in the kitchen, frantically searching for food, who was more scared than they at being discovered. In his panic, he uttered to Elizabeth that he also had a son. She fed the man and took him down to her cellar to lay low.

There was a further remembrance from Elizabeth. Whistles had shrilled as the SS encouraged escapees out of the homes. When appearing warily in the doorways, the SS had ruthlessly cut them down with their machine pistols. One who ran had his legs shot away and he collapsed by a lamppost begging for water. Elizabeth and her son didn't dare go out and help.

The experience of Wilhelm Sommer, then aged 13, was equally terrifying. Wilhelm had lived in Fuhrbergerstrasse and he had seen 'men in striped clothing with matching rimless hats running like hares' in the heathland behind the back gardens and ducking down behind the bushes. 'Just like a hare hunt', recalled Wilhelm, they popped up again and ran. He had been ordered by two SS and a local member of the Volkssturm to help carry ammunition cases up the Wittesstrasse to the Lönsweg and into the 'Mulde' where bodies were strewn throughout the clearing. Wilhelm heard one SS say, '"they are all dead"' and to make certain, the soldier broke off a birch twig and thwacked one around the face. Shocked, Wilhelm had seen the eyelids flutter. The SS man stood over the prostrate häftlinge and shot him in the head. Wilhelm ran away, hid for a while in the Wittesstrasse, and then ran home. He didn't venture out again.

I began this account of the appalling events that occurred in Celle over two days in April 1945 with a reminder, if one was needed, on how the persuasive pull of Nazism had permeated deep into every level of Germany's social and cultural fabric. The testament of Vasily Krotjuk,[24] who was not a witness in the Celle trial, illustrates that even the young had been caught up in the moment.

Vasily had been caught up in the blast on the train and gaining consciousness, he found himself lying amongst vegetables in a garden by the side of the track, about 35 metres away from the train bleeding profusely from a shattered leg. 'Everywhere around was burning', said

---

[24] Account held in the Neuengamme Gedenkstätte.

Vasily. Despite his terrible wound, he crawled further up the track to a concrete shelter where he found eight others. After about 20 minutes, two boys, aged about 14, Vasily estimated, came running towards them firing wildly. As the other prisoners ran in panic, Vasily was alone and fortunate to live. One boy had shouted at the other, "'we have run out of cartridges, let's run home and our mother will give us some more'".

Vasily was liberated by the British army from Oetzmann's Heide Kaserne hellhole.

The RAF war crimes team agreed that most prisoners had been shot either in the head or in the neck. 'They never stood a chance', stated Able. 'In their weak condition they were soon caught and cried out for mercy despite the pleas from several that they were German'.

Sadly, there were few like Frieda Wolter, who had stood defiantly amongst the concentration camp inmates in her garden at Fuhrbergerstrasse No 40 and gave them water, Elizabeth Henschel, who at great risk to herself had hidden a prisoner in her cellar, and Louise Basse, the courageous air-raid warden, who had propped up a severely wounded prisoner, before being brushed aside by two members of the town's fire service, bent on killing.

▼ OVERLEAF: The Güterbahnhof in Celle where the prisoner train was bombed. Bodies were buried in the bomb craters where some still lay.
Source: Nigel Bance

A WITNESS STATEMENT IN FULL

This statement to witnessing some of the massacre was given to a British interrogator in Celle on January 24, 1946 by Wolfgang Helms, who lived in Fuhrbergerstrasse No 52. Wolfgang was aged 14 at the time of the killings.

'On April 8, 1945, the English attacked the railway station in Celle. Between other trains in the station were an ammunition train and a transport of concentration prisoners. They fled to the woods during the attack to save themselves from the bombs. They remained in the woods during the night as the station was burning.

'On Monday morning, I was attracted by the sound of shooting. Naturally I was interested. That is when I saw people in concentration camp uniform running wild.

'As I looked into the wood I saw many policemen from Celle, Luftwaffe soldiers and SS men, with pistols and rifles shooting the prisoners. Soldiers were also in the street, lining up prisoners and dragging them along by their collars. I then met my friends. I was later a witness with a neighbour, Helmut Born, to Otto Amelung, the boxer, who lived in Fuhrbergerstrasse No. 82, bringing four prisoners through our garden from the nearby wood.

'I further saw from a 50-metre distance, a policeman handing over his pistol to Amelung. Then I saw the prisoners getting down on their stomachs. Otto Amelung was bending over and shooting them through the back of the neck. My aunt called me home. In the afternoon we saw still more prisoners with most shot in the neck.

'On Wednesday, the prisoners were buried at the rear of our garden by Hanna Wolynski, Anna Wolynski, their father, Ernst Ebeman and Helene Helms. I later saw three soldiers – airmen – shooting 20-30 prisoners. An airman related to me that he broke his rifle over a prisoner. I also saw a fellow, about 17 or 19 years old, with a smashed head and another body was near him. One day when I was coming home my mother told me that the dead were dug up and were now buried in the cemetery.'

STORY CHARACTERS

★ Able, Sergeant Ernest: member of Special Investigations Branch attached to No 84 Royal Air Force, War Crimes Group.

★ Ahlborn, Helmut: Celle policeman, member of killing squad. Accused of war crimes.

★ Ahrens, Constable: Celle policeman, driver of the killing squad crew car.

★ Amos, Corporal William: member of Special Investigations Branch attached to No 84 Royal Air Force, War Crimes Group.

★ Basse, Louise: air-raid warden, witness to a killing.

★ Behrens, Gustav: Celle policeman, member of the killing squad.

★ Bohlau, Ernst: Celle policeman, witnessed killings.

★ Cahn, Rosa: Jewish Celle resident, transported and murdered in Chelmno.

★ Carlowitz, Oskar: Luftwaffe, Fuhrbergerstrasse resident, accused of war crimes.

★ Compass, Peter: translator attached to the Special Investigations Branch attached to No 84 Royal Air Force, War Crimes Group.

★ Decker, Senior Sergeant Jacob: Celle policeman, member of killing squad, accused of war crimes.

★ Detzloff: Celle policeman, member of the killing squad.

★ Dümeland, Albert: Fuhrbergerstrasse resident, witness to brutality.

★ Dzierzawa, Erdmann: Wietzenbruch resident, witnessed killings.

★ Einfeldt, Ludwig: forester and Fuhrbergerstrasse resident, witnessed killings, but there were accusations against him.

★ Fischer, Master Sergeant Ernst: Celle prison officer, Fuhrbergerstrasse resident, accused of war crimes.

★ Foste, Frau: neighbour of Ahlborn, the Celle policeman, in Rolandstrasse.

★ Fromme, Wilhelm: Volkssturm, witnessed killings.

★ Genthe, Karl: Hitler Youth Leader, not tried for war crimes, missing.

★ Gottwald: Celle policeman, member of the killing squad.

★ Giesemann, Heinrich: Former Todt, Volkssturm, Fuhrbergerstrasse resident, accused of war crimes.

★ Götee, Dr: Hattendorferstrasse resident, witnessed killings.

★ Gründer, Georg: Hattendorferstrasse resident, witnessed killings.

★ Haarstrich: Celle German Red Cross leader.

★ Helms, Major: head of the Luftwaffe armoury.

★ Helms, Wolfgang: young boy who lived in Fuhrbergerstrasse, witnessed killings.

★ Henschel, Elizabeth: Sophie-Dorothea-Strasse resident, witnessed killings.

★ Hilbig, Frau: Fuhrbergerstrasse resident, witness to brutality.

★ Hoessler, Franz: Belsen's Camp No 2 commandant.

★ Hoffman, Unterbrandmeister Heinz: fire station commander, Wietzenbruch, accused of war crimes and released.

★ Homann, Marta: Birkenstrasse resident, witnessed a killing.

★ Joost, Fritz: Birkenstrasse resident, accused of war crimes.

★ Jürgen, Ruth: Fuhrbergerstrasse resident, witnessed a killing.

★ Just, Ernst: volunteer fireman, witness to a killing.

★ Klein, SS Dr Fritz: Belsen, Camp No 1.

★ Kniep, Berta: Fuhrbergerstrasse resident, witnessed a killing.

★ Koch, Senior Lieutenant: Celle policeman, deputy to Oetzmann the police chief.

★ Kohls, Adolph: Jewish Celle resident, transported and murdered.

★ Kohls, Edith: Jewish Celle resident, transported and murdered in Auschwitz.

★ Kohls, Elsa: Jewish Celle resident, transported and murdered in Auschwitz.

★ Kohls, Lieselotte: Jewish Celle resident, transported and murdered in Auschwitz.

★ Kommel, Paul: Rotthagen resident, uncle of Ahlborn.

★ Klingemann, Elfriede: Fuhrbergerstrasse resident, witnessed killings.

★ Koninczeny, Louise: Fuhrbergerstrasse resident, witnessed killings.

★ Kramer, Sergeant Ernst: Celle policeman, member of the killing squad. Committed suicide.

★ Kramer, Josef: Belsen's Camp No 1 commandant.

★ Kuckuk, Deputy commander: Celle Volkssturm.

★ Lambrecht, Theo: young boy, Fuhrbergerstrasse resident, witnessed killings.

★ Lautenbach, Friedrich: Hattendorfstrasse resident, accused of war crimes.

★ Loth, Friedrich: Celle stationmaster and rail traffic superintendent, questioned.

★ Luhmann, Heinrich: Luftwaffe, accused of war crimes.

★ Marell, von der Renate: Fuhrbergerstrasse resident, witnessed a killing.

★ Meinken: Celle policeman, member of the killing squad.

★ Mengershausen, Ortsgruppenleiter: senior NSDAP officer, Fuhrbergerstrasse resident, accused of war crimes but released.

★ Meyer, Edward: Celle policeman, member of the killing squad.

★ Meyer, Ernst: regional Oberbürgermeister, or mayor.

★ Meyers, Senior Lieutenant: Celle policeman, deputy to Oetzmann, the police chief.

★ Milewski, Willy: Celle's SS Kreisleiter.

★ Müller, Hermann: Wietzenbruch resident, witnessed a killing.

★ Müller, Lieschen: Fuhrbergerstrasse resident, witnessed killings.

★ Neuer, Friedrich: Fuhrbergerstrasse resident, witnessed killings.

★ Oetzmann, Major Hermann: Celle police commander.

★ Peters: Celle policeman, member of the killing squad.

★ Prater, Augusta: Carstenstrasse resident, witnessed killings.

★ Rautenkranz: industrialist, whose family owned the ITAG plant in the Güterbahnhof.

★ Reinecke, Gertrud: Hasenwinkel resident, questioned.

★ Schmidt, Karl: Hattendorferstrasse resident, accused of war crimes.

★ Schmitz, Wilhelmine: Hattendorferstrasse resident, witnessed killings.

★ Schnabel, SS Doctor: Belsen, Camp No 1.

★ Schuchardt, Alwin: Celle fireman, accused of war crimes.

★ Schwandt, Lieutenant Otto: Celle policeman, head of killing squad, accused of war crimes.

★ Sievert, Lieutenant Albert: Celle policeman, joint head of killing squad, accused of war crimes.

★ Sommel, Frau: Fuhrbergerstrasse resident, witnessed a killing.

★ Sommer, Wilhelm: young boy, Fuhrbergerstrasse resident, witnessed killings.

★ Stahl, Staff Sergeant Heinrich: Celle police.

★ Telschow, Gauleiter Otto: Reichstag member for the Eastern Hanover district.

★ Tzschökell, Erika: wife of Paul Tzschökell, Wehrmacht commander.

★ Tzschökell, Major General Paul: Celle Wehrmacht garrison commander.

★ Unknown SS Hauptsturmführer: in command of the häftlingen train, name never disclosed by Celle's police, major participant in the SS killings.

★ Wegmeyer, Heinrich: Celle fireman, questioned.

★ Weu: Celle policeman, member of the killing squad.

MAIN SOURCES

★ National Archives, Kew – summaries, testimonies, statements and correspondence relating to the accused and witnesses, Summary Court and war crimes trial papers, subsequent pleas to commute the death sentences, and documents relating to No 84 Royal Air Force, War Crimes Group.

★ Neuengamme Gedenkstätte archives

★ Belsen Trial papers, 1946

★ Gedenkstatte Bergen-Belsen, Forschung und Dokumentation, (Department of Research and Documentation)

★ *The War Illustrated*, Amalgamated Press, published monthly in WW2

★ *Celler Kriegs* – brief, as cited in several written papers, including Strebel, 2010

★ Cellesche-Zeitung.de

★ Bertram, Mijndert: '*April 1945, Der Luftangriff auf Celle und das Schicksal KZ-Häftlinge aus Drütte*', Celle, 1989

★ *Die Zeit*

★ Central Intelligence Agency

★ Hendrik Altmann: found-places@live.de

THE CELLE HARE CHASE

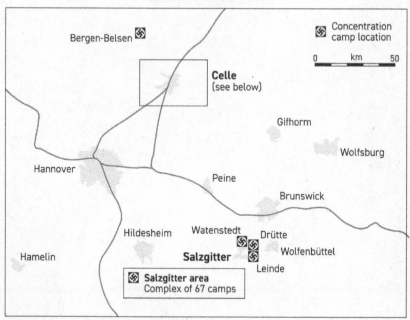

Celle and nearby region of Northern Germany

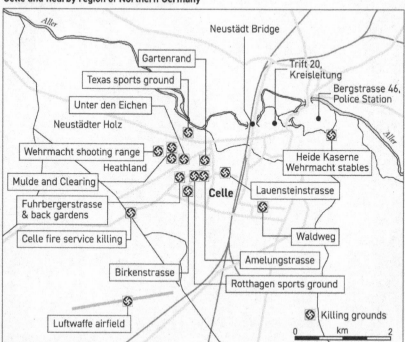

Celle's killing grounds

IV

THE CHARNEL HOUSE

STORYLINE

Gardelegen is a WW2 atrocity site barely known in Germany but what happened on the outskirts of this town, 200km to the west of Berlin, with the American army only a day's march away, deserves to be heard by a far wider domestic and international audience.

Stepping off the train, the town appears uninviting to a first-time visitor. Its bahnhof – the station – is boarded up, derelict, like many others on the line from Stendal, the hub to Berlin. The windows are smashed and graffiti is daubed on every wall of a once attractive building. Formerly in East Germany, Gardelegen is one of many towns where reunification hasn't lived up to the promise that Berlin intended.

Blame for the slaughter that took place on April 13-14, 1945, lay not only with the SS and Luftwaffe paratroopers. The Volkssturm, Germany's huge part-time army, was in the mix whose members included a schoolteacher, finance manager, cattle merchant, flourmill manager, lumberjack, musician and two butchers. Young boys of the Hitler Youth and Gardelegen's firemen made their contribution. The US army doctor who cared for the survivors was unequivocal in an emotional letter home: 'The people of Germany' were responsible.

A clergyman, fearing that the US army commander would execute 200 local men in retribution pleaded on his knees to the colonel, whose troops had uncovered the site where more than 1,000 beaten and starved concentration camp prisoners had been burnt to death in a barn. The Americans never had any intention in doing so but it did use the scene as a photo opportunity to starkly portray back home in America the murderous capability of the Nazis. Gardelegen will forever be scarred as the site of one of the most harrowing mass killings committed in the final weeks of the war. During the Cold War, it was commemorated more as a victory for communism over the evils of fascism.

◀ This horrific image of death by fire encapsulates the brutality and bestiality that was the Third Reich.

Yet again, the main perpetrator of this massacre escaped justice, its architect immersing himself into a vibrant West German economy using a false name, and in 1974 he would start collecting his pension, the state, supposedly, none the wiser to his hideous past.

Inside this barn in Gardelegen prisoners had died where they had crawled, their bodies roasted.

HÄFTLINGEN... in the hundreds they came, filling the narrow roads into Gardelegen from almost every direction, under watchful and trigger-happy SS guards. Gardelegen hadn't been their ultimate destination but it would be here these concentration camp inmates, deemed looters, rapists and murderers by the local authorities, would die, put to death in Gardelegen's very own charnel house.

As the columns approached Gardelegen, escapes intensified and outside one hamlet, five Dutchmen, one a 62-year-old former town mayor, slipped away and hid in a ditch to await the cover of darkness. When it was safe to do so, they warily entered the town in the hope that a church might provide shelter.

Rapping on the first church door, the Dutchmen encountered a Nazi stalwart, one of many in the German Protestant clergy known as a 'Deutsche Christen' so bitten were they by Nazi ideology. From the pulpits these Hitler disciples preached the Aryan code, shaped by a persistent demand for the removal of all Jewish references in the Bible. This movement overtly embraced the swastika in its symbolism. Churches were often draped in swastika flags.

This 'Deutsche Christen' sent the Dutchmen packing and fearing he would alert the police or military the group swiftly moved on into the night. One split away so four later knocked on the front door of the Pfarrhaus, or rectory, of another pastor, who readily took them in. After his wife had fed the Dutchmen, this humanitarian led them to a barn behind the Pfarrhaus that housed the family pig to hide.

Watching what had unfolded was a 14-year-old daughter, who would recall her story years later.

The Dutch grandchildren of one of those shielded by the pastor and his family relived their grandfather's experiences in 2015, walking with 60 young people from Gardelegen along the same death march route to Gardelegen from nearby Mieste railway station.

Thanks to Pastor Friedrich Franz, the four Dutchmen had been spared the horror of the Isenschnibbe charnel house that claimed 1,016 lives.

Gardelegen easily stands comparison with the torching of Oradour-sur-Glane in south-west France on June 10, 1944. In this French village, SS division Das Reich had slaughtered 642 villagers whose troops had mockingly looked on as the women and children burnt to death inside the church. The menfolk had been shot. The torching was duly photographed for the archive that always travelled with the division.

From the outset of war, the military had conducted atrocities in buildings. In one of the earliest, on May 27, 1940, in the French village of Le Paradis, SS Totenkopf, the notorious 'Deaths Head' division, had herded 99 British PoWs into a village barn to be machine-gunned and finished off with bayonets. These were men of the Royal Norfolk and the Royal Scots regiments left behind to cover the British army retreat to Dunkirk.[1]

Culpability in Gardelegen for the annihilation of concentration camp prisoners during April 12-14, 1945, cannot be laid fully at the hands of the SS, even though an SS Kreisleiter, a schoolteacher before he joined the military, was its chief architect. Luftwaffe paratroopers did their share of the killing as did willing residents of Gardelegen. Its Volkssturm, a drilled military force of part-timers, hadn't waivered from the order to kill nor had those zealous young men, even boys, of the Hitlerjugend, the Hitler Youth. Gardelegen's part-time fire service, too, had picked up weapons: its chief shooting a survivor to set an example to his men. The war had less than a month to run yet the people still paid lickspittle service to their Nazi masters.

---

[1] Miraculously, two had survived and their evidence sent Hauptsturmführer Fritz Knöchlein to the gallows in January 1949.

▲ The American army only uncovered the horror at Isenschnibbe on Monday, April 15, the day after it had arrived in Gardelegen. As to who discovered the burning barn that was Lt. Jim Hansen according to the reminiscences of several 405th Regiment members. In his Jeep, Hansen had ventured into a part of the town that hadn't been investigated and after an angry encounter with an SS colonel, who hadn't bought into the German military surrender, he saw smoke rising in the distance and investigated.

The photographs that follow of the torched barn and its victims were taken by members of the 405th and 406th Regiments of the US 102nd Infantry, official US military photographers and *Time Life* magazine. Eisenhower had ordered maximum exposure back home in America.

The day after American troops had entered Gardelegen on April 14, the civilised world had recoiled further as the British army liberated Bergen-Belsen.

VICTORY OVER FASCISM

As WW2 ended and the Cold War cast its long shadow, the hard line diktat that prevailed in East Germany memorialized the Gardelegen dead through a political not a compassionate lens. With the exception of one wall, the Isenschnibbe barn was demolished in 1953 and each year local communist party apparatchiks, townspeople and Gardelegen's young had walked solemnly to the site. The young placed flowers at the foot of each headstone. Isenschnibbe had become an official memorial to honour the victims as Communist resistance against the Nazis: a victory over fascism.

Gardelegen is another example of how so few Nazi war criminals were prosecuted. Kreisleiter Gerhard Thiele, the SS administrative head in the Gardelegen district, enjoyed a long life post-war and picked up his state pension in 1974. Moving from city to city in West Germany he had finally settled in Düsseldorf in 1957 where his backstory of being just an ordinary former Wehrmacht soldier was never challenged. There were rumours but it took to 1997 – more than four decades since the barn torching – before the Düsseldorf authorities opened an enquiry of sorts where it emerged that Thiele had actually died three years earlier in its midst.

When I visited Gardelegen, I was accompanied to Isenschnibbe by the director of the Sachsen-Anhalt Memorials Foundation, based in Berlin, which has many WW2 Holocaust sites under its management. Very few visitors came to the site that day. The director related that some 30,000 visited annually but that number was only an estimate given it lacked a visitor centre and with regional expenditure budgets tight, arguments had long persisted on who should build one.[2] The lack of protection had been another issue with headstones vandalised and daubed with the Nazi swastika. There are 1,023 of them, seven more than the initial number recovered inside and outside the barn. These others had been executed in nearby locations and reburied in Isenschnibbe. The French exhumed 34 remains in 1946 for reburial in France. The Belgians, too, exhumed a number who could be identified.

I enquired whether there were people in the town who might still recall what happened in April 1945. There were, replied the director, but the town had long deigned to forget its notoriety.

Before the American army had left Gardelegen – after first conducting a war crimes inquiry – it commissioned and erected a large and damning memorial plaque, in English and German. That plaque was removed as the Red Army occupied Gardelegen on July 1, 1945, with the town merged into the Soviet occupation zone. On site now is a replica of that original that had been dumped in a local shed for decades.

Surprisingly there had been barn survivors: seven. Frantically they had dug with their bare hands and crawled under the blazing brick barn, somehow avoiding being gunned down outside. When the barn doors were slid back the following day, Kapos – prisoner functionaries armed by the SS guards – willingly sifted through the smouldering piles of bodies to shoot hiding survivors, as did the Volkssturm. Those who had climbed the rafters to avoid the flames were callously shot down. According to the director, one survivor remained alive but too feeble to visit from his home in France.

The victims of Gardelegen had been used as slave labour for the Third Reich in several concentration camps in Germany – 146km apart – and as to why they died in Gardelegen we need to begin our story in July 1943.

LABOUR FOR BATTERY PRODUCTION

Ensuring a ready supply of batteries to the Kriegsmarine U-boat fleet had necessitated the building of the Stöcken concentration camp in the suburb of Hannover, one of 96 satellite camps in the

---

[2] Funding was finally provided to construct a memorial, documentation and exhibition centre, which was formerly opened on September 15, 2020 by Federal President, Frank-Walter Steinmeier. Given Covid restrictions few were allowed to participate in the ceremony.

Neuengamme complex. Accumulatoren-Fabrik AG, the battery manufacturer, needed a slave labour force to operate the hot counter-rotating rollers. Worker protection was minimal and the accident rate was high. Post-war, that battery manufacturer became Varta AG and it grew into a global battery exporter. Only 402 deaths for Stöcken workers were 'officially' recorded but that number failed to take into account the many deaths in the satellite camp itself and the sick workers who were transferred back to Neuengamme. Only a metal statue of two stooped victims at a corner of a busy road intersection now commemorates the site.

The final SS commandant of Stöcken was the notorious Hauptsturmführer (Captain) Kurt Klebeck who had form in working prisoners to death. His previous posting was as deputy chief of SS-Construction Brigade 1, based at the Sylt concentration camp on Alderney, in the Channel Islands, where mainly Russian PoWs constructed gun installations all around the island. Under Klebeck's watch at Sylt, prisoners were shot and dumped in Alderney's harbour or strung up on the camp's fences, their bodies left to rot as a macabre warning. His favourite execution site were the steep cliffs outside Clonque, the Victorian fort. Victims, often roped together, were thrown alive onto the rocks below. Klebeck needed no lectures in dishing out brute force.

As the US 84th Infantry Division advanced closer to Hannover in early April 1945, Klebeck followed his SS orders and executed the incapacitated, hurriedly dumping hundreds of bodies in shallow trenches within the camp. For the remainder, they were to be force-marched or taken by train to other camps not immediately threatened by the Allied advance. Those considered still capable of work, some 1,500, were to be removed to Bergen-Belsen to the north, a 57km march. This convoy arrived at Belsen on April 8 but many had been executed on the road. Klebeck, too, had evacuated Stöcken but within days he was up in front of an SS-Gestapo military court, with another SS officer, for disobeying orders on another matter.

For the remaining 400 at Stöcken thought too ill to walk to Bergen-Belsen, they were boarded onto freight wagons in Hannover on April 8, with no food or water. Their destination was to be Sachsenhausen concentration camp, north of Berlin in Oranienburg. Wolfsburg, a distance of 115km and due east of Hannover, was enroute… as was Gardelegen.

DEATH IN THE RAILWAY STATIONS

With aerial superiority, the Royal Air Force and US airforce were targeting railway lines and hubs as a priority. News came through to the driver of the Stöcken train that the Wolfsburg to Gardelegen line was ruptured. He pulled into the village of Mieste, some 18km to the west of Gardelegen, on the afternoon of April 9 where it remained. There were numerous attempts to escape.

Mieste was the unexpected halt for a second train with an even larger contingent of prisoners. These were from the Rottleberode, Ellrich-Bürgergarten and Ilfield satellite camps of Dora-Mittelbau, near Nordhausen, collectively holding 1,000 prisoners. Rottleberode had a particularly atrocious death rate as its slave labour force converted the nearby historic gypsum caves into an underground production site for the Dessau Junkers aircraft manufacturer. All the 39 Dora satellites were evacuating to Neuengamme, Sachsenhausen and Mauthausen in Austria. Equally notorious was the Stempeda satellite and in its final week, the 400 inmates were to swell the number in Rottleberode.

Lagerführer, or SS camp leader, for Rottleberode was Erhard Brauny. A 59-year-old Hauptscharführer, master sergeant Friedrich Teply, was his deputy. Together, they took charge of 600 prisoners transferring to Neuengamme. On April 6, it set off on a 17km march to Niedersachswerfen station. At Niedersachswerfen, other walking prisoners, similarly in bad condition, arrived from Ellrich-Bürgergarten and Ilfeld. After the war, Erich Scholz, Ellrich-Bürgergarten's Lagerführer, claimed he had added the sick of his camp to Brauny's Rottleberode group so not to hamper his own evacuation from Niedersachswerfen.

For three days Niedersachswerfen station was a squalid holding centre and Brauny made no attempt to alleviate the conditions for his charges. The train eventually arrived and the prisoners were loaded up. At Osterode station more wagons were added with the prisoner

▲ In their desperation to escape, prisoners had dug under the barn.

▲ Three local bürgermeisters were ordered to view bodies.
None took their hats off in respect.

▼ The 405th Regiment of the US 102nd Infantry prepared a pamphlet on the massacre. This is the front cover. Standing amongst the headstones, an American bugler sounded 'Taps', the traditional military lament for the fallen, and rifle shots were fired in a final salute.

Gardelegen

▲ Before the American army had left Gardelegen, the war crimes inquiry quickly concluded, it commissioned and erected a large and damning memorial plaque, in English and German. That plaque was removed as the Red Army occupied Gardelegen on July 1, 1945 with the town merged into the Soviet occupation zone. On site now is a replica of that original that had been dumped in a local shed for decades.

▲ On the day of the ceremony, April 25, Gardelegen's suitably attired residents had filed solemnly to Isenschnibbe. The top-hatted Pastor Friedrich Franz on the left had risked his life to save four prisoners.
Source: Karl-Heinz Reuschel

233

count now close to 2,000 but given Allied straffing it now headed east towards Berlin and Sachsenhausen. Enroute was Gardelegen.

With the Stendal railway hub blocked, both trains unloaded at Mieste railway station much to the anguish of Adolf Krüger, its SS bürgermeister. In urgent phone calls to his opposite number in Gardelegen, acting mayor Karl Leppe, Krüger demanded that only Gardelegen had resources to take them.

A third train had arrived in the Gardelegen area, this one halting at Letzlingen station, 12km south-west of the town, on April 11. It, too, was enroute to Sachsenhausen and it carried between 1,000 and 1,200 prisoners from four camps near Dora: Mackenrode, Nüxei, Wieda and Osterhagen. In command of this train was SS-Scharführer Kemmnitz, a sergeant from Wieda.

Workers from these four camps had constructed the Helmetalbahn railway line to Nordhausen. Wieda, a small collection of huts nestling in a scenic valley at the edge of a stream, housed not only inmates but the SS construction administration block and at one stage up to 100 prisoners worked in the well-stocked SS kitchens. The Luftwaffe provided guards for the camps and conditions were lenient but in July 1944 the SS took over, marching the entire workforce to Dora and replacing it with a new contingent, mainly Poles, Russians and French.

In Mieste and Letzlingen stations, prisoners were dying or being shot if attempting escape. The locals desperately wanted them gone. Volkssturm, Hitler Youth and farmers hunted them down. Unable to cope, the SS camp guards were joined by a Fallschirmjager unit, Luftwaffe paratroopers based close to Gardelegen. A trench was dug outside Mieste station to dump bodies.[3]

An Allied fighter attack on Mieste station was the catalyst to evacuate. Mass execution had been considered but rejected given the impracticality of killing such a large number in the station vicinity. Those who could walk were split into groups, the rest were left to die in the train wagons or killed by the paratroopers and SS. Avoiding

---

[3] There is a memorial at Mieste, simply engraved '13.4.1945' to commemorate the death march and the 80 or so who died or who were executed here.

the open road to Gardelegen, the prisoners and guards trudged through the fields and woods. Brauny and Teply had assumed overall command of the march directly east from Mieste to Gardelegen. Bodies littered the route, mainly in the villages of Wernitz and Solpke. Another group went north of Mieste in a loop to Gardelegen. Here, too, the bodies piled up with multiple shootings in Breitenfeld, Zichtau and Berge. The largest massacre took place in the village of Estedt. In the woods behind its railway station, Luftwaffe paratroopers had ordered 104 escapees to dig three trenches, their graves. The US army would only discover this killing ground on May 12 after a tip-off from a Polish worker. The local bürgermeister was ordered to call up all able-bodied villagers to disinter them.

The Volkssturm of Kloster Neuendorf, a neighbouring village of Gardelegen, had also seen action, rounding up escapees in the forest to the south-east of the town. Arno Brake, a 44-year-old lumberjack, and Wilhelm Biermann, a 49-year-old musician, will eventually pay with their own lives for committing war crimes. Two Slovak escapees were found by the Volkssturm and taken to the command post at Forsthaus Lindenthal, a house in pre-war days in a much-favoured area popular with holidaymakers. The musician knew his orders. The Slovaks were summarily executed.

PANIC IN GARDELEGEN

Gardelegen was awash with rumour that it was shortly to be swamped with marching häftlingen – up to 2,000 camp prisoners deemed rapists, looters and murderers. Gerhard Thiele, the 34-year-old Kreisleiter, took charge ordering Rittmeister Josef-Rudolf Kuhn, the cavalry master sergeant in charge of the now-empty Remonteschule, the cavalry barracks, to make ready. Attached were stables and a large parade area. Regarded as one of the biggest and most modern of the Wehrmacht's riding schools, the army had vacated the site just days earlier.

At Letzlingen station, the condition of the 1,200 prisoners held in the train had worsened by the day. Kemmnitz with a group of 600 struck out for the Elbe to the south-east and the remainder were left to fend for themselves as all the SS guards had deserted. The village of Dolle witnessed a massacre as its inhabitants took exception to häftlingen in their village. Local Volkssturm, aided by townspeople, rounded up 66 prisoners and shot them down. This mass grave would only be uncovered in 1949. In the village of Javenitz, more had been shot, and survivors were marched into Gardelegen. Some would return to Javenitz and avoid the burning of the barn.

In the weeks before the Americans moved out of Gardelegen and before the Red Army occupied the town in the first week of July, three officers in the US Ninth Army War Crimes unit arrived to conduct an investigation: Lt. Colonel Edward Cruise, Lt. Colonel William Callanan and Captain Samuel Weiss. Initially these investigators came up against a bulwark of silence but the team persisted, conducting 99 interviews in the short time it had.

Thiele was quickly acknowledged by investigators to have been the architect of the atrocity, working closely with Rudolf Jordan, Magdeburg's district SS gauleiter, who had already given the blanket order that escaping häftlingen on the marches to Gardelegen had to be shot on sight. Further approval was solicited from the three Ortsgrüppenleiters, senior officers in Gardelegen's Volkssturm. Hans Debrodt, a civilian financial administrator in his day job, Waldemar Schumm and Otto Palis saw no difficulty in the employment of the town's part-time soldiers. Karl Lepa, Gardelegen's acting bürgermeister, and Rudolf Ringstmeyer, the town's police chief, had also bought into Thiele's plan for mass execution.

Cord von Einem, the chief of the Fallschirmjager, the Luftwaffe paratroopers, was additionally supportive but his opposite number at the Luftwaffe airfield, Colonel Walter Miltz, dissented, arguing that the prisoners should remain in the Remonteschule for the Americans to find and look after.

In the early hours of Thursday, April 12, the Remonteschule was choked with starving and sick prisoners and in the hours to come, Thiele repeatedly told Kuhn that the Remonteschule was the ideal execution site given its size. Kuhn suggested an alternative: a barn large enough to hold all the häftlingen on the Isenschnibbe forest estate outside the town. Reluctantly, Thiele had ordered a local lad to cycle over and reconnoitre whether it was empty.

That evening, Thiele confirmed to Kuhn that the barn was indeed suitable. According to the US war crimes investigators, 'Kuhn couldn't find Brauny so he passed the order to Brauny's deputy, Friedrich Teply, but advising him to get the order in writing.' Of the elusive Brauny there was no sign but reportedly he had shared his reservations on Thiele's plan to Debrodt, one of the Volkssturm commanders. Thiele had telephoned Debrodt from his home around midnight and on hearing Brauny's reluctance, he reacted angrily. Thiele had exclaimed, 'if the convoy commander won't do it, hang him.'

Thiele still couldn't locate Brauny the following day, Friday, April 13. A rumour had spread that he had fled Gardelegen on a bicycle, destination unknown. Thiele had to move quickly, the arrival of the US army was imminent.

THE LAST WALK

It was 6pm when the prisoners were ordered to assemble on the Remonteschule's parade ground in three groups, the prisoners duped into believing they were being marched off to yet another location. Those unable to walk were loaded onto wagons: some were shot. Thiele had assembled 80 assorted military: 30 SS camp guards, 30 Luftwaffe paratroopers and 20 from the Volkssturm and Hitler Youth.

With Brauny absent, Teply led out the first group through the gates onto Bismarker Strasse and facing was the municipal cemetery: a portent of what was to come. The other two columns followed. Residents would have witnessed these long columns of starving and emaciated prisoners in their striped clothing trudging through their streets.

It took about an hour for the groups to converge at the large bricked barn at Isenschnibbe, then as now, in an area of ploughed lowland. The sick on the wagons were carried or dragged inside by the prisoner Kapos and at gunpoint the rest were herded in to sit amongst the gasoline-soaked bales. The realisation and panic must have been unimaginable as the large wooden doors, set on runners, were slid shut and locked. With Thiele looking on, a door was then slid slightly ajar and the 16-year-old SS-Unterscharführer Braun, a section leader guard from Dora-Mittelbau's Ilfeld satellite camp, threw in a lit rag… laughing as he did so. The door was then closed and the machine-gunners waited for any breakout. A number of the Kapos were now shot dead by the SS.

Beating out the first fire, the prisoners were powerless as the guards entered again this time firing signal flares into the bales, setting the barn fully ablaze. Some Russians succeeded in beating down a door on the north side but were gunned down. Hand grenades were thrown inside to swell the flames and the Luftwaffe paratroopers added their own firepower piercing the walls with panzerfausts, their antitank weapons. Any part of the body that did appear under the doors or walls was riddled with bullets.

There was an unexpected witness.

Observing from a distance was Dr Friedrich Herwig, a 76-year-old senior warden in the huge Gardelegen forest reserve adjacent to Isenschnibbe. He also had a license to hunt. Hearing intermittent shots and seeing rising smoke, Herwig had ventured closer and he immediately recognised Waldemar Schumm, one of the Volkssturm officers. Alarmed, Schumm, a friend, came over. When others aggressively waved at Herwig to turn around he fled the scene.

At 10pm, the paratroopers were stood down at the barn and they returned to their local base.

Thiele had already departed and in his office in the Kreisleitung he was quickly on the phone, he hadn't done.

THE COVER UP

In the early hours of Saturday, April 14, the same day that the 405th Regiment of the US 102nd Infantry would arrive in Gardelegen, the barn continued to smoulder. The smell of fire and death must have permeated the air for some distance around, maybe even drifting into the town. During the night some of the SS guards had deserted.

Thiele had summoned up more assistance for what he had in mind. Kloster Neuendorf's Volkssturm had joined their Gardelegen counterparts. Rallying to the cause were members of the Technische Nothilfe, the uniformed paramilitary organisation responsible for the security of vital public services, and the 15 members of Gardelegen's fire service. In all, Thiele had assembled 170 men. Drums of petrol from the Kreisleitung garage had been conveyed onsite at 3am. Thiele knew that if captured the Allies would call him to account. The bodies had to be buried and incinerated.

As dawn broke the barn doors were slid open. Prisoners had died where they had crawled, their bodies roasted. Thiele's men cautiously stepped inside, their first task to execute anyone still living. Needing no encouragement, the Kapos relished the task still aiming to please their SS masters who might grant them freedom. One, Kazimierz Drygalski, a Polish Jew, had no qualms in finishing off those who cried out for mercy. Some prisoners had climbed the rafters in a bid to avoid the flames. Schernikau, the fire chief, shot a survivor dead to encourage his wary firemen to do the same. Gustav Palis, a member of Gardelegen's Volkssturm, also had reservations, but Pannwitz, a schoolteacher who taught art, had no such misgivings.

With an acute awareness that the American army was now close, the digging of the four trenches on two sides of the barn took on some urgency. According to the US army record, 586 of the still smouldering dead had been pulled outside by Thiele's men and dumped in them before word had come through that the US army had been seen in Estedt only 8km away and an advance unit had called on Gardelegen's military to surrender. Thiele never had time to use his petrol to incinerate the bodies. He left the scene: so did everyone else. The Volkssturm returned to their day jobs, keeping their heads down.

It was dark when Arno Brake, the professional lumberjack in Kloster Neuendorf's Volkssturm, left his home with his rifle. At the barn he would later record that 'he heard a groan' and 'there was a bad smell'. He never admitted to killing survivors but he did admit being at the scene with a spade to help in the digging of trenches. When he got home he spent the rest of the day in bed and never related to his wife what he had done.

Some hours had passed before the Luftwaffe colonel, Walter Miltz, as the senior German officer in the Gardelegen area, appeared punctually at the agreed time of 7pm on the Estedt road. White flags flew from his staff car and his motorcycle escort. Miltz surrendered all military to the 405th Regiment and his vehicles guided the Americans into Gardelegen with white flags appearing outside the homes. The military had already neatly stacked its weapons. Miltz

▲ The Remonteschule in Bismarker Strasse had housed the prisoners in its square and stables before they were marched off in three columns to Isenschnibbe. This empty cavalry riding school, one of the biggest and most modern in the Wehrmacht, looked after by Rittmeister Josef-Rudolf Kuhn, the cavalry sergeant, was the intended execution site but Kuhn suggested to Gerhard Thiele, the Kreisleiter, that the Isenschnibbe barn was a more suitable choice.

▲ As WW2 ended and the Cold War cast its long shadow, the hard line diktat that prevailed in East Germany memorialized the Gardelegen dead through a political not a compassionate lens. With the exception of one wall, the Isenschnibbe barn was demolished in 1953 and each year local communist party apparatchiks, townspeople and Gardelegen's young had walked solemnly to the site. The young placed flowers at the foot of each headstone. Isenschnibbe had become an official memorial to honour the victims as Communist resistance against the Nazis: a victory over fascism.

◀ Inside what is left of the barn after it was dismantled.

▶ Another massacre had taken place in nearby Estedt. In the woods behind its railway station, Luftwaffe paratroopers had ordered 104 escapees to dig three trenches, their graves. The US army would only discover this killing ground on May 12 after a tip-off from a Polish worker. The local bürgermeister was ordered to call up all able-bodied villagers to disinter them.

◄ SS Kreisleiter Gerhard Thiele had disappeared. Now masquerading as a Wehrmacht soldier he was picked up and held by the Americans, who were none the wiser to who was in its custody. Let go in 1946, and using the alias of Gerhard Lindemann, he worked in a number of jobs in several West German cities including Karlsruhe, Cologne and Düsseldorf. Despite the East German authorities knowing full well of Thiele's role at Gardelegen, little or no attempt was made to inform the West Germans who were seemingly ambivalent. There was an investigation of sorts in 1961 by the Munich Court of Justice but it went nowhere as co-operation between East and West Germany broke down. The case against Thiele reappeared in 1997 - some 52 years after the event - and only then did it emerge that Thiele had died in Düsseldorf on June 30, 1994, aged 85.

◄ Magdeburg's SS district Gauleiter, Rudolf Jordan, who gave his authorisation to kill the prisoners, had earlier given the blanket order that escaping häftlingen on the marches to Gardelegen had to be shot on sight.

◄ Kazimierz Drygalski, the 22-year-old Pole, was one prisoner Kapo seen finishing off barn survivors.

► Erhard Brauny, the Rottleberode camp leader who had played a key role in the marches to Gardelegen, was to be the sole member of the SS ever probed about the Isenschnibbe atrocity in an American war crimes court. He was in US custody and provided testimony in the Nordhausen/Dora-Mittelbau element of the Dachau Trials. Under questioning, he was asked about the Gardelegen massacre but Brauny fended it away saying he had left the town before it happened. No one could contradict that statement.

► Brauny is second on the left in this photograph of the Dora accused.

had refrained from mentioning the events that had taken place in Isenschnibbe in the past 24 hours.

The American army only uncovered the horror at Isenschnibbe the following morning, Monday, April 15, and in the memories of several 405th Regiment soldiers, it had been Lt. Jim Hansen who made the discovery purely by accident. Hansen had ventured into another part of the town in his jeep and after a nasty confrontation with an SS colonel, who hadn't bought into the Miltz surrender, he saw smoke rising in the distance.

Soldiers quickly descended on Isenschnibbe including an army doctor. Somehow seven prisoners had survived and some were later able to provide first-hand accounts despite their condition. Geza Bondi, a former lieutenant in the Hungarian army, who had been incarcerated at Flossenbürg, Dora-Mittelbau and its Ilfield satellite, had successfully dug underneath the barn and somehow crawled away unnoticed. Bondi had been on the train brought to a halt at Mieste station. Georges Cretin, one of four French survivors, had hidden under piles of bodies. When found, the Americans took him to the hospital on the Luftwaffe airfield. Two Polish survivors, Wlodzimierz Wozny and Eugenius Siradzki, shared their experiences. Wozny was on the Letzlingen train. A former medical student and inmate of the Lublin Ghetto and Buchenwald before Wieda, he had escaped through one of the barn doors, avoided being shot and ran for his life. Siradzki, like Cretin, had hidden under bodies. He had been in Gross-Rosen, Dora-Mittelbau and Ilfield and was on the Mieste train.

HUMANITARIAN EFFORTS

Brigitte Franz, the 14-year-old daughter of Pastor Friedrich Franz, had grown accustomed to low-flying American aircraft over the town. In the Pfarrhaus, the church rectory, her room was on the top floor, and vulnerable, so her father moved her into a room downstairs next to the front door. When bombs had rained down on Gardelegen on March 15, 1945, the church took a direct hit. The roofs had collapsed leaving it a ruin.[4] The Pfarrhaus was unscathed.

There were some in Gardelegen, none more so than Pastor Franz and his family, who restored a level of humanity amidst the slaughter at great risk to themselves. Forever etched in Brigitte's memory was the day that she joined the residents column to Isenschnibbe, under US army escort, with sheets and tablecloths to shroud the dead. In the years after the war, Brigitte had married a Scotsman and they set up home in South Africa. Brigitte died in November 2018, just six months after what was to be her final visit to Gardelegen to visit old school chums. During that trip she had related in significant detail how her parents had shielded four Dutchmen, who had escaped from one of the death marches into Gardelegen, subsequently sparing them from almost certain death in Isenschnibbe. It is a warming account of a family that had put their own lives on the line to save others.

One march from Mieste railway station had taken a circuitous route, approaching Gardelegen from the north-west. Outside the village of Ackendorf, five Dutchmen slipped away, hid in a ditch and waited for darkness. When they thought it was safe to do so, the Dutchmen took to the road and sought out the churches in the hope that one might offer shelter from the SS.

Their first encounter might have led to recapture and almost certain execution if the authorities were called. From his doorway, Pastor Friedrich Liederwald, one of many in Germany's clergy who as a 'Deutsche Christen' actively collaborated with Nazi ideology and its objective to totally exclude Jews from the German nation to the extent of eradicating any mention of the Jewish faith in a rewritten Old Testament. Liederwald had sent them packing. Reduced by one, and nothing is known of his subsequent fate, the group knocked on the door of the Pfarrhaus, behind the Church of St. Nikolaus.

Awoken by the knocking, Brigitte opened it, noticing the growing brightness in the east. First light was not far off. She saw four frightened, emaciated and hungry men. Her father quickly appeared. Grasping the situation, the pastor peered cautiously around to ensure no one was watching before he ushered them inside. Brigitte was told to return to her room and stay put. Later in the morning, the inquisitive girl asked her father what the men had

---

[4] The Church of St. Nikolaus was built in 1196. The Bell Tower was restored in 1991 but the rest remains a ruin.

wanted to which he replied 'they just asked for directions'. It didn't take long for Brigitte to discover the truth but at the time she didn't realise the significance of the actions of her parents. Harbouring häftlingen could incur the death penalty. There was even the real possibility that the three children, Brigitte was the middle one, might also suffer punishment.

The pastor led the four Dutchmen, one of whom was the 62-year-old Mathieu Lambert van Geen, the respected mayor of Putten in the Netherlands before his arrest by the Gestapo in 1941, into the kitchen to be introduced to his wife who immediately prepared tea and food. Before they ate, the four knelt down in thanks and to pray for their rescue. Ravenous, they ate quickly. The pastor now led them to the rear of the Pfarrhaus and to the barn beyond, the home of the family pig, 'Julante', that was looked after by the children. Above Julante was a platform where straw was stored, an ideal hiding place. Brigitte sensed something was up when she and a sister were barred from the barn to do their regular chores, their father attending the pig.[5] After the US army entered Gardelegen and commandeered the Rathaus as its headquarters, Pastor Franz had relinquished his charges into its safety.

An accountant in Gardelegen's hospital had also aided escaped prisoners. For years Pastor Franz had been very grateful to Otto Wendt for contributing free bookkeeping services to the church as his own such abilities were poor at best. On April 12, Wendt had cycled into the forest to collect firewood and as he dismounted he noticed a fearful face staring at him in the undergrowth. An emaciated man appeared in striped clothing, followed by three others. They were French and Wendt didn't understand a word. In sign language he did manage to tell them to stay put. Returning home, Wendt mugged up on some basic French before he set off with food and drink. He would cycle into the forest several times over the next three days, taking blankets on some occasions. Once Gardelegen was fully occupied by the Americans Wendt led his group out of the forest. They, too, had been spared the Isenschnibbe charnel house.

---

[5] Julante was eventually slaughtered to feed the family given the hardship that prevailed in Gardelegen as the war ended.

▲ The humanitarian pastor, Dr Friedrich Franz, with his wife in Gardelegen.
Source: Karl-Heinz Reuschel

ALERTING THE WORLD'S PRESS

Within hours of the discovery, US Army Signal Corps photographers arrived to document the war crime. Word had already reached General Eisenhower and he insisted on full public exposure. In the course of the next few days, the bodies were left *in situ*, exposed and unburied. GI's were encouraged to come to Isenschnibbe and see the scale of the horror for themselves, and hundreds did.

One of those, Sergeant Fred Strauss, recorded in 2011 that he had photographed what he witnessed with a camera found on his regiment's advance across Germany. 'I remember taking a picture of this man who had tried to dig himself out of the blaze from under the blazing barn. Only his hand and head were sticking out and the Germans had shot him in the forehead. He had died on the spot'.

Gardelegen had been long seared into the wartime memory of Henry Skwirut, a radio operator and driver in the 406th Regiment. He, too, had picked up a German camera and used it regularly, sending photographs of his war to his wife in East Orange, New Jersey. Skwirut had heard over his radio that the 405th was working on a war crimes site. With a sergeant, and his camera, he drove over to Gardelegen to see for himself. Reminiscing in the *Tampa Bay Times* in 2013, Skwirut stated "'I'll never forget it. The smell of burning flesh was horrible and bodies were everywhere'". Skwirut had sent the 25 Gardelegen photographs home and a note to his wife to keep them safe and never show them to anyone. Retired with his wife in Florida, his three adult children were unaware of their existence until just a few years before his death in 2017, aged 96. Why had Henry never shown the photographs, except to his wife? He had informed the *Tampa Bay Times* readers that "'they were not the kind of photos you show to people.'"

Associated Press, the wire service, had posted its story on April 18 and *The New York Times* ran it the next day, its headline 'Americans seize murderer of 1,000' but it didn't name Thiele as the 'German ringleader' in custody. That 'ringleader' couldn't have been Thiele who was masquerading as a Wehrmacht soldier with a new identity in a US detainment camp, some distance from Gardelegen. The *New York Times* report was short and it also included the news that the

British had liberated Belsen. *The Washington Post*, too, carried the Gardelegen story. In Britain, its press had focussed on Belsen with British Pathé vividly relaying this German abomination directly into the cinema.

The day that *Associated Press* had wired its story, the US army rounded up every bürgermeister and anyone else in authority from all the villages, assembling them in front of the Rathaus in Gardelegen's market place. With a tank in the rear, the column walked to Isenschnibbe and forced to view what had been committed on the town's behalf. Over the next few days, the able-bodied were marched out with spades to clear the barn of bodies, disinter those that Thiele's men had slung into the four trenches and to dig seven parallel trenches in an area designated as the burial site. There was a report that on one occasion, GIs had lined up some men against a wall of the barn in a mock execution. The US army film unit covered the residents forced march to Isenschnibbe, each man carrying a cross: 'Unbekannte' – unknown – was the inscription. The decision had been taken to bury the dead individually and not in a mass grave.

SALUTING THE DEAD

The column of townspeople, suitably attired given the occasion, stretched into the distance on April 25 as it now ambled to Isenschnibbe. With the troops maintaining a wary eye and the film unit recording this final salute to the dead, the service of commemoration began. Church leaders mourned the victims, as did the chaplain of the US Ninth Army. In his speech, Colonel George Lynch, the battalion commander of the 102nd Infantry, barely suppressed his loathing.

'The German people have been told that stories of German atrocities were Allied propaganda. Here, you can see for yourself. Some will say that the Nazis were responsible for this crime. Others will point to the Gestapo. The responsibility rests with neither – it is the responsibility of the German people.

'Your so-called Master Race has demonstrated that it is a master only of crime, cruelty and sadism.'

Standing amongst the headstones, an American bugler sounded

▲ *Then:* The Pfarrhaus, or rectory, connected to the Church of St. Nikolaus.
Source: Karl-Heinz Reuschel

▲ And now.
Source: Karl-Heinz Reuschel

▲ Then: The building behind the Pfarrhaus where Pastor Friedrich Franz hid his escapees, sharing it with the family pig.
Source: Karl-Heinz Reuschel

▲ And now.
Source: Karl-Heinz Reuschel

▶ Gardelegen was long seared into the wartime memory of Henry Skwirut, a radio operator and driver in the 406th Regiment. Skwirut had sent 25 photographs he took of Isenschnibbe to his wife and asked her to keep them safe and never show them to anyone. His family was unaware of their existence until just a few years before his death in 2017, aged 96. Why had Henry never shown the photographs, except to his wife? He had informed the readers of the Tampa Bay Times in Florida, where he lived, that "'they were not the kind of photos you show to people.'"

▼ Before the American army had left Gardelegen, the war crimes inquiry quickly concluded, it commissioned and erected a large and damning memorial plaque, in English and German. That plaque was removed as the Red Army occupied Gardelegen on July 1, 1945 with the town merged into the Soviet occupation zone. On site now is a replica of that original that had been dumped in a local shed for decades.

Jhr. M. L. VAN GEEN
met ingang van 1 Oct. a.s. benoemd
tot burgemeester der gemeente Putten

Uitgave Nieuwsblad voor Stad en Land
Nijk. VA. (Uitg. Nolpit)
Agentschap Putten W. Aberbergen

▲ Mathieu Lambert van Geen, one of the Dutchmen hidden by Pastor Franz, had been the mayor of Putten in the Netherlands.

'Taps', the traditional military lament for the fallen, and rifle shots were fired in a final salute. Of the 1,016 dead only an initial four could be named and for some others a prisoner number was recorded. In all, 586 bodies had been exhumed from the trenches and 430 recovered in the barn. In later weeks more bodies were brought in, escapees from the Letzlingen train. In the years to come, only 305 victims were ever identified: mainly Russian, French, Dutch and Belgian. One was from Mexico. Not all were Jewish.

In a radio broadcast from US-held Luxembourg, a captured senior Wehrmacht officer sought to absolve the army from any blame at Gardelegen. Brigadier-General Kirstheim stated 'in the present situation no German soldier must feel bound by an oath of allegiance and those who are still in doubt must be persuaded by the news from Buchenwald and Gardelegen. The German army is not guilty of these murders. No German general knew anything about them'. Kirstheim also pleaded to Field-Marshal Keitel, as head of the German High Command, to include the Volkssturm, who he referred to as 'military amateurs', in any military surrender.

The full graphic horror of Gardelegen appeared in the May 7th edition of *Time Life* magazine, headlined 'The Holocaust of Gardelegen'. In the short time the American army had before Gardelegen was to become part of the Soviet zone, the three war crimes investigators concluded their examination and a pamphlet was published on the slaughter.

LACK OF A TRIAL

Of Kreisleiter Gerhard Thiele there was no sign. Thiele, like so many SS, had opted for the comparative anonymity of a Wehrmacht uniform and ID in his escape. Gardelegen's Wehrmacht recruitment officer, Major Stobbe, had provided Thiele with a false identity in the name of Gerhard Lindemann. The US interrogators would extensively interview Rosemarie, his wife, but she proved unhelpful. In the 1960s, prosecutors in Magdeburg and Göttingen did try and determine Thiele's whereabouts with regard to a trial but both attempts reached a dead end. Thiele had been held in an American holding camp but his new ID, and luck, held and he was eventually let go in 1946.

Moving west, Thiele travelled in and out of the British and American occupation zones. Rosemarie claimed in 1970 that the last time she saw him was on April 14, 1945, when she kissed him goodbye outside their home at Stendaler Strasse 89 in Gardelegen but rumours persisted that they had kept in touch long afterwards. Thiele, the architect of Gardelegen's charnel house, had escaped accountability and justice, dying in Düsseldorf in 1994, aged 85.

In the time it had before Gardelegen became part of the Soviet occupation zone, the US interrogation team had conducted 99 interviews. Two of the first to be arrested, Otto Palis, a Volkssturm officer, and Dr Hintze, a member of the town's Kreisleitung, committed suicide in custody. In all, 28 were arrested including 13 Kapos and four members of Thiele's Kreisleitung staff. Of Gardelegen's Volkssturm, nine were in custody, including the manager of the local flourmill, a schoolteacher, a cattle merchant, and two butchers. The Americans had rounded up 10 Kapos, the prisoners who had been armed by the SS at the barn.

Kazimierz Drygalski, the 22-year-old Pole, was one prisoner Kapo seen finishing off survivors. In a US photograph, several captured Kapos sit in the Rathaus with an investigator. On the floor, lying on his front, Edward Antoniak, a survivor, demonstrates how he had feigned death before pointing an outstretched arm towards Drygalski. Another photograph has Drygalski leaning on the bonnet of a US jeep. Josef Pamuta never confessed to any culpability and he was let go. On the 20th anniversary, Pamuta, with four other Poles, either barn survivors or death march escapees, visited Isenschnibbe but his backstory was never revealed. One of the worst of the Kapo killers, according to Aurel Szobel, a 26-year-old Hungarian survivor, had been the German concentration camp inmate, Adolph Pinnenkämper. Most of the named 39 SS guards were never located. Assessing the culpability of Rittmeister Kuhn, the sergeant in charge of the Wehrmacht cavalry stables, was never satisfactorily determined as he repeatedly changed his account on the role he had played in the decision to kill the prisoners but absolving himself on any blame.

The Gardelegen war crime investigation posed a major logistical difficulty for the American legal authorities, which intended rolling all such enquiries into one central trial location – termed the Dachau

Trials. US troops had liberated Dachau, Flossenbürg, Mauthausen, Nordhausen/Dora-Mittelbau, Buchenwald and Mühldorf, and all were in the American occupation zone. With Gardelegen now in the Soviet zone and with little co-operation expected, the decision was taken to exclude this particular war crime. When the Dachau Trials did open in November 1945, 1,672 individuals were charged and after 489 separate proceedings that ended in August 1948, 1,416 had been convicted of which 297 were sentenced to death. A large number received life sentences.

With no trial, the Americans handed over most of their files to the Russians, who conducted a military tribunal in August 1946. Long sentences were handed out but in 1950 the East German authorities assumed responsibility of the convicted. Two members of the Kloster Neuendorf Volkssturm, Wilhelm Biermann and Arno Brake, were subsequently executed in 1951. Where and how they were buried became a controversial issue several decades later.[6] Gustav Palis, a Gardelegen Volkssturm officer, would also be executed.

Rudolf Ringstmeyer, Gardelegen's chief of police, a member of the senior coterie that had supported Thiele, was released in East Germany and he moved to Bielefeld in West Germany in 1960 to again assume a police job. His role in the Gardelegen massacre was questioned in 1961 and his denials of any culpability were accepted.

Erhard Brauny, the Rottleberode camp leader who had played a key role in the marches to Gardelegen, was to be the sole member of the SS ever probed about the Isenschnibbe atrocity in an American war crimes court. He was in US custody and provided testimony in the Nordhausen/Dora-Mittelbau element of the Dachau Trials. Under questioning, he was asked about the Gardelegen massacre but Brauny fended it away saying he had left the town before it happened. No one could contradict that statement.

---

[6] After execution, their ashes were placed in unnamed urns in a part of the Gertrauden-Friedhof cemetery in Halle that held the remains of 117 dead or executed between 1950 and 1953 in the notorious Fort Zinna jail in Torgau. During the war, Fort Jinna had housed prisoners convicted by the Reich's military courts with large numbers executed in a gravel pit near the prison or in the moat on the north side of the castle. Only in 2004 did the relatives of Brake and Biermann discover the existence of the urns.

'THESE ARE THE PEOPLE OF GERMANY'

Henry Swann, the US army doctor who had attended the handful of barn survivors, expressed no ambivalence in determining where the culpability lay in an emotional letter home to his wife: 'The people of Germany', he wrote.[7] Swann named the SS Kreisleiter but he equally attributed blame to the Volkssturm.

Swann described the event.

'At the barn some prisoners had been asked if they could fire a rifle. Some said they could. These they stood in a line about 15 yards from the barn, with Volkssturm and SS standing behind them with pistols in their ribs. The rest of the prisoners were herded into the barn. Some refused to go, knowing what was in store. These were shot. Then the big wooden doors were slid shut. The ones with rifles were ordered to start shooting through the doors. The machine guns began to rattle. Some bazookas were fired through the walls. A 16-year-old boy threw a burning faggot through a hole in the wall. The straw began to burn, and soon inside was an inferno – then the prisoners who had had the rifles[8] were shot in the back of the head.

'I went out to the barn and it was a sight to banish sleep. Emaciated bodies, twisted in grotesque shapes. Some charred, others just blackened by the smoke. Piled on top of each other, four, five, ten deep, especially near the doors and corners. One had dug with his hands a pit in the dirt of the doorway just enough so he could get his face out – struggling to get air to breathe! The agony is frozen on his face. Some had others in their arms, as if to protect them. One oldish man was just a head on a body. The legs and arms were burned right off.

'It seems hard to believe, but several people lived to come out of the barn alive. One lay unconscious under a pile of bodies until Sunday. They are in an evacuation hospital near the town. I have seen them and talked with them through an interpreter. They will probably survive.

'Gardelegen is a county seat, a rural town of about 20-25,000

---

[7] The letter, dated April 21, 1945, is held in the US National Library of Medicine.
[8] Swann is referring to the Kapos who helped push the prisoners into the barn.

people and 25 miles to the north of Magdeburg. It is a farming community and almost 100% Nazi. These are the people of Germany. These are the men, and women, and boys, who could burn alive over one thousand, sick, and starving men!

'This is only one incident, apparently. There are others on a much vaster scale elsewhere.

'That doesn't seem possible, does it? But don't be deceived. These are the German people in their naked brutality.

'Let as many people as possible see this letter. Let them know, and try to understand. Let them remember this when they talk about the peace to come. When the time of retribution and punishment of war guilt arrives, let them visualise that barn in Gardelegen on the afternoon of Friday, April 13.'

POSTSCRIPT

An extraordinary story emerged post-war on whether Colonel Lynch, the battalion commander of the US 102nd Infantry, had threatened to shoot 200 local men and raze public buildings to the ground, such was his disgust to what he and his men had witnessed. Feelings had certainly run high as the bodies were deliberately left *in situ* for several days to be viewed and photographed by the American press. Eisenhower had used Isenschnibbe as a photo opportunity to starkly portray back home in America the horrors that the Allies were uncovering.

Kloster Neuendorf historian, Karl-Heinz Reuschel, has extensively researched into the massacre and believes the threat story is compelling after speaking to Brigitte Thompson when she visited from South Africa to see her old school chums. Reuschel also travelled to the Netherlands to interview a close friend of Mathieu Lambert van Geen, one of the Dutchmen hidden in the barn behind the rectory.

Pastor Franz had already visited Lynch in his Rathaus office but on this occasion the visit had urgency. On his knees, the pastor had impassionedly pleaded with Lynch to rescind his execution threat but that act of fealty failed to sway the US commander, runs the account. Pastor Franz wasn't done. He now enlisted the support from van Geen, who had endured four years of Nazi captivity and torture in Neuengamme and its satellite camps. What van Geen articulated to Lynch proved to be a powerful testament as to the respective disciplines of Allied and German armies. "Taking revenge on civilians is an act only conducted by German soldiers", expressed van Geen, "American and Dutch soldiers are respectful and would never conduct themselves in such a way".

This 62-year-old Dutchman is remembered by some as 'the man who had saved Gardelegen', an epitaph difficult to swallow amongst others in the town affronted that a Jewish concentration camp inmate is accorded that accreditation.

If van Geen had had access two weeks later to the May 1 edition of *The New York Times*, he might have revised that opinion on the behaviour of US troops. The headline ran 'Dachau captured by Americans who kill guards, liberate 32,200'. Dachau concentration camp, 10km outside Munich, had been liberated and so shocked were the US troops they embarked on their own orgy of mass execution. Estimates of the SS dead ranged from 300 to more than 500.

A US doctor in the 116th Evacuation Hospital, Captain David Wilsey, had witnessed the killings. When the family home was cleared in 2008, a collection of 280 letters and photographs was discovered in a trunk, detailing Wilsey's war. The SS guards had been made to stand for hours with both arms raised high above their heads before they were gunned down against a wall in the camp. In his letter home to Emily, his wife, Wilsey had written that the swift justice meted out was necessary 'because they had it coming'.

A photograph exists of the executions.

THE GARDELEGEN KILLING GROUNDS

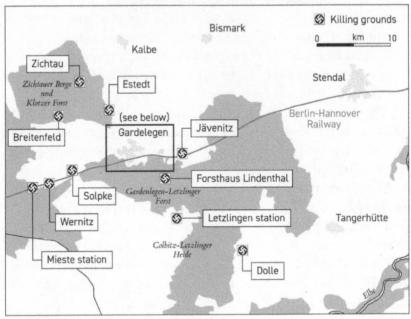

Gardelegen - on the railway line to the Stendal hub

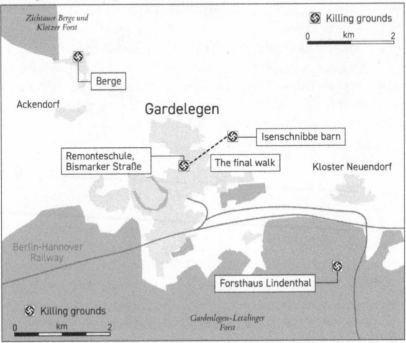

STORY CHARACTERS: AFTERMATH

★ Biermann, Wilhelm: A member of the Kloster Neuendorf Volkssturm, he was handed over by the Americans to the Soviet authorities and stood trial with others on March 28, 1947. Russia subsequently handed over a group convicted for the Gardelegen war crime to the East German authorities in 1950. He was executed in November 1951.

★ Brake, Arno: Another member of the Kloster Neuendorf Volkssturm and handed back to East German authorities. He was executed in April 1951.

★ Braun, SS-Unterscharführer: This 16-year-old section leader from the Ilfeld satellite camp, who laughed when he started the fire in the barn, was never found after the war.

★ Brauny, SS-Lagerführer Erhard: On the run and wearing a Wehrmacht uniform, the Americans picked him up. The Soviets also questioned him. In the trial of Dora-Mittlebau commandants during the Dachau trials, Brauny was questioned over Gardelegen but he denied any culpability in the massacre as he had supposedly fled the town before it happened. Given a life imprisonment over his actions at Rottleberode, his life was cut short by leukaemia and he died in Landsberg jail in June 1950, aged 46.

★ Drygalski, Kazimierz: This Polish Kapo was among the group handed back by the Soviet authorities. He quickly disappeared.

★ Holtz, Hermann: Volkssturm member who disappeared in 1955, after he with others were handed back to the East German authorities.

★ Jordan, Gauleiter Rudolf: He was tried by a Soviet court and sentenced to 25 years in the Gulag. His release in 1955 was part of the amnesty agreed by Adenauer and Khrushchev. Jordan died in Munich in October 1988, aged 86.

★ Klebeck, SS-Hauptsturmführer Kurt: Shortly after he had arrived at Bergen-Belsen, upon leaving the Stöcken-Hannover camp, he was arrested with Theodor Breuning, another SS officer, for disobeying SS orders. A Gestapo judge tried them. After being investigated by the British War Crimes Group while being held in Hamburg-Fuhlsbüttel prison, Klebeck was sentenced to 10 years in September 1947 for his actions at Stöcken-Hannover, and released after five. An SS colleague, Roland Puhr, who had worked with Klebeck in Sachsenhausen and Alderney, defended him in August 1963 stating that there was no truth in Klebeck deliberately starving prisoners to death. 'I often saw him bringing in food in suitcases into the camps', said Puhr. A Hamburg court in 1970 charged Klebeck with executing 125 Jews in Belarus and he was acquitted. Another charge of working 250 slave workers to death in Alderney was later laid against Klebeck but a proposed trial was abandoned due to his death on May 5, 2004 in Hamburg, aged 98.

★ Kuhn, Rittmeister Rudolf: The cavalry sergeant was interrogated first by the Americans and later by the Soviets who handed him over to East Germany. Sentenced in 1950 by the Chemnitz Court of Appeals in Waldheim, Kuhn was released in 1955.

★ Locke: One of several SS guards from the Ilfeld and Ellrich satellite camps who disappeared after the war.

★ Miltz, Colonel Walter: The commandant of the local Luftwaffe station was sentenced in Chemnitz and released in 1955.

★ Palis, Gustav: Another Volkssturm member handed back by the Soviets to East Germany. He was executed April 1951.

★ Pinnenkämper, Adolph: German Kapo released from East German custody in 1955.

★ Ringstmeyer, Rudolf: Gardelegen's chief of police was arrested by the Soviets, charged and imprisoned in East Germany. He was later released and moved to Bielefeld in West Germany in 1960 and re-joined the police service. He was questioned in February 1961 about Gardelegen.

★ Fritz, Rose: One of the SS guards from the Ilfeld and Ellrich satellite camps who disappeared after the war.

★ Teply, Friedrich: Brauny's ageing deputy appeared at the Dora-Mittelbau case in the Dachau Trials and gave testimony on Brauny's war crimes at Rottleberode.

★ Thiele, Kreisleiter Gerhard: He did a runner before the Americans arrived in Gardelegen, disappearing shortly after he had ordered the cover up and the digging of the trenches outside the barn. The main architect of the massacre ditched his uniform and went into hiding before being held on April 17 – three days after the massacre – by the Americans in a holding camp. After being let

▲ Kreisleiter Gerhard Thiele, a former schoolteacher, was never brought to justice.

go by the Americans in 1946, Thiele disappeared. In the subsequent Soviet investigations and trials, Thiele's name was added to the list of the accused, *in absentia*.

Using the alias of Gerhard Lindemann, he worked in a number of jobs in several West German cities including Karlsruhe, Cologne and Düsseldorf. Despite the East German authorities knowing full well of Thiele's role at Gardelegen, little or no attempt was made to inform the West Germans who were seemingly ambivalent. There was an investigation of sorts in 1961 by the Munich Court of Justice but it went nowhere as co-operation between East and West Germany broke down. The case against Thiele reappeared in 1997 – some 52 years after the event – and only then did it emerge that Thiele had died in Düsseldorf on June 30, 1994, aged 85. His wife, Rosemaria, consistently related after the war that the last time she had seen her husband was at Stendal, a day or so after the burning, but her evidence was deemed unreliable.

★ Unvertorben, Fritz: This brutal Ellrich camp guard was one of the very few SS guards found by the Americans. He was part of the group that was released into East German hands in 1950.

▲ Local residents uncover the bodies in the trenches.

▲ The Isenschnibbe cemetery. Most of the graves are marked 'Unbekannt' or 'Unknown'. *Source: Nigel Bance*

MAIN SOURCES

★ Yad Vashem archives
★ *Massacre at Gardelegen*, After the Battle, No 111, London, 2001
★ *The Death Marches*, The Final Phase of Nazi Genocide, Blatman D., 2013
★ *The New York Times* archives
★ *The Times* archives
★ *The Washington Post* archives
★ *Die Welt*
★ Testimonies and memories of US troops present at Gardelegen
★ Sachsen-Anhalt Memorials Foundation
★ Neuengamme Gedenkstätte

★ Special thanks to Karl-Heinz Reuschel in Gardelegen, who from his own extensive research, is very familiar with the Gardelegen story.

V

THE CAMP THE WORLD FORGOT

STORYLINE

The camp's location is known but because of its location on the perimeter of private land, owned and regularly patrolled by one of Germany's largest munitions companies, few care to venture amongst these ruins in the woods. This company is the largest employer in the village and it doesn't welcome the curious who stray off the permitted pathways. There are no signs or plaques in commemoration to the horrors perpetrated here. The village doesn't like to be reminded about its sinister past.

'The Camp the World Forgot' is a very apt title for KZ Tannenberg, the concentration camp outside the village of Unterlüss, 83km to the north east of Hannover and half that distance from the administrative town of Celle, the post-war home of the British Army during the Cold War.

Conditions in Tannenberg were brutal and a chief dispenser was a 22-year-old former shop girl who trained in Ravensbrück, an equally notorious concentration camp. When the inmates returned from a typical backbreaking day lugging rubble around the village, this sadistic SS guard awaited them outside the camp gates with her whip and truncheon tucked into her belt.

Unterlüss wasn't just the location of Tannenberg, a satellite of Bergen-Belsen. A plethora of other camps provided slave workers to fulfil orders for Germany's military machine. The 'Baby Camp', where women gave birth under primitive conditions, and a Gestapo 'AEL' camp, a 'correction' centre for errant workers, were cogs in this substantial complex sited close to two huge facilities that developed missile systems that could have reversed Allied aerial superiority even in the dying months of the Third Reich.

Some foundations still remain of this concentration camp in the woods. Nearby are warning signs positioned by Rheinmetall that trespass will incur a substantial fine. With the camp fully cleared by the SS on April 10, 1945, the female inmates were transported to Bergen-Belsen where few survived.

Source: Nigel Bance

263

'*HILLE entered the Dental Room with a prisoner, a Hungarian woman of about 42 years of age. HILLE had her rubber truncheon and whip. The other patients and myself were ordered out of the room. I went to my block, situated opposite Block I, and there I could hear the screaming and moaning. The screaming lasted for 20 minutes, after which HILLE came to tell me that I could return. When I did so, the prisoner had gone. Later, the prisoner's little daughter came to fetch me to attend to her mother who was in great pain. There were numerous red and blue bruises all over the length of her back and buttocks as a result of the savage beating. Barely able to stand, she had to go on Appelle next morning and go out to work.*'

These words belong to Lola Teichner, a 31-year-old Polish woman, an inmate of the Tannenberg concentration camp in Unterlüss, Lower Saxony, and a village then-as-now dominated by Rheinmetall, a major German weapons manufacturer. Lola had survived the war. Her incarceration had begun in the Sosnowiec Ghetto in Poland and after it was cleared by the SS, Lola with other ghetto inmates were transported to Auschwitz-Birkenau. A slave labour selection in Birkenau took Lola, with 800 other women, to Tannenberg. Her final destination was the notorious Bergen-Belsen. A British army officer attached to the No.1 War Crimes Investigation Group, had interviewed Lola on November 24, 1945, in the Belsen-Hohne camp, formerly the Wehrmacht barracks that bordered Belsen, which in the immediate months post-war housed more than 15,000 former prisoners and displaced persons.

THE 'BROWN ONE'

Susanne Luise Pauline Hille was a 22-year-old sadist, so described by an SS male guard in Tannenberg when interrogated and by several Tannenberg survivors. She had enrolled as an Aufseherin, a female SS concentration camp warder, and taught the craft of brutality and torture in the Ravensbrück all-women concentration camp. To these Aufseherinnen, the use of rubber truncheons and whips became standard. With Tannenberg a satellite camp of nearby Belsen, Hille would stand comparison with notorious Belsen female warders such as Irma Grese, Elizabeth Volkenrath, Juana Bormann and Ilse Forster, who exacted similar retribution on women prisoners. Forster, in charge of Kitchen No 1 in Belsen, would later attempt to convince the prosecution at the Belsen Trial that she must be viewed as a 'fairy godmother' to the 38 women 'internees' who worked under her, even though she revelled in breaking heads with her truncheon.

Tannenberg, usually referred to in concentration camp records as 'Unterlüss', is on the west side of the village. Out of earshot, inmates referred to Hille as 'Die Braune', or the 'Brown One', so enthusiastically had she embraced Nazism and everything it stood for. The unfortunate victim in what passed as Tannenberg's dental room that evening in January 1945, an episode vividly described by Lola Teichner, had risked a beating by queuing twice for soup given her extreme hunger. It was the end of another day of hard graft for the Tannenberg women, felling trees, filling armour-piercing rocket shells with deadly phosphorus, or lugging heavy handcarts of rubble for the foundations of another Rheinmetall-Borsig facility.

NO CAMP MEMORIALS

All attempts to erect memorials to Tannenberg and the slave labour camps in the village have been blunted by obfuscation from past local and regional authorities. No signs commemorate the Sauglingsheim, known as the 'Baby Camp' and the Arbeitserziehungslager, the Gestapo-run AEL 'correctional' camp that 're-educated' recalcitrant slave workers. Rheinmetall has consistently objected to any signposting on its land. Unterlüssers had breathed a collective sigh of relief in April 1964 when the wooden Hubachstrasse barracks were pulled down, the last visible vestige of its slave labour past.

Rheinmetall has grown into an international weapons monolith and a world leader in high-precision laser weapon technology, with a political clout to match. In January 2019, the company threatened to sue the Angela Merkel government for loss of earnings on Germany's decision to ban arms exports to Saudi Arabia after the murder in Istanbul of Saudi journalist, Jamal Khashoggi. Later retracting this extraordinary challenge, Rheinmetall's CEO, Armin Papperger, reported that the company remained ready to ship 120 military trucks as soon as Berlin should grant an export licence.

In many areas of Unterlüss, Rheinmetall maintains a tight grip on security with warnings not to stray and threatening fines of Euro 5,000. Company security patrols are frequent and CCTV proliferates. The only pointer to the company's murderous backstory is in the village cemetery but even here there is no mention of the camps. There is a board with a listing of just some of the dead slave workers, and children, but even its erection in 2017 caused rancour and heated argument even as to how Russian child deaths should be described: 'Russian children' or 'Children of Russia'. The company must have maintained records because the recorded dead on the board have full names and dates of death. Tannenberg's women are notable omissions. Not far into the cemetery are two very small gravestone memorials: one says in German 'here lay four Italian and 23 Polish children', the other '34 dead Russian children'.

In September 2018, there was a first-ever commemoration at KZ Tannenberg but it took the form of a protest at the lack of memorials and signposting. Between 80-100 protestors gathered in Altensothrieth, to the west of the village, and they trod the same path down to the camp in the woods walked by the Birkenau women when they had arrived in Unterlüss in August 1944. Some brick foundations are still visible under the dense moss and bracken. No public officials attended and only an online newspaper agreed to cover the event.

None of the KZ Tannenberg commandants were brought to justice at the end of the war. Several had gone on the run as had Hille. Information on Tannenberg is minimal in the files of the Gedenkstätte Bergen-Belsen[1], Yad Vashem in Israel and in the British archives. What is known on how Tannenberg operated is mainly through the reminiscences of survivors. Tannenberg was empty when the British army occupied Unterlüss: the bulk of its inmates having been transported to Belsen that in its last months and days of operation had become known as a Krankenlager – a concentration camp for the sick and dying.

Sadly, through the long lens of time, KZ Tannenberg is the camp the world forgot and to gain some insight of what happened here, and in Unterlüss, we should begin with Auschwitz-Birkenau and its infamous senior doctor.

THE ROLE OF JOSEF MENGELE

'The second time I saw Dr Mengele, he was accompanied by two SS women.[2] It was August 1944. We had been in Auschwitz almost four months. Mengele's presence was required for it was another selection.

'Once again we stood before the handsome doctor. Once more we took off all our clothes. The able looking, he sent back to the barracks. The Muselmänner[3] he put to one side. While we waited our turn, I watched as the SS women marked the Muselmänner with red X's over their chests. We were next. Mengele was momentarily distracted. Mother stood in front of me – by now she looked very emaciated – and when he glanced away, I pushed her into the barracks. Luck was again with us and we were not observed. We breathed a sigh of relief. Too soon, I'm afraid, for our ordeal had just begun. Our guards led us away saying we were going for a shower. The bathrooms with their border of geraniums came into view. Each of us thought, "It's our turn now"'.

These were the remembrances of Valerie Furth.[4] They did have a shower but of water, not gas crystals, before being herded to Birkenau's infamous railway ramp and made to stand in the pouring rain to await the train. As night fell they were still standing, as they were in the morning. An SS officer barked out an order to strip. They stood naked and cold for several more hours.

The train didn't arrive and the prisoners were marched off to different barracks. Two days had passed until a loudspeaker blared, 'the 800 women selected from Camp C should come to the tracks'. Women ran from all directions to get in the cattle cars and in the

---

[1] Gedenkstätte Bergen-Belsen, Forschung und Dokumentation, (Department of Research and Documentation, on the site of the former camp).

[2] One of those women may have been the Aufseherin Irma Grese, who worked in Birkenau before Belsen. Grese was known to attend selections with Mengele for slave labour transportations to German industry. According to one deposition in the Belsen Trial, if Grese saw a mother or daughter, or sisters, trying to get together in selections, she would beat them senseless.

[3] The German term for concentration camp prisoners deemed too sick and unfit for work.

[4] *'Cabbages and Geraniums'*, Valerie Jakober Furth, Social Science Monographs, Boulder, Columbia University Press, New York, 1989. She died March 24, 2011.

rush, Valerie lost hold of her mother. 'Frantically, I searched for her among the masses of shaved heads and naked stumbling bodies. I saw her and fought my way toward her and gripped her. We didn't want to lose our one chance of escaping from Auschwitz. We surged toward the cattle car and hands reached out to us, pulling us into the open car. Minutes later, the doors slammed shut'.

Several days later the train pulled into Unterlüss, in the dense Lüsswald Forest on the southern rim of Lüneburg Heath, south of Hamburg. As the RAF pounded the Rheinmetall-Borsig plants in Berlin and Dusseldorf, Unterlüss had taken on a secret and additional capability in July 1944. Revolutionary new shells were being manufactured, as were prototypes of ground-to-air liquid-fuelled guided missiles that if successful might radically alter the Allied aerial dominance.

The column of Birkenau women was marched away from the bahnhof, guarded by SS guards with their dogs. It wound up Müdener Strasse, the main thoroughfare through Unterlüss with slave labour camps on either side with high perimeter fencing. Approaching the fork in the road, with Rheinmetall facilities and proving grounds to the north and the Neulüss plant a distance away to the right, the column continued to the left, past the Wehrmacht barracks and the Eschengrund, the large munitions factory. The column finally arrived at Altensothrieth, a collection of farm buildings. Opposite was one of several Rheinmetall testing ranges. The track between the buildings took the column to a small bridge and fields. Beyond were the woods and the camp under the trees.

'It had taken three days to arrive in hell', reflected Valerie Furth.

THE 'CANNON CHRIST'

'Cannon Christ' was the chief Rheinmetall-Borsig[5] weapons inventor, the Christ-like appearance of Dr Carl Waninger, with his head of hair and a voluminous beard belying a genius who designed munitions for the Nazis considered way superior to Allied designs.

---

[5] Full name of the company.

The cannon he built for Düsseldorf's carnival in the mid-1930s displayed the depth and breadth of his innovation, as it fired sweets into the crowds. Waninger had cleverly overcome the pervading odour of gunpowder. After the war, Waninger would write a book about his time at Rheinmetall, entitled 'Knallbonbons', or 'Crackers', that described some of his weapon patents.

Waninger was a Nazi but not a member of the NSDAP, unlike other senior staff and board members. Why he didn't acquire membership is explained in the Rheinmetall archives. Documents confirm that Waninger applied but was rejected for being a Freemason, an order Hitler had tried to ban believing its Lodges harboured influential and wealthy Jews. In Nazi-occupied Europe many Freemasons were dispatched to the concentration camps.

Being a Freemason didn't affect Waninger's employment at Rheinmetall. Such was his importance to the Third Reich that he went on record to the Berlin-based Transocean News Agency in April 1943, disclosing that Rheinmetall had secretly designed weapons during the inter-war years despite the supposed scrutiny of the Allied Military Control Commission and the ban on German rearmament post WW1. Rheinmetall and other munitions firms had discretely geared up for war. Waninger's sobering comments gained an international audience through *The Times* in London and *The New York Times*. Dr Robert Ley, the head of the German Labour Front and a key minister in industry's use of slave labour, added further substance to the claim that Germany had built up a huge arms capability right under the noses of the Allies.

During those inter-war years, Waninger and his design team had moved around Germany, primarily in Berlin and the Düsseldorf head office, secretly preparing blueprints behind closed doors. As the war began the team was based in Düsseldorf but in the Transocean report, Waninger alluded that it was repositioning 'somewhere in the Lüneburger Heide', the Lüneburg Heath, a reference to Unterlüss.

The RAF had long been aware of the importance of Rheinmetall. The industrial heart of Düsseldorf endured a spate of bombing raids in the summer of 1942 and *The Times* reported that its plant had been a key target. Believing the job to be done, the raids ceased but aerial photoreconnaissance confirmed in January 1943 that plants deemed irreparable had been brought back into production. An RAF pilot, sanctioned by the Air Ministry, graphically described the scene below in the massive raid on January 23 by Lancaster and Halifax bombers. It was a week before the German surrender at Stalingrad. 'In less than 20 minutes, shortly after 8pm, many 4,000-lb bombs had been dropped. The noise was like a thunderbolt and there were great fires.' This was the 51st time Düsseldorf had been attacked.

An even more devastating raid took place on June 11, 1943, leaving Ost Strasse, a major Düsseldorf thoroughfare, a wasteland with incendiary fires burning for a week. Rheinmetall transferred significant production to the east and into occupied Eastern Europe. Plants in Guben, Apolda and Sömmerda and Hundsfeld in Poland became key. The RAF bombed the Derendorf and Rath facilities in November 1944.

In Berlin, the RAF was further crippling industry in its nightly raids. According to RAF analysts, 326 factories in the capital had been damaged between November 18, 1943 and February 15, 1944. Britain's Ministry of Economic Warfare maintained a list of 103 of the most important industrial sites in Berlin, the biggest number in this category than for any other German city. Of that number, 44 had been hit, of which 29 very heavily. Of the eight factories given the highest priority by the RAF, five were owned by Rheinmetall including the Altmärkische Kettenwerke (Alkett) tank manufacturer, regarded by the British as the most important in Germany. Rheinmetall's Berlin facilities were hit multiple times. The company had run a public newsreel in 1941 with super-heavy tanks attached to chains seemingly 'floating from one position to the next in a factory hall'. An 'extraordinary sight' ran one report. The name and location of the manufacturer was not revealed.

Albert Speer, the munitions minister, had ordered a new generation of 'super-tanks', one being the 'Mouse', a misnomer of a name. This Alkett tank was to be the heaviest armoured vehicle in the Wehrmacht, weighing in at 188 tons. With two prototypes built, the Wehrmacht placed an order for 150 but it was cancelled in 1944 as the tank proved impractical under battlefront conditions. The 'Mouse' was too heavy to cross bridges and too wide to negotiate tunnels. It was also thirsty, consuming 3,800 litres of diesel to cover 100km. One prototype, according to Rheinmetall archives, ended up in Moscow after the Red Army dismantled the Alkett site as war booty.

As relentless Allied bombing sapped Germany's industrial base, Unterlüss took on a more significant role in the war effort. Commissioned before the outbreak of war, the location was perfect for testing new weaponry. Taken over by the Reichswehr, the area was not easily visible from aerial surveillance given the forestation and could be protected from prying eyes but there was a constraint. With the single proving ground in constant use by Rheinmetall, the Luftwaffe and the Wehrmacht, confusion usually reigned if the three were on the range together, firing from their respective firing positions. When measurements were conducted testing had to cease. Inaccurate firing often bombarded the nearby area of Brambostel, its inhabitants forced to vacate when the range was in use.

With the volume, Rheinmetall submitted a proposal to the Lüneburg authorities in 1941 to build a second range with consent granted in November 1942. Brambostel homeowners were forcibly dispossessed despite their vocal opposition. A further request for an extension was submitted in November 1944 and by the end of the war four proving grounds were in operation.

The 'Canon Christ' began working permanently in Unterlüss three months after an unexpected bombing raid on the village by the Americans. A large force of B-17s was on a mission on March 29, 1944, to bomb the Brunswick steel and munitions works to the south. During the raid, a formation of 20 aircraft split away to head north to seek further targets. A distance of 60km from Brunswick took the B-17s over the densely wooded southern perimeter of the Lüneburg Heath and through the cloud cover, hutted camps, explosives dumps and large multi-bay buildings were discernible as were proving ranges. Running in formation from the west at 1.24pm they dropped an 830-bomb payload on the unknown sites below but all missed, dropping well short of Unterlüss. The raid ended at 2.18pm. The RAF photoreconnaissance specialists in Medmenhem, Buckinghamshire, confirmed that these facilities were unknown and never before photographed. Unterlüss now became what the RAF

▼ Altensothrieth is a small community of restored properties, like this one. We visited Altensothrieth on an early spring day with the sun shining. Hendrik Altmann, a knowledgeable and respected researcher, who for years has tramped through woods and underground in northern Germany in the search for forgotten wartime locations, had agreed to take us to Tannenberg. There is no memorial signposting. 'It had taken three days to arrive in hell', reflected Valerie Furth.

▲ Much of the brick infrastructure is visible in the undergrowth.

◀ An Allied view shows the camp clearly visible through the wispy cloud and the track now barred. That follows a route east to join another that eventually leads to the Eschengrund plant that needed significant slave labour. The track from Altensothrieth to Tannenberg can be seen. Just outside the camp, the visible first building housed the SS guards and a small building next to it was the camp kitchen.

▶ A clear map of the Tannenberg concentration camp, a short walk from Altensothrieth, west of Unterlüss.

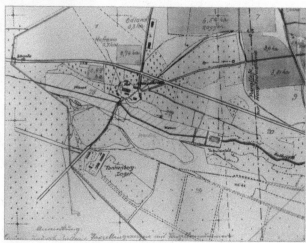

◀ A sketch of Tannenberg camp drawn by survivor, Ilana Hironsky.
Source: Gedenkstätte Bergen-Belsen

referred to as a 'target of opportunity'.

Whether the Allies, since that first sighting, obtained intelligence on the rocket development in Unterlüss isn't clear but given the village was immediately closed down by the British on later occupation we should assume they did. Rheinmetall had developed and tested ATOs (Assisted Take-off Rockets), a revolutionary new generation of weapons. The Allies bombed Unterlüss a second time, on April 4, 1945, and this time the bombs didn't fall short. One target fully destroyed was the secret rocket propellant filling plant in Neulüss, a short drive east from the village centre.

The records of that raid don't mention sightings of the slave labour camps where there were many victims, including children in the 'Baby Camp'.

INDUSTRY'S RECOURSE TO SLAVE LABOUR

All the main Rheinmetall-Borsig factories – Düsseldorf, Berlin, Unterlüss, Sömmerda and Hundsfeld[6] – had recourse to Ostarbeiten, foreign workers, or Häftlingen, Jewish concentration camp prisoners. The Düsseldorf plant garnered prisoners from 10 camps. The Sömmerda weapons factory, in Thuringia, sourced from Buchenwald, 24km to the south. Berlin industry had the biggest call on slave workers with approximately 500,000 transported into the city, of which 30,000 were put to work in the Rheinmetall factories.

There is a report of an Rheinmetall employee named Möller visiting Birkenau yet his name doesn't appear in the Rheinmetall archives and nor do the records of the centralised department that handled slave labour requirements. It isn't clear how many camps existed in Unterlüss but the figure could be as high as 20. Some, certainly in the first years of the war, just housed German workers to staff the large munitions factory or to work on the construction sites. As the Wehrmacht sucked in vast numbers of conscripts with the invasion of the Soviet Union in June 1941, so the domestic labour force dwindled. With orders from the Wehrmacht, Luftwaffe

---

[6] In occupied Poland, now renamed Psie Pole.

and Kriegsmarine piling up, Rheinmetall's need for slave labour was insatiable. Rheinmetall confirmed that slave labour accounted for 81% of the Unterlüss workforce at its peak.

The Nuremberg trial of industrialist Friedrich Flick and five of his advisors, who held powerful positions in the management of the Reich's war economy and official trade bodies, was the first post-war trial of a major German company. It began in April 1947 and lasting for eight months the trial illuminated the depth of German industrial need for slave labour. In Germany and the occupied East, concentration camps were constructed near new industrial complexes.[7]

Accountability was the prime charge laid against Friedrich Flick, the powerful and titular head of the 'Flick Concern', a swathe of 300 industrial enterprises, including coal and iron ore mines, steel production and manufacturing. Daimler-Benz was in Flick's portfolio. After the Soviet invasion, Flick was the first to exploit its mining and smelting sectors.

The court didn't dispute that the Reich had originated and marshalled Germany's slave-labour programme at every level. Labourers, involuntary and voluntary, were procured under Reich regulations and industry never had authority in the programme's administration conducted only through the Reich's labour offices. Plant management couldn't object to slave worker allocation and not fulfilling the Reich's strident output targets sometimes led to charges of sabotage and in extreme cases death sentences were imposed on plant managers. No one dared challenge the Reich's slave labour programme.

Flick's defence counsel provided evidence that plant managers had often voiced objections when sick labourers were removed by the SS for execution but given they had no jurisdiction over slave labour management such protest was refused. As to whether slave labourers had worked under inhumane conditions in Flick's plants, defence counsel took the line that ill-treatment and neglect was isolated and didn't conform to plant management policy.

---

[7] The Flick Trial: trial of Friedrich Flick and five others, US military tribunal, Nuremberg, April 20-December 22, 1947.

Despite every attempt by the defence counsel to exonerate the company and deflect all culpability directly onto the Reich, Flick was found guilty of committing war crimes. He and his companies were accountable. They had employed large numbers of slave labourers and bespoiled public and private property in the occupied territories.[8] Flick's strong links to the SS and other Nazi organisations that had wantonly murdered and committed atrocities were also deemed criminal, an uncomfortable conclusion for many other German companies. The court had considered and illuminated another illegal crime. Flick, with other industrialists, had annually paid lip service to Himmler.

FRIENDSHIP WITH HIMMLER

Rheinmetall was one company that had this particular skeleton rattling in its corporate cupboard, being among the 30 or more from the business and banking communities associated with Himmler's personal slush fund known as 'Freundeskreis', also referred to as 'Friends of Himmler' or the 'Keppler Circle'.

Wilhelm Keppler, an economic advisor to both Hitler and Himmler, had been the originator as soon as the NSDAP assumed power in 1933. As chairman of a major subsidiary of I.G.Farben that manufactured synthetic gasoline utilising the technology of its US partner, Standard Oil, Keppler had powerful contacts with deep pockets both home and abroad.

Hitler was short of such friends in his climb to power and his speech to Düsseldorf's Industry Club in January 1932 was one of several attempts to bolster support. His vision of a vast political and business internal market created out of Lebensraum, the 'new living space', captivated the 650 business leaders who awarded Hitler with a tumultuous ovation. To Hitler, if he did take Germany to war he could only sustain and win it with a strong industrial base. So enthused were several US companies that had bought into the rhetoric, business relationships were cemented with German

---

[8] Flick was sentenced to seven years and the other accused received lesser terms.

companies, especially in the vehicle and chemical sectors.

Initially, Hitler was the driving force behind the Freundeskreis but Himmler, aided by his chief of staff, SS-Gruppenführer (Lt. General) Woolf, took it under his wing. Dinners and meetings took place around the country. In 1936, Himmler personally escorted a group of his key funders around Dachau concentration camp. The 'Sonder Konto S', known better as the 'S account', was set up for members of Himmler's exclusive club to make contributions and at the onset of war the account was with a Schroder banking subsidiary. The funds were subsequently credited to Himmler's personal accounts, numbered 30-6640/41, in the Behrenstrasse head office of Dresdner Bank in Berlin.

Germany's three largest banks, Dresdner, Deutsche and Commerz, made annual payments ranging from RM50,000 to RM75,000. Flick, one of the largest contributors, stumped up RM100,000, a tenth of the one million Reichsmarks that was channelled annually into Himmler's slush fund. Membership to this exclusive club wasn't compulsory but it brought benefits and enhanced company profits.

There is no record of any Rheinmetall contribution paid into the 'S account' by its chairman, Hellmuth Röthnert, and nor would there be in the company archives given the secrecy of such payments. *Der Spiegel*, in a 1965 article on the Freundeskreis, however, did report that Röthnert had attended a dinner in Berlin in 1941. In his company that day was Carl Krogmann, the Hamburg banker, who had become the city's wartime bürgermeister, and as a hard-line Nazi his office had been a participant in the sacking of Jewish businesses and the deportation of Jews to the Polish death camps.

Röthnert, an NSDAP member, held the chairmanship of the Waffenblock, the overarching weapons and mechanical engineering sector in Hermann Göring's Reichswerke structure. Göring had visited Rheinmetall's plant in Berlin-Tegel in late 1939, just after Britain had declared war on Germany. Such was the strategic importance of the Waffenblock that by 1941 the combined workforce in this sector held more than 600,000. Röthnert was a close friend of Albert Speer, the munitions minister, but how he viewed Nazism and industry's use of slave labour isn't known. If Röthnert did have doubts, in those quiet dinners and meetings of the Freundeskreis it is unlikely that anyone dared to express views to the contrary.

Despite Berlin being systematically reduced to rubble, the capital remained as the official headquarters of Rheinmetall-Borsig.[9] Unscathed, Unterlüss, now housed all company documents and financial accounts. Röthnert had also relocated, moving into the Haus Waldfrieden, the company's palatial guesthouse in Unterlüss that had been acquired some decades earlier. He would most certainly have been advised that 81% of his workforce was forced slave labour of numerous nationalities. From his chauffeur-driven car, Röthnert would have witnessed emaciated women from KZ Tannenberg, personally selected by Mengele in Birkenau, with their shorn hair and dressed in typical striped concentration camp clothing, lugging heavy handcarts laden with building rubble on the road into Neulüss.

THE UNTERLÜSS CAMPS

To my questions as to how Rheinmetall had managed the Unterlüss camps, the company responded that their day-to-day operation was left to the SS or other military but company staff did dictate the type and scale of work. Once the inmates were marched back to their respective camps after a long working day, Rheinmetall had abrogated all responsibility. Plant managers never had unlimited access to the camps and only visited with permission. Any available company property was used to house the slave labourers but as the war wore on the prisoners were forced to build their own huts.

When the Tannenberg women, accompanied by SS guards, set out in the morning from Altensothrieth in their respective arbeitskommando, or working party, the two SS-Aufseherinnen colleagues of Susanne Hille went with them. Compared to Hille, these two were less inclined to dispense harsh punishment. Hille usually remained in the camp and often used this free time to ride in the woods. Residents who witnessed the women in the village said they

---

[9] Berlin remained the headquarters up to June 27, 2000.

appeared cowered as they pulled their carts to several facilities. Quite often the women were subjected to hostility. A survivor recalled an incident when a woman bystander encouraged her young daughter to throw stones at them. The SS guards merely looked on, grinning. At the end of a long day, they were marched back to Tannenberg to be greeted by Hille with her whip and truncheon tucked into her belt. She would order an immediate rollcall.

Whose responsibility it was to feed the Tannenberg women as they worked is unclear but camp survivors who had worked at sites in the village related that the construction companies, working on behalf of Rheinmetall, provided only limited water. Escapes did occur mainly from work parties in the woods or in open fields. No attack on any Rheinmetall personnel in Unterlüss is recorded in the company archive. Indeed, only one such episode was ever recorded in those records and that was at the Gispersleben factory, on the outskirts of the city of Erfurt. This facility was quickly constructed in 1944 to save the production from the Sömmerda plant that was under sustained aerial attack. A factory leader had been tortured to death by slave labourers and what happened to the assailants is not known but assuredly the SS or Gestapo would have summarily dealt with them.

Through an imagined drive with company chairman, Röthnert, we can describe the individual camps that littered Unterlüss. Leaving the Neulüss facility, his car would have crossed the railway line, spurred to the village bahnhof, which led to Rheinmetall's own loading and unloading ramp. In Müdener Strasse, the main thoroughfare through the village, a turn right took the chairman north into Neuensothriether Strasse where on the right the five barracks of the Arbeitserziehungslager, or AEL, were visible. This was the Gestapo-run 'correctional' camp for errant workers.

There were eight of these Gestapo camps in Germany in 1940, according to Berlin's Bundesarchiv, and in the final year of the war the number in Germany and in the occupied territories had reached 200 with many strategically sited next to munitions plants. The AEL in Unterlüss was established in 1941. German labourers, initially, were imprisoned in them for the official period of between 21-56 days but as the camps grew in number foreign slave labourers became the majority and the length of imprisonment was open-ended. Says the

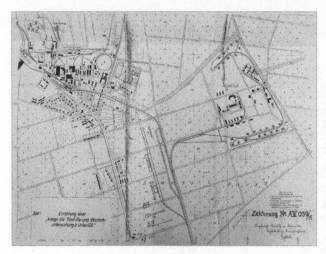

◀ The Rheinmetall sites in 1942.

▲ Dr Carl Waninger, known as 'Cannon Christ', was the chief Rheinmetall-Borsig weapons inventor. Waninger was a Nazi but not a member of the NSDAP, unlike other senior staff and board members. He later co-operated with the British. This photograph was taken in 1960.
Source: Rheinmetall archive

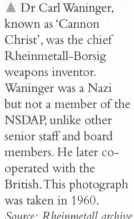

▲ The Waldfrieden company guesthouse, pre-war.
Source: Rheinmetall archive

◀ Hellmuth Röthnert, acquaintance of Himmler and Göring and close friend of Albert Speer, the munitions minister, was Rheinmetall's chairman. He had moved to Unterlüss and lived in the Waldfrieden company guesthouse where he later committed suicide. As to method and circumstances there has never been clarification. Rheinmetall's illustrious chairman might have been murdered.

◀ A clear Allied aerial view of the Rheinmetall sites destroyed after the second US raid on April 4, 1945. Laboratories were devastated, as were the smelting house, with its four large boilers, and the production halls. The propellant facility in Neulüss, a key target for the bombers, had been completely destroyed. All the financial records evacuated to Unterlüss in the final weeks and months of the war from Berlin, Düsseldorf, Leipzig, Sömmerda and Hundsfeld production sites were lost in the firestorm.

▶ Unterlüss was first bombed on March 29, 1944. A large force of B-17s was on a mission to bomb the Brunswick steel and munitions works to the south and a group of 20 aircraft had split away north to seek further targets. Running in formation from the west at 1.24pm they dropped an 830-bomb payload on the unknown sites below but all missed, dropping well short of Unterlüss. The RAF photoreconnaissance specialists in Medmenham, Buckinghamshire, confirmed that these facilities were unknown and never before photographed. Unterlüss now became what the RAF referred to as a 'target of opportunity'.
Source: National Archives

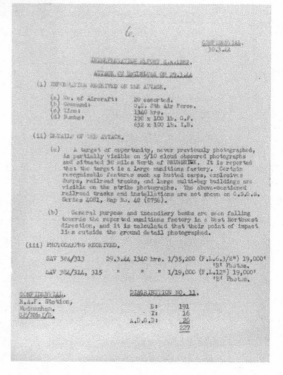

Bundesarchiv, reasons for detention included going for a walk, refusing to work or even not responding to the traditional German greetings. Women were detained for more than labour offences. Approximately half a million people had been detained in the AELs and conditions began to resemble those in the concentration camps with executions the norm. Frequently AEL prisoners were transferred to them.

Administrative responsibility for the Unterlüss AEL lay with the Gestapo office in Lüneburg but operational control was ceded to Celle whose Gestapo chief was the notorious Hermann Kühn, who often visited to assess its functioning and determine whether punishment was tough enough. According to Jürgen Gedicke, who wrote a 'Chronik', or chronicle, of wartime Unterlüss, this camp held 300 prisoners at its peak.[10] Of the foreign nationalities in the AEL, most were Polish and Dutch. The guards were usually Ukrainian who throughout the Nazi camp system were renowned for their cruelty and in the last months of the war the death rate of inmates in this AEL increased. Upon occupation, the British ordered a local doctor, Dr Alfred Schwarz, to determine the cause of death of 11 disinterred bodies. They had been executed between April 4 and April 13, 1945, and inspection reported that seven had been shot in the neck, two were strangled and the other two had had their skulls bashed in. There were many others who had died in Neuensothriether Strasse[11] during the course of the war.

Returning to Müdener Strasse and heading south, Röthnert in this imaginary drive around the Rheinmetall estate, under his watch, would have passed slave labour camps on both sides of this thoroughfare.

First on the left was Männerlager III, Lager Tielemannsort, holding Polish, French and Serb prisoners.[12] In early 1942, some 400 children were among them. Adjoining Tielemannsort was Männerlager II, established in 1943. Originally it held 358 German prisoners and 507 Russians but later, Italian PoWs joined them.

---

[10] *Chronik der Politischen Gemeinde Unterlüss*, Jürgen Gedicke.
[11] The Gestapo camp is now a small housing estate.
[12] This camp was on the present-day site of the sports field.

South of Hubachstrasse was Männerlager I where today a renovated wooden barrack can be seen down a lane behind the fire station: it is now a home with a shop fronting onto Müdener Strasse. This camp housed the first slave labourers in Unterlüss. They had been forcibly transported from Poland in April 1941, and of the 700 put to work by Rheinmetall, approximately half were women. Later, more barracks were erected for Czech, Russian, Serb, French and Belgian prisoners.

A short distance away was the bahnhof, the final stop for the slave labour train transports. South of the bahnhof, a small collection of barracks housed Poles who mined kieselgur, the ore that when crumbled turns into a white powder, and is widely used by industry as an insulator and a chemical additive. The area around Lüneburg Heath is rich in the material.

Asking his chauffeur to now turn the car around, coming quickly into view on the left side of Müdener Strasse was the Frauenlager complex of three camps close to the shooting range. Röthnert would have been familiar with the work of their inmates. Frauenlager I slave labourers built Rheinmetall infrastructure and the Polish women in Frauenlager II, Lager Heidkamp, slaved in the Eschengrund, the huge ammunition plant with its three production halls: Presserei, Hammerei and Harteofen. Each hall was connected to the assembly line and working conditions were primitive and hard. Labourers were easily recognisable by their reddish hair, the result of filling shells with phosphorous. Life expectancy was short. Several Eschengrund buildings remain and they have had several uses over time but now the area is off-limits with the usual Rheinmetall signs threatening heavy fines for trespass. Over the road, trees and high double wire fences shield a Rheinmetall proving ground. CCTV cameras maintain a constant surveillance.

Might Rheinmetall's erstwhile chairman felt a modicum of guilt and shame over Frauenlager III, whose responsibility lay with Rheinmetall and the Deutsche Arbeitsfront, the German labour service known as DAF? Probably not. This was the Säuglingsheim, or 'Baby Camp'. Paul Guse, who held the military rank of Oberst, or Colonel, was the Rheinmetall employee charged with its day-to-day management. Amongst the barracks was a maternity ward of 60 beds looked after by four Polish prisoner nurses and a Polish midwife. Not only women from the Unterlüss camps gave birth in this ward with its primitive conditions, pregnant women were transported here from labour camps in and around Celle. Gedicke, in his Unterlüss chronicle, reported that Guse often complained to DAF on the shortage of nappies and bedding but nothing was done.

And then there was Tannenberg, Belsen's satellite in the woods at Altensothrieth, 2km outside the village to the west and out of the sight from the curious. The company chairman would have been aware that Unterlüss had its own concentration camp, now full of women after the Italian PoWs had been moved out to accommodate them in August 1944. Röthnert's vehicle would have proved unsuitable to navigate the track down into the dense wood and as to this camp's description and operation, the memoirs of survivors are rich in detail. Readers of their respective memories are not spared the horrors.

One such survivor sketched a diagram of the camp that is held in the Belsen archives. Through the guarded gate were two wooden barracks on the right, the first, the camp kitchen and the second, the quarters for the 18 male SS guards, the three Aufseherinnen and the commandant's office. Whether the commandant lived onsite or in quarters in Unterlüss isn't clear. To the left was another tall fence, with a guarded gate into the Appellplatz, or parade ground. Facing were the three blocks that housed the prisoners, numbered one to three, in which 900 inmates were housed in the final months of 1944. The washroom and latrines were in a block to the right.

Valerie Furth, in her memoir *'Cabbages and Geraniums'*, included drawings that are dark and sinister with high trees. Jotted among them are fences, plenty of them. Through the trees she drew her first glimpse of the huts. Her first job was to work on the night shift in the munitions plant until 4am and she reminisced that she had struggled to stay awake. If workers did drop off, SS guards prodded them awake with their rifle butts.

No surviving inmate would forget the Aufseherin, Susanne Hille. 'Even the guards feared her', recalled Valerie. 'Astride her horse, she looked down on us with strangely piercing eyes. Once during rollcall, she whipped a friend of mine, a very pretty girl who worked in the office. After the beating my friend was unable to move for days'. In her memoir, Valerie portrayed those stark eyes and grimace in a drawing with the caption, 'We called her the 'Brown One''.

After two months in Tannenberg, Valerie worked in a construction detail to prepare foundations for a new building somewhere on the Rheinmetall estate. 'The work was bad in our weakened state' she wrote, 'but Tannenberg was a distinct improvement compared to Birkenau'. A good worker, Valerie became a foreman, which brought some benefits. Her mother, with whom willing hands had pulled both off the Birkenau ramp and onto the departing train, had been lucky with her work in Tannenberg. She was on kitchen detail.

Also on the transport from Birkenau to Tannenberg was Irene Gluck, a 20-year-old Czech, and she described several incidents involving Hille. Irene was in Block 2 and an orderly. Angry at the supposedly untidy state of the hut, Hille ordered everyone out, with the orderlies and the block leader in the front of the line-up. Hille 'then proceeded to strike every girl with the palm of her hand on the face'. In another episode, Gluck recalled one bitterly cold winter morning. Hille had chosen the Block 2 inmates for a particularly gruelling outside work party. Being poorly clothed, there was a general reluctance to go so Hille ordered Gluck to fetch her truncheon. When Gluck handed it over, Hille went from one to one, including Gluck, swiping it hard across the face and head.

Dina Kraus, a Hungarian teacher who would almost later succumb to typhus in Belsen, regularly risked her life in Tannenberg to give a spiritual comfort to inmates. Her family had been part of Eichmann's systematic emptying of the large Jewish population in Hungary's rural communities between March and July 1944. Dina, her mother, and young brother, Jidu, were transported to Birkenau. Dina had been in the selection for Tannenberg and these first-hand experiences would be included in her memoir *'The Secret Seder at Unterlüss'*. In Hebrew, the term 'Seder' is a prescribed order of prayers and readings. Being fluent in German, Dina was assigned as block leader and the distributor of the daily ration of soup. As Passover was approaching she was asked to conduct a secret Seder and writing in pencil she wrote down her first words from the Haggadah, 'this year we are slaves, but next year we will be free'. Profound words. She would be proved correct but in her hushed and attentive audience some would soon perish in Belsen. If the SS guards manning the main gate and patrolling inside the camp compound had heard Dina's whispered text, everyone in the hut would have been punished. Dina had survived the war, but her mother and Jidu were gassed in Birkenau.

Another survivor, Sarah Berkowitz, also risked a severe beating by committing some of her experiences to paper, which she concealed under her bed. There was always a chance of discovery as SS-Unterscharführer (Corporal) Hans Stecker, one of Tannenberg's deputy commandants, regularly searched the barracks for banned objects and material. Sarah remembered Stecker as tall, grim-faced, and vicious.

In *'Where are my Brothers?'* [13], Sarah recorded that Stecker's entire family had been wiped out in an Allied bombing raid and he sought brutal retribution on the Tannenberg women. A Pole from the Lodz Ghetto, Sarah had been in a group of 200 women taken to Birkenau. Weeks later, the group was transported by a freight train to Belsen, via the German port of Cuxhaven, and was amongst the first to enter this concentration camp not far from Celle. Tents had been erected as temporary housing and the camp was still occupied by Germans. Conditions then were certainly better than in the latter months of its existence. On their arrival, the German guards in the main were sympathetic to their plight and a truck pitched up with its Russian inmate driver handing out hot black coffee. Line-ups were conducted casually, said Sarah, and the women received bread with salami or margarine. Coffee was available daily. 'Here we felt so free that we even sang some songs', recalled Sarah, but they unwisely complained of being idle. That 'freedom' quickly terminated. After a five-week stay in Belsen, around 100 women were taken to the railway ramp in nearby Bergen, in August 1944, to board boxcars to Unterlüss.

As she and her colleagues were marched into the woods by SS guards to halt at the camp gate, Sarah bitterly regretted those unthinking remarks in Belsen that now brought her here to Tannenberg. The commandant at that time, SS-Hauptsturmführer

---

[13] *Where are my Brothers?*, Sarah (Bick) Berkowitz, Helios Books, New York, 1965

(Captain) Friedrich Diercks, wrote down their names and dates of birth and gave each of the new arrivals a number: Sarah's was 1832. In the coming months, Sarah and the women had to endure Susanne Hille. This woman with 'an olive complexion, dark eyes and brown curly hair, tied back', recorded Sarah, they called a beast.

Sarah had quickly discovered that blankets were a vital commodity and needed safeguarding. Sarah's was stolen so her nights were spent uncovered until she summoned the courage to steal one back. With the three blocks crammed with 900 women, fighting amongst them was a daily occurrence especially between the Poles and Hungarians, the former accusing the latter of grabbing the best jobs in the camp.

The first whistle of the morning would blow at 5am but some women had been up an hour or so earlier stealing food from the kitchen. If the 'Brown One' caught them, she would order them to spend an entire night on the cold concrete floor of the washroom, naked. If that wasn't enough, afterwards she thrashed them. Breakfast was usually what passed as hot potato soup but only rarely did it contain an actual potato. When the second whistle blew, all prisoners had to line up within five minutes. Orders were given for the work parties. Sunday was a camp rest day, but often the SS guards amused themselves by calling the women to line up in the cold to endlessly pass a brick amongst themselves. Those who objected were dealt with.

Lunch on the work parties was usually nothing or bread kept from the previous evening's meal. Male prisoners from some of the numerous slave labour camps often joined them onsite but they were kept apart by the SS guards. Lifting heavy shovels of lime and cement for building construction was an arduous task on an empty stomach so the women were thankful if the men threw them some of their food. Sarah specifically remembered the kindness of one German woman in Unterlüss riding her bicycle. Out of sight of the SS guards she handed the Tannenberg women some carrots.

The lack of food was a constant anxiety. Mushrooms had become a staple, the women picking them on working parties and concealing them in their clothing. Every evening, huddled around the barrack stove they were cooked and eaten, not knowing if some were poisonous. If they were, they soon vomited. One prisoner in Sarah's barrack, named Sala, had somehow managed to hide her gold watch, which she had brought from Birkenau concealed in her mouth. Sala did a deal with the German cook in Tannenberg, handing over the watch in return for more food, an act that duly antagonised other inmates as she assiduously coveted her increased ration.

Sarah by now was regularly chosen for the tree-felling detail, a back-breaking and hazardous task, and it was on one of these trips into the local woods when she badly lacerated a foot. Hille committed her to the camp sickroom to join 50 others on the cramped bunks but the deep wound was left unstitched and it bled. With the pain now wracking her body, Hille placed her on one of her selections of the ill for transportation to Belsen. Sarah was now in Belsen for the second time and the condition of the foot worsened. Polish doctors in Belsen were unable to help but eventually she underwent an operation by a German doctor, which helped her to recover and survive the last weeks before liberation by the British.

Ilana Hronsky, who had been transported from the Munkács Ghetto in Poland to Birkenau in May 1944, had related her experiences in February 1995 to Dr Thomas Rahe, the senior archivist in the Gedenkstätte Bergen-Belsen. Her two sisters had also been in the Birkenau selection and transported to Tannenberg.

Ilana wrote:

'In spite of the tragic circumstances that had brought us to this camp, it seemed that we had come to a more human place. It was an area that could be identified with the planet earth, which was impossible in Auschwitz. Clean air of the woods replaced the smoke-filled air of Auschwitz and we did not have to see the flames of the crematoriums day and night. We were given new clothes. Although they were striped prisoner outfits with the yellow star on them, they were warmer than the rags we wore in Auschwitz. We also received lightweight coats and shoes. In the camp's kitchen we had a German chef who also prepared food for a nearby camp of French prisoners. We were Jews, they weren't, so they were better fed than us. When some of their food did find its way to us it felt like a special holiday.

'Upon entering through the gate of the camp, on the left was a fence and three barracks for prisoners, Blocks 1 to 3. The second block also *housed a tiny infirmary for minor injuries that needed bandages. Serious health problems were not reported, and if they became obvious, the inmates were taken away and never heard from again. Only after the war did we hear that these women had perished in Bergen-Belsen.*

'We were awoken at 5am and we rushed to dress. Before our line-up, we were given a slice of bread and a small amount of ersatz jelly. We always dreaded if the 'Brown One' was in charge of the line-up. She was exceptionally evil. Among the SS guards there were a few who showed us some compassion, and one, Josefine Holub, stands out. When she marched us off to work, we marched without fear. In the winter we marched in the dark. Some of us worked in Neulüss and involved in munitions. There was plenty of lifting and some munitions were brutally heavy. The environment was filled with dangerous gasses. In a very short time, the women resembled walking shadows with discoloured skin and hair.

'Other groups cleared areas where roads were to be built; others dug ditches for the construction of underground shelters. My sisters and I worked most of the times at these sites. Sometimes we had to chop down trees. We were always undernourished and this existence took its toll. For those who couldn't take the work and fell sick, they were taken to Bergen-Belsen.

'In the evenings we were marched back to camp and as we passed by the kitchen our evening meal was doled out. Most Sundays we didn't work and we were given a slice of horsemeat. We would always concentrate on trying to keep ourselves clean and we only had access to cold water. After working, we were exhausted. There were outside latrines but during the night we were given a large bucket to use after we were locked up. Some girls volunteered to empty them because they would be excused work and earned some extra food.

'In March 1945 we began to notice the planes and we realised that signalled the ending of the war. Our hopes soared. One of the older SS secretly hinted that the war was not going well for Germany. It was around this time that I went down with a high fever. My right hand and wrist swelled to the size of a grapefruit. I took myself to the infirmary and joined 23 others in the sickroom. We were given no medicine.'

That transfer to the infirmary would save Ilana's life.

In the latter part of 1944, Tannenberg was under the command of SS-Hauptsturmführer (Captain) Friedrich Diercks, who the survivor, Irene Gluck, described as having little or no interest in the day-to-day operation of the camp. Berlin's Bundesarchiv provided me with his SS record that had begun at Esterwegen, one of the earliest concentration camps in Germany, followed by Sachsenhausen. Diercks' deputy in Tannenberg was SS-Hauptsturmführer Rudolf Wandt, who temporarily left, returning in February 1945. His SS file in the Bundesarchiv is missing. In Wandt's absence, Stecker assumed operational control and according to Irene Gluck he was even worse than Hille. Stecker's records at the Bundesarchiv are incomplete but he was aged 20 when he dished out punishment in Tannenberg.

During the cold winter of 1944/45, the Tannenberg women tried as best they could to keep warm and a favourite ploy was to wrap blankets and paper around their bodies, under their thin concentration camp clothes. Aware to the practice, the camp's three Aufseherin guards conducted spot checks at the daily parade when the women were given their working detail orders. Some panic-stricken women let the blankets fall to the ground at their feet but that didn't spare them from a thrashing. Hille's two Aufseherin colleagues, Holub and Chani, usually ignored such misdemeanours and treated the women leniently but Stecker and Hille ordered them into Block 3 where each were whipped 25 times across their buttocks before re-joining their fellow inmates outside. A beating was no excuse for not working. Stecker never held back and he beat some women to death, one being Helene Goldinger, who was strong and healthy. On her own, she was marched into Block 3, and she would linger in the camp's sickroom for days before finally succumbing to her wounds.

In February 1945, Hille called a parade of all 900 women, including those in the sickroom, and ambled amongst the ranks picking out the weak, those she considered no longer capable of heavy work, and the inmates she personally disliked. When she'd done, around 500 had been selected for transportation to Belsen, a camp the women knew was a virtual death sentence. For the 400 that remained, there was relief even if that was tempered by having to endure more of Hille's savagery.

TANNENBERG... THE FINAL DAYS

An SS order came through that Tannenberg was to be fully cleared in April. The first to go were women in the sickroom.

Ilana Hironsky was still in the sickroom and she described an extraordinary chain of events:

'It was obvious to us that the battle zone was drawing closer. We heard the sound of aircraft and air raids.[14]

'On April 10, 1945, some SS guards entered the sickroom and told us to quickly get ready. We were leaving and all we could take was a blanket but no food. Panic broke out and some girls left to join their relatives in other blocks. This fear of separation grew to hysterical proportions. My sisters quickly joined me in the sickroom. There were 24 of us.

'A military truck was waiting on the Appellplatz with an SS soldier sitting beside the civilian driver. We were told to board and sit on the benches on either side. As we sat, we shivered violently. I do not recall how long the ride took through the wooded areas but it seemed endless. It was dark when we were told to get out of the truck and stay together. They said they would soon return and take us to a hospital.'

The truck drove off. Its driver and SS guard never did come back.
'In a way we were free', wrote Ilana. *'There was a fear of running into a dangerous situation so we went deeper into the woods and huddled together to keep warm and keep our spirits up. Most of us were very sick and feverish.'*

After several hours the women saw flashlights and two German soldiers appeared, demanding to know who they were. 'There was no point in pretending', said Ilana, 'our prisoner outfits told the story.' One soldier left and the other, an officer, offered to find some shelter for the women. 'In the darkness and blackout, we followed this man to the nearby village of Häcklingen'.[15]

---

[14] Ilana was referring to the April 4 bombing of the Rheinmetall plants in Unterlüss.
[15] Häcklingen is 6km south of Lüneburg.

'We came to a farmhouse and the soldier went in and came out with a very nervous lady of the house. She cautioned us to keep very quiet and to follow her into a barn, which had thick layers of straw on its floor. We quickly fell asleep. In the morning, the woman reappeared and this time with two young men who we discovered later were Russian prisoners of war who worked on the farm. They carried milk and cooked potatoes and warned us not to leave the barn. The woman brought us clothes and the Russians burnt our camp outfits in a local field.'

Those two Russians were a great help to the Tannenberg women further bringing news that the Allies were close but warned that the barn might become a target. With the first sounds of gunfire the women were to follow the men and hide in the field ditches.

It was eight days after the women had left Tannenberg that the war did arrive in Häcklingen and gunfire echoed around the farm. The women ran for the ditches with the Russians. Only when the gunfire subsided did the group walk cautiously into the village centre. The sight that greeted them was freedom, at last.

'There were British military vehicles, trucks and jeeps lining the street as far as the eye could see. Hundreds of soldiers were resting, chatting and eating. We didn't approach, we just stood there, watching them, not knowing what to expect and besides, our English was extremely poor. But they had noticed our little group and the moment they realised who we were, we now had British protection.

'They carried huge boxes of food into the barn and stayed with us for hours, constantly reassuring us that we were now safe. They told us that Bergen-Belsen had been liberated on April 15, five days earlier. There was no need to be fluent in English to understand how stunned they were at the unspeakable horrors that they had witnessed. It was only later that we discovered that our fellow prisoners in Tannenberg who were transported after we had left, had been taken to Belsen.'

The British army took the women to the City Hospital in Lüneburg to be treated for severe malnutrition and various diseases. All 24 had survived the war but the ending for some didn't end well. It was July when 21 were discharged from the hospital. Of the other three, one had been operated upon for bone tuberculosis, another had lost her sanity and jumped off the roof at the hospital, and the third never had the strength to recover from her ordeal in Tannenberg.

Ilana Hronsky and her fellow inmates did eventually travel to Belsen but only to receive travel documentation from the British authorities. 'We needed papers to travel home and we needed to register in Belsen. So began our trip home to Prague to begin our fruitless search for friends and relatives and to somehow rebuild our lives.'

BELSEN... THE FINAL DAYS

Ilana and the other women from the evacuated sickroom in Tannenberg had been lucky. With Tannenberg being cleared, the remainder were herded aboard trucks by the Volkssturm on April 10, and driven to Uelzen, to the east of Unterlüss, but the local authorities refused to accept them. The Volkssturm then conveyed them to Belsen, which in its final days lived up to its reputation as the Krankenlager for the dead and dying.

As to numbers on how many were taken to Camp 1 in Belsen, no exact numbers exist apart from one document. An SS document in the Belsen archives does document a figure of 517 women being held in Tannenberg in March 1945 and after Hille's selection the month before.

In Camp 1, those walking, or immobile on the ground, resembled living skeletons. Bodies were stacked in the open and in piles. At this stage any record keeping of arrivals had ceased. Arriving death marches swelled the numbers and incoming trains, terminating at the ramp in Bergen, added to the influx. Efforts were made by the Tannenberg women to locate their fellow inmates from the February transport but all attempts were futile leading to the assumption that most must be dead.

All power supplies had been cut off after an Allied bombing raid on Hannover in early April took out the relay transformers. In charge of maintaining electricity supplies in Belsen was SS NCO Paul Steinmetz, who had previously done the same job in Auschwitz-1. Later interrogated by the British, he described his futile attempts to keep the generators operating that drove the water pumps.

Approaching Kramer, the commandant, for permission to draw petrol from stores he was refused. Steinmetz then claimed he approached the Wehrmacht commander in the nearby Bergen-Hohne barracks but was again snubbed, this time on the basis that the Wehrmacht had priority, not Camp 1 prisoners.

As the situation grew ever desperate, Steinmetz claimed he used the camp's small fire pumps to pump in water from a local river but that attempt failed. Steinmetz reported to Kramer that even his men were suffering, and might even die, with the lack of fresh water. Kramer characteristically responded, "When all your men die, I'll send you some women!"

Contaminated bodies floated in the stagnant tanks that still had some water and inmates ignored the risk. Disease spread further. Latrines were locked, and overflowed, and the inmates were too sick to build new ones. Bread supplies had ceased, as had the staple of turnip soup. Increasingly, the SS abrogated its guard duties to the Hungarian Army whose members rampaged through the huts, revelling in taunting and indiscriminate killing.

Cannibalism broke out across Camps 1 and 2, so described by Dr Fritz Leo, a doctor of medicine from Dresden. Miraculously, since his arrest in May 1935, he had survived a decade of slave labour and concentration camps. Leo had arrived in Belsen in February 1945 to work as a doctor and quickly contracted typhus. He would later relate in the Belsen Trial how cannibalism started in Block 10 in Men's Compound No.2, a stone-walled block with its inmates suffering from violent diarrhoea and dehydration, defaecating where they lay. The floors were thick and slippery with excrement and slime. Leo was called in and shown a body with its liver hacked out. He would witness another 300 cases. Parts of bodies were cut off to eat immediately or they were put in pockets to cook and eat later. If the SS found the culprits they were immediately hung.

In the days before the British were expected at the gates of Belsen, Dr Horstmann, an SS doctor, made strenuous efforts to clean up the camp and conceal the piles of bodies but it was a hopeless attempt given the number. On the day of liberation, Horstmann was observed with his watch in hand, looking at it hourly, and harrying prisoners to hurry away with the corpses.

UNTERLÜSS REVEALS ITS SECRETS

A sombre and impromptu gathering took place in the village of Ellerndorf, to the north of Unterlüss on June 6, 1945.[16] Germany's capitulation to the Allies was now four weeks past. Max Wessing, the head of Rheinmetall-Borsig's supervisory board, hadn't travelled far. He was living in Eimke, close to Ellerndorf, in the home of a local farmer named Otte. Wessing addressed the four board members that included his son-in-law, Herbert Pavel.

Hellmuth Röhnert, the influential chairman, friend of Speer, and a probable contributor to Himmler's slush fund, was dead, his body discovered the previous evening in Haus Waldfrieden in Unterlüss, Rheinmetall's guesthouse, very close to the company's plants. The official verdict was suicide but as to method and the circumstances there has never been clarification. Rheinmetall's illustrious chairman might have been murdered.

The Ellerndorf minutes reflected not only the mood but also Wessing's condemnation of the past when Rheinmetall was fully subservient to the Reich. 'The Hitler system had been both corrupt and criminal', he stated, 'the war was over and Rheinmetall needed a new sense of direction, unfettered by intrigue dictated by party politics'. Post-war would mark a new era of collaboration, explained Wessing, this time with the Allies, but he questioned the calibre of the present management and supervisory boards in the challenge. Some senior staff had already quit, among them, Dr Waninger, the 'Cannon Christ', who resigned on May 8, the day of Germany's surrender.

Across Germany, the company had effectively been closed down. What had remained of Rheinmetall's Berlin factories and the plants in Sömmerda and Hundsfeld plants had been lifted and transported away by the Soviets on trains. The damage caused by the April 4 raid on Unterlüss had rendered the Rheinmetall facilities incapable of restarting production. Laboratories were devastated, as was the

---

[16] 'Rheinmetall - Vom Reiz, im Rheinland ein grosses Werk zu errichten', Greven Verlag, Cologne, Vols 1 and 2, 2014, Dr Christian Leitzbach, p429.

smelting house, with its four large boilers. The propellant facility in Neulüss, a key target for the bombers, had been completely destroyed. All the financial records evacuated to Unterlüss in the final weeks and months of the war from Berlin, Düsseldorf, Leipzig, Sömmerda and Hundsfeld were lost in the firestorm.

The Seaforth Highlanders had warily approached Unterlüss on April 13 and immediately put the village into lockdown. Days before, the Rheinmetall management had concealed as much as possible. Designs and files were stored in underground tunnels and crated rocket and exploding shell prototypes were buried deep in the surrounding woods.

Troops guarded every Rheinmetall facility to stop the wholesale plundering that was taking place. Every vehicle was confiscated and driven away. The proving grounds were put off limits. Within days, British Intelligence moved in, accompanied by specialist munitions engineers flown in from Britain, and an inventory was drawn up of what was found in the ruins.

Photographs were taken throughout the Rheinmetall estate that included the slave labour camps. According to Rheinmetall records, only 2,800 slave workers had remained. KZ Tannenberg was empty. The SS contingent had gone on the run.

Waninger and his design staff, including Dr Klein, his deputy, were vital to the British in uncovering Rheinmetall's secrets. Before his move to Unterlüss, Klein had been Rheinmetall's chief of rocket development for the Luftwaffe in Marienfelde, Berlin. Klein and his staff had evacuated to Unterlüss with a large number of ATOs (Assisted Take-Off Rockets) manufactured on the site. Scientists and engineers from other research and manufacturing locations had joined in the general exodus to Unterlüss, many of them members of Rheinmetall's key Weapon Research and Development Organisation, the WRDO.

Whether Waninger had agreed to co-operate with the RAF-led seven-man team of experts from Britain, but assist he did. His final 65-page report to two secret London committees, the Combined Intelligence Objectives Subcommittee (CIOS) and the British Intelligence Objectives Subcommittee (BIOS), was carefully scrutinised by the Royal Aircraft Establishment in Farnborough and the weapons research facility in Fort Halstead in Kent.[17] The British later escorted Waninger to Brunswick where the Hermann Göring Air Research Institute was based.[18]

According to British records, Klein underwent 'an intense interrogation'[19] to reveal further information on the Rheinmetall projects. Other members of the WRDO experienced the same and in short order the intelligence committees had compiled a full description of Rheinmetall's munitions and rocket development across all sites. In total, 10 WRDO staff underwent interrogation. Dr Vüllers, Klein's successor in Marienfelde, with Klein, were flown to Britain for direct questioning by weapons experts.

Klein had revealed the location of the hidden documents and prototypes and taken away in eight truckloads were 40 crates of rocket drawings and 20 crates of other material for transportation to Britain.[20] With over 300 buildings on the main Rheinmetall site and another 100 on the Neulüss propellant-loading facility, the British search was intense.

The questioning revealed that Rheinmetall was refining weapon systems that without the interruption of Allied bombing might well have turned the direction of the war. It is worth recalling what the British investigators had uncovered.

The Rheintochter programme, R1 and R3 guided missiles, had been set in train by Göring's air ministry in 1942. Designed with the explosive punch of 200lbs, the R1 was first trialled in August 1943

---

[17] CIOS report: 'Was die Englander 1945 in Unterlüss Vorfanden was sie fragten und was man ihnen antwortete' - referenced Item No 2, File No: XXVII -35, by von C Waninger. Essentially, that translates into what the Englishmen found in Unterlüss in 1945, their questions and answers. It ran to 65 pages.

[18] Waninger later returned to work for Rheinmetall and lived in Unterlüss. As a Freemason, the British never required him to go through the de-Nazification programme and in 1956 he became a main board member of Rheinmetall GmbH and established Defence Company Rheinmetall, which is still based in Unterlüss. He represented the company in talks with the Defence Ministry in the development of the Leopard 1 tank. In 1960, Waninger retired and he died the following year aged 79. Many former members of Rheinmetall had really enjoyed his book *Knallbonbons* about his time in the company, which was full of anecdotes, and the many patents he registered.

[19] The phrase used in a CIOS report.

[20] CIOS report: Item No 4, File No: XXVII - 65.

▶ The Deutschelandhalle was one of the main facilities destroyed on April 4.
Source: Rheinmetall archive

◀ The destroyed Rheinmetall railway ramp.
Source: Rheinmetall archive

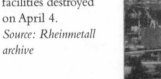

▶ The Marinehall was also hit.
Source: Rheinmetall archive

◀ Present-day Neulüss facility.

◀ Part of the enormous Eschengrund ammunition plant still exists. Polish women in Frauenlager II, Lager Heidkamp, were among those who slaved in the three production halls, Presserei, Hammerei and Harteofen. Labourers were easily recognisable by their reddish hair, the result of filling shells with phosphorous. Life expectancy was short. The area is off-limits with Rheinmetall signs threatening heavy fines for trespass.

▶ Site of what was the AEL camp off Neuensothriether Strasse, run by the Gestapo as a 'correctional' centre for errant workers, holding 300 prisoners at its peak. The guards were usually Ukrainian. In the last months of the war, the death rate of inmates increased. Upon occupation, the British ordered a local doctor to determine the cause of death of 11 disinterred bodies. They had been executed between April 4 and April 13, 1945, and inspection reported that seven had been shot in the neck, two were strangled and the other two had had their skulls bashed in. There were many others who had died in Neuensothriether Strasse during the course of the war.

▼ Hubachstrasse, present day. Wooden slave-worker barracks, part of the Männerlager complex, had once occupied this site. They were pulled down in April 1964.

▲ This area was once the site of Frauenlager I, part of the Frauenlager complex of slave worker camps.

▲ A typical slave worker barrack in Unterlüss, there were several hundred and many remained occupied post-war. *Source: Unterlüss Chronik, Jürgen Gedicke*

at the Rheinmetall testing site in Leba on the Baltic Coast in Poland but the results were disappointing. The rocket was underpowered and with its short burn it couldn't achieve the sufficient height to bring down high-flying aircraft as intended. Alternative firing mechanisations and propellants were tested yet in the second R1 trial its revolutionary liquid motor blew up in flight. In all, 70 trials took place in Leba up to January 1945. Klein admitted to the British that liquid motors had not been a success. Two were located in the shattered ruins of Neulüss with fuel and pressure tanks.

Rheinmetall placed greater store in the R3 using a combination of solid and liquid motors and this rocket had achieved a height of 12km in the five tests at Karlshagen on the Baltic Coast, very close to Peenemünde where the V-rockets had been developed. Guided by radio waves from the ground and with the introduction of close proximity fuses in the nose, the R3 packed a deadly punch. The British, too, had used such fuses in shells that successfully brought down V-1 rockets. The R3 had the height, however, but not the speed. Never achieving more than 250mph the chance of hitting fast flying aircraft was negligible. The British Mosquito fighter/bomber could reach a maximum speed of 378mph and the Lancaster and B17 bombers had a top speed of near 290mph. A permanent launching system was required for the R3, a 25ft-diameter and 10-ft deep pit, known as a 'Ringbahn'. RAF photoreconnaissance experts had identified a circular pit in Unterlüss after the April 4 bombing.

In the last months of the war, the Luftwaffe had changed priorities moving away from further rocket development to pursue jet engine advancement, resulting in the cancellation of a mass test firing of 15 enhanced R3s planned for February 20. Rheinmetall ploughed on with a number of joint ventures of the Rheintochter. Partnering with the Hermann Göring Air Research Institute, it was a key component in the radio-guided Feurlilie multi-stage flak rocket similar to Rheinmetall's design of the Wasserfalle, and the company was in partnership on a flak rocket with Telefunken at Schönfeld, outside Berlin. One highly ambitious idea was a manned R3 with the pilot escaping by parachute when a course had been set.

Rheinmetall had a raft of other weapon designs. The Kzt 1000, the codename for the weirdly named Short Term Obstacle, had been a joint venture between the Neulüss and Dusseldorf plants. A parachute was released from a fired rocket with multiple hanging wires connected to TNT. Only a few actually reached development. Much store was placed on the Rheinbote, a long-range multi-stage rocket for use on ground targets with a 100km range and carrying 30kg of explosives. Scale models were used in 50 trial firings. In Neulüss, the British discovered 50 crated ATO rockets, destined for the Rheinbote. Flight sections were also found. A derivative, the R100 BS, designed for launching from interceptor aircraft, had been dispatched from Neulüss to several Luftwaffe airfields to test in combat, but they had remained crated. A small-scale Rheinbote and a complete R100 BS were located in the ruins and removed to Britain.

Only photographs of the Walze, and its derivative, the Kurt 2, with stabilizing fins, were located. Commissioned by the Luftwaffe, the Walze, a rotating cylinder of explosives, was designed to blow holes in ship hulls, but tests concluded that it was erratic in heavy seas. Rheinmetall had designed several missiles for the Kriegsmarine, including the Launcher that could be fired from a submerged submarine when under aerial attack. Commissioned in 1944 from Unterlüss, the first tests were positive. Once launched, this missile could fly up to 6,000 metres but by the time it was fully ready, the war was effectively lost.

It was clear to the British weaponry experts that Rheinmetall-Borsig had developed many revolutionary weapons during the Third Reich's 12-year existence. Just for the Wehrmacht, revealed Klein, Rheinmetall had tested and manufactured 20 by July 1944. In its rocket development programme, Rheinmetall had designed 14 systems and the drawings for most of them had been located by the British in the hidden crates.

Rheinmetall's scientists and engineers were certainly an invaluable catch in the growing Cold War with the Soviet Union but the British needed to assess whether the Unterlüss site should be rebuilt. Rocket superiority in the new era of the jet engine was uppermost in the minds of a BIOS team that visited in November 1946. Its members had to determine whether the Unterlüss rockets had the capability to bring down fighters flying at a speed of 630 mph and bombers at 500 mph.[21] The report was not encouraging. At best, the rockets only had a 55% chance of hitting their target and even that figure supposed a volley of rockets in a scatter pattern. In a follow-up visit in May 1947 the Royal Aircraft Establishment declined to send a representative, providing no reason as to why.

Outside the Unterlüss evaluation, the demands were growing louder, especially by the Russians, for a complete dismantling of German industry in lieu of reparations. In the Soviet Occupation Zone, teams of NKVD specialists had already systematically dismantled whole factories and used thousands of trains to transport the parts back to the Soviet Union. Large numbers of captured scientists and engineers, especially in the nuclear and munitions sectors had been coerced into working for Stalin.

In the Anglo-American Zone, the final dismantling terms were agreed on October 17, 1947, with statements issued simultaneously in Berlin and London. Initially the number of factories to be dismantled was 1,636 but that target was considered too drastic if the new West Germany was to recover. It was pared back to 682. That reduction didn't save any of the Rheinmetall-Borsig plants in the zone that had produced weapons, including Unterlüss, whose ranges were now being used by the RAF. To help in the dismantling process in Unterlüss, the British drew up a map, dividing the village into districts identifiable by a letter and name. Every Rheinmetall facility was marked including the four proving grounds and the shooting range south of the Eschengrund ammunition production site, not far from KZ Tannenberg. Areas were colour-coded for the degree of damage in the April 4, 1945 bombing. Several labour camps were identified.

Brambostel, part of the proving ground that had been commandeered early in the war, was to be returned but its dispossessed owners could only return to blasted buildings and fields littered with unexploded ordnance. Compensation claims were filed against Rheinmetall but the company tossed them aside with the

---

[21] BIOS report: BIOS 7/Exploitation. Unterlüss, November 23, 1946.

statement 'as the dispossession had taken place at the order of the German Navy, the company had reaped no benefit, only a cost burden'. Claimants remained determined and Rheinmetall reluctantly paid up in 1955.

No longer permitted to manufacture munitions, the Borsig element of Rheinmetall was allowed in 1950 to manufacture product for civil use and it became a major supplier of boilers and refrigeration systems. A convicted war crimes criminal took a majority shareholding in Rheinmetall in 1956, sensing new opportunities in a renascent economy. The ageing steel entrepreneur, Hermann Röchling, a personal friend of Hitler, had seized control in June 1940 of 12 French steel plants and never shied away from the use of slave labour for the rest of the war.

In June 1948, Röchling and his son-law were hauled in front of a military tribunal in the French Occupation Zone and at the age of 73, Röchling was sentenced to seven years. That sentence was subsequently considered too lenient and Röchling had another three years added to his term. It isn't clear what political wrangling ensued but in August 1951, Röchling was conditionally discharged and free to continue running the family businesses. The purchase of Rheinmetall-Borsig was a key element in his portfolio as the Western Allies considered West Germany the front-line military buffer against the Soviet Union. Röchling wanted Rheinmetall to restart weapon production and one of his first actions was to hive off Borsig to a buyer.

The timing of Röchling's takeover was fortuitous. It coincided with West Germany making its first overtures to the Allies for the restoration of sovereignty.

CALLS FOR A SECOND BELSEN TRIAL

The Belsen Trial had begun on September 17, 1945. Of the 42 accused of war crimes, first in Auschwitz-Birkenau and then Belsen, nine were sentenced to death by hanging. One to hang was the notorious Aufseherin Irma Grese.

Sentences were imposed on November 17, 1945 but during the trial the British No.1 War Crimes Investigation Group, led by Lt.

Colonel Thomas Tilling, hadn't scaled back its Belsen investigation. The former Wehrmacht barracks in Hohne, a part of which had been Camp 2 during Belsen's operation, were now crammed with 15,000 Vertriebene, or Displaced Persons, amongst them several thousand former Belsen inmates, still recovering or awaiting repatriation.

Despite such a major humanitarian and logistical challenge, Major Frank Caolo, No.1's senior investigator, saw a tremendous opportunity to gather evidence for a second Belsen trial of guards that would include the war crimes committed in Tannenberg and Waldeslust, two of Belsen's satellites. By the end of December, more than 200 new witnesses had come forward to provide testimony in the interview rooms set aside in the Hohne barracks. Some of the accused were already in custody and held in eight civil internment camps throughout the region. Celle's jail held others, including many Hungarian army guards who had run amok before Belsen's liberation.

Corroboration was vital so Caola's staff photographed each of the accused that were in custody and prepared an album named FPC/1. This was shown to any new witness, and only after identification was a sworn statement taken. In the event that a witness had named a person but was unable to identify a photograph, the questioning focused on identifying the rank, duties and dates of the accused, and only if the answers agreed with what was known from other sources, did the investigators proceed. Using FPC/1 as the central photographic database, investigators subsequently compiled a series of extensive dossiers on the accused, FC/1 running to FC/16. If possible, the Judge Advocate General's office wanted at least three witness statements on each of the accused.

Not in this FPC/1 album were photographs of Hauptsturmführer (Captain) Friedrich Diercks, Hauptsturmführer Rudolf Wandt, Unterscharführer (Corporal) Hans Stecker and the Aufseherin, Susanne Hille. Their names had appeared on wanted notices since November 1945 after Tannenberg survivors, including Irene Gluck, had provided their names, as had one SS guard, Unterscharführer Franz Kalitowski. He was in custody.

A baker by trade, Kalitowski had come late into the war joining SS-Totenkopf in July 1944 followed by a posting to Belsen before a transfer to Tannenberg in September that year. Kalitowski was ordered back to Belsen the following January. Interrogated at the Fallingbostel internment camp, Kalitowski stated that while at Tannenberg he guarded the perimeter and the outside work parties. He told the British that the 54-year-old Diercks, who commanded Tannenberg in his time in the camp, reported directly to Kramer, the Belsen commandant. Diercks had one very notable characteristic: his hair was ginger. In the opinion of Kalitowski, Hille committed the worst beatings of prisoners describing her as a 'sadist'.

Kalitowski used the same description for the 51-year-old Sturmscharführer (Staff Sergeant-Major) Heinz Reddehasen, the former commandant of Waldeslust, who had become a key aide of Kramer in Belsen after Waldeslust was cleared. 'He was one of the worst types', Kalitowski recollected.

Waldeslust, to the west of Celle and close to the village of Hambühren, had a similar history to Tannenberg with its 400 Polish and Hungarian women prisoners also selected in Birkenau. Ita Cytryn had been one, aged 16 when the SS and Wehrmacht cleared the Lodz Ghetto in Poland. Her stay in Birkenau lasted two days before she stood in a selection parade in August 1944. Another Waldeslust survivor, Ester Brunstein, would later record her stay in the camp.[22] It was an abandoned potash mine to be used as an underground production site for the Bremen aircraft manufacturer, Focke-Wulf. The women laboured for Hochtief, Germany's largest construction company, which was preparing the facility. Ester recorded that the starved women were worked close to death and she recalled being thrashed by a German guard who raised his gun to finish her off. Despite her wounds, Ester ran off lucky to live.

The young Ita Cytron, in her account of Waldeslust given to a British war crimes investigator, had no difficulty in recognising the photograph shown to her of Reddehasen. This Nazi would forever leave a lasting memory. Reddehasen had severely beaten up a fellow prisoner, Genia Kalichman, with a rubber truncheon for the innocuous 'crime' of looking at a French inmate. The friend fell to

[22] Imperial War Museum, London, 'Oral History' record.

the ground as Reddehasen kicked her repeatedly in the head and elsewhere on her body. Bleeding profusely, Genia was carried away. Another 16-year-old prisoner from the Lodz Ghetto, Sala Najman, witnessed an equally ferocious Reddehasen episode with his truncheon and boots.

Reddehasen, thick set with an oval face, had form beginning in Mauthausen, before being handed the command of Waldeslust in August 1944. Living with his family in Winsen, very close to Belsen, he was one of many SS who fled but had been tracked down and was in custody.

Kalitowski, the SS guard, would not face charges.

With such a volume of evidence, London decided to prosecute a second Belsen trial but its venue needed careful consideration. Bergen-Belsen was the natural choice but the presence of 15,000 DPs in the immediate vicinity was considered a serious threat to maintaining order if any of the accused was acquitted or the sentencing was too light. Celle was considered. The British didn't want this trial to drag on, a likely outcome given the large number of accused. Cases would be heard together if those accused were involved in the same crime. Trying everyone separately was ruled out.

Under pressure to complete the interrogations Tilling expanded Caola's team. To add to the workload, a previously large and unknown group of former SS guards at the civil internment camp in Munster had been identified. Tilling decided to concentrate primarily in securing evidence only in cases where evidence already existed so any new cases were ignored.

The second Belsen trial did go ahead and it lasted for six weeks, beginning on May 16 and terminating on June 30, 1946, with Celle and Lüneburg the joint locations. Security concerns finally ruled out Bergen-Belsen. With haste the overriding factor, the decision was taken to prosecute only 10 cases where evidence was strong and with multiple witnesses. Reddehasen was one, and he, with three others, was hanged in Hameln jail on October 11, 1946.

No SS guard, commandant, or Aufseherin in Tannenberg was ever charged. Wanted notices on Diercks, Wandt, Stecker and Hille remained in force and thanks to survivor and Kalitowski's descriptions, the British could issue detail apart from height and facial features. Diercks had ginger hair, Wandt was muscular with a Hitler-style moustache, Stecker had a hare-lip and wore glasses, and Hille was unusually tall for a woman. The survivor, Irene Gluck, had described her as pretty with good teeth.

THE COMPENSATION CLAIMS BEGIN

With Israel awarded nationhood in May 1948, its government lobbied the four occupation powers – Britain, America, Russia and France – to resist all West German efforts for sovereignty restoration until compensation was awarded to Jewish survivors of the concentration camps. Reluctant to enter into dialogue with Israel or any Jewish group, Federal Chancellor, Dr Konrad Adenauer, finally succumbed to Allied demands to do so and a deal was struck in The Hague on August 28, 1952. West Germany would pay Israel DM3bn, not in cash but in goods, with an additional DM450m to cover personal claims by world Jewry. That settlement led to the establishment of the Claims Conference to provide the logistical and legal support to claimants[23] and in Benjamin Ferencz, an American lawyer, it had an advisor exceptionally well qualified to champion the cause[24].

As an enlisted man under General Patton, Ferencz had fought in several European theatres. With Nazi atrocities being uncovered in the Allied advance, Ferencz had transferred to the newly created war crimes team of the US army to gather evidence in Dachau, Buchenwald and Mauthausen. As the war ended, he returned to practising law in New York but was quickly co-opted into the

---

[23] The Claims Conference is still maintained and since its first agreement with West Germany in 1952, it has organised more than $70bn in payments to more that 800,000 survivors. It took until February 2018 for the German government, under Claims Conference pressure, to recognize the general claims of 25,000 still-living Algerian survivors who had been in Vichy France.

[24] *Less than Slaves - Jewish forced labour and the quest for Compensation*, Benjamin B. Ferencz, published in association with the United States Holocaust Memorial Museum, Washington D.C., 1984: one of the best accounts of the long and bitter battle between German industry and claimants.

American prosecution team at Nuremberg and became its lead prosecutor in the Einsatzgruppen trial, which *Associated Press* headlined 'the biggest murder trial in history'.

German industry had no intention of facing up to its wartime responsibilities, contributing nothing to the August 1952 settlement but it couldn't forever hide behind the shield of a compliant West German legal system, stuffed with former high-ranking Nazis, and influence in government.

The first compensation claim took aim at I.G.Farben, arguably the most notorious corporate symbol of the Nazi regime with its manufacture of the poison crystals that had gassed millions in the camps. This pharmaceutical and chemicals conglomerate with holdings in BASF, Bayer, Hoechst, and many others, had already been in court in 1947 to defend itself in its trial at Nuremberg. Among the 24 defendants was former SS-Obersturmbannführer (Lt. Colonel) Heinrich Bütefisch, the member of I.G.Farben's supervisory board who had direct responsibility for the company's plant in Monowitz, the vast purpose-built industrial complex known as Auschwitz-3. In Nuremberg, the disbelieving court listened to Bütefisch feigning complete ignorance of both his plant's operation and I.G.Farben's use of 30,000 prisoners from Buna, an Auschwitz satellite. Bütefisch had been a die-hard Nazi and a long-standing member of the 'Freundeskreis', Himmler's slush fund.[25]

Norbert Wollheim filed his claim against I.G.Farben in the Frankfurt District Court in 1953, fearful of what he was pitted against. He also had a dire shortage of funds to prosecute his case. According to Ferencz, this Buna survivor could only offer DM150, or $30, as a fee down payment to his Frankfurt lawyer. The Claims Conference and primarily Jewish groups in the US came to his aid. Wollheim's wartime backstory was so typical: a sister, wife and child were among victims gassed in Auschwitz. The West German press speculated on the outcome as the case was a litmus test for others

---

[25] After serving a short jail spell, Bütefisch served on many company boards and in 1964 he was awarded Germany's Great Cross of Merit for his services to the country. After protests, Federal President Lübke had the award overturned given Bütefisch's wartime record.

that would surely follow.

To everyone's surprise Wollheim won but I.G.Farben immediately challenged the verdict. Thereafter, the claim would be engulfed in legal opinion on whether German industry, despite working for the Reich, had assumed 'moral duty' for the welfare of its slave labour force. Friedrich Flick, with his 300 companies, including Daimler-Benz, was unequivocal in his statements. Flick was adamant that the slave labour survivors used in his plants must be paid nothing.

Over the next three years I.G.Farben obfuscated at every turn but in an early statement there was mention of a payment but only as a 'gesture of goodwill' rather than the 'discharge of an obligation'. I.G.Farben hoped that Wollheim would give up and walk away and many times Wollheim considered doing exactly that. He persevered.

What almost scuppered Wollheim's claim was a demand from the Appellate Court in 1956 that he provide written proof of being a Buna inmate and a slave worker for I.G.Farben. Six months later, probably due to political pressure, I.G.Farben did make an offer and extended it to other Buna workers but only on the understanding that the company accepted no legal responsibility whatsoever for its use of wartime slave labour. Although surprised at this unexpected corporate change of heart, the Claims Conference considered the DM5,000 offer per claimant insufficient, countering with DM14,000, a figure I.G.Farben immediately rejected. The final settlement agreed in February 1957 was DM7,000.

Despite the settlement, Wollheim was bitter at the treatment he had received from the German courts and the company in his four-year battle for compensation. Upset, too, were I.G.Farben's shareholders who believed that the settlement created an open-ended financial liability given that the settlement was open to thousands of Buna survivors. The German stock market was delighted, however, the company share price rising 10% on the news.

The German, British and American governments ratified the settlement and in a move to mollify the shareholder objection, they forcibly imposed a nine-month time-clause for all further claims. Given the near impossible December 1957 deadline, the Claims Conference urgently set up settlement committees in London, New York, Oslo, Melbourne, Vienna, Prague, Budapest and Sao Paulo.

Claimants were given questionnaires to complete but I.G.Farben set a high bar for acceptance and many were turfed out as incomplete or illegible. That December deadline was missed but the Claims Conference, with the help of Ferencz, continued to submit claims.

For the next four years, according to Ferencz, I.G.Farben and its shareholders continued to be downright awkward. At one stage, in 1961, I.G.Farben even demanded a refund on what it had already disbursed, in order to fund non-Jewish slave labour, mainly Poles, excluded from the compensation settlement. Ominously, I.G.Farben threatened to embargo any further payments to Jews.

To discredit the company claim that large numbers of non-Jewish Poles were employed in Buna, Ferencz located a document in Poland recording that in late 1944 only 5% of Buna inmates were Polish. That disclosure went unanswered by I.G.Farben whose shareholders further raised the bar for Buna survivors to claim, dashing their expectations as 'unacceptable' and in this corporate statement was an extraordinary comment: 'The Jews had lived under harder conditions and with the knowledge that they would be gassed'.

For Norbert Wollheim, the Buna survivor, his life would be memorialised after his death in New York in November 1985, aged 85. That memorial is on the site of the I.G.Farben building in Frankfurt, now housing the humanities and cultural studies departments of the Goethe-Universität.

The month before Wollheim had settled in February 1957, the Claims Conference filed the first claim against Rheinmetall in a Berlin-Charlottenberg district court on behalf of two Holocaust survivors, known as Helen R. and Rachel B.. Both women, living in New York, had survived Buchenwald, the concentration camp that provided slave labour to Rheinmetall's Sömmerda shell production plant. Aged 17 and 11 respectively at the time, they worked in Sömmerda with 1,200 other Buchenwald women between July 1944 and March 1945 under inhumane conditions. Rheinmetall directors and senior management involved in Sömmerda demonstrated no compassion in the treatment meted out to its slave labour force, stated counsel for Helen and Rachel. Rheinmetall, in its defence, argued that prisoners from Buchenwald had been forced upon it against its will and for every slave labourer

310

employed the Reich had demanded a payment. [26]

The timing of the claims was embarrassing for Rheinmetall, as only months had passed since the Allies had approved the creation of the Bundeswehr, the West German armed services. Although only for light weapons, the company had been permitted to restart its armaments programme. Redevelopment had begun in Unterlüss and the proving grounds were put back in use.

Mirroring the I.G.Farben case, Rheinmetall stalled. The Claims Conference and its German lawyer, Karl-Heinz Schildbach, believed defeat was inevitable as ranged against them was a vociferous supervisory board, stuffed with former Nazi party members, including the formidable Otto Kransbühler, its vice chairman. Rheinmetall had no intention of caving in. As a former naval lawyer, Kransbühler had expertly and successfully prevented a death sentence for Grand Admiral Karl Dönitz in Nuremburg. Post-war, not only was he a Rheinmetall board member, he had turned his legal expertise to representing Krupp and I.G.Farben in defending against compensation claims.

Despite the doubts the claim continued but the Berlin court set a number of conditions precedent before it would allow the case to proceed. Schildbach needed to submit a raft of documents that would test the ability of any lawyer or researcher. He needed to find written evidence that Rheinmetall had actually owned Sömmerda, the names of the Rheinmetall staff managing the plant, and documentation that clearly illustrated the company had utilised Buchenwald labour.

If those conditions weren't onerous enough, Schildbach had to locate actual details of Helen and Rachel's service in Sömmerda with witnesses to corroborate. The final prerequisite was to establish the comparable 1944 wage for unskilled conditions in the German munitions industry against what slave labourers were paid. Schildbach did track down a wage scale from the Federation of Labour Union for a comparison. [27]

Oral arguments began in February 1959 but in a cynical move,

---

[26] Ferencz, B., p130.
[27] Ibid p131.

the court threw out the case on the grounds that the litigation had begun too late.[28] Astonishingly, it had arbitrarily decided that the end of 1951 had been the deadline for compensation claims to be submitted against Rheinmetall. An appeal was immediately filed in the Bundesgericht, the West German Supreme Court.

As the Supreme Court deliberated, Rheinmetall turned a tin ear to any further dialogue with Schildbach and the two women but in the silence over 800 survivors contacted the Claims Conference in new claims against the company, a number from Tannenberg. When Rheinmetall did agree to restart talks, the Claims Conference put forward the proposal to settle all claims for DM3-5m, an average of DM5,000 per person. That was rebuffed.

Multiple compensation claims now stacked up against a number of German companies and a decision in London marked a further bitter blow. Under the terms of the London Debt Accords, signed on February 27, 1953, West Germany had DM15bn of its DM30bn debt written off by Allied governments to rebuild its economy. Further debt repayments were only payable if the country ran a trade surplus. Compensation claims by nationals of the former German-occupied territories fell under the agreement's remit.

In the London aftermath, the appeals in the Supreme Court of Helen R. and Rachel B. were thrown out, as were the claims of other Sömmerda prisoners. Rheinmetall believed it was off the hook.

THE COMPENSATION BATTLE SHIFTS TO AMERICA

What unexpectedly broke the deadlock wasn't an edict from a German court or a sudden change of mind by Rheinmetall, it was an appeal letter sent to the US President, Lyndon Johnson, the contents of which were publicly aired in the December 3, 1964 edition of the *Springfield Daily News*. The Springfield Armory, one of America's largest and oldest munitions plants, was on the potential closure list of 95 such factories across the country. Defense Secretary, Robert McNamara wanted to shed 30,000 jobs across the sector in

---

[28] Ibid p131.

312

a major cost-cutting exercise.

The appeal to Johnson, signed by the local US Congressman and Springfield's straight-talking mayor, Charles Ryan, wasn't only a plea to block the closure of the Springfield plant. McNamara was intent on buying a West German-produced gun and Ryan was incensed that Springfield jobs were being sacrificed for an import to save money.

At first, the Defense Department denied that an import contract was even in the offing but in the first week of January 1965, it admitted that negotiations were in progress. The *Springfield Daily News* didn't let up, reporting that Ryan was hustling to discover the German firm's identity. His brother helped by visiting the West German consulate in Washington but its diplomats refused to disclose the name. The story went mainstream in the national press, describing the impending deal as the 'Big Secret'. Under extreme pressure, the Pentagon went public on January 14, naming Rheinmetall but Ryan wasn't done. He denounced Rheinmetall as one of several munitions companies that had rearmed Nazi Germany and used concentration camp prisoners in its operations. Protest letters poured into the White House and Congress. In the minds of the press, the story was not only to reverse the Springfield Armory closure but the government's preparedness to engage a company with such a sinister backstory.

Adding to the public clamour were several US army chiefs who doubted the abilities of this Rheinmetall 20-mm gun, calling it sub-standard. If the US required a weapon of this type, it must at least be superior, they said, to a comparable weapon in the Russian armoury. In Düsseldorf, Rheinmetall's frustration turned to anger as US media now targeted those directors with Nazi backgrounds. The anti-Rheinmetall lobby across the US intensified and Jewish groups openly claimed the company was guilty of murder.

When international press reports stated that the deal had been quietly signed in March 1966 – the West German defence minister attending the signing in Washington – the protest groups were outraged. Even at this late stage, there remained hope that the Rheinmetall contract could be overturned but the deal was fully ratified in May by the US army who issued a statement on what had been purchased. The order was for 1,080 guns, known as the G3,

◀ SS-Unterscharführer (Corporal) Hans Alfred Stecker, aged 21, pictured here in his SS file, was on the post-war Allied wanted list. Remembered by survivors as tall, grim-faced, and vicious, Stecker regularly searched the Tannenberg barracks for banned objects and material. His entire family had been wiped out in an Allied bombing raid and Stecker sought brutal retribution on the Tannenberg women.
Source: Bundesarchiv SS file

◀ Another of the drawings by the Tannenberg survivor, Valerie Furth.

▲ The initial thought of survivor, Valerie Furth, was that "it was better than a death camp". As time passed, her opinion would alter.
Source: Cabbages and Geraniums, Valerie Jakober Furth, Columbia University Press, New York, 1989

▶ The only memorial in Unterlüss to the slave workers who died in the war has recently been erected in the town cemetery. The numbers are incomplete and do not include those who were in the Tannenberg concentration camp.

▲ Ben Ferencz, the claimants' champion for compensation against Germany's largest companies, including Rheinmetall. The photograph shows Ferencz at Nuremburg as the chief US prosecutor in the Einsatzgruppen trial.

▲ Otto Kransbühler, Rheinmetall's vice chairman and former member of the Nazi party, had no intention of caving in on the compensation claims. Kransbühler's legal rhetoric at Nuremburg had helped his client, Grand Admiral Karl Dönitz, avoid the death penalty.

▲ Almost all of the Tannenberg women ended up in Belsen, including the 500 sent here earlier by Susanne Hille in February 1945. This graphic photograph in the Imperial War Museum's Belsen collection shows SS Aufseherinnen, under British army guards, filling one of the vast tranches with dead.

which had the capacity to fire 900 rounds a minute. The Swiss arms firm, Hispano Suiza, had first produced the weapon. Included in the $74m deal were spare parts and four million rounds. Further orders would extend the contract value to $150m and first deliveries were expected in the summer of 1967. *The New York Times* and *The Wall Street Journal* questioned the integrity of the deal given that army chiefs had publicly discredited the weapon.

Several newspapers including *The New York Times* turned their attention onto Julius Klein, a Chicago public relations expert and Rheinmetall's chief lobbyist in the US. Klein enjoyed considerable influence in Washington and had been instrumental in landing the deal.[29] Thanks to Klein, believed Benjamin Ferencz, Rheinmetall had powerful friends.[30] Despite being a past champion of Jewish war veterans in the US, Klein had sent a six-page letter to the US State Department refuting all slave labour allegations against Rheinmetall, even arguing that its use by German industry had never been properly investigated.[31] Klein demanded that the US government shouldn't cave in or be influenced by the noisy public campaign. The gun contract must stand.

Adding his support to Ryan, Springfield's mayor, Ferencz met the Defense Secretary, Cyrus Vance, to suggest that his department, at the very least, might publicly express sentiment to the Rheinmetall slave labour survivors struggling for even token compensation in Germany. Vance listened, outwardly sympathetic, later shuffling the request over to the State Department.

Ferencz met Klein in Frankfurt but Rheinmetall's PR man ridiculed the claims, saying that the Claims Conference had relied on extortionate demands rather than appealing to 'Rheinmetall's corporate conscience'. The meeting went badly. A meeting was arranged with Rheinmetall's managing director, Otto Caesar, another with a Nazi past, but before it took place the US embassy in Bonn advised Ferencz to meet a senior official in the German ministry of

---

[29] *The New York Times*, August 13, 1966.
[30] *Less than Slaves - Jewish forced labour and the quest for Compensation*, Benjamin B. Ferencz, p134.
[31] Ibid p135.

defence. At least this meeting was productive with the official offering to write to Caesar to suggest that Rheinmetall should pay what he considered to be a modest amount. The Düsseldorf meeting with Caesar failed to solve the impasse and shortly afterwards the Claims Conference received a formal Rheinmetall letter: "After careful consideration of all the circumstances, our Board of Directors came to the conclusion that our company cannot recognize the merits of your demands".[32]

The opposition to Rheinmetall in the US reached fever pitch and some company directors, according to Ferencz, queried its heavy-handed decision. The headlines of association with the SS in some of the worst concentration camps didn't abate. The White House, Senate, Congress, the State Department were all in the front line of criticism. Springfield's proactive mayor never waivered in his campaign resulting in Rheinmetall's Washington's office pushing out a statement that a new post-war Rheinmetall had emerged, unrelated to its past. In Congress, calls to block the gun contract grew louder. Rheinmetall's reputation was being shredded as the Defense Department announced it was rethinking the award. Klein was scathing and put the blame squarely on the interference of Ferencz.

THE LADY IN MINK

Ferencz received an unexpected visitor in his New York office, 'a woman wearing a mink coat, a mink hat and with an alligator skin handbag'. She introduced herself as the wife of Canadian businessman, John Hecht, who had dealings with Rheinmetall in Düsseldorf. She came armed with an offer.

This lady in mink did make a compensation offer, of sorts, roughly averaging DM2,000 per claimant. That offer was checked out and had some basis. Yet, as more negotiations followed between all parties, Ferencz wasn't surprised when the hardliner Rheinmetall vice chairman, Otto Kransbühler, personally took charge of the discussions. At first, the compensation package offered was for

---

[32] Ibid p137.

DM3m in total but the Claims Conference held out for DM5m and was prepared to negotiate. The lady in mink re-emerged to report that 'Kransbühler was keen to settle' but any settlement needed to be ratified by the board.

It certainly wasn't ratified and what seemed to be a conclusion for the claimants ended with a resounding response of no deal from Kransbühler. Seemingly, Rheinmetall and its vice chairman were more obdurate than ever. Several West German publications took the side of Rheinmetall with Ferencz castigated for his part in the vociferous campaign to ruin the reputation of one of the country's largest companies. In US government circles, officials figuratively wrung their hands, wanting to appease the worsening public outrage but eager to honour the Rheinmetall contract.

Ferencz as a matter of urgency expanded his research on Rheinmetall's use of slave labour in other locations, not just in Sömmerda. Calls were made to the bürgermeister in Unterlüss and exhaustive efforts were conducted by Jewish organisations to find as many Rheinmetall slave labourers they could.[33] Many had died or had emigrated. Of the 800 women in the Tannenberg concentration camp, 261 were found and asked to submit compensation claims. Many had to be rejected because facts couldn't be verified.

The deal that was eventually struck was worth DM2.5m with Rheinmetall never formerly recognizing any claim, including the joint claim of Helen R. and Rachel B.. Ferencz reflected that the settlement equated to a very small percentage on the profit of the US gun deal. That contract, the first post-war weapons import from West Germany, was never reversed but some of the later additions were quietly dropped. Rheinmetall's reputation in the US may have been sullied but it was only temporary. The company would later win large orders from the American military.

I.G.Farben's eventual one-time settlement was $375 to $1,250 to each of the 5,855 former prisoners whose claims were approved. Krupp averaged $825 to 3,090 qualified claimants, AEG-Telefunken paid $500 to 2,223 and Siemens $825 to 2,200. Dynamit-Nobel's

---

[33] Ibid p150.

contribution, negotiated in 1980, was one of the last settled. It made a one-time payment of DM2,000, equivalent to $1,000, to 2,500 slave labourers. Rheinmetall's payment was amongst the smallest, paying out an average of $425 to 1,507 approved claimants. Some were Tannenberg survivors. The Flick Concern, the umbrella entity for 300 companies, paid nothing.

For the 5,855 I.G.Farben claimants who were successful by the end of 1973, the total compensation disbursed was DM27.8m, more than half of the total DM51.9m paid out by itself, Krupp, AEG, Siemens and Rheinmetall.[34] In addition, I.G.Farben paid out DM3m to non-Jewish workers. All payments were described as reparations. The I.G.Farben payments at least made the lives of the Buna survivors 'just a little easier', recorded Ferencz.

Krupp and Rheinmetall, West Germany's largest two munitions companies, had been models of obfuscation. Both had dispatched staff to Birkenau to oversee slave worker selection, yet they had stood behind their defence of assuming no responsibility whatsoever for their employment. The owners of both companies were stained with convictions for aiding and abetting war crimes. Alfried Krupp and 10 others were convicted at Nuremburg, their sentences later reduced, and members of the Röchling family, the post-war owners of Rheinmetall, had also been charged. Krupp had instructed his lawyers to play hardball in every compensation lawsuit. Wrongly, the Claims Conference had hoped that Krupp would voluntarily settle. He would be forced to do so, which was also the case for Rheinmetall eager to save its gun contract with the US Defence Department.

The first claim against Krupp had been filed in January 1954 with the claimant asking for DM40,000. With the Krupp lawyers immediately responding that the claimant must deposit into the court sufficient funds to cover court costs, the claimant reduced his claim to DM2,000. In a highly disputed move, the Americans had returned

---

[34] Ibid pp209-211. The individual amounts, and destination of payments, by these five companies had been audited and prepared by a New York accounting firm as at end December 1973.

to Krupp all his confiscated wealth and assets. Alfried Krupp, forever preaching that he had been unjustly treated at Nuremburg, travelled widely doing deals and *Time* magazine put him on a cover with the caption 'The Richest Man in the World'.

By the late 1990s, pressure had grown for a further, probably final, compensation settlement from corporate Germany. The Swiss, too, felt the brunt of condemnation after Jewish researchers had uncovered a huge cache of secret documents gathered by US and British intelligence agencies during and after the war. The Swiss banking system had shielded and laundered substantial looted Nazi wealth.[35] Intelligence had also been obtained pointing to the Swedish banking system that had laundered plundered Nazi funds through several large US banking giants including Chase Manhattan and JP Morgan. These files had been kept secret as they illuminated the extent of US co-operation with the Hitler regime.

German Federal President, Johannes Rau, called for German industry to step up and contribute DM5bn into the German Slave Labour Fund.[36] 'We owe it to the victims', he urged an industry audience. Gerhard Schroder, Germany's Chancellor, hoped companies would make good previous pledges but the response was pitiful and in May 2000, there were calls in the German media to name and shame. Rheinmetall was among the list that had contributed with a nominal payment of DM1m into the fund in December 1999, a sum of $500,000 in the-then currency equivalent. The DM5bn target was never achieved.

Many survivors who had slaved for German industry were broken in body, mind and spirit. They had endured appalling hardship and cruelty and had witnessed harrowing scenes. Death was never far away in the camps. Compensation was justly deserved but it was never accompanied with sincere regret or an apology and for that German industry should forever hang its collective head in shame.

---

[35] The Swiss Bank Holocaust Settlement is now closed to claimants. It paid out $1,285bn to 458,400 victims and their heirs. Part of the total covered payments to the Claims Conference, which totalled $252m for 173,000 for claimants used as slave labour by German companies with their wealth and property confiscated by the Nazis after incarceration in the slave labour and concentration camps.
[36] The Stiftungsfonds der deutschen Wirtschaft.

LACK OF CLOSURE

Tannenberg has become the concentration camp the world has forgotten, as have the other slave labour camps in Unterlüss. None are signposted or memorialised despite the best efforts of the village's present-day bürgermeister, his deputy, the Gedenkstätte Bergen-Belsen, and private individuals, who have pursued the cause. I asked Rheinmetall if it would engage with these parties. On principle, Rheinmetall was not *per se* against signposting of camps, it had agreed to several in Düsseldorf in 2017, but the company was adamant that none would ever be erected on Rheinmetall grounds. Under that policy, Unterlüss may remain bereft of any indication of its sinister backstory apart from an incomplete list of dead on a board in the village cemetery.

Children had died in the Sauglingsheim, the 'Baby Camp', and amongst its Polish casualties was Stanislav Solinski, who had been transported with his mother. He succumbed on December 30, 1943, aged five months. Vladislav Musial had been born in Unterlüss in October 1943 and was nine months old when she died in January 1944. There are 34 dead Russian children named on the board including Nikolaus Korniejenko, who was aged one month, and Vera Kondareschka, born near Leningrad in November 1942, who lived only a month longer.

In the research and writing of this story, one major loose end was apparent. What had happened to Susanne Hille, the 22-year-old SS-Aufseherin from Tannenberg, referred to by inmates as the 'Brown One'? The British had put out wanted notices across Germany.

Our search for Hille took us to a graveyard in a quiet village in the former East Germany. Her death is surrounded in intrigue and worthy of a separate chapter. It is a fitting conclusion to our six accounts of what occurred in the last days of the Third Reich.

The two memorial headstones for the Italian, Polish and Russian children in the cemetery

MAIN SOURCES

★ The Belsen Trial, *Trial of Josef Kramer and forty-four others*, published papers of the trial, 1946

★ Gedenkstätte Bergen-Belsen (Department of Research and Documentation)

★ National Archives, Kew, London: various military files on Rheinmetall, bombings of the Rheinmetall plants, including Unterlüss, interviews and interrogations conducted by officers from the Royal Artillery, members of No.1 War Crimes Investigation Group, based in Belsen-Hohne

★ Bundesarchiv, Berlin, including the Berlin Document Centre, the SS personnel files, and the records of the Ministry of State Security of the GDR

★ Bernd Horstmann, *Encyclopedia of Camps and Ghettos 1933-1945,* Indiana University Press 2009

★ *Chronik der Politischen Gemeinde Unterlüss,* Jürgen Gedicke

★ Bürgermeister and deputy Bürgermeister, Unterlüss

★ Rathaus – Unterlüss

★ Hendrik Altmann

★ Yad Vashem

★ *Cabbages and Geraniums,* Valerie Jakober Furth, Columbia University Press, New York, 1989

★ *The Secret Seder at Unterlüss*, Dina Kraus Ehrenreich

★ *'Rheinmetall – Vom Reiz, im Rheinland ein grosses Werk zu errichten'*, Dr Christian Leitzbach, official historian, Rheinmetall, Greven Verlag, Cologne, Vols 1 and 2, 2014

★ *The Times*, London

★ *The New York Times*

★ *Die Welt*

★ *Springfield Daily News*

★ Benjamin Ferencz: *'Less Than Slaves – Jewish Forced Labour and the Quest for Compensation'*, published in association with the US Holocaust Memorial Museum, 2002

★ CIOS (British Combined Intelligence Objective Sub-Committee) reports on Rheinmetall – London

★ BIOS (British Intelligence Objectives Subcommittee) – its technical reports on Unterlüss were held under BIOS 7/Exploitation – London

★ The Flick Trial: Nuremberg summary and sentencing, December 1947

★ Special thanks to Dr Leitzbach, official historian, Rheinmetall, who answered my many questions.

★ Special thanks also to Hendrik Altmann, who took us to Tannenberg and who shared his knowledge of the camp and village.

UNTERLÜSS, THE SECRET ROCKET FACILITY IN THE WOODS

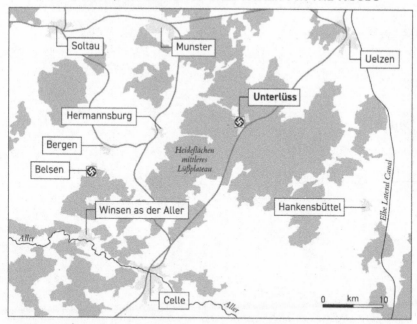

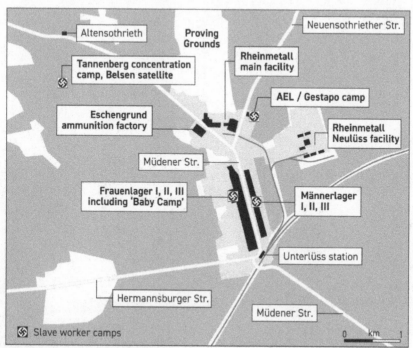

Rheinmetall's slave worker camps

VI
THE VILLAGE THAT KEEPS ITS SECRETS

STORYLINE

Two reminders of Susanne Hille's savagery in Tannenberg:

VALERIE FURTH, A SURVIVOR

She remembered this SS warder, one of three female warders in the camp, for the rest of her life. 'Even the guards feared her', she had poignantly related in her book, Cabbages and Geraniums, *with her own drawn illustrations. 'Astride her horse, she looked down on us with strangely piercing eyes. Once during rollcall, she whipped a friend of mine, a very pretty girl who worked in the office. After the beating my friend was unable to move for days'. A caricature pencil drawing in the book is of Hille, with stark bulging eyes, spiky hair, and an SS symbol sewn into the neckline of a dress.*

'We called her the 'Brown One''.

FRANZ KALITOWSKI, A MALE SS COLLEAGUE

'Hille was responsible for most of the atrocities, maltreating the inmates and beating them up.' He further remarked in his interrogation statement –
'Good looking. Sadist.'

◀ Picher church - front entrance.
Source: Nigel Bance

ACCORDING to records of Picher church, the body of a 22-year-old woman, a 'salesgirl', was buried in its grounds on the very last day of war in Europe. Yet, was the body that of Susanne Hille as the records state?

In the frenzied death rattle that was a crumbling Third Reich, incriminating files and documents were being wantonly destroyed. Fearing Allied charges of war crimes, those responsible had gone on the run, changing uniforms and identities. Some would eventually disappear into Nazi-friendly South America, courtesy of compliant Vatican paperwork, or into the Middle East, namely Egypt and Syria. German communes in Namibia, then known as the former German colony of South West Africa, would be just as welcoming.

War criminals mingled with three million ordinary soldiers, who had only done their duty for the nation, in Allied detention camps across Germany, many former concentration camps. Given the volume, few could be seriously interrogated and most were allowed to go home with discharge and travel papers. Lawyers, doctors and other high-ranking Nazis, who had arrogantly strutted in their SS uniforms, determining life-or-death situations for so many, seamlessly resumed their careers and achieved high office, some at the very highest level of government. Notable examples are West German chancellor, Georg Kiesinger, who as a radio propagandist in the wartime foreign ministry had worked closely with the Reich's arch propaganda minister Joseph Goebbels. Kurt Waldheim, an Austrian, throughout his glittering post-war political career tried hard to conceal his murky past. As a Wehrmacht intelligence officer attached to military units active in the Balkans, Waldheim's signature adorns documents relating to massacres of Yugoslav partisans and the deportation of Greek Jews to the Polish death camps. Waldheim would be elected as Secretary-General to the United Nations and later was Austria's president.

In what would become East Germany, there were a myriad of places to hide and in plain sight. The new Soviet occupiers in the post-war era rarely researched into backgrounds. Russia's new enemy was the West not former Nazis: war crimes were quietly ignored.

Once the British had been aware of the horrors of Belsen and its three satellite camps, including Tannenberg in Unterlüss, 'Wanted

Notices' were distributed across Germany for the arrest of Hille and Tannenberg's three commandants. Hille was the top target. Fully cleared of inmates by April 12 and with all documents burnt, Tannenberg's guards hadn't hung around. They were gone.

Susanne Hille had headed east to Mecklenberg, in the direction of Ludwigslust, close to the Elbe where the Wehrmacht was putting up a stout retreat resistance against the Red Army. It is likely she had a companion, maybe Josefine Holub, an Aufseherin colleague in both Ravensbrück and Tannenberg, who, like Hille, had been named in survivor testimonies to British war crimes investigators. The hunt was on.

TRACKING DOWN SUSANNE HILLE

Two letters in the archives of the Gedenkstätte Belsen immediately held our attention. An independent researcher[1] in 1999 had requested the Deutsches Rotes Kreuz, the German Red Cross, to conduct a trace on Hille. Its Munich-based service disclosed that she had died in the former East German village of Bresegard bei Hagenow on May 7, 1945. The village is now renamed Bresegard bei Picher. As part of the trace, a letter from the-then pastor in 1999 of the Evangelisch-Lutherische Pfarre church in Picher, a village 2km away from Bresegard, had confirmed that Susanne Luise Pauline Hille had been buried in Field 6 in the churchyard, the day after her death. Her date of birth was recorded as June 26, 1922, with place of birth noted as Altenburg in Thüringia. Cause of death wasn't logged. The pastor further wrote that sometime in the 1980s, this part of the cemetery was dug over.

Susanne Hille had died at the age of 22, ironically on the very last full day of the war when all around the country German armies had already surrendered. Had her death been violent or had she succumbed to an illness or disease rife in the concentration camps she had worked in? Allied airstrikes had ended apart from isolated incidents so the chance of dying in one was slim indeed.

---

[1] Peter Heine.

▲ Picher's church dominates the village, this side view facing the main street. The cemetery on this side and in the front is divided up into areas for each village in the diocese.

▲ The other side of the church has been left to grass and was probably the area dug over in the 1980s under East German regulation that all unkempt sites were unproductive. Field 6, in which Susanne Hille was buried, we think was here but the present parson, Matthias Galleck, in post for the past 20 years, has no document to confirm.

▲ The imposing home of Friedrich Drenkhahn, the local Nazi dignitary and registrar for local births and deaths. His house in Lindenstrasse faces the rear of the church.

▲ Only one grave in this area has been left intact. This belongs to the Polish PoW, Stanislav Bartuk, who while employed as a farmworker in Picher, had a banned local relationship, and as to who killed him on September 16, 1943 is unclear. Towards the end of the war, his former employer, a woman, sympathetic to the state of the Jewish prisoners passing through Picher on the death marches, was often seen by the side of the road handing out food to the desperate.

▲ The parsonage where Wilhelm Köhn lived is also on Lindenstrasse.

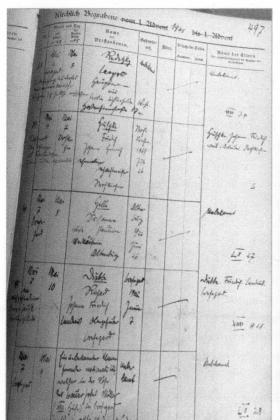

▼ The church burial book would add to the twists and turns in the death of Susanne Hille. Wilhelm Köhn, pastor since 1932, had completed the record of her burial.

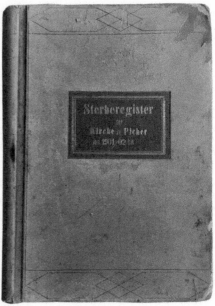

▲ The third entry on the relevant page recorded Hille as being buried on May 8 - in a grave marked LII 27. Köhn had written that she was a 'Verkäuferin', or salesgirl. This entry had marked the demise of Susanne Luise Pauline Hille, the feared sadist from Tannenberg who enjoyed thrashing her victims to death.

What caught our attention was the last entry on the page, an 'Unbekannt', an unknown, had also died in Bresegard, in Hufe, in the vicinity of the Möller Hof, and on the same day that Hille had died. What further heightened the intrigue over Hille's death was that its finder, Wilhelm Möller, had also been the finder of her body. This unknown was buried in L11 28, next to Hille, but again this death raised doubts that there was more to the death of Susanne Hille. In Köhn's handwriting the parson recorded Hille's burial as No. 40. The next burial, No. 41, has nothing to do with our story but for the Unbekannt, Köhn recorded no number. It should have been No. 42. The present pastor could offer no explanation. He, too, was baffled.

The Deutsches Rotes Kreuz trace was the conclusive confirmation that she had died and there the matter of her death should have ended for us but the burial record in Picher's church raised a flag of serious doubt in my mind. In those end-days of war, how had Picher's pastor in May 1945 obtained such biographical detail on Hille including her three forenames and the date and place of birth? Was she known in Bresegard or did she have a local relative who might have supplied the detail? Given the speed of her burial, parental contact in Altenburg, south of Leipzig, was certainly not feasible.

We began by looking into Hille's first employment as an SS Aufseherin in the notorious Ravensbrück concentration camp, the training ground for hundreds of female SS camp guards before their transfer elsewhere. The camp was in Furstenberg on the Havel and to the south of Mecklenberg's three large lakes. With records almost non-existent since most were destroyed in the camp's final weeks, a list of Aufseherinnen was compiled in 1949 as a result of the first two trials of Ravensbrück staff and survivor testimonies given to British war crimes staff.[2] The list was far from definitive but Hille is on it.

Initially, Hille was understood to have been a guard in the experimental and 'correctional' camp in the Ravensbrück complex for girls and young women, the Jugendschutzlager. It had opened in June 1942 and was the only camp of its type in Nazi Germany for females. The inmates, aged 16-19, were referred to as Zoglingen, or 'pupils', and the intention of the Kriminalpolizei, or Criminal Police, which ran the Jugendschutzlager, was to administer strict discipline but without punishment beatings. With jurisdiction later passing to the SS Concentration Camp Inspectorate, humiliation, food deprivation, torture, and whippings became the norm in this 'correctional' process. By January 1945, the Jugendschutzlager had grown from the original two blocks to 17 and it held 1,200 girls and young women. The Gestapo had sole use of one block that held the

---

[2] Those trials took place in 1946 and 1948 by British military courts. Of the 10 found guilty, nine were sentenced to death. A camp commandant, Max Koegel, had already committed suicide in prison. There were subsequent Ravensbrück trials. The Soviet tribunals were lenient in sentencing and most found guilty were released in the mid 1950s. East Germany later prosecuted some of the camp guards.

children of captured partisans. Zoglingen worked arduous shifts at the nearby Siemens plant with other parties of young girls' felling and dragging large trees onto trucks. For those who still refused to conform to the Nazi ideals, the Aufseherinnen carried out selection detail for transportation to Buchenwald or the Polish death camps.

The Gedenkstätte Ravensbrück now believes that Hille might also have worked as a guard in the main women's camp. In January 1945, Ravensbrück and its subcamps held over 45,000 women and 5,000 men and during the course of the war, over 130,000 women had passed through its system and up to 30,000 perished. Hille's employment at Ravensbrück, according to records, began on August 14, 1944, at a starting wage of 50 Reichsmarks paid through the Stadtsparkasse Neustrelitz in Fürstenberg. The account number was 4043. That account was still open in 1949 and it might have remained open for many years. Previously she had worked as a Verkäuferin, or salesgirl, probably in her hometown of Altenburg. Young women like Hille were encouraged to join up. An education wasn't necessary, only an adherence to National Socialism.

Hille and Josefine Holub were transferred from Ravensbrück to KZ Tannenberg on January 5, 1945, a date confirmed by their final salaries being paid into the Stadtsparkasse Neustrelitz.

All members of the SS, including the Aufseherinnen, carried an identity card referred to as an Ausweis and given Gedenkstätte Ravensbrück had no copy of Hille's card we asked for a copy of another to check what details were included. The Gedenkstätte sent us the ID for Marianne Minges, who would twice be sentenced to death by hanging.[3] There is little space on it for much biographical detail: a signed photograph of Minges, a typed-in name with just one forename, and her Aufseherin number. The-then commandant of the women's camp, SS-Hauptsturmführer Fritz Suhren[4], added his expansive signature before the card was officially stamped. Such limited space on the Ausweis only heightened our suspicions on

---

[3] Minges was freed in 1950 when the West German judicial authorities, in a surprise decision, no longer determined Jugendschutzlager detention as a war crime.
[4] Suhren was hanged in 1950.

Hille's death in Bresegard. Staging your own death to avoid facing justice over war crimes was a common practice in the final days of the Third Reich.

After Tannenberg was fully cleared of its inmates on April 15 where had Hille gone and how had she landed up in Mecklenberg?

Hille might have fled to the comparative safety of this area of Germany but there is the possibility that Hille and her two Aufseherin colleagues in Tannenberg, Josefine Holub and Chani[5], were recalled to Ravensbrück, to help in the camp's last and largest forced 'evacuation'. In late March, 5,600 women had already been taken to Mauthausen in Austria and Bergen-Belsen and in late April, fitting into the Hille and Holub timeline, 20,000 women began a death march towards northern Mecklenberg. Wöbbelin, the transit camp for inmates on death marches from other camps, just 2km to the north of Ludwigslust, might have been its first intended destination but enroute, the Red Army intercepted the long column and liberated the women. Many of the SS guards had already fled.

INTRIGUE AND MURDER

Bresegard bei Picher, today, has a population of 295 humans and 300,000 livestock. The 'Hitler Oak', planted in its Hitler Platz, still thrives. Post-German reunification has brought regeneration. Many of its traditionally constructed homes, with attached large brick barns in their rear, are now modern dwellings and heated by state-of-the-art biogas boilers. The endless fields that grow the corn that feeds the animals that provides the organic waste to manufacture the gas are a stark reminder of the once authoritarian dead hand of East German state planning. There is no crop diversity. Mechanisation has largely replaced human labour in the vast animal sheds outside Bresegard and the hamlet of Picher. Wild boars roam the cornfields and when the fields are cropped the boars run into the crosshairs of the hunters in their watchtowers.

---

[5] Her full name is unknown. Her name might have been incorrectly noted in survivor testimonies.

Tensions emanating from successive state land and property grabs remain. Villagers turfed out of their homes post-war in favour of state-approved dwellers only rarely had their property returned to them. One bitter Picher resident, for the rest of her life, walked past her former family home fearing personal harm if she ever began redress proceedings for its return. A Bresegard villager confided to us quietly during our visit that there remains a 'Brown' sentiment, with modern-day elements of fascism stitched into the very fabric of the village's social community.

Bresegard and Picher have their own bürgermeisters, or mayors, who despite their main jobs still provide the time to solve local issues. The Evangelisch-Lutherische Pfarre church brings the communities together. Externally, this Picher edifice is magnificent in style and size but inside, scarce funding has left it somewhat bereft of character. The long wooden pews are in need of care and polish. In the burial ground, the large grassy area surrounding the church is bereft of headstones that should have given a glimpse of the church's ancient history with its roots extending into the 12th century. Under an East German edict, the headstones were either removed or ploughed into the hallowed ground in the early 1980s, as much of the burial ground was overgrown. All land, even sacred sites, had to become productive. Only recent deaths have headstones.

These two villages, not far from Ludwigslust, figure prominently in our account of Susanne Hille's final days. It is an account of intrigue and murder, a secret that is still kept by the few who still remember and little did we know that our research would lead us to a second wanted SS war criminal, who had lived in plain sight for the rest of his life concealing his past to both his two families. We ventured whether there was a connection between him and the death of Hille.

Before our visit we needed to find a death certificate but doubted whether such paperwork had even existed with the collapse of local and regional administration at the time but to our astonishment the Hagenow Standesamt, the regional registry office that included Bresegard, informed us that the death had been recorded. It sent us a certified copy. Hagenow is a short distance north of Bresegard bei Picher. Hille's certificate had been completed in Sütterlin, the flowing German handwriting script taught in German schools from 1915 until 1941, but we knew someone who expertly deciphered it.

To facilitate our visit to Bresegard and Picher, the respective bürgermeisters readily accommodated our requests to arrange respective gatherings of villagers, several of whom were children who lived through those final days of war. Duly presenting ourselves, our audiences were curious as to why an English writer and his fellow English researcher, who lives in Germany, had taken such an interest in their villages. Astonishment clearly registered when we explained that a wanted SS war criminal, a woman, was buried in the grounds of its community church.

Sadly, a key Bresegard resident declined to attend, a former bürgermeister who we believed knew the truth of Hille's time in the village, as related to her by her mother who had been in a position to know.

DEATH STALKED THE COUNTRYSIDE

Mecklenburg had long been a favoured hunting playground for top Nazis, such as Hermann Göring, whose shooting parties hunted elk whilst staying in the grandeur of the hunting lodge in the tiny hamlet of Jasnitz, just north of Picher. An encounter with Göring in Picher in the mid 1930s is still recalled. Göring had stopped his car at the sight of a young man, enquiring 'where are we?' which received the gruff response of 'Picher'. Göring took exception to his attitude and warned the young man before waving his driver on.

Now, with the war only weeks to run, any such sporting pleasures were over. Death stalked this countryside, the area adrift with refugees clogging up the roads and tracks. German Volksdeutsche, encouraged in the first successful flush of the war to take over confiscated farms and property in the occupied eastern territories, now trudged west into the German heartland and away from the Red Army advance. Sharing the narrow roads were inmates on death marches from camps in Poland, and columns of Allied PoWs.

Emaciated and ill concentration camp prisoners could never withstand the rigours of daily walking and those that succumbed were summarily dealt with. There is a record of one sympathetic Picher resident, sitting by the side of the road, offering what sustenance she could to these prisoners passing through, in their concentration camp clothes. This same woman had employed a Polish PoW, Stanislav Bartuk, on her farm earlier in the war but the local authorities had him shot in September 1943 after a relationship with a Picher woman. His headstone is still visible in Picher's church graveyard and is maintained, one of the very few that were not ploughed into the soil in the early 1980s.

On March 21, a forced march of RAF PoWs, enroute to the PoW camp in Fallingbostel, near Hanover, was in the south of Ludwigslust. Cecil Room, a PoW, recorded his experiences.[6] 'The going was very hard', he said, the guards never letting up: 'we had to walk 14 miles a day on a diet of two slices of bread and two spuds. Blokes died every day'. As the PoWs headed to Bresegard bei Eldena[7], Room and his mates encountered a German farm worker and bartered 15 cigarettes for a chunk of sausage. When they reached Bresegard bei Eldena, the column split up and occupied several barns, roughly 100 men in each.

Room shared out the sausage meat and they drank from a water tap in the yard, their first running water for days, before falling into an exhaustive sleep. At 5.30am, off they started again. 'It was a glorious day', wrote Room, and he sweated in his RAF greatcoat. Needing to relieve himself, he veered off from the column only to receive a bone-crunching blow in his back from the rifle butt belonging to a German sergeant. He fell reeling from the pain. Summoning up all his strength, Room staggered to his feet and then he ran back to the column deliberately outpacing the portly sergeant running behind, flushed and panting. Room loudly shouted, 'I'll do him one fine day!'

The RAF column did reach Fallingbostel with the body count continuing without a pause. The stay was short with Montgomery's army close. Even the guards were experiencing the extreme fatigue. Outside Bergen in the daily burial ritual, 15 PoWs were laid into the hastily dug graves. As their still-living colleagues trudged away,

---

[6] BBC: *WW2 People's War*, archive of memories written by the public and gathered by the BBC. Recorded October 2005.
[7] There are two villages with the name of Bresegard in this region, Bresegard bei Eldena is to the south of Bresegard bei Picher.

above them a dogfight was in play. RAF Typhoons and Spitfires were beating up a Luftwaffe station and FW190s encountered them in combat. Later, one British aircraft came in low over the column, to loud cheers, dropping leaflets proclaiming that the end of the war was close. The guards were curious.

HILLE FLEES LUDWIGSLUST

Ludwigslust, 13km to the east of Picher, had been a bolthole for Hille and other SS for several days before the surrender on May 2 of the remnants of the 200,000-strong 21st German Army, under Major General Kurt von Tippelskirch. Renowned for its palace, once owned by a German prince and described as the 'Versailles of the north' given its splendour, Ludwigslust was bursting with thousands of refugees competing for shelter and food. Hiding out on a farm was Hille.

A sergeant in the 325 Glider Regiment, 82nd US Airborne, Larry Gourlie, recollected the first two days of Ludwigslust's occupation.[8] In his commandeered basement room, the loud and regular rhythm of German jackboots on the cobbles above prevented any sleep. American machine gun posts were embedded each side of the road as this beaten army came in to be disarmed. Vehicles had to be abandoned and the weapons piles grew, as did the quantity of watches dumped into disused oil drums. The town's citizens were also ordered to hand over weapons, without exception. Makeshift camps for the German PoWs were set up spreading for miles outside Ludwigslust, into the fields and the villages.

On the eastern perimeter of the town, observing the surrender, the Red Army stood off with orders not to interfere. That didn't stop it firing the large German ammunition dump and for three days the fire raged and Ludwigslust was enveloped in a dense pall of smoke that contaminated fresh water supplies. Fraternisation occurred all along this Allied front as Americans swapped cigarettes for strong Russian alcohol. German pistols became popular mementoes for the Americans and in one amusing but painful episode, as a trooper

---

[8] Memoir held in Gedenkstätte Wöbbelin.

fiddled with the gun to show off to his colleagues, it fired. A colleague was hit in the hip.

An incident in the town was to leave a marked impression on Gourlie. In a jeep with two glider regiment colleagues, a commotion brought it to a sharp halt. Three 'naked male skeletons'[9] were shuffling around inside the front window of a clothing shop, striped clothing strewn on the floor. The gathering crowd laughed at the spectacle, some jeered.

These living skeletons were pulling on their new clothes, oblivious to their audience. When none of the three responded to questions in English or German, Gourlie tried in broken French. One was indeed a Frenchman and he said he came from Wöbbelin concentration camp just 2km to the north, and the guards had fled. The camp was unknown to the Americans. Gourlie and his colleagues drove to Wöbbelin and the gates were open. Inside, they were met with the sight of bodies and the pervasive smell of putrefying flesh. Gourlie described the very basic brick barracks that had only narrow slits for windows and all were blocked up. Inside, the dead competed with the living for the filthy straw. The locked door to what should have been the washroom was prized open and upright corpses literally tumbled out. The SS had used it as a warehouse to store the dead. With no water pipes installed, the only washroom in the camp had never functioned.

Another member of Gourlie's glider regiment later described the sight of bodies stacked high in two railway boxcars on the siding into the camp. In open view were two open pits and the soldiers put on their gas masks to stifle the smell. Inmates shuffled aimlessly around, begging their liberators for food and water.

After the Wöbbelin discovery, Gourlie quickly returned to Ludwigslust to report. The town's bürgermeister was summoned to the palace, now commandeered by the US army, and bluntly ordered to select civilians for the following morning. They were to go to Wöbbelin and prepare bodies for burial. No Ludwigslust resident would admit to knowledge of this concentration camp in its midst.

---

[9] The actual phrase used by Gourlie.

It was a sombre service on May 7 when 200 of the Wöbbelin dead were buried in the manicured front lawns of Ludwigslust palace with every able-bodied person in Ludwigslust ordered to attend as well as Wehrmacht officers, including 12 generals who looked on dispassionately. To the side of the dug graves the dead had been wrapped in sheets with the face exposed for maximum effect. Gourlie and his regiment watched edgily from the perimeter, their weapons loaded. Snipers still operated. This was just one mass grave. There would be seven in total. A mass wartime grave of Wöbbelin dead was discovered in the 1960s, in the dense forest of Neu Lüblow and very close to the concentration camp. With the camp overflowing, the aptly named 'Corpse Unit' of prisoners had been ordered by the SS to transport bodies to a number of locations.

Wöbbelin, initially named 'Reiherhorst', was to house captured Allied aircrew but it was left unfinished and its use changed dramatically with the arrival of death marches from emptying concentration camps, the first being 500 prisoners from Neuengamme near Hamburg. For some arrivals the stay was merely days, as they were moved out on new death marches. The body count soared when SS-Obersturmbannführer (Lt. Colonel) Paul Werner Hoppe, the former commandant of the main Stutthof concentration camp to the north, near Gdansk, and his Stutthof deputy, Hauptsturmführer (Captain) Theodor Meyer, took over on April 20. A contingent of Stutthof guards accompanied them. With the arrival of Hoppe, Wöbbelin would become one of the final monstrous monuments to German barbarity. In the 10 weeks of its existence, from when it opened in February 2 to when the camp was liberated on May 2, more than 1,000 died out of 5,000 inmates from 25 nationalities.

Dorothy Forester, a member of an American Red Cross unit of seven nurses, had written home about what she was experiencing in Ludwigslust describing the scene as if she was an extra in an epic Hollywood movie, the analogy in this instance played out with thousands of refugees, and starved former Wöbbelin inmates.[10] In the courtyard of a large stable, large numbers were sorted by

---

[10] Memoir held in Gedenkstätte Wöbbelin.

nationality: Czechs, Russians, Poles, Hungarians, Italians, French, and many more. Dorothy had set up a soup kitchen to feed them but the food always ran out and American soldiers struggled to keep order. Flares from countless campfires around the town and beyond lit up the night sky as horses were skinned and roasted.

When possible, women and children were given better shelter. In Ludwigslust's hospital, with so few beds, every ward was piled with bloodied straw and rubbish. Dorothy and her nursing colleagues worked with a French doctor, a former Wöbbelin prisoner, and a Dutch sea captain, another inmate, who took over the management of the hospital.

With the Americans moving out, the British had command and Dorothy persuaded officers to order local German police to go into every home in Ludwigslust to demand at least one complete outfit of clothes from the women. The clothes handed over were shabby but fights ensued on the hospital wards for them. Those who couldn't raise themselves from their beds got nothing. The Red Cross nurses had to restore a level of fairness.

The Red Army camped around the eastern perimeter of Ludwigslust maintained its observance, an unnerving presence for the town's residents, the refugees and the large number of German PoWs in the temporary detention centres. A sense of inevitability hung over the town. No one wanted the British to leave. The British would not stay long.

Ludwigslust's bürgermeister with his daughter committed suicide.

For Hille, she and an SS companion – maybe Josefine Holub, another Tannenberg Aufseherin – had already fled west of Ludwigslust in the direction of Bresegard bei Picher on stolen horses.

FLEEING TO BRESEGARD

Between them, Wilhelm Bartels, Bresegard's bürgermeister, and Fritz Dubbe, its Ortsbauernführer, upheld Nazi policy in Bresegard. When Hitler's birthday was celebrated at the Hitler Platz, these two pillars of authority would probably be in uniform in the salute to their Führer but obsequious acceptance couldn't dispel the growing recognition that the Russians and Western Allies were dancing on the grave of the once glorious Third Reich. The columns of escaping Volksdeutsche that had come through had spoken of towns and villages set afire by the Red Army. Bresegard had experienced its first real taste of war in March 1945 when an Allied aircraft shot up a column of 200 Volksdeutsche outside the village, enroute to Hagenow, resulting in many dead and wounded.

Picher had its own pillar in Ortsbauernführer Friedrich Drenkhahn, who lived in a grand house adjacent to the church. In addition to his party functions, Drenkhahn acted as the local registrar for births and deaths. When 82nd US Airborne moved into the outskirts of Picher on May 2, a messenger went ahead to order residents to hang anything white from their homes in a show of surrender. When the soldiers arrived at its centre dominated by the church, there was no opposition. Drenkhahn would have been in the reception committee. Villagers still recall the time of occupation: 2pm, precisely.

That day of occupation coincided with the Red Army winning the battle for Berlin.

The soldiers warily moved on towards Bresegard with two young Picher men cycling in the front, together holding an unfurled white sheet but word had gone ahead and homes were already displaying white surrender items. One house hadn't and with no answer, the front door was kicked in and shots fired. It was subsequently torched. The family next door had hung sheets from their windows and withdrawn into the cellar where they heard the shots. A Polish worker later entered the smouldering embers and took two pairs of boots from the ruins.

Bartels, the bürgermeister, formerly greeted the senior American officer who asked if any Nazis or German soldiers were in his village, the standard question in the advance. He replied there were none. He may not have known that as the American army had approached Bresegard, two German officers had committed suicide with their firearms, their bodies hastily buried in the local woods.

One resident, then a young child, recalled to us that eight US tanks had parked up in the family farmyard. She and friends excitedly scrambled aboard asking for chocolate. All the local schools had closed with no immediate date for reopening. Beds for the troops were scarce so the men grabbed cushions from chairs and sofas to sleep on.

Bresegard and Picher residents were ordered to accommodate the American soldiers and the relationship was generally cordial but there were incidents. In one Picher home a soldier took a dislike to the family cat, shooting it dead in front of the traumatised children. In a show of conciliation, each day he gave them sweets but the mother threw them back in disgust. With so many soldiers in the villages, the women hid their bottles of schnapps but as the days passed they were shared. Poles, Ukrainians and other nationalities sought shelter and food wherever they could find it. Some told the Americans they had been mistreated by locals. Not equipped to handle the numbers, the Americans simply told the Poles to walk back to Poland, an unpalatable alternative given that it was now under Soviet control. A Ukrainian brother and sister, working as farm labourers in Bresegard, did leave in the hope they might somehow get to England. One Pole who left returned to the village 48 years later to recall his experiences.

The fear of rape by the occupiers was to be unfounded, that would come later when the Red Army moved in after the Americans and British vacated. There were numerous assaults at gunpoint and families still movingly recall the shameful incidents that left unwanted pregnancies.

Susanne Hille was now holed up in Bresegard.

THE EXTRAORDINARY STORY TOLD BY JOHANNA TREICHEL

Prior to our visit to Mecklenberg, we had spoken to Peter Heine, the researcher who had initiated the Hille trace in 1999. We needed to know if he had pursued his research after the revelation that she had deceased in Bresegard on May 7, 1945. He had, and he had telephoned the Bresegard bürgermeister at the time hoping she might flesh out some detail. Unexpectedly he found himself talking to the bürgermeister's mother, Johanna Treichel, who spoke freely and she related an extraordinary tale.

According to Johanna Treichel, Hille was in possession of valuables in Bresegard including gold jewellery and currency. For whatever reason, and Treichel hadn't elaborated, Hille, with another, took off on horseback but two men, probably others in the Bresegard hideaway gave chase. The chasers wanted the valuables and Hille was murdered. Again, Treichel didn't enlarge on the sequence of events. The call abruptly terminated when Heine asked to visit to find out more. Treichel and the bürgermeister, who had been listening to her mother's conversation, responded sharply that no one in the village would be prepared to speak to him. That abruptness had terminated Heine's search.

When we visited in 2019, through an intermediary we asked that now former bürgermeister, who still lives in the village, whether she might attend our gathering of interested villagers in the Bresegard Gemeindehaus, the meeting house. She declined. A second attempt was made for a meeting, this time in private, and that too was rejected. Whatever she knew about Hille's death from her mother, she had no intention of sharing any detail with us.

Wöbbelin had been the first stop on our visit to the area to check whether Hille with other female Tannenberg colleagues had been transferred to this camp after April 15 when Tannenberg was emptied. Given that Hille had been in Ludwigslust there was the possibility. The Gedenkstätte Wöbbelin informed us, as far as it knew, that no Aufseherinnen had been employed as guards. What did arouse our curiosity was a file held by the Gedenkstätte on an SS guard named Rottenführer Ernst Treichel, who we discovered had married Johanna Lewerenz post-war in Bresegard, the same Johanna who Heine had spoken to in 1999. Had Treichel been part of the SS contingent that had accompanied Obersturmbannführer (Lt. Colonel) Paul Werner Hoppe from Stutthof on assuming command of Wöbbelin? The Gedenkstätte couldn't provide a definite answer given the lack of available documents on the camp's operation.

We were trying to uncover the truth behind one wanted war criminal in Bresegard and now we had stumbled on a second in the same location.

Berlin's Bundesarchiv furnished me with Treichel's SS record, at least up to 1944, and a record from Polish archives that clearly confirmed Treichel's employment in Stutthof with Hoppe's signature as his commandant. As a Rottenführer, or Lance corporal, Treichel would have carried out orders from his superiors to punish and execute. A trawl through US archives revealed that Treichel had been placed on one UNWCC (United Nations War Crimes Commission) wanted list in 1945 for his activities prior to Stutthof. Another file, this one in the archives of the USHMM (US Holocaust Memorial Museum) in Washington, explained why. Treichel had been named as a participant in several massacres of Poles in two historic cities in northern Poland, Swiecie and Grudziadz (now Graudenz), between October and December 1939 during the German invasion.

That revelation took us back to his SS personal file that confirmed his membership at this time in the Selbschutz Westprussia paramilitary unit, a 17,000-strong group of armed ethnic German Volksdeutsche, part of the wider Selbschutz organisation that comprised 100,000 men in uniform. For much of its short existence, it operated with the support of the newly formed SS Einsatzgruppen whose lax terms of operation supplemented the clearing and extermination of ethnic Poles in this part of Poland, especially the upper and educated classes. Standartenführer (Colonel) Ludolf Hermann von Alvensleben, with other members of his family, ran the Selbschutz units and there was a strong demand within the Volksdeutsche communities to join up. At the age of 34, Ernst Treichel, living in the hamlet of Studzianka, in Rypin County, Dobriner Land, with his partner and two children, had heeded the call to enlist.

So sickened were two Selbschutz paramilitaries by the atrocities in Swiecie, they filed a report to the German military authorities, an account that remains in the German federal archives. Events in Graudenz were equally as awful with hundreds shot in five large pits. If the children thrown into them were still alive, the Selbschutz climbed down and smashed in their heads with spades. Even by the murderous standards of the SS, von Alvensleben's methods were shocking which finally led to the disbandment of Selbschutz Westprussia in the spring of 1940. A large number of paramilitaries, including Treichel, were enrolled into the SS and Gestapo. In the last three months of 1939, Selbschutz Westprussia and the Einsatzgruppen had wantonly murdered up to 10,000 ethnic Poles and Jews.

Only 1,700 paramilitaries could later be identified, Treichel being one. A mere 10 would face trial and Treichel wasn't one of them.[11] Treichel would also avoid the six Stutthof war crimes trials that took place in Poland, all but one held in Gdansk.[12] Had Treichel never been located by an arm of justice? We never found any evidence he had. Up to 65,000 ethnic Poles and Jews had perished in Stutthof and its subcamps during the war. Stutthof had a killing speciality. In January 1945, several thousand inmates were marched to the Baltic coast by SS and Ukrainian guards and forced into the sea. If they didn't drown they were machine-gunned. A similar episode occurred in late April when some 5,000 prisoners met their end. Stutthof achieved further notoriety in scientific experimentation. The main camp, where Treichel worked, provided the human 'feedstock' for Dr Rudolf Spanner and his team in the Danzig Anatomical Institute.[13] Heads were severed and with torsos they were transported to a local factory for the manufacture of soap, referred to as Rein-Judisches-Fett, or 'Pure Jewish Fat'. Large vats boiled the body parts. A Polish investigation in 2006 into this aspect of Stutthof's operation labelled the process as 'one of the darkest pages of the Second World War'.

With the SS guards fleeing Wöbbelin in the US army advance, escape routes were limited. Escaping east was unlikely given the closeness of the Red Army front. The Baltic to the north and a boat to the comparative safety of Flensburg on the German/Danish border was an escape route taken by Hoppe. To the west, the American and British armies were scything through this part of Germany but outside the large towns, the sympathetic 'Brown'

---

[11] Ludolf Hermann von Alvensleben, the commanding officer, would die in a car crash in Dortmund in 1953, leading to speculation that he had been summarily dealt with.
[12] The Stutthof concentration camp was again in focus in late 2019 when a former guard, identified in the Hamburg court as Bruno Dey, was charged and later found guilty as being an accessory to the murder of 5,230 inmates. Oddly, this 93-year-old was charged in a juvenile court because he was only 17 when he worked in the camp. On the first day of the trial he gave dramatic testimony about the camp's gas chambers and crematoria and the screams he heard. Dey had denied any participation in murder.
[13] Post-war, the West German authorities dropped an investigation into Spanner's work. His only punishment was dismissal from the University of Cologne but only after intervention by the British. He later worked as an ordinary physician in Schleswig-Holstein. His patients, supposedly, were none the wiser to his past.

hamlets offered refuge. Franz Kafesei, one Wöbbelin guard, had remained in plain sight working in a bakery in Ludwigslust before being picked up by the German police in 1946. He would later be acquitted over war crimes as several Wöbbelin survivors testified that he had been a very rare exemption in the camp, a guard who treated inmates with a modicum of humanity. Erich Happke, another guard, was picked up by the Americans in Hagenow, 11km to the north west of Bresegard.

None of Ernst Treichel's dependants from his two relationships ever knew where their father had spent his immediate months post-war, nor did they know his backstory as an SS guard and Selbschutz paramilitary. Alina Schielke was Treichel's first partner and a daughter told us that he had re-joined the family in late 1945 or early 1946. Only in 2005 did they learn of Treichel's Stutthof connection.

As the Red Army had moved closer to Studzianka in the winter of 1944/45, Schielke, now with three children, Bruno, aged 16, Elsa Gertrude, aged 13, and Edeltraud, aged three, joined the extended Treichel family in fleeing west. The large party included eight children. The trek took its toll and the horses struggled in the snow and ice. An older family member succumbed and the women were at the mercy of Russian soldiers. Eventually all the horses were stolen and the group continued on foot. They had no change of clothes. Reaching the hamlet of Kreien, some 55km to the east of Ludwigslust, they were given temporary accommodation in the school but the Kreien bürgermeister turfed them out and sent them back. As they reached the Oder, the Russians turned the group around. They returned to Kreien where they remained.

When Ernst Treichel did eventually meet up with the family in Kreien the conditions it lived in were dire given the harshness of post-war austerity. None of the villagers wanted Vertriebene, or refugees, in their midst and they were ostracized. After five years, the East German state provided funds enabling Treichel to build a small farm in the village. He would not have known that he was on a United Nations wanted list as a war criminal but assuredly Treichel would have been worried when the first Stutthof trial of 17 guards and Kapos took place in Gdansk in April 1946. The horror of the concentration camps had become an international outrage and the

▲ When the Americans discovered the Wöbbelin atrocity, Ludwigslust's residents were forced by gunpoint to recover bodies for burial in the palace grounds. This site marked the first proper and respectful burial ceremony on May 7, 1945.

▲ During that ceremony on May 7, 1945 the bodies of 200 victims had been placed in white shrouds and with their faces visible to the attending German military officers.

▲ The Gedenkstätte Wöbbelin gave us access to its archives. We were eager to pursue whether Hille and the other two Aufseherinnen from Tannenberg had been transferred here when the Unterlüss camp was evacuated. With Wöbbelin quite close to Bresegard there was that possibility. However, nothing in the Gedenkstätte's records implied that female SS guards had worked at Wöbbelin in its very short existence, but those files are incomplete given that the SS ceased maintaining personnel files in the latter stages of the war. What did gain our immediate interest was its file on Ernst Treichel. He might have been a member of the Stutthof contingent of SS guards transferred here. There is no record as to the identity of these guards and what is known has only come from arrests at the time and survivor memories. One guard, Erich Happke, was arrested by the Americans in Hagenow, 11km north of Bresegard. Another, Franz Kafesei, had remained in plain sight working in a bakery in Ludwigslust before being picked up by the German police in 1946. He would later be acquitted over war crimes as several Wöbbelin survivors testified that he had been a very rare exemption in the camp, a guard who treated inmates with a modicum of humanity.

There are several burial sites to the Wöbbelin dead in the vicinity, including Ludwigslust, but this symbolic monument with its winding path in the brick surface marks the actual entrance to the camp through the woods.

◀ A grandson in Ernst Treichel's first family contacted us and provided a post-war photograph of this former SS concentration camp guard. As a young boy, he had innocently asked Treichel about the war and why people had to kill each other. Treichel had smiled at the question, saying that the war was not so bad and that he had spent much of the time sunbathing with his friends. Treichel told the boy not to believe what he had heard about the war and that people lied. That grandson saw his grandfather several times and he believed that his relative had secrets that he wouldn't divulge to anyone.

◀ Berlin's Bundesarchiv sent us its SS records for Treichel. This is his Stammkarte, its last entry July 26, 1944. Centrally updating SS records in the final months of the war was practically non-existent.

▶ Before Treichel had been transferred into the Waffen SS and employed in Stutthof, the records confirm that he had enrolled in the murderous Selbschutz Westprussia paramilitary group on September 10, 1939.

search was on across Europe to bring the perpetrators to justice. The crimes of Hitler's Germany would have to be paid for. There would be a reckoning.

Alina died in 1957 and a year later Ernst Treichel, now aged 53, married Johanna Lewerenz, aged 37, in Bresegard where he started another family. Treichel's name first appears in the records of Landkreis Ludwigslust-Parchim in 1958 as a resident of Bresegard and if its villagers were aware of Treichel's wartime activities, we couldn't ascertain. Almost certainly, none would have known about his paramilitary days in the murderous Selbschutz Westprussia.

An elderly woman in Picher with a phenomenal memory of the war recalled for us the first time that Treichel appeared in Bresegard, and it's a tale befitting the intrigue we were uncovering.

A STRANGER NAMED SCHIELKE

A stranger had moved into Picher in the last weeks of the war, a relatively affluent one given the size of his horse-drawn wagon. His name was Schielke and whether he was a relative of Alina Schielke, Treichel's partner, is unclear. There was an assumption that this stranger, probably an ethnic German Volksdeutsche from the east, had money. Shortly after his arrival, Schielke brought three men, also strangers, into the area. One was Ernst Treichel and he was accommodated in Bresegard.

The other two, named Neumann and Gube, were given lodging in Picher and in the nearby hamlet of Gross Krams respectively. Schielke gave no details of where the three came from, or his own background, but there is now conjecture that given Treichel was an SS guard, their backstories, including Schielke, were similar. Had Schielke and his two other charges also been Selbschutz and Stutthof kamaraden, hoping to evade Allied justice?

Thanks to the mysterious Schielke, Ernst Treichel, wanted for war crimes, had gone to ground in Bresegard, remaining in the village for a period of several months before joining Alina Schielke and his three children in Kreien. He might have met his future second wife, Johanna Lewerenz, who he would marry in 1958, during this time. We can only contemplate whether Treichel might have had an involvement in Hille's demise.

Treichel died in 1977 aged 72. Johanna died in 2006 and both are buried in the same grave in Bresegard's community graveyard. Years earlier, the Kreien farm had been handed over to Bruno, Treichel's son with Alina.

Johanna Lewerenz is well remembered. With her knowledge of English she had saved the immediate life of a black American airman who had parachuted into the local woods in early 1945 after his plane was downed. The hunters cut him down from the trees and paraded the airman through the village. Being black, his appearance created quite a spectacle. The hunters wanted to shoot him but Johanna stepped in and after negotiation, the airman was locked into the tiny village jail next to the fire station behind the Gemeindehaus for his own safety. The military eventually took the airman away, his fate unknown. Johanna had later acted as translator for the Americans and British who occupied the village.

A grandson in Ernst Treichel's first family contacted us and clearly Treichel hadn't expressed any remorse even towards the end of his life. As a young boy, he had innocently asked Treichel about the war and why people had to kill each other. Treichel had smiled at the question, saying that the war was not so bad and that he had spent much of the time sunbathing, with his friends, lying under an apple tree. Treichel told the boy not to believe what he had heard about the war and that people lied. That grandson saw his grandfather on several occasions in various locations, including Bresegard and Vienna, recalling him as a sincere, silent and even philosophic type but with secrets that he wouldn't divulge to anyone. Whether Johanna had been privy to those secrets isn't clear.

OUR SEARCH FOR A MÜLLER OR MÖLLER

Unable to speak to Johanna Treichel's daughter was a blow but we had other avenues to pursue. The Hille death certificate we had obtained had named the Bresegard individual who had found the body and the present Picher pastor, Matthias Galleck, in post for the past 20 years, had helpfully offered us sight of the church burial book, a village record that was to add even more twists and turns to our story of the death of Susanne Hille, the Tannenberg sadist.

If some of the elderly members in our attentive audiences in Picher and Bresegard did have information about the murder of a 22-year-old German woman in May 1945, or indeed just the death, no one admitted to the fact, even after I had read out some of the Tannenberg survivor testimonies that illuminated the brutality of this Aufseherin whose body lay in the Picher churchyard. In hamlets the size of Bresegard and Picher, the murder of a young German woman, even during the confusion of the last day of war, would have stimulated village gossip and that recall would have come down the generations. Our audiences could recant for us many wartime incidents, in great detail, yet no one remembered the violent death of a young woman on the last full day of the war. Very quickly we had the sense that whatever had occurred would not be disclosed to curious outsiders. Word soon spread in the villages that two British researchers were keen to talk to anyone that might provide us with leads.

What had the translation of the Sütterlin in Hille's death certificate revealed? One word was key that of 'Baueraltenteiler', a traditional German expression implying an old farmer who has passed over control to a younger generation, usually a son.

The certificate did have full details including all three forenames, her date of birth, where born, and that she had deceased on May 7, 1945. Cause of death is left blank and residency is recorded as Bresegard. Friedrich Drenkhahn in his capacity as registrar of local births and deaths had completed the certificate with the phrase 'Registered in a verbal report by Baueraltenteiler Müller, Bresegard, and he is known to the registrar personally'. This Baueraltenteiler had obviously lived in the Bresegard community for many years. Under the section 'Read, Approved and Signed', is the signature of Müller. We showed the certificate to people in Picher and Bresegard and several insisted that the name was Möller, the low-German language for Müller and often used in this part of Germany.

Müller or Möller are common names so we again engaged the help of our archivist contact at the Landkreis Ludwigslust-Parchim to search the records, and in 1945, two Müller families were recorded as resident in Bresegard. Had we got the man who had found the body of Hille and reported it to Drenkhahn? We had, because one

Müller had been recorded as a Baueraltenteiler, and the other Müller was away in the war and didn't return from captivity until September 1947. We were subsequently advised that both these Müllers' were known in Bresegard as Möller. Henceforth, we used Möller in our research.

Our Baueraltenteiler was Wilhelm Möller, aged 64, with two children, Bernhardt and Liesbet. Bernhardt was probably in the military. This Möller lived at Häuslerreihe 13, a road on the western fringe of Bresegard with open fields to the front and rear. 'Häuslerreihe' literally means a row of houses and most, including No. 13, had barns attached in the rear and were working farms with small acreage. Had Wilhelm Möller discovered the body of Susanne Hille on his family land?

The second Möller family lived in the Möller Hof a short distance away in Hufe, a quiet road with large properties surrounded by trees, and was definitely not related to the Häuslerreihe family according to the Landkreis Ludwigslust-Parchim records. The Möller Hof might have direct relevance in the death of Hille, which we will explain shortly. With her husband away, Erna managed the property helped by her two sons, Walter, aged 13, and Gunter, aged eight. If there was a living Möller grandfather in this family, he didn't live in Bresegard and Gunter would later contest that he never knew or saw him at any stage in his childhood.

It is worth reiterating that almost certainly, Hille would have ditched her Aufseherin uniform and SS Ausweis, her identity card. However, in the belief that she had just done her duty for the Reich she might have maintained her name but that doesn't answer the key question as to how Baueraltenteiler Wilhelm Möller obtained such biographical detail including Hille's three forenames, date of birth and place of birth.

Möller had conveyed the body to Picher in a horse and cart on a side road that for generations ceremoniously ferried the Bresegard dead to the church, pulling up first at Drenkhahn's house close to the church on Lindenstrasse. Once the death certificate was completed, the next stop was Wilhelm Köhn in the parsonage just a few doors away. Köhn had been the pastor since 1932. Very likely, Hille's body would have been stored in an outbuilding. We know

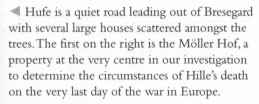

Hufe is a quiet road leading out of Bresegard with several large houses scattered amongst the trees. The first on the right is the Möller Hof, a property at the very centre in our investigation to determine the circumstances of Hille's death on the very last day of the war in Europe.

Some remedial work to the property had taken place after the German re-unification but funds had run dry.

The rear entrance to the Möller Hof. A Bresegard resident, a young boy at the time, recollected that the brazier was always alight in its courtyard as the refugees cooked their foraged rabbits and other game. In the community there was anger towards their presence.

A view of the abandoned Möller Hof from Hufe. The barn on the right was a post-war addition. In the final weeks of the war the house and outbuildings were crammed with refugees. Erna Möller with her two young sons, Walter and Gunter, were pushed into one room. During our visit to Bresegard, on our behalf, two very helpful villagers, one an old school chum of Gunter, drove over unannounced to Redefin, a village nearby, to see him. Gunter was somewhat taken aback and after the pleasantries, the conversation had turned to Hille, the SS camp guard. Gunter feigned any knowledge of a dead woman in the Möller Hof that is until the extraordinary prompt from his wife – 'Go on, tell them about the woman'.

▲ Wilhelm Möller, a Baueraltenteiler, or old farmer, who lived at Häuslerreihe 13, Bresegard, had found two bodies in the village on March 7. These Häuslerreihe properties have attached barns in the rear and were working farms with small acreage.

▼ The Gedenkstätte Ravensbrück provided us with a typical SS Ausweis, an ID card, so we could see what Hille might have had on hers. This one for Marianne Minges, an Aufseherin from Ravensbrück, confirmed to us that the ID, always kept by the holder, is devoid of much biographical detail.

from the church burial book that she was buried the following day – May 8 – in a grave marked LII 27, in Field 6 of the churchyard. A simple small wooden cross would have marked the grave.

Köhn completed the entry in the church burial book and wrote in 'Verkäuferin', salesgirl, even though that occupation wasn't stated on the death certificate. That entry and the simple burial supposedly marked the end of Susanne Luise Pauline Hille.

How she died was not recorded but Drenkhahn, as the community registrar, must have been curious. If she had died of natural causes, why didn't he record it as such? Might the body have bullet wounds or shown signs of hanging? Johanna Treichel had said in 1999 that Hille was murdered. Very likely, Drenkhahn knew the cause of death but didn't want it officially recorded in case questions were raised. We need to remember that Picher and Bresegard were now under US army occupation even if its physical presence was limited to military vehicles and troops passing through. The Americans had left the bürgermeisters and other Nazi officials, like Drenkhahn, temporarily in post during the transition.[14] If Hille's SS past was known, Drenkhahn might have been minded to instruct Pastor Köhn to register in his burial record that the deceased was simply a salesgirl.

Our investigation would take an extraordinary turn.

'TELL THEM ABOUT THE WOMAN'

During our stay in Bresegard and Picher we were repeatedly drawn back to the second Möller family and for good reason. To fill in the background of what occurred in the Möller Hof, in Hufe, in the last days of the war, we twice interviewed one Bresegard villager who had a strong memory of this family. He also knew the present whereabouts of Gunter, the youngest son, now aged 82.

With Bresegard flooded with refugees, large houses such as the Möller Hof were forcibly occupied and with Walter Möller away in military service, Erna, his wife, and her two sons were reduced to

---

[14] Drenkhahn was immediately dismissed once the Red Army took control.

living in a single room. Behind the property, in the courtyard, a brazier was always alight. Rabbits and other game were foraged by the refugees in the local woods and fields, much to the annoyance of villagers. A local farmer badly mistreated Polish refugees he employed on his farm and threatened with a lynching, he was lucky to live.

The Möller Hof now stands derelict and has been for many years. Its run-down wooden barn, not built until after the war, is used by a Hufe neighbour to stable her horses. Picher's bürgermeister, who knew her, gained permission for us to wander around and he was our guide. We were happy to have him with his extensive knowledge and community contacts. He runs an electrical business and is the local fire chief.

At some stage after German reunification, a new owner had started to clad the external brick and wood fascia with a brick skin, but with money tight and the over-optimistic political promises failing to deliver, the renovation floundered. The brick outbuildings with their pens that once held livestock, and refugees, are now full of rubbish. Like any ruinous house surrounded by large trees and unruly undergrowth, this one oozed with mystery. We needed to talk to Gunter Möller.

On our behalf, two very helpful Bresegard villagers, one an old school chum of Gunter, drove over unannounced to Redefin, a village nearby, to see him. Gunter was somewhat taken aback and after the pleasantries, the conversation turned to Hille, the SS camp guard. Gunter feigned any knowledge of a dead woman in the Möller Hof that is until the extraordinary prompt from his wife – 'Go on, tell them about the woman'.

From what we were told afterwards, the atmosphere in this impromptu meeting turned even more febrile. Gunter had no intention of elaborating, apart from the curious statement that at the time, women had disguised themselves as men. Nor did he want to pursue his later revelation that he had witnessed a body in an outbuilding wrapped in a green canvas sheet, the type of covering used on farms. Had that been Hille? If not, we now had a second body.

There had indeed been a second body and it may have been the one recorded in Picher's church burial book. Not only had this person died on May 7, the same day as Hille, astonishingly, Wilhelm

Möller, the Baueraltenteiler from Häuslerreihe, was again the finder. As to the body's location, Pastor Köhn noted in his church record that it was found in Hufe close to the Möller Hof. If this body was not the one observed by Gunter in the green canvas, had our body count now climbed to three?

Pastor Köhn had recorded the second body found by Wilhelm Möller as an 'unbekannte', or unknown. His scrawling writing was difficult to read but it appears that the male victim had been hung. Nationality was another unknown, wrote Köhn, and the victim might have been a camp guard. Where had Wilhelm Möller gleaned that snippet of detail for Köhn?

There is a further oddity. This 'unbekannte' was buried a day later than Hille and next to her in Field Six. Hille was No 41 in the burial book, another local death on May 7, and unrelated to the Hille story, was No 42. The 'unbekannte' should have been No 43, but Köhn had deliberately omitted numbering this burial. We asked the present pastor, Mathias Galleck, for a possible explanation to this curious flaw. He could only shake his head.

Köhn had had a busy first week in May. Poles had killed a German in Jasnitz and an Allied aircraft had strafed and killed three other villagers outside its railway station. Buried on May 5 was Leopold Rededski, a Wehrmacht officer from Lichterfelde in Berlin. He had shot himself in Picher the day the Americans arrived on May 2. A Picher villager, a depressed Nazi, had hung himself on May 4 in his home.

It was the discovery of the 'unbekannte' that confirmed to us that the Möller Hof was at the very heart of the intrigue over the death of Susanne Hille. That interjection from Gunter Möller's wife – 'Go on, tell them about the woman' – is compelling, as are her husband's statements about seeing a body wrapped in green canvas and that women had disguised themselves as men. The fact that Wilhelm Möller had found it in Hufe clearly implicates the Möller Hof or somewhere close. Had this farmhouse become a temporary bolthole for Hille and others and might their real SS identities have become known to the Polish refugees? To them, many had suffered terribly in the concentration camps in their homeland and vengeance was deserved. As the 'unbekannte' had been hung, according to the Picher burial record, might Hille have endured the same fate?

THE VILLAGE THAT KEEPS ITS SECRETS

DID HILLE FAKE HER OWN 'DEATH'?

Despite our best endeavours, we couldn't conclusively determine the account given over the phone to Peter Heine in 1999 by Johanna Treichel. We questioned whether her story was even genuine. Her marriage to a wanted SS war criminal, who had successfully concealed his notorious past to both his families and to the village, had somewhat tainted its veracity.

We can only question why Johanna's daughter was disinclined to share with us what her mother had imparted to her on Hille's death. A member of the Bresegard community had taken us aside with the suggestion that Hille might be the 'big secret', an untold story that even to this day remains locked in the minds of those who know. Something violent and sinister had happened in Bresegard on the last day of the war resulting in at least two deaths with the possibility of a third.

Pivotal to our story has been Wilhelm Möller, the Baueraltenteiler from Häuslerreihe, and we searched for a reason behind his involvement. The answer might be straightforward if he had simply found Hille's body on his property or on adjoining farmland. Yet, he had found two bodies, one definitely in Hufe, and there is no satisfactory explanation as to how he provided the information he did on Hille for the death certificate. If he had found Hille's Ausweis, her SS identity card, Gedenkstätte Ravensbrück confirmed to us that only the basic information would have been on it. As far as we could ascertain, Hille had no relatives in the area that might have assisted Möller with details.

If Hille had been murdered in the Möller Hof, Erna Möller, living on her own with two boys, and her home and outbuildings swamped with displaced persons, would have needed urgent help. Erna might have turned to Wilhelm Möller, well known in the village, to take both her body and that of the 'unbekannte' to Picher for burial. What cannot be discounted is whether Wilhelm Möller had willingly shielded Hille and others in his Häuslerreihe farmhouse. Had Hille and someone else fled this farmhouse and got no further than Hufe? The 'unbekannte' might have been the body wrapped in green canvas, maybe the woman disguised as a man, as remembered by Gunter?

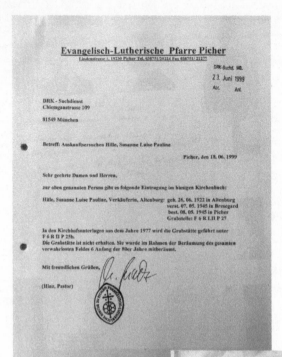

Evangelisch-Lutherische Pfarre Picher
Lindenstrasse 1, 19230 Picher Tel. 038751/20224 Fax 038751/21227

DRK-Suchd. MB.
23. Juni 1999
Abt.   Az.

DRK - Suchdienst
Chiemgaustrasse 109

81549 München

Betreff: Auskunftsersuchen Hille, Susanne Luise Pauline

Picher, den 18. 06. 1999

Sehr geehrte Damen und Herren,

zur oben genannten Person gibt es folgende Eintragung im hiesigen Kirchenbuch:

Hille, Susanne Luise Pauline, Verkäuferin, Altenburg; geb. 26. 06. 1922 in Altenburg
verst. 07. 05. 1945 in Bresegard
best. 08. 05. 1945 in Picher
Grabstelle: F 6 R LII P 27

In den Kirchhofsunterlagen aus dem Jahre 1977 wird die Grabstätte geführt unter
F 6 R II P 25b.
Die Grabstätte ist nicht erhalten. Sie wurde im Rahmen der Beräumung des gesamten
verwahrlosten Feldes 6 Anfang der 80er Jahre mitberäumt.

Mit freundlichen Grüßen,

(Hinz, Pastor)

In the archive of Gedenkstätte Bergen-Belsen is a confirmation by Pastor Hinz, dated June 1999, the-then incumbent pastor in Picher, that Hille had been buried in Field 6, in plot L11 27. Yet, that letter to the tracing service of the German Red Cross opened up a further intrigue. It states that in the cemetery documents from 1977, Hille's body had been numbered plot 25b despite the church burial record book clearly stating plot 27.

The Hagenow Standesamt gave us a certified copy of Hille's death certificate that had been completed in Sütterlin by Drenkhahn, using information provided to him by 'Baueraltenteiler' Wilhelm Möller, aged 64, who lived in Häuslerreihe 13, Bresegard. Under the section 'Read, Approved and Signed', is the signature of Müller. We showed the certificate to people in Picher and Bresegard and several insisted that the name was Möller, the low-German language for Müller and often used in this part of Germany.

Illus. 33. "We called her the 'brown one.'"

▲ Had the 'Brown one' died in Bresegard on the last day of the war or had she staged her death? There are still those in the village and Picher who know the truth about Susanne Hille, the sadist of Tannenberg.
Drawing taken from *Cabbages & Geraniums* by Valerie Furth – a survivor of Birkenau Tannenberg and Belsen. She died in March, 2011.

We shared our findings with those who had taken an interest in verifying how Hille had died and two theories had common ground. Either Hille's details had been deliberately left on the body for Wilhelm Möller to find, obviously by someone she knew well, or the body was not that of Susanne Hille.

In the former scenario, we know from a Tannenberg survivor testimony to the British that Hille came from Altenburg. If that detail with other personal information were known in the camp, then the person that had deliberately placed Hille's details on the body would have been another SS Aufseherin, probably Josefine Holub. She might have accompanied Hille all the way to Bresegard.

In the latter scenario, Hille was not the victim but probably a murderer. The body purporting to be Hille may have been anyone, maybe a Polish refugee, and there were many in Bresegard. Her SS accomplice, if there was one, would have been complicit in the conspiracy, as might Wilhelm Möller and even Drenkhahn. With her 'death' officially registered with Drenkahn and recorded in the church burial book, Hille could now restart her life with a new identity, unfettered by her past.

A WALL OF SILENCE

As with every story in this book on episodes that took place in the last days and weeks of the Third Reich, our research delved deeper than just unearthing documents in dusty archives. To relate each account with a high level of accuracy, we interviewed a great many people, who, although very young at the time, and despite the passing of seven decades, had astonishing recall of events.

Thanks to the respective bürgermeisters of Bresegard and Picher and their valuable assistance, we spoke to groups of villagers, and several individually. With our visit at an end, contact was maintained with a number who tried to obtain answers to further questions.

Thanks to sight of the church burial book that Pastor Galleck arranged for us to view in his parsonage, we knew the exact plot in the cemetery where Hille was supposedly buried alongside the 'unbekannte' but, sadly, after enforced ploughing by the East German authorities, that precise location in the grounds has been forgotten.

However, we do have an indicator to the location of Field 6, the site of Hille's burial. The side of the church facing the main street in the village is now scattered with gravestones in plots for each hamlet in the community, not just Bresegard and Picher. Yet, the other side of the church is bereft of gravestones apart from a pile left along the side of the hedge. We believe that part of this area was Field 6, and historically it was probably given over to the dead who had died without funds for a bespoke plot or gravestone.

The lack of a positive confirmation of the site is just one of the many unknowns in this story of unravelling the truth behind Susanne Hille's death on the very last day of war when all around the European continent the guns had fallen silent. That makes Hille's death all the more intriguing.

There were many unknowns in our investigation, the 'unbekannte' being one. Why hadn't Pastor Köhn in May 1945 accorded a burial number in his records despite its burial next to Hille? The reticent Gunter Möller never shared the truth behind the body he had witnessed wrapped in green canvas in the Möller Hof and nor would he elaborate on the remark that women at this time disguised themselves as men. Had this been a specific reference to Hille? Through an intermediary, we contacted relatives in the village of Wilhelm Möller, the old Baueraltenteiler, who had found two bodies in Bresegard and conveyed both to Picher for certification and burial. The bad health of one relative, who might have helped, precluded further discussion. Why had Joanna Treichel, wife of a long dead Stutthof guard, and her bürgermeister daughter, effectively barred Peter Heine from travelling to Bresegard on the grounds that no-one would be prepared to speak to him, and why had this daughter steadfastly refused our requests for an interview?

Hille was only a marginal character in the shaping of the most barbarous regime in the twentieth century yet she is a classic example on how Nazism had filtered down into every level of society, class and education. Trained in Ravensbrück with hundreds of other young women who would become guards in Germany's concentration camp system, she lacked any moral sense and was oblivious to the suffering she inflicted on her victims. To Susanne Hille, the Aufseherin who readily wielded the whip, rubber truncheon and used her bare hands to brutalize, the rhetoric and ambition of the Führer to conquer and occupy was without fault. To her, ridding the continent of Jews and other ethnic communities in the worst genocide in human history was a necessary price for that domination.

We can only conjecture but some villagers do know what did happen to Hille but a wall of silence pervades. Bresegard bei Picher and Picher have no intention, just yet, of yielding up what one villager described to us as the 'big secret'. If Johanna Treichel had known the facts on Susanne Hille then others were conversant with events of May 7, 1945.

Faking one's own death wasn't unusual for those who desperately sought to literally bury their past and avoid justice. There are countless wartime examples of those who did. Willing helpers, villagers remaining loyal to the Nazi cause even in ignominious defeat, might have gladly shielded a 22-year-old German woman who convinced them that she, too, was a victim of war.

Had Susanne Hille, the 'Brown One', staged her own death and remained in Bresegard, maybe Picher, with a new identity and protected by villagers? If still alive when we conducted our research, this Tannenberg sadist would be aged 97.

The Tannenberg survivors would never confront Hille in court.

THE VILLAGE THAT KEEPS ITS SECRETS

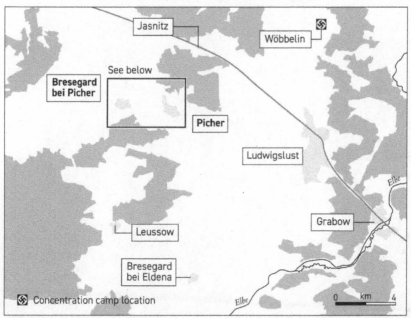

Susanne Hille, wanted SS war criminal - from Tannenberg to Bresegard

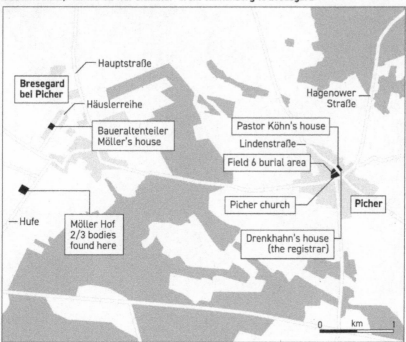

Picher church - Hille's final resting place, or was it?

▲ Heinrich Himmler parked his vehicle in this shed where Hans Heinrich Otzen, a boy at the time, chattered to him. Himmler took him for a drive. Sadly, since I took this photograph Hans Heinrich has died.

▲ SS-Obersturmführer Arnold Georg Strippel, the concentration camp careerist and hardened torturer and killer, always avoided justice for the horrors he perpetrated in the basement of the former Hamburg school.

▲ In this clearing in the Neustädter Holz, the Celle police murdered 60 concentration camp prisoners, maybe more, who had run for their lives after surviving the bombing of the train in the Güterbahnhof. We followed the specific map drawn for the RAF war crimes investigators by Helmut Ahlborn, one of the accused.

▲ One of the worst atrocities of the war was committed in this barn in Gardelegen. Few of the dead were ever identified.

▲ Only few of the Tannenberg women survived Belsen. The SS
Aufseherinnen, the women guards employed in many concentration camps, are
often considered to have been even more brutal than their male counterparts.

▲ Had one SS Aufseherin in Tannenberg, Susanne Hille, faked her death in Bresegard? The entry in the Picher burial book only adds to the intrigue. Some villagers know the truth but the 'big secret' continues to this day.

THE AUTHORS

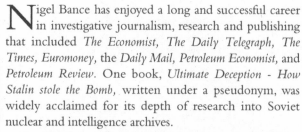

Nigel Bance has enjoyed a long and successful career in investigative journalism, research and publishing that included *The Economist, The Daily Telegraph, The Times, Euromoney,* the *Daily Mail, Petroleum Economist,* and *Petroleum Review.* One book, *Ultimate Deception - How Stalin stole the Bomb,* written under a pseudonym, was widely acclaimed for its depth of research into Soviet nuclear and intelligence archives.

In 2005, in Moscow, he was presented with a prestigious award by a Russian defence institute for that research that had included interviews with intelligence officers and nuclear scientists in the US, Britain and Germany. He interviewed one of the last surviving German nuclear physicists who worked for Hitler in the wartime race to develop the atomic bomb, revealing for the first time that he had personally briefed Hitler's deputy, Rudolf Hess, on the very latest German nuclear developments just days before his historic flight to Scotland. What Hess shared with the British still remains classified. Some of the author's past work has been published in Russian.

In recent years he wrote regularly on security issues in the global oil and gas industry, in particular the growing threat of terrorism, kidnapping and piracy. In 2016, in his book, *The Liquidation of Raoul Wallenberg,* he was allowed a unique access in Moscow into the personal files of Colonel-General Ivan Serov, who ran the KGB and its intelligence sister, the GRU, to finally determine how and why the Russian Intelligence Services murdered this Swedish diplomat in 1947.

This new book, *Himmler never gave me Chocolate,* involved many interviews with those who still remember the events in northern Germany in the last days and weeks of WW2. That generation, who witnessed so much, is fast passing,

Diana Petersen-Büchse provided invaluable assistance in researching this book. She studied at Goldsmiths College, University of London, and had a long and distinguished career in teaching that began as a member of Voluntary Service Overseas in the Punjab, India. She has lived in Schleswig-Holstein, northern Germany, since 1972, and has taught in German schools as well as teaching English to several large international companies. For over 20 years, Diana taught members of the Bundeswehr (German Armed Forces), including the German Navy in Flensburg and the Luftwaffe near Hamburg, finishing her career at the University of Applied Sciences in Flensburg.